D1423563

— Garden and Landscape History —

— DESIGNS UPON THE LAND —
Elite Landscapes of the Middle Ages

Leeds Trinity University

LIBRARY

**This book is due for return on or before
the last date stamped below**

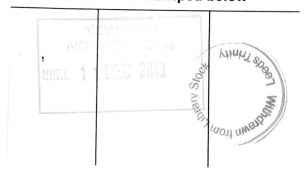

UNTIL 1 1 DEC 2013

LEEDS TRINITY LIBRARY

303045 9

— *Garden and Landscape History* —

ISSN 1758-518X

General Editor
Tom Williamson

This exciting series offers a forum for the study of all aspects of the subject. It takes a deliberately inclusive approach, aiming to cover both the 'designed' landscape and the working, 'vernacular' countryside; topics embrace, but are not limited to, the history gardens and related subjects, biographies of major designers, in-depth studies of key sites, and regional surveys.

Proposals or enquiries may be sent directly to the editor or the publisher at the addresses given below; all submissions will receive prompt and informed consideration.

Professor Tom Williamson, University of East Anglia, University Plain, Norwich, Norfolk, NR4 7TJ

Boydell & Brewer, PO Box 9, Woodbridge, Suffolk, UK, IP12 3DF

LEEDS TRINITY UNIVERSITY

Previously Published

Designs upon the Land: Elite Landscapes of the Middle Ages
Oliver H. Creighton

Richard Woods (1715–1793): Master of the Pleasure Garden
Fiona Cowell

Uvedale Price (1747–1829): Decoding the Picturesque
Charles Watkins and Ben Cowell

Common Land in English Painting, 1700–1850
Ian Waites

— *DESIGNS UPON THE LAND* —
Elite Landscapes of the Middle Ages

Oliver H. Creighton

THE BOYDELL PRESS

712.09420902
CRE
3030459

LEEDS TRINITY UNIVERSITY

© Oliver H. Creighton 2009

All Rights Reserved. Except as permitted under current legislation
no part of this work may be photocopied, stored in a retrieval system,
published, performed in public, adapted, broadcast,
transmitted, recorded or reproduced in any form or by any means,
without the prior permission of the copyright owner

The right of Oliver H. Creighton to be identified as the author of this work has been
asserted in accordance with sections 77 and 78 of the Copyright, Designs and Patents
act 1988

First published 2009
The Boydell Press, Woodbridge
Reprinted in paperback 2013

ISBN 978 1 84383 446 5 hardback
ISBN 978 1 84383 825 8 paperback

The Boydell Press is an imprint of Boydell & Brewer Ltd
PO Box 9, Woodbridge, Suffolk IP12 3DF, UK
and of Boydell & Brewer Inc.
668 Mt Hope Avenue, NY 14620–2731, USA
website: www.boydellandbrewer.com

The publisher has no responsibility for the continued existence or accuracy of URLs for
external or third-party internet websites referred to in this book, and does not
guarantee that any content on such websites is, or will remain, accurate or
appropriate.

A CiP catalogue record of this publication is available
from the British Library

Designed by Tina Ranft

Papers used by Boydell & Brewer Ltd are natural, recycled products
made from wood grown in sustainable forests

MIX
Paper from
responsible sources
FSC
www.fsc.org   FSC® C013604

Printed and bound in Great Britain by
CPI Group (UK) Ltd, Croydon CR0 4YY

— Contents —

— List of Illustrations —

To Peggy

— *Acknowledgements* —

I am grateful to the British Academy for providing a grant that supported the research and fieldwork behind this volume.

The author is indebted to all those who generously provided guidance, advice and information during the writing of this book. Particular thanks are due to: Stuart Ainsworth; Mick Aston; Terry Barry; Graham Brown; Neil Christie; Catherine Clarke; Piers Dixon; Penny Dransart; Chris Dyer; Paul Everson; Chris Gerrard; Martin Gillard; John Goodall; Peter Herring; Robert Higham; Andrew Jackson; Matthew Johnson; Brian Kerr; Robert Liddiard; Tom McNeill; Stephen Moorhouse; Kieran O'Conor; Alastair Oswald; Tadhg O'Keeffe; Richard Oram; Nicholas Orme; Paul Pattison; Steve Rippon; Allan Rutherford; Paul Stamper; Christopher Taylor; Rick Turner; and Liz Whittle.

I am also grateful to individuals at a number of archives and record offices for their assistance and help locating appropriate aerial photographs, including staff at the National Monuments Record Centre in Swindon, Cadw in Cardiff, the Royal Commission on the Ancient and Historical Monuments of Wales in Aberystwyth and the Royal Commission on the Ancient and Historical Monuments of Scotland. Acknowledgements of copyright are given in the individual captions for illustrations. Special thanks are also due to Mike Rouillard and Adam Wainwright for their generous help in preparing the illustrations and to Caroline Palmer of Boydell and Brewer for suggesting that a book on medieval designed landscapes was long overdue. I am also grateful to an anonymous reader whose comments have improved the text enormously. My family and friends have also provided unwavering support and encouragement: thanks in particular to Suzie, Ramona and Peggy, Gary and Julie Walker, Anthony and Rachel Garrett, David Gedge and Ian Robins.

— *Chapter One* —

Introduction: Approaching Designed Landscapes

In British historical scholarship the phrase 'designed landscape' is most commonly used to describe the parks and gardens laid out around the great country houses of the post-medieval period; it conjures up images of famous places such as Blenheim, Chatsworth and Stowe. Its quintessential form is the eighteenth-century 'English landscape garden' of William Kent, Lancelot 'Capability' Brown and Humphry Repton, whose commissions made sweeping changes to estate landscapes, representing what has come to be regarded as a specifically English contribution to garden-making and the visual arts. The contrived, naturalistic parkland settings created around these grand residences were far more than places where their owners could walk, talk, ride, hunt and entertain. Alive with imagery and rich in symbolism, these 'polite landscapes' were also vehicles for contemporary elites to showcase their wealth and sophistication.[1] The principal purpose of this book is, quite simply, to show that in the Middle Ages the houses of the social elite could be embedded within settings that were also 'designed' for essentially similar reasons of social expression and visual impact. It is argued that the image projected by these landscapes was that of elite authority rather than simple beauty and that, together, buildings and their settings provided contrived environments for structuring networks of social power. These were landscapes meant to display but also to conceal and to exclude – artificial environments to which access was tightly controlled, commanding views that were carefully managed.

This approach is new but not revolutionary: the 'designed landscape' concept has already been applied in a limited way as a means of understanding features such as gardens, ponds and parkland that were appurtenances to elite medieval residences (particularly castles) and served, at least in part, to enhance their visual appearance.[2] The theoretical leap required to recognise the existence of 'design' in the medieval landscape is not without its problems, however. What makes the notion immediately contentious is that, traditionally, the story of the designed landscape in Britain starts in the sixteenth century with an outburst of park and garden creation led by ambitious Renaissance-inspired elites. In an English context, the early Tudor period is often seen as *the* benchmark against which to examine the subsequent history of garden and landscape design, with buildings and estates newly acquired through the Dissolution of the monasteries supplying the raw materials while an ostentatious monarchy provided the lead.[3]

Numerous general books on the subject have overlooked altogether the possibility of medieval ancestry to the practice of landscape design, their coverage starting with the Renaissance.[4]

The central argument of this book is that polite landscape design has a largely unacknowledged 'prehistory' that extends back into the later medieval centuries, taken here to span the period *c*.1050–1550. This is not to say, however, that the history of designed landscapes exhibits a smooth sequential development, emerging from dim medieval beginnings to culminate in the glories of the early modern period. At one level the application of the concept of the 'designed landscape' to the Middle Ages is appealing, but it also has its problems, not least because of the cultural baggage from the post-medieval period that the phrase carries. While it might seem attractive to portray medieval elite landscapes in the same way as the polite settings of eighteenth-century gentry houses, we should be careful not to crudely back-project ideas and concepts of the modern age on to much earlier landscapes, where societies had quite different value systems and people experienced space, place and visuality in different ways.

That said, there are essential similarities between the polite estate landscapes of the eighteenth century and the elite landscapes of the medieval period which mean that the label 'designed landscape' is applicable, with caution, to both (*Black and White Plate 1*).[5] The role of hunting and leisure activities as key mechanisms for the expression of status and as a means of communicating social differentiation transcends the medieval and post-medieval periods, of course. Designed landscapes of all periods were far more than arrangements of earth, water and buildings; they embodied ideas and reflected how their owners and users understood the world around them. Of absolutely central importance to any understanding of the 'designed landscape' concept is the idea of control over nature – creating order from chaos in order to fashion an environment that was visually appealing and somehow 'tasteful'. The taming and reshaping of nature could be manifested in many ways, perhaps most obviously by 'internalising' it in small pockets through the creation of gardens. At a broader scale it could be expressed through the manipulation of water in the landscape to form lakes and ponds, through the introduction of animals for visual display and hunting, and through the arrangement of trees and other flora.

The term 'designed landscape' should not, however, disguise the fact that these landscapes were far more than inanimate objects for aesthetic appreciation. The ways in which they were intended to be experienced were not simple. Elite medieval landscapes certainly had the capacity to impress: great residences, whether castles, palaces or great country houses, often had frontages that expressed splendour as well as proclaiming function. But designed landscapes also represent more than the naked expression of power. They embodied deeper symbolic and perhaps religious and political values that reflected the outlook of their owners and, arguably, something of the worldview of contemporary society. They were not intended to be experienced from any single point

Plate 1. Powderham castle (Devon), showing the site of a medieval deer park redesigned in the late eighteenth century as a landscape garden, with fallow deer grazing in the foreground. (Photograph: Oliver Creighton)

alone, and the idea of movement within medieval as well as post-medieval elite landscapes, giving a viewpoint that was flexible rather than fixed, is crucial to understanding their contemporary meanings. The routes by which these buildings were approached and the ways in which access to their gardens and settings were managed could convey an element of theatre, intended to enchant and even surprise observers. They were, therefore, not simply areas for private recreation and contemplation but were sometimes intended as 'stage sets' for social display. The audiences at which such landscapes were aimed might also range far beyond the owning family. They contained different meanings for social rivals within the elite and their households, as well as members of the lower classes who might experience them more sporadically or from afar, and their impact on the senses of course depended on the circumstances of the individual.

While it is tempting to portray 'designed landscapes' as exclusively elite spaces, it is also important to remember that they often accommodated more mundane day-to-day activities, often in intriguing ways. The settings of great medieval and post-medieval residences were certainly intended for activities such as hunting but also found room for various forms of agriculture. These occasionally included arable cultivation as well as grazing and myriad forms of animal exploitation. For these reasons, medieval estate landscapes might also convey impressions of lordly benevolence and careful management, in the manner exemplified by the ordered and idealised demesne settings of the *Très Riches Heures du Duc de Berry*, for example.[6] There is clearly a complex interplay between gardens and pleasure grounds as represented in art and literature and those realised in the landscape: crucially, the 'imagined' garden of the medieval romance could be emulated on the ground, but literary sources also made quite deliberate references to 'real life' examples of parks and gardens. We are concerned here with the manipulation of physical components of landscapes, but also the manipulation of the memories these represented in the minds of contemporaries. Early modern designed landscapes were often punctuated by faked antiquities – 'Gothick' grottoes and cottages or 'Classical' temples and fountains – as well as 'real' features of the past reused as eyecatchers,[7] and it was not unknown for the medieval nobility also to draw on the imagery of the past to bolster their positions. The range of reactions and attitudes to symbols and images of earlier regimes ranged from complete eradication to their reinstatement, re-creation, and even their forgery. This reuse of the past emerges as another key theme that links the study of medieval designed landscapes to their post-medieval counterparts.

Aims and scope of the book

Examining these themes and others, this book explores the concepts as well as the actuality of elite landscape design in the Middle Ages. It seeks to understand the character and appearance of the settings of elite buildings and to come to grips with what they meant to those who created and visited them. In undertaking this, it has four key aims.

First and foremost, this study aims to cut through some deeply ingrained preconceptions about the medieval world to demonstrate that designed landscapes were indeed a fact of life in the period, albeit for a privileged minority, and endeavours to translate to studies of the medieval landscape something of the outlook of the 'new garden history'.[8] This sees traditional narratives based on familiar 'classic' sites at the sharp end of contemporary design surpassed by scholarship that takes full advantage of a greater variety of source material to explore a broader spectrum of sites.

Second, while an enormous body of scholarship has addressed the various component parts of medieval elite landscapes, this study aims to examine them *in toto*. Not only has the subject of medieval gardens attracted its own voluminous literature, but there exist detailed monographs on many of the key features of the medieval demesne and estate landscape, including deer parks,[9] fishponds,[10] rabbit warrens,[11] and dovecotes.[12] Such structures and resources might seem of marginal importance at most to our understanding of medieval landscape, representing little more than the minutiae of lordly exploitation. A central tenet of this book, however, is that they articulated together to form sophisticated and multi-layered environments for aristocratic residences and settings for elite discourse. Furthermore, studies of the castles, greater houses and royal palaces of the period have developed along quite separate lines, with their own gazetteers, research volumes and works of synthesis. Park history has similarly emerged as a distinctive sub-discipline in its own right in the same way as garden history. But it is of course artificial to compartmentalise the medieval landscape in this

Plate 2. Bodiam castle (East Sussex) from the air, showing the late-fourteenth-century castle within its watery setting. (© Crown copyright: English Heritage)

way and to disaggregate what contemporaries experienced as a whole. Rarely, it seems, have the interlinkages and interrelationships between these various components of elite landscapes (of which house and garden are only the most obvious manifestation) been examined. Accordingly, this study is all about joining up medieval landscapes, examining the ways in which different elements articulated together to create elite settings at different scales.

Third, while several excellent studies of individual examples of medieval designed landscapes have been published, scholarship to date has drawn back from overview and shirked explanation. This book aims to broaden our understanding of the phenomenon of elite landscape design in the medieval period beyond the fortified residences of major magnates on which work to date has largely focused. Bodiam castle in East Sussex *(Black and White Plate 2)* was the first major example of a designed landscape of the medieval period to be recognised as such,[13] showing how our understanding of elite buildings that are apparently well understood could be revolutionised by looking at their wider settings. For this leap forward in our understanding, particular tribute must be paid to the work of Christopher Taylor of the Royal Commission on the Historical Monuments of England (RCHME, later merged with English Heritage) who, alongside colleagues such as Paul Everson, identified for the first time the potential to characterise such elite settings as designed landscapes.[14] The existing body of work has, however, focused largely on the recognition, cataloguing and in some cases the planning of individual examples, while their meanings, uses and social contexts remain under-studied. Furthermore, work carried out on the subject to date has been published largely in the form of scholarly articles and contributions within specialist academic monographs, while other relevant material exists in the form of semi-published 'grey literature', with very limited distribution. This volume aims to fill this lacuna by addressing the topic of medieval landscape design within a single book. It aims to synthesise and contextualise the existing body of information in order to provide a survey of the current state of knowledge, but also, crucially, recognises that any meaningful study of the subject should be more than a collection of examples distributed in time and space.

The fourth key aim of this book is, therefore, to explore the symbolism of medieval designed landscapes and ultimately to extract something of their contemporary meanings – how they were perceived, understood and valued by the people who lived and moved in and around them. Generations of essentially functionalist approaches to the understanding of the medieval countryside, with emphasis on its management for essentially pragmatic reasons, have arguably retarded any ambition towards understanding its deeper-rooted symbolic meanings. Traditional histories of the medieval landscape have understood settlements and fieldscapes as an essentially workaday world – subsistence bases in an economic space and as resources to be 'exploited'. Contrary to what we may suppose, not all areas of medieval estates were managed to maximise production and profit, and it is crucial that we look at the deeper meanings that these landscape elements had for medieval men and women. While in the working world of medieval agriculture nature may well have been perceived as something that was struggled against, it also provided a backcloth for life and leisure, especially in the upper echelons of society.

The notion of landscapes manipulated for ritual and symbolic effect is familiar to prehistorians and, arguably, some of the concepts employed in the study of these prehistoric landscapes could be applied to the understanding of the 'designed' spaces and landscapes of historical periods. While medieval archaeology has tended to play down the importance of perception in the past, this type of approach has obvious potential for any study of the concept of landscape 'design'. Prehistoric archaeology arguably has much to offer the medieval landscape historian interested in understanding the experiential dimension of past land use. In interpreting prehistoric monuments within their settings, it has become almost standard practice to think in terms of how they would have been experienced by those moving through the landscape in different ways, with emphasis on the ever-changing visibility and intervisibility of sites and features. Tilley's *Phenomenonology of Landscape* pioneered an ethnographically informed experiential approach to the study of prehistoric ritual landscapes,[15] and studies of Neolithic and Bronze Age landscapes have since led the way,[16] although Iron Age studies are catching up.[17] Certain concepts – in particular that of visibility and sensory impact – have application to the medieval period, although precise methodological applications remain to be refined.

How can we begin to reconstruct medieval society's own views of elite landscapes? Alongside the material evidence of the landscape itself that is central to this study, visual sources and literary and poetic material provide important starting points, but reconstructing medieval conceptions of 'landscape' remains intensely problematic.[18] In particular, we need to pay attention to the 'symbolising faculty of the medieval mind'.[19] To those who inhabited it, the medieval landscape was full of symbolism, packed with references to religion and the work of God.[20] It was inherent, in a way now almost unimaginable, for medieval people to disaggregate 'natural' surroundings and see flora and fauna as symbols for higher things – in short, to transform the countryside into allegory. Hermeneutics are important here: medieval texts that described the natural world also tended to allegorise nature, attributing hidden spiritual meanings to plants and animals.[21]

It can be tempting to create a rigid division between these 'ritual' or 'symbolic' attitudes to landscape and its more practical and utilitarian functions. The various components of elite landscapes discussed here had, at one level, economic rationales: for example, fishponds, dovecotes and rabbit warrens provided sustainable foodstuffs, while deer parks gave venison and grazing, and therefore, ultimately, it would be misleading to create a false dichotomy between what might be labelled 'landscapes of pleasure and leisure' and 'landscapes of production'. The boundaries between the two were mutable rather than fixed, while many of the components of landscapes discussed in this book manifestly meet both definitions – features whose utility values are undeniable but whose symbolic connotations were also important, if underestimated in the scholarly literature of the modern world, to medieval contemporaries.

This book is also characterised by the fact that it examines an area of overlap between three areas of scholarship: studies of medieval buildings; landscape history; and garden history. Each of these approaches has something important to offer the study of medieval designed landscapes, but none alone can provide an all-embracing approach. The fact that these fields of scholarship have developed along quite separate paths, with their own traditions and historical baggage, presents particular challenges. For example, studies of medieval buildings have benefited in recent years from fresh approaches that emphasise the social meanings of architecture and built spaces – concepts that can usefully be extended to the designed environments around them. Yet a deeply ingrained tendency towards a 'building-centric' mode of enquiry has generally neglected these settings and the ways in which they and the buildings were experienced *in toto*, although studies of castles in particular have made important steps forward in this regard.[22] Landscape studies, meanwhile, offer the benefit of a more holistic view of the medieval countryside and one grounded in the evidence of the historic landscape as a document in its own right, but have been long dominated by essentially functionalist modes of interpretation that neglect the symbolism and the social construction of landscape.[23] Finally, garden history deals more explicitly with the creation, diffusion and meanings of designed spaces. It has developed as a field of medieval studies in its own right, led by Harvey's seminal *Medieval Gardens*.[24] Yet garden historians in general have tended to downplay the significance of developments before *c*.1500, which are often ignored completely or marginalised as an insignificant prelude to a post-medieval flourishing of garden design.[25]

The fact that the subject of medieval landscape design sits a little uneasily across these three areas is perhaps the key reason why its recognition as a phenomenon of the Middle Ages has taken so long. Another reason is that the British sites and landscapes on which this book focuses might seem to compare poorly to some of their equivalents in continental Europe. For example, on a broader European scale the contribution of British monasticism to the practice of medieval gardening has been portrayed as 'second rate'.[26] The glories of secular garden design exemplified by the palaces of Norman Sicily or the water gardens of Islamic Spain do not have obvious equivalents in Britain.[27] Nevertheless, while some of the sites examined in this study unquestionably push the boundary of the definition 'designed' landscape, it is clear that the evidence from Britain should not be dismissed as merely derivative or substandard: rather, it is a rich source of social history in its own right.

Approaching medieval designed landscapes

A study of any form of cultural landscape from a historic period must, by definition, be interdisciplinary in scope. While this book accordingly makes use of a wide range of source material embracing historical documents as well as literary, poetic and pictorial material from the Middle Ages, it should be noted that this is also a volume that is firmly rooted in the study of material evidence, whether buildings, excavated deposits or the countryside itself, which is used as a basis from which to explore the social dimensions of elite landscapes in the past.

It is a central tenet of landscape history that landscapes reflect the societies that created them. Nowhere, it can be argued, are these links between society and landscape more explicit than in the case of designed landscapes whose configurations reflect not only contemporary systems of social organisation as well as tastes, fashions and ideologies, but also the idiosyncrasies and motives of individual landowners. The Renaissance is often seen as signalling a new and unequal type of relationship between humanity and nature in which the latter is dominated.[28] A key theme of this book, however, is that the conscious manipulation of nature for reasons beyond utility had a deeply rooted medieval ancestry. This study stresses, moreover, that landscape was a space that not only mediated social relations, but whose meanings were socially produced, maintained and reproduced. The artful incorporation of buildings into pleasure grounds and wider designed settings had many effects; architectural space and elite landscapes not only structured social practices but also projected images of power. Far more than simply a collection of resources to be exploited, therefore, the medieval landscape can be conceptualised as a web of performances and activities but also of meanings; it was structured outwardly and from above by the power-holders within society but also from within by the communities and individuals who inhabited the everyday working world.

In terms of chronological coverage, the core of this book is concerned with the period *c.*1050–1550, although there are glimpses both backwards to antiquity and forward to the Renaissance and the post-medieval legacies and reuses of these landscapes. Definition of the word and concept of 'landscape' is not so straightforward, however; different disciplines have their own definitions and the term has often been used uncritically. The word originated in the Dutch language (as *landschap* or *landscap*) in the Middle Ages, where it meant the perception of the ability to live on the land (something that was felt rather than seen), before its adoption into English to describe a genre of painting following the Renaissance.[29] Here, landscape is understood broadly, both in the archaeological sense as a tract of territory, and as a view captured by the eye, although we should of course remember the absence of a medieval tradition of landscape painting in any accepted sense of the word. 'Ways of seeing' altered in the sixteenth century with perspective and realism.[30] We should be careful to remember, however, that 'landscape' and 'landscape art' are two quite different things. In charting the history of landscape representation in art, Crandell has claimed that: 'The sense of detachment and security necessary to stand back and look at the landscape appreciatively was simply not existent during the Middle Ages'.[31] Conventionally, landscape perception 'proper' is a product of a modern consciousness.[32] The cloistered medieval mind saw and represented nature as discrete objects with spiritual meanings rather than as an object of beauty.[33] 'Pure' landscape painting as strictly defined implies a depiction free of the pictorial conventions and narrative content that characterised medieval art, equating to a view from one vantage point – through an 'illusionistic window'.[34] It is not until the fifteenth century and the advent of linear perspective that 'imitative art' displaced the 'landscape of symbols'.[35]

For evidence of depictions of landscape scenery in art in the period under discussion, we have to look beyond Britain. Ambrogio Lorenzetti's famous frescos on the walls of Siena's Palazzo Pubblico, painted in the period 1338–40, have been identified as being perhaps the very first landscape paintings in the modern sense.[36] Depicting on one wall scenes representing the effects of good government and, on the other, the effects of tyranny and bad government, these allegorical frescos depict a countryside punctuated by rounded hilltops stretching away from the walled city to the horizon. The rural and urban worlds are intimately bound up to create an idealised composition of the city-state and of a commercialised rural hinterland tied to an urban hub. Critically, it is in this context – of the rural idyll as perceived from the town, viewed, as it were, from the city walls – that the concept of landscape art is rooted. At a broader level the concept of 'scene' – of perspective, realism and structure – in medieval art can gradually be detected in works of the fourteenth and fifteenth centuries. In the middle of the fifteenth century, for example, the Burgundian manuscript illustrations of Jean Froissart's *Chroniques* used compositional devices including receding perspectives to depict idealised castles, cityscapes and their hinterlands from vantage points in order to showcase the self-confidence of the Valois dukes.[37] Again, it was from the urban milieu that these tastes emerged, in particular from the industrial heartlands of northern Italy and Flanders, reminding us that, in art at least, the first medieval representations of landscape were from an essentially urban perspective. Embodying a deeper aristocratic ideology, such images are contrived and are not 'realistic' depictions of landscapes in any conventional sense, of course. The perspective of the October scene of the early-fifteenth-century *Très Riches Heures du Duc de Berry*, showing Paris, for instance, is altered to include fields immediately outside the walls.[38] Medieval encyclopaedias afford other glimpses of contemporary sensitivity to the concept of landscape. For example, Bartholomeus Anglicus's *De proprietatibus rerum* ('On the properties of things'), written in the second quarter of the thirteenth century and comprised of 19 books on subjects such as 'the birds', 'the earth' and 'trees and plants', was supplemented in various later forms with illustrations exhibiting a sense of landscape structure seen only sporadically within the text. Bartholomeus's *Pays et Provinces*, for instance, recognised regional sub-divisions of Europe not simply in terms of their resources and physical geography, but also as distinctive culturally moulded entities and textured landscapes.[39]

The work of historical and cultural geographers has sometimes given the impression that the ability to perceive landscape was an innovation of the fifteenth century.[40] While paintings show little evidence of the observation of the landscape as an object of beauty until the development of linear perspective from this time, this study shows that the viewing of compositions of elite features is apparent from landscape and architectural evidence. Inhabiting the medieval world was a rich and complex sensory experience, but one which was also culturally conditioned. In the Middle Ages physical sensations and the senses were understood and affected human behaviour in ways very different to those of today.[41] Medieval people thought the senses a two-way process, with sight in particular understood in a very different and more affective way, almost as a feeling, closely linked to concepts of memory.[42]

Notwithstanding these differences between past and present observation of surroundings, scholarship drawing on the behavioural sciences reminds us of the fundamental habits of perception that guide and condition, if not dictate, our response to scenery; essential concepts such as 'prospect', 'refuge' and 'hazard' arguably transcend time, place and cultural context.[43] These are also relevant to the present study. The visual effect of, for instance, perceiving a building on an elevated position, across water, or via an approach that ensures that scenery is revealed quickly and dramatically features in a tradition of medieval landscape design that conveyed distinctive meanings, intentions and symbolism. But again, perceptions of the countryside are culturally conditioned; different societies have very different interpretations of what constitutes 'beauty' in the landscape, and it would be utterly wrong to project our ideas, or those of the eighteenth century, onto the medieval period with which this book is concerned.

In an age of emulation, the medieval nobility embodied a culture of competition in which the need for the physical display of status was ever present. While a huge body of scholarship exists on the subject of medieval elite societies, only rarely has this literature extended to address aspects of the physical evidence that defined the aristocracy.[44] Beyond the study of residences as forms of elite display, scholarship on the material culture of the medieval aristocracy has included discussion of the insignia of the higher nobility (e.g. banner, sceptre, and coronet) as well as that of lesser magnates and the knightly classes (e.g. shield, seal and heraldry).[45] What characterises this book is that it endeavours to examine the material culture of these societies in terms of their residences and their settings.

A major impetus to the realisation that medieval landscapes could be designed for dramatic effect and symbolic impact has come from castle studies. While this field of study was for long dominated by site-centric approaches and militaristic explanatory frameworks, fresh approaches from the late 1980s and the 1990s have seen new emphasis on social, domestic and symbolic interpretations of castles. One crucial plank of this approach has been the realisation that the environs of castles could represent vehicles for social display in the same way as the buildings themselves. Scrutiny of evidence for the projection of power in Norman landscapes is particularly important given that most individually researched examples of medieval designed landscapes date to the period *c*.1350–1500, and have become entwined with arguments regarding the supposed decline of military imperatives in castle-building. The relationship between residence and setting can work in more than one way, however. In stressing that landscapes were laid out explicitly to complement buildings, this book is also careful not to overlook the possibility that the reverse might also be true – that buildings were also designed as parts of landscapes.

While studies of castles have progressively broadened out to examine the landscapes in which these residences were embedded, the same cannot always be said of studies of other types of elite medieval residence. Another way in which this study aims to advance our knowledge about design in the medieval landscape is thus by examining non-fortified as well as fortified seats of lordship. A broad spectrum of aristocratic sites with and without defences existed, and designed qualities were not restricted to residences belonging only to those on the uppermost rungs of aristocratic society. This book therefore aims to broaden the range of sites around which designed landscapes are known to have been created, and extends to examine palace sites, both those of ecclesiastical magnates and the monarchy, as well as great houses and other aristocratic sites such as moated manors. Studies of medieval palaces have taken time to catch up with castle studies in examining the settings of these great residences. Some syntheses have neglected this wider context entirely,[46] or extended to cover gardens and the material culture of hunting but not wider landscapes of leisure and recreation.[47] Some individual case studies have emerged, however, including excellent analyses of the multi-period parkscapes of Clarendon and Windsor.[48] But it is important to remember that the medieval world saw no real hard and fast distinction between these 'categories' of residence, and that labels such as 'fortified manor', for example, are post-medieval coinages and academic jargon rather than authentic medieval concepts. In medieval England, documentation relating to the gardens of royal properties invariably records these properties as the 'king's houses', making no distinction between residences with and without fortifications.[49] The book also extends the coverage of elite landscapes to embrace certain aspects of religious landscapes (particularly those around monasteries), while acknowledging that a fuller study of the imagery and meanings of the settings of religious communities is a priority for the future.

By looking at this broad range of residential sites, this book therefore also deals with the social 'elite' in a broad sense. In particular, this study aims to extend the study of medieval landscape design beyond those created for kings, queens and major magnates, which have perhaps received more attention, to encompass the residences of the lower nobility and gentry classes. While overall the households of these social groups comprised no more than 1 or 2 per cent of the total population at the most, their impact on landscape reorganisation was profound. These patterns did not remain static, however. We can detect differing attitudes within the various levels of 'elite' medieval society, and these changed through time as the social order transformed, just as sites themselves were invariably developed through long-term histories of occupation. As well as comparing how landscape design was or was not realised across different strata of medieval elite society, this book is also concerned with the search for areas of commonality in noble attitudes to landscape, and thus further explores the concept of an underlying aristocratic ideology. These landscapes represent one under-studied dimension to the materialisation of elite medieval attitudes and arguably a wider elite ideology and worldview.[50]

This volume aims to build on a long-established tradition of archaeologically based studies of the social use of space within medieval buildings. While castles have been the main focus of enquiry, the planning of manor houses and palaces has similarly been interrogated as a source of information about contemporary social organisation.[51] By reconstructing patterns of access and flow within these structures, such studies reveal how circulation patterns reflect the increasing complexity of the medieval household through time. By extension, they can also shed light on concepts such as privacy, hierarchy and the gendered nature of space.[52] The walls of the structures in question have usually bound the definition of space within these studies, however. In contrast, this study aims to apply some of these notions to fresh contexts – moving beyond buildings to explore their settings and landscapes and how these too were arranged for social reasons.

For the post-medieval period, approaches to polite landscapes rooted in art history have tended to sever mansion houses and their settings from the countryside and communities beyond the park pale. In the medieval period the households of larger medieval landowners could certainly be isolated from the workaday world, especially as most lords oversaw far-flung federated estates rather than consolidated chunks of territory.[53] Yet an intriguing dimension to the study of designed landscapes that unites the medieval and post-medieval periods is the way in which the settings of elite buildings combined function with beauty. Adopting an approach rooted in archaeology and focused on the physical landscape, this study advocates a more complex discourse of the designed landscape that endeavours to acknowledge the impact of landscape reorganisation on settlements and communities. A focus on the upper echelons of society could be seen as restrictive – politically incorrect even – and contrary to the principle that archaeology tells the history of the undocumented. We should also remember that the elite 'landscape' with which this book is concerned took up relatively small areas of space: in fourteenth-century England, for instance, non-agricultural land uses, including hunting and other recreational facilities, took up a mere 5 per cent of the total areas of demesnes.[54] Yet the social impacts of these activities were enormous considering the relatively modest areas over which they occurred.

A major challenge here is to critically address assumptions about what constituted a garden in the medieval period. It is a point of orthodoxy in traditional accounts of British garden history that the medieval garden equated to the *hortus conclusus* – a small-scale and cloister-like space whose defining characteristic was its enclosure.[55] The role of the garden in elite culture more generally was out of all proportion to its impact on the ground, however, with its prominent allegorical role in art and literature well attested.[56] As represented in late medieval manuscript illustrations, these spaces were adjuncts to elite residences that provided bubbles of social exclusivity and microclimates for horticulture. Inward-looking and segregated from the wider settings of residences, it is difficult to see the medieval garden as traditionally understood as constituting a 'designed landscape' in any sense.[57] Medieval usage of the term 'garden' was, however, more elastic than is often realised, covering everything from small square plots to complex pleasure gardens, while archaeological fieldwork is showing how gardens were embedded within wider elite settings.[58] This book demonstrates that gardens were very often single components in far wider tracts of territory structured for leisure and pleasure, often serving to link and mediate between residences and their wider landscapes, and influencing how these settings were perceived by contemporaries.

In exploring designed landscapes it is important not to rely wholly on a 'top down' approach that concentrates on the activities of the social elite, but also to consider how these aristocratic landscapes fitted into the wider world. It would certainly be misleading to suggest that landlords imposed their will upon the landscape irrespective of wider communities, and negotiation or brokerage may lie behind outwardly grandiose schemes of design. How might other members of society outside the social elite experience and perceive designed landscapes? How exclusive were these spaces? What is the relationship between the everyday 'taskscapes' of those living in and working from surrounding settlements and the sphere of the social elite? As well as examining the wider impacts of elite landscape design, the present study also attempts to assess whether traces of dissatisfaction and even resistance to it can be detected within wider communities. It was arguably not only those 'beyond the pale' of parks and gardens that were affected,[59] but those who worked, lived and moved within elite spheres of the landscape more generally.

The study of design in the medieval landscape has developed unevenly in a geographical sense. A key problem is that the existing body of scholarship is largely restricted – beyond anecdotal examples – to lowland England, which is unsurprising given the longstanding bias in landscape history towards the study of areas of southern and midland England.[60] Accordingly, this book aims to highlight something of the potential for the study of medieval designed landscapes across landscape types of different character and texture and extends to include examples in Ireland, Scotland and Wales as well as in northern and western England. The different regions and, indeed, different countries, covered in this book have experienced very uneven study and exhibit divergent traditions of archaeological fieldwork and scholarship. Our understanding of fashions of gardens and landscape design in medieval Wales, for example, has arguably been retarded by provincialism, with garden history in general developing relatively late.[61] In Scotland, while garden designs dating before *c.*1700 were traditionally seen as exceptionally rare, the number of recognised sixteenth- and seventeenth-century antecedents is growing and the existence of medieval equivalents is a tantalising possibility.[62] Ireland presents different circumstances. Here, the notion that later medieval landscapes could demonstrate elements of aesthetic and symbolic design is especially recent, and lingering perceptions of the Irish medieval landscape as a violent place mean that scholarship on this topic in Ireland has a long way to go.[63] This can be attributed not only to the relative youth of medieval archaeology in the Republic of Ireland, with the study of rural landscapes in particular in its infancy,[64] but also politics: castle studies have traditionally adopted quite a military emphasis, so that the social and symbolic roles of medieval elite sites have been underplayed.

Discussing medieval landscape design: the structure of the book

This introduction to the aims and content of the book concludes with a short case study of the landscape around Restormel, in Cornwall, which is intended to bring into sharper focus the actuality of landscape design in the Middle Ages. Following this, Chapter Two, 'Sources and Approaches', examines in more detail the key categories of data on which our understanding of medieval elite landscapes will be based. The next two chapters explore the physical structure of elite landscape design. Our understanding of medieval designed landscapes is sufficiently far advanced to recognise that many feature essentially similar elements, and the account works outwards from the elite buildings that were invariably their focal points to examine in turn ornamental features in close proximity (the 'inner core') and those that formed the broader setting (or 'estate landscape'). A range of case studies from across Britain is used to identify these tell-tale features and explain how they articulate together to form the 'anatomy' of a medieval designed landscape. Chapter Three, 'The Inner Core: House, Garden and Setting', looks at the relationship between buildings and the designed spaces in their immediate vicinity as well as at a wide variety of artificial water features, including moats, meres and ponds. Chapter Four, 'Shaping Nature: Animals and Estates', looks at the significance of ponds, warrens and dovecotes as symbols of status and authority and assesses the significance of the elite species of animal that inhabited these environments. Chapter Five, 'Parkscapes and Communities', takes a wider perspective and looks in particular at hunting landscapes. Perhaps the most important elements of these were deer parks, which formed privatised enclosed landscapes in their own right. Designed landscapes were far more than mere compositions of physical features around buildings; they were rich in symbolic and allegorical meanings familiar to medieval aristocratic culture. These are assessed in Chapter Six, 'Seeing and Believing: Understanding Designed Landscapes', which also turns to the wider vernacular landscapes in which elite parks and gardens were embedded and assesses the wider social implications of these schemes. Against this background, Chapter Seven, 'Touchstones to the Past: Legacies', looks at the influence of medieval gardens on Tudor landscape design and explores their longer-term histories. It also includes a brief examination of the parks and gardens around Tudor-period palaces – places such as Hampton Court and the 'lost' palace of Nonsuch. This subject is far more fully covered in other literature, but it is important to acknowledge these developments as they provide the link between the medieval period and the great designed landscapes of the post-medieval era. The conclusions presented in Chapter Eight include a critical commentary on the 'designed landscape' concept as well as a chronological summary. Within this discussion, evidence is explored through a series of case studies, and particular attention is given to illustrating the physical traces of designed landscapes from a variety of perspectives – for instance, through aerial photographs, archaeological survey drawings and ground-level views.

Land and lordship: the case of Restormel

> It is seated in a park upon the plain neck of a hill, backed to
> the westward with another somewhat higher, and falling every
> way to end in a valley watered by the fishful river of Fowey … a
> palace so healthful for air, so delightful for prospect.[65]

The celebrated antiquary Richard Carew of Antony, writing in the late sixteenth century, was well aware of the aesthetic qualities of Restormel castle,
which still stands in splendid isolation amidst rolling green countryside in
southern Cornwall (*Black and White Plate 3*). This building and its surrounding
landscape provide a short but instructive introductory case study that highlights
a little more clearly several of the themes that run throughout the structure of
this book.

Occupied as a seat of lordship from the eleventh or twelfth centuries and
abandoned by *c*.1540, the site's heyday was as a residence of the earls and
dukes of Cornwall after 1265, when the administrative centre of the duchy
was moved here from Launceston, some twenty miles to the north-east.[66] The
castle's principal surviving vestige is a circular masonry 'shell keep' that is
visually striking not only because of its battlemented silhouette but also
because of its position on a false crest on one side of the valley of the River
Fowey. Notably, its builders chose not to utilise a higher position to the west (as
noted by Richard Carew), where the earthworks of a former Roman fort can still

Plate 3. Restormel (Cornwall), showing the shell keep standing within an area of former medieval
parkland. (Photograph: Oliver Creighton)

be made out, but rather a spur fully intervisible with the whole of the valley below. The castle looms up on the skyline dramatically and quickly for the visitor and observer within the park around it and in the valley below. Such locations were more common for castles than we might imagine; visual needs were not always served by a location on the highest point within a locality, but more often by places that were intervisible with valley floors and sides.[67]

Purportedly an archetypal example of a shell keep, Restormel has slotted neatly into a traditional narrative of castle typology and evolution presented in numerous textbooks.[68] Accounts of the castle have generally suggested that the visible masonry remains are of two phases, and that these replaced an earlier earth and timber castle based on a 'ringwork' (i.e. a simple circular embanked and ditched enclosure). However, a detailed structural analysis suggests that the stone castle was built as a masonry edifice of one phase in the late thirteenth century (although on the site of an earlier earth and timber fortification), and embodied an unusually innovative design whereby domestic apartments were disposed around a central circular space (*Figure 1*: top).[69] Despite its circular plan, the castle design ensured that it presented quite different images from different viewpoints. A detailed survey of the manor recorded in the Caption of Seisen in 1337 makes it clear that the shell keep was accompanied by a series of functional farm buildings within the bailey, including two stables either side of the gatehouse.[70] The fact that a major masonry building at the cutting edge of contemporary design was accompanied throughout its lifetime by a bailey enclosure packed with agricultural facilities and whose defences remained of earth and timber presents an apparent contradiction. It may well be significant that this less impressive 'working' area of the site was largely hidden from view, tucked away in the manner of a post-medieval kitchen garden.

What is of particular significance here, however, is not so much the architectural detail of this structure as how the building was 'keyed into' a local setting that was manipulated, at least in part, with an eye for aesthetic value, thus amounting to a designed landscape (*Figure 1*: bottom). Three elements in particular are important: a deer park that enveloped the castle; other lordly structures associated with or appended to it, including a chapel and garden enclosure; and the small medieval port town of Lostwithiel, located on the lowest crossing point of the river, just within view to the south.

The castle sat almost centrally within an oval-shaped deer park. Probably laid out in the 1160s by the Cardinham family, who owned an earlier castle on the site, this took on a new significance following acquisition by the duchy, and by the 1370s it was stocked with some 300 deer, making it the largest in the county.[71] The financial accounts of the Duchy of Cornwall make it clear that medieval parks in the county were not run primarily for profit, at least by the fourteenth century, which represented Restormel's heyday. The exclusivity of this hunting landscape certainly did not deter and may well have actually attracted park-breakers. Offences are recorded in large numbers from the 1270s and individuals were regularly employed to plug gaps in the fenced park

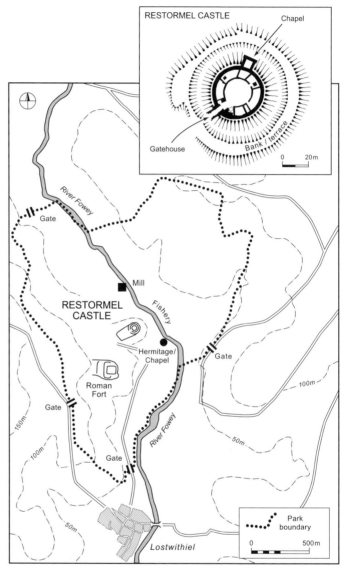

Figure 1. The elite landscape around Restormel castle (Cornwall). Based on Thomas 2000 and Herring 2003, with additions.

boundary. Expenditure on the repair of pales, lodges and the payment of parkers was considerable, while grazing rights generated scant profit and were minimised prior to visits by the dukes in order to boost the deer population.[72] It was nonetheless a carefully maintained environment. In the winter of 1355, the parker provided hay and 'rake houses' for the deer, while other fourteenth-century records detail the painstaking removal of mossy patches that created problems for grazing animals.[73] While most seigneurial parks were appended to residences, here the parkland completely enveloped and secluded the seat of lordship, and anybody approaching it would have done so via one of several timber gates within the pale. First depicted in cartographic form in one of Henry VIII's coastal charts,[74] the park had a bowl-like topography that ensured the castle was not only its central point but also its visual focus. The castle was intervisible with most of the park, with the natural lie of the land disguising the fact that the deer park actually had limits; the impression from within was thus of rolling, boundless parkland.[75] The notion of parkland that appears to stretch into infinity was not alien to the medieval mind and is represented vividly in manuscript illustrations such as the much-reproduced early-fifteenth-century *Très Riches Heures du Duc de Berry* (see p. 84).

Secluded within the deer park on the banks of the Fowey below the shell keep was the hermitage and chapel of the Trinity, noted by the sixteenth-century antiquary John Leland and founded in the late thirteenth century by a lord of the castle, perhaps Richard, Earl of Cornwall.[76] As the religious needs of the household were served by a chapel neatly incorporated within the shell keep the purpose of this structure was rather different, being associated with an isolated hermitage that, like many others within castle parks, added to the mystique of hunting landscapes and sometimes featured in medieval romances (see p. 139–40). It was one of a number of hermitages founded or supported by the duchy, including another secluded in their castle park at Liskeard.[77] When first recorded in 1296–7, Edmund, Earl of Cornwall, was paying the hermit in the park, then Brother Philip, an annuity of £2 13s 4d, an arrangement which was maintained through the fourteenth century.[78] Other features of the manorial landscape included within this parkland setting included a valuable fishery and a watermill in the river below, as well as rabbit warrens, all recorded by the middle of the fourteenth century.[79]

Seigneurial aggrandisement was also expressed through settlement planning and promotion contemporary with the construction of the shell keep. A suburban zone of Lostwithiel was incorporated into the existing town in a charter of 1268 and the double borough was given new market rights and urban privileges.[80] While the lords of Restormel had been closely associated with the growth of the market town from its origins in the late twelfth century, the town was not physically appended to the site of the lordship. Characteristically for the largely dispersed settlement landscape of the South West, the castle-borough developed separately but within sight of the seat of lordship. Parallels elsewhere in the region include Okehampton (Devon), where castle and borough developed as discrete entities from the late eleventh century, and Berry Pomeroy (Devon), where the lords removed their residence from the town they had founded (Bridgetown Pomeroy) to a new secluded parkland setting in the fifteenth century.[81] Park-gate towns were not uncommon in medieval Britain and represent an important way in which the social order was embedded within the configuration of landscape.[82] They represented an equivalent to the 'castle-gate' town, but ensured even greater exclusivity for their founders, highlighting the separateness as well as the status of lords who kept their

Plate 4. Interior of the shell keep at Restormel (Cornwall), showing windows and parapet walk commanding views over the surrounding park. (Photograph: Oliver Creighton)

distance spatially as well as socially. This planned borough lay on the very fringes of the castle's emparked setting, terminating the view down the Fowey valley to the south – the borough boundary following the line of the park pale in places.[83] The period of Lostwithiel's promotion in the later thirteenth century saw the administrative and legal apparatus of the duchy established in the borough and the administration of the Cornish stannaries transplanted from nearby Bodmin (as represented by the Duchy Palace in the centre of Lostwithiel, where the duchy regulated the tin industry and extracted taxes).[84] While it is customary to consider castles as administrative centres, here the day-to-day machinery of lordship was conducted quite separately from a castle whose lords remained a discreet distance upstream.

The fabric of the castle itself provides the most compelling indications that this was a building whose visual relationship with the surrounding landscape was carefully managed. Particularly telling is the fact that the parapet walk crowning the shell keep (*Black and White Plate 4*) was accessible via a stair from the lord's 'inner hall'. Access to the most panoramic views of all was thus directly available from the 'deepest' and most private space within the entire site. On the same (southern) side, large windows that must surely have compromised any serious military value for the site opened from the solar, hall and private chambers out over exquisite parkland views, onto the river valley and towards the borough, which remained on the very edge of the 'viewshed' (i.e. the area visible from it). The garden recorded in *c.*1300 probably also lay on this side, as revealed by geophysical survey, where, again, it would have been visible from the large windows. The earthworks lying beneath and around the masonry edifice are also not all they seem. Most importantly, the great grassy mound from which the shell keep appears to rise is something of an illusion. Its appearance is actually the result of piling earth against the exterior of the shell keep, the walls of which extend well below the present ground surface. The probable explanation is that its builders were trying to give the impression that the structure was built on top of a motte, by then an anachronistic feature but one that would give the visual impression of lordly dominance and perhaps permanence and continuity. Worthy of comparison is the castle and stannary prison at Lydford, on the edge of Dartmoor in Devon, where a false motte was similarly thrown up around the rebuilt tower in the late thirteenth century.[85] A broad outer bank surrounding the shell keep represents the vestiges of the first castle at Restormel, and gives the impression of having been rescarped and levelled contemporary with the shell keep in a manner suggestive of a terrace from which the site's dramatic sylvan setting and activities in the park could be observed.

The apparent exclusivity of the site's landscape setting should not disguise the fact that it was sporadically accessed and experienced by elements of the wider community. Many entered the park illegally, as indicated by the incidents of park-breaking and poaching detailed frequently in the duchy records and by commissions to control trespass set up in the fourteenth and fifteenth centuries.[86] But there were other ways in which the burgesses and merchants of Lostwithiel and the peasants of the surrounding manors interacted with Restormel's parkscape. They might take part in hunts, sometimes in almost ritual fashion. In the fourteenth century all villein tenants on the manor of Restormel were obliged to assist with the lord's 'chace' once every year or contribute 1d in lieu, a payment known locally as *huntyngsylver*.[87] Tenants might perform labour service on the repair of the hedges, pales and earthworks around parks in a county where such arrangements were otherwise extremely rare and had by the fourteenth century usually been converted into cash payments. In the 1340s, service on the park pale was costed at 1¼d or 1½d per perch and performed at Restormel as well as other duchy parks at Climsland and Liskeard.[88] Another less obvious way in which the seat of lordship was linked to its surroundings was through the obligation of castle-guard performed by the tenants on outlying estates. Alongside the Duchy of Cornwall's other principal castles at Launceston and Trematon, in the fourteenth and fifteenth centuries individual fief-holders at Restormel were responsible for erecting designated lengths of timber 'hourding' along the castle's battlements and storing them again for the winter.[89] This duty was primarily symbolic rather than perpetuated out of military necessity and highlights a less obvious way in which feudal organisation of the surrounding human landscape was displayed and materialised in the physical fabric of the castle. On other occasions tenants might enter the park because of the duchy's control of the tin industry: in 1312 tin-workers and merchants carried their produce to the castle, presumably from the borough via the 'Towney Gate' in the park pale.[90] The social signals confronting those entering this exclusive domain would have been very clear. Arguably, the castle and its setting formed a carefully composed ensemble that proclaimed the unmistakeable message of lordship to anyone who approached it on the ground. It would also have made a striking impression on anybody passing it on the river that snaked through the valley immediately below, which was navigable until at least the late fourteenth or fifteenth century and represented the lifeblood of the tin trade on which the wealth of the castle lords depended.

The case of Restormel highlights much of the interest in and potential for conceptualising the settings of such elite medieval buildings as 'designed landscapes'. But it also hints at some of the difficulties and paradoxes in this approach – not least that this is a 'designed landscape' without a known designer! Methodological and theoretical difficulties will be considered in this book, which features a concluding critique of the applicability of the 'designed landscape' label to the medieval period (see p. 218–23). For the time being, four points of broader significance emerge from this case study that can be identified as key threads that run through the book, linking together its chapters and subsections.

First, it is clear that recognition of evidence for 'design' in medieval landscapes requires us to consider the relationships between buildings and their settings in new ways. Just as it would be wrong to conceptualise a medieval designed landscape without considering the principal residence with which it was associated, it is also wrong to think of buildings in abstraction from their settings. The realisation that Restormel castle in its principal masonry phase was not a primarily military structure is also sharply at odds with the image of the castle in popular imagination and, indeed, as perpetuated by the heritage industry, and reminds us of the need to cut through lingering preconceptions about the functions of structures. Likewise, as we encounter different types of medieval building throughout this study, including ecclesiastical structures, manor houses and palaces, it is important to consider their symbolic roles as well as their day-to-day functionality. Secondly, it is crucial that we think about how these landscapes were seen, perceived and experienced by contemporaries and vital that we consider not only how landscapes were viewed from buildings, but how buildings were viewed from landscapes. In addition, the importance of considering routes of approach to buildings (including those across water as well as land) and the fact that many structures were embedded within hunting landscapes reminds us that views of these buildings and their settings were ever-changing. Thirdly, we should take care not to adopt a simple 'top down' approach to the study of elite landscapes. They clearly had meanings to others beyond the elite groups who created them, and the position of wider settlements in relationship to designed landscapes warrants careful thought, as do attempts to resist their creation or imposition. Fourthly, it is clear that medieval lords did not have in mind a definitive blueprint for any sort of 'ideal' designed landscape, but tailored the development of landscapes around their houses to the locality. This is another reminder that elite settings were not elevated above and entirely separate from the vernacular world, but enmeshed into the regionally distinctive character of the countryside more generally.

Chapter One Notes

[1] Williamson 1995.

[2] Liddiard 2005a, 119–21.

[3] Bettey 1993, 45–57.

[4] See, for example, Mosser and Teyssot 1991; Quest-Ritson 2001.

[5] Cummins 2002, 33.

[6] Longnon and Cazelles 1969.

[7] See, for example, Wainwright forthcoming.

[8] Williamson 1995, 4–9.

[9] Liddiard 2007b.

[10] Aston 1988.

[11] Williamson 2006b; 2007.

[12] Hansell and Hansell 1988.

[13] Taylor *et al.* 1990; see also Coulson 1990; Everson 1996a; 1996b.

[14] See, for example, Taylor 1989a; 1991; 1996; 1998a; 2000; Everson 1998; 2003, 143–5.

[15] Tilley 1994.

[16] See, for example, Bradley 1998.

[17] See, for example, Miles *et al.* 2003, 8–10, 243–68.

[18] Howe and Wolfe 2002.

[19] Clark 1949.

[20] Eco 1986, 52–64.

[21] Hoogvliet 2000, 28.

[22] Johnson 2002; Creighton 2005b; Liddiard 2005a.

[23] See Johnson 2007.

[24] Harvey 1981; see also McLean 1981; MacDougall 1986b; Landsberg 1996; Jennings 2004.

[25] See, for example, Mowl 2004.

[26] Hadfield 1985.

[27] Ruggles 1999.

[28] Thomas 1983, 13–41; see also Cosgrove 1993, 139–66, on 'Water in the Palladian Landscape'.

[29] Van de Noort and O'Sullivan 2007, 79–80.

[30] Woolgar 2006, 270.

[31] Crandell 1993, 48.

[32] Mitchell 1994, 10–13.

[33] Crandell 1993, 48–9.

[34] Deam 2000, 116, 137.

[35] Eade 1987, 2.

[36] Clark 1949, 6; Andrews 1999, 154.

[37] Ainsworth 2000, 102.

[38] Alexander 1990, 451.

[39] Cahn 1991, 21–2.

[40] Cosgrove 1984, 1–2; see also Cosgrove and Daniels 1988.

[41] Woolgar 2006, 2–3; Nichols *et al.* 2008; see also Eco 1986, 4–6, 65–73.

[42] Giles 2007, 106–7; see also Graves 2007, 515–17.

[43] Appleton 1975; 1990.

[44] See, for example, Steane 2001.

[45] Crouch 1992, 177–247.

[46] Keevil 2000.

[47] Steane 1999.

[48] For Clarendon palace see Richardson 2005; James and Gerrard 2007; for Windsor, Roberts 1997; for parks associated with royal palaces generally, see Richardson 2007.

[49] Colvin 1986.

[50] See Hansson 2006, 11–44.

[51] See Hillier and Hanson 1984 for theoretical context and methodology; see Faulkner 1963; Fairclough 1992; King 2003; Richardson 2003a; 2003b for medieval applications.

[52] Emery 2005, 151–2.

[53] Campbell 2000.

[54] Campbell 2000, 65–7.

[55] Thacker 1979, 84–4.

[56] Pearsall and Salter 1973, 76–118; see also Albers 1991.

[57] See Crandell 1993, 58.

[58] Henisch 2002, 153.

[59] Johnson 2002.

[60] See Johnson 2007.

[61] Briggs 1991, 128; 1998, 65.

[62] Hynd 1984, 269–70; Cruft 1991, 175–6; McKean 2001, 75–8.

[63] See O'Keeffe 2004.

[64] See O'Conor 1998.

[65] Quoted in Halliday 1969, 213.

[66] Elliott-Binns 1955, 248.

[67] See, for example, Liddiard 2000a, 175–6, on Castle Rising, Norfolk.

[68] See for instance Brown 1976, 86–7; Platt 1982, 34.

[69] Thomas 2000, 28–30.

[70] Hull 1971, 41.

[71] Herring 2003, 38–9.

[72] Hatcher 1970, 179–80.

[73] Henderson 1935, 161.

[74] Chandler 1993, 78.

[75] Herring 2003, 38–9.

[76] Henderson 1935, 161; Chandler 1993, 78.

[77] Elliott-Binns 1955, 248.

[78] Orme 2008b.

[79] Hull 1971, 40–4.

[80] Beresford 1967, 406–8.

[81] Higham 2006, 97–8.

[82] Creighton 2005a, 178–9; 2005b, 151–63.

[83] Pounds 1982–84, 91, 111–13.

[84] Pearse 1963, 28–36.

[85] Saunders 1980.

[86] Hatcher 1970, 184.

[87] Hatcher 1970, 65; Hull 1971, xxxix.

[88] Hatcher 1970, 224.

[89] Coulson 2003, 279.

[90] Herring 2003, 48

── *Chapter Two* ──

Sources and Approaches

Any sophisticated approach to the subject of elite landscape must be inter-disciplinary, synthesising the results of historical, literary and art-historical as well as archaeological research, ideally enriched by theoretical input from these disciplines and others. This chapter reviews the key data sources on which this study is based, affording critical insight into their strengths and weaknesses and assessing their complementary contributions. What are the main sorts of evidence through which medieval designed landscapes can be recognised, reconstructed and understood? They fall into two main categories: physical and historical. Of foremost importance under the category 'physical evidence' is the historic countryside itself, in particular the earthwork vestiges of ornamental and other features. Evidence for medieval gardens and designed landscapes is by its very nature unstable and ephemeral, however, and long-term continuity in the occupation of elite residences also often means that such evidence can also be transient, as one favoured style has replaced another. The second part of this section will draw attention to the great diversity of documentary material relating to designed landscapes, which extends to embrace pictorial and carto-graphic sources.

In attempting to reconstruct and understand the ways in which medieval elites moulded the settings and wider environments of their residences, the most important source of information is the landscape itself – the 'richest historical record'.[1] The existence or otherwise of medieval landscape design was certainly not a concern of the founding fathers of landscape history. For W.G. Hoskins in *The Making of the English Landscape*, designed landscapes were a product of the sixteenth-century 'age of great houses'.[2] And while O.G.S. Crawford devoted chapters of *Archaeology in the Field* to deer parks and ponds, it was their physical character rather than aesthetic qualities that interested him.[3] It is important to remember here that the recognition of the various features from which medieval designed settings were composed is nothing new; rather, it is our transformed understanding of the ways in which they were arranged and inter-related that is relevant.

Part of the appeal of this landscape evidence is its tangible and accessible nature. For example, the boundaries of relict medieval parks may be visible in present-day field boundaries, while elements such as ponds and gardens can leave telltale traces in the form of earthworks. A key issue when comparing and contrasting designed landscapes of varying dates in different regions concerns the durability of such evidence. By their very nature, designed landscapes and gardens are subject to redesign and decay as fashions change. Their identification and reconstruction presents many other challenges, not least in unpicking early phases of design where landscapes have been drastically altered. An illustrative example is the landscape of Wardour (Wiltshire), where the luxurious castellated late-fourteenth-century house of John, fifth Lord Lovel, was subsequently integrated into two major schemes of landscape redesign.[4] The construction of a new house nearby in the 1680s was associated with the creation of a new series of formal gardens that incorporated the medieval building as a picturesque centrepiece. A century later the removal of the seat of lordship to 'New' Wardour castle, a little over 1 kilometre to the north-west, saw the creation of an associated Brownian landscape park that found another new role for the old castle as a romantic relic and 'eye-catcher'. These developments obscure the likelihood that the castle itself was originally embedded within its own 'original' designed setting of the late fourteenth century, comprising a compartmentalised deer park and a string of ornamental ponds.[5] Another part of the problem is that medieval buildings preserved and protected as heritage sites in the present landscape invariably represent single components of originally far more extensive settings that have frequently been redesigned.[6] Guidebooks are often guilty of abstracting sites from their settings, although there are signs that this is improving.[7] Prescribed tours are inevitably contained within the walls, while reconstruction drawings too often fail to depict surroundings in realistic fashion. For example, the heritage site of Bishop's Waltham Palace (Hampshire) now under guardianship represents the inner court of a once far more extensive complex embedded within a magnificent setting that showcased the classic appurtenances of lordship. To the north lay the outer court with its gatehouse; to the south an enormous garden was embraced within a turreted brick wall and, beyond that, a vast park of over 4,000 hectares; to the east lay the mill and a planned town; and to the west a great string of fishponds.[8]

Garden archaeology

An archaeological approach has particular potential to illuminate the garden features that were integral components of elite landscapes. Surviving physical traces of medieval gardens of any sort are extremely rare, but given sufficient conditions of preservation, archaeology can help to show how design varied across the social hierarchy and how gardens were embedded within their own wider physical settings; and, in focusing on remains that were disused, it can illuminate examples unchanged by post-medieval redesign.[9] Excavation is only one of the tools of 'garden archaeology', which is an umbrella term embracing a broad range of techniques that, judiciously deployed, can be complementary to one another.[10] All these points can serve as a counterbalance within a subject where documentary and art-historical approaches have traditionally dominated, at least until the late 1980s, after which the pioneering work of figures such as Chris Currie not only established garden archaeology as a serious subject but also helped set an ambitious research agenda.[11]

The most tangible archaeological traces of medieval gardens are those defining the perimeter of the garden space, such as walls, banks and ditches. Within, evidence might include arrangements of beds and the small stone or timber revetments for them, as well as stone-lined pathways, raised benches, ponds and even fountains. The most crucial point of all is that garden archaeology should not be inward-looking but should extend to explore the place of these small designed spaces within wider landscapes. Early examples of garden archaeology are known from the 1930s, one of the first excavations being that at the Elizabethan Renaissance house of Kirby Hall (Northamptonshire).[12] The great modern success story of the subject was, however, the excavation in the 1960s of a remarkable formal courtyard garden accompanying the Roman palace of Fishbourne (West Sussex), and it is worth considering briefly how archaeology has contributed to our understanding of gardens of the period.

ROMAN GARDENS

Although the Roman garden remained a relatively neglected subject until the 1980s, energetic co-operation between ancient historians and archaeologists has since showcased the value of garden study to our broader understanding of elite society in the Classical world.[13] Nowhere is the intimate relationship of house and garden preserved more dramatically than in the Vesuvian landscape sealed in AD 79.[14] In addition to arrangements of enclosing fences, walls and the characteristic trelliswork sometimes portrayed on wall paintings, the immediate settings of Roman gardens were landscaped with terraces, sunken areas and water features and punctuated with seats, temples, shrines and pavilions. In Britain, the outstanding contribution of archaeology to the understanding of Roman gardens is the palace-like villa complex at Fishbourne, near Chichester (West Sussex).[15] Here, the local heavy clays ensured that Roman gardeners dug deep bedding trenches for their plants, leaving outstandingly clear evidence of a formal garden plan that survived centuries of ploughing. Occupying a courtyard-like space between the main entrance and a sumptuous audience chamber, the gardens were surrounded by a continuous colonnaded walkway and divided symmetrically into two portions by paths lined with hedges aligned using an ornate system of recesses for statues or garden furniture; other features included deliberately dug pits for trees, post-holes for trellis work, and an elaborate piped water system. The formality of this scene contrasted with the more natural and rugged aesthetic embodied by another, larger, garden on the south side which featured clumps of trees, a stream and ponds lending a naturalised appearance to an artificially moulded terrace that extended down towards the sea's edge, with extensive views over the coastline. Moreover, the wider setting of the palace had the flavour of a landscape contrived for visual effect: the area to the east of the complex was kept open to afford an uninterrupted view from a formal approach road that skirted, on one side, a series of rich gardens and, on the other, the serene scene of a stream gently flowing to the harbour.[16]

In other cases, archaeology has shown Roman villa and town-house gardens to be second-rate equivalents to those well known from Mediterranean contexts, although our sample of sites remains limited. A notable example is the formal garden created early in the fourth century to visually complement the villa at Frocester Court (Gloucestershire), which included an arrangement of two beds in front of the house and a pair of longer beds and a hedge flanking the approach road.[17] Elsewhere the perimeter walls of attached walled gardens have been excavated but their interiors are unknown, as at Great Witcombe (Gloucestershire);[18] other relevant sites include Bancroft (Buckinghamshire), Barnsley Park and Chedworth (Gloucestershire), Eccles (Kent) and Latimer (Buckinghamshire).[19] Within towns, meanwhile, larger domestic complexes could be organised around or fronted onto garden spaces, as with the possible *mansio* at Silchester (Hampshire) and a winged villa-like building at Wroxeter (Shropshire).[20] Water had an important place in the Roman garden: ornamental cisterns are known, while fishponds were clearly objects of pleasure as well as providers of food. More than a dozen examples are known, including good excavated evidence from the villas of Eccles (Kent) and Bancroft (Buckinghamshire), showing these features to have been stone-lined, quite unlike their medieval equivalents.[21] Other ornamental water features were linked to shrines, as at Blunsdon St Andrew (Wiltshire), where a suite of terraced gardens descends a hillside towards a complex of ceremonial buildings, ponds, courtyards and a bathhouse.[22]

THE ARCHAEOLOGY OF MEDIEVAL GARDENS
A key problem in reconstructing the physical appearance of medieval gardens is that the number of excavated sites and the quality of evidence compares poorly to the Roman and post-medieval periods. Among the more important post-medieval garden excavations are Castle Bromwich (Warwickshire) and the Privy Garden at Hampton Court (Surrey).[23] Those excavations that have taken place on medieval sites have been prompted largely by restoration needs rather than research, so that our data have remained small and biased towards more prestigious sites. Furthermore, the results have often been limited by the ephemeral nature of remains: paths and beds for plants are particularly elusive, as are the shallow depressions for ornamental ponds. For example, investigation of the gardens north of Antrim castle in the early 1990s hoped to recover something of the formal gardens laid out next to the massive Plantation-period castle, but twentieth-century disturbances left little of any value.[24] Negative archaeological evidence can sometimes be helpful, however, where an absence of buildings within an enclosed space suggests a likely garden function. This was the case at the medieval moated site of Rest Park (Yorkshire, West Riding), for instance, where a grid of test holes revealed an area of sterile soil within the moated com-

plex that was interpreted in this way.[25] Similarly, analysis of the soil profile within a rectangular open space enclosed by the ranges of Denny Abbey (Cambridgeshire) suggested that this had been cultivated in the medieval period, probably by the Franciscan nuns who occupied the site in its final monastic phase.[26]

A further challenge is that many excavations of key sites were carried out before the potential of garden archaeology was realised. At castles, manor houses, palaces and, perhaps most markedly, at monasteries, the remains of gardens were simply not on the radar of early excavators. References in the Liberate Rolls make clear that Clarendon Palace (Wiltshire) had among the most elaborate arrangement of medieval royal gardens anywhere in Britain, including designed spaces for the king and queen integrated with their domestic lodgings, but they were totally ignored at the expense of the buildings themselves in extensive excavation campaigns of the 1930s, 50s and 60s.[27] Other excavations have doubtless entirely overlooked evidence for gardens. In the case of moated sites in particular, excavations that have apparently failed to reveal evidence of occupation on internal 'islands' may have been sampling garden areas (see p. 90–2).

The fashion for restoring historic gardens has presented great opportunities for archaeological study.[28] It is critical, however, that such interventions are targeted and integrated into broader management plans for sites. Some early examples of garden reconstruction or restoration occurred without any serious archaeological input, as at Edzell (Angus).[29] No garden restoration can be neutral; most have been based at least partly on conjecture and all embody the values of their restorers.[30] Traditionally, reconstructions of historic gardens have tended to place more weight on the evidence of texts than on that of archaeology. Numerous examples of 're-created' medieval gardens exist, as at Tretower (Brecknockshire) (*Black and White Plate 5*). Although there is no positive proof for the existence of a medieval garden on this site, a pleasure garden was re-created here along authentic lines in 1991, the fifteenth-century design being based on extensive documentary research.[31] Another carefully researched reconstruction is Queen Eleanor's Garden in Winchester,[32] while re-creation of Kenilworth's Elizabethan gardens in 2007 was preceded by excavation and analytical field survey that identified errors in the Elizabethan-style beds laid out in the 1970s.[33]

Other excavations of medieval gardens have occurred either as spin-offs or component parts of work focused elsewhere. Experience also shows that we have remarkably little idea of where medieval garden remains might be encountered archaeologically. The well-preserved medieval gardens revealed by excavation and restored at Haverfordwest Priory (Pembrokeshire) in the 1980s and 90s were entirely unexpected.[34] Comprising at least eight square and rectangular beds, some of them raised and delimited by revetment walls and paths, this garden complex was laid out on low-lying ground within the south-east corner of the monastic complex, between the church and one of the claustral

Plate 5. 'Medieval' garden at Tretower Court (Brecknockshire). (Photograph: Oliver Creighton)

ranges (*Colour Plate 1*). One compartment of the garden was distinguished by an entrance-type feature and a central square plot seems to have been an arbour.[35] It is medieval monastic gardens such as these about which archaeology has been most informative,[36] although our understanding is biased towards the Carthusian order, where the individual – and indeed personalised – gardens attached to the cells of monks are well known, as exemplified by Mount Grace (Yorkshire, North Riding) *(Black and White Plate 6)*. Despite a superficial level of standardisation in the sizes of the individual walled gardens appended to the monks' gardens around the Great Cloister at this site, excavation suggests that they were designed and managed rather individualistically, largely as pleasure grounds rather than for growing vegetables, at least in their fifteenth- and sixteenth-century phases.[37] Thus the garden of cell nine featured an L-shaped arrangement of three square beds or knots separated with grass paths, while at cell ten the gallery that functioned as a private cloister looked out onto a square grassed garden with a decorative layout beyond it; the garden of cell eight showed, in contrast, that a formalised arrangement had been replaced in the sixteenth century with a more utilitarian vegetable garden.[38] Other good examples of monastic gardens known through excavation include those of Denny Abbey (Cambridgeshire), Hull's Augustinian priory and York's Gilbertine priory, where the plans of gardens complete with trenches have been revealed, making it quite clear that principles of monastic planning were extended to include gardens which were designed along regular formal lines.[39] Occasionally, archaeology can show us that monastic gardens were not the idealised designed spaces we might imagine: the large and varied bone assemblage revealed from the well in the fifteenth-century garden of the London Greyfriars was indicative of a marshy and unkempt environment in the final years of the friary's existence.[40]

Examples of excavated gardens from medieval secular contexts are fewer in number. One of the major contributions of garden archaeology for the future must be the study of medieval gardens below the level of the Crown and the front ranks of the aristocracy, about which virtually nothing is known. Radford's clearance of the medieval walled garden at Tintagel (Cornwall) for the Ministry of Works in the early 1930s (*Figure 2*) represents an exceptional example worth examination in more detail, although this excavation was an incidental component part of a more extensive investigation into a presumed early medieval monastic site.[41] The results of these excavations, supplemented by a detailed archaeological survey carried out in the late 1980s, afford a uniquely detailed view of a medieval secular garden and its context.[42]

Occupying a slightly irregular quadrilateral area with maximum dimensions of *c*.20 x 14 metres, the garden was surrounded by a low stone wall pierced in the south-east side by a single entrance positioned slightly off-centre. This trapezoidal shape may even have conveyed the impression that the garden was larger than it really was. It enclosed two equally sized and approximately rectangular beds, divided and surrounded by a path defined with edge-laid stones, leaving another narrow bed around its circumference. In isolation, this information gives little indication of the garden's purpose, which is only clear upon consideration of its setting. Given its incredibly exposed, wind-blasted

Plate 6. Recreation of a medieval garden adjacent to the cell of a Carthusian monk at Mount Grace Priory (Yorkshire, North Riding). (Photograph: Oliver Creighton)

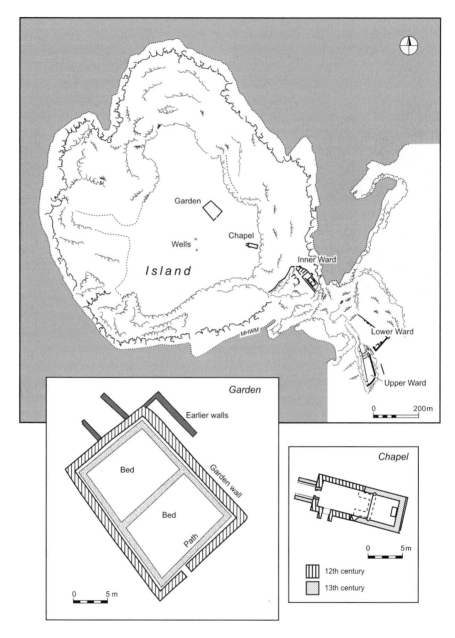

Figure 2. Tintagel (Cornwall): the setting of the medieval garden and castle. Based on Radford 1935; Rose 1994, with additions.

position on a rocky coastal promontory, there is no chance that the garden was intended as a utilitarian feature. Set on the exposed plateau of Tintagel Island, the garden was one element in a castle complex now thought to have been created for Richard, Earl of Cornwall and 'King of the Romans' in *c*.1230. Located some

Plate 7. Tintagel (Cornwall), showing the wild headland setting of the medieval castle. (Photograph: Oliver Creighton)

distance from the lower and upper wards that were the domestic focus of the castle (*Black and White Plate 7*), the garden stood within 50 metres of a chapel and a well, these features giving an impression of order against the background of a naturally wild environment. They were clearly complementary: the garden was positioned in the direct line of sight from the (earlier) chapel porch, for instance.[43] There are also very good reasons to think of this little collection of features as a medieval literary landscape made real. Geoffrey of Monmouth's *History of the Kings of Britain*, completed in the late 1130s, saw the place-name *Tintogel* celebrated across Europe as the seat of the Cornish ruler Gorlois and the place of the magical conception of Arthur, while the place's romantic connections were further amplified by romances such as Tristan and Isolde.[44] The castle itself referenced the fortress of King Mark; the garden recreated the venue for lovers' trysts; and the chapel echoed the place from which Tristan made a miraculous escape.[45] A garden in a similarly spectacular position was attached to the coastal castle of Dunluce (Co. Antrim). Here, earthworks under pasture clearly indicate a series of associated terraces and beds within a cliff-edge garden sited precariously amidst wild scenery, although this part of the site has not been subject to any archaeological study and remains undated.[46]

ENVIRONMENTAL EVIDENCE AND MATERIAL CULTURE
The skeletal information of archaeological structures alone tells us little of the flora that lent medieval pleasure gardens not only their visual beauty, but also the aromas that were integral to the complex sensory experience that a garden

provided and the impression of Paradise it invoked.[47] Direct archaeological evidence for the types of plants grown in medieval gardens comes most usually in the form of macrofossils – in particular the remains of seeds. There is evidence of peony from the gardens of Winchcombe Priory (Gloucestershire), for example.[48] Excavations in the Sewer Lane area of the Old Town of Hull, immediately inside the line of the medieval wall, have provided insight into the sorts of plant species that might be expected in a 'typical' medieval urban garden and how these changed through time; species from the late thirteenth or early fourteenth century included coriander (a relatively early import), with later deposits indicating a diversification in the range of herbs and vegetables and, by the sixteenth century, the growing of shrubs and fruit trees.[49] At its most ambitious, environmental analysis of excavated garden deposits can shed new light on the appearance and functions of gardens, as with a programme of research into the medieval medicinal gardens of Soutra hospital, near Edinburgh.[50] Such data can supplement information from documentary sources such as Alexander of Neckham's late-twelfth-century list of 77 garden plants and Thomas Fromond's list of garden herbs of the late 1520s.[51] In terms of indicating the early presence of introduced species, archaeological evidence can be conservative, however: a long time lag is likely between when the exotic plants are first mentioned in historical records and when they enter the archaeological record.

Excavated deposits within the barbican ditch of the castle at Oxford have afforded an unlikely snapshot of activities within the royal garden in the late fourteenth to mid fifteenth centuries. Among the edible plants were *Vitis vinefera* (grape) and *Ficus carica* (fig), which may well have been imported, while the clipped leaves of *Taxus baccata* (yew) and *Buxus sempervirens* (box) presumably show us that the hedges of the castle gardens were well maintained.[52] Archaeological evidence of box has also come from monastic gardens: excavated deposits of leaves from ornamental hedges have been recorded at Romsey Abbey (Hampshire) and Oxford Blackfriars.[53] An excavated pit in the garden area of Wood Hall moated manor (Yorkshire, North Riding) similarly contained debris from the pruning of shrubs, including holly and rose.[54]

The archaeobotanical record is notoriously biased by the different ways in which plant remains are incorporated into and preserved within below-ground deposits, however. In the archaeological data set for flora within the gardens of late medieval and early modern London, for instance, fruit cultivation is over-represented while cereals, pulses and common vegetables are detected very infrequently, largely because they were invariably harvested before seeding.[55] While three seasons' excavation of the designed setting of Aberdour castle (Fife) revealed the layout of the late-sixteenth-century terraced gardens in precise detail, the site's taphonomy ensured that despite extensive sampling not a single scrap of information about its horticulture was revealed.[56] Environmental sampling of archaeological deposits from garden features can present other challenges of interpretation where excavated fills from beds may reflect post-abandonment flora and fauna. This was certainly the case at Hill Hall (Essex), where interpretation of deposits from a sixteenth-century garden was limited by the fact that these related to a derelict phase, when areas were back-filled with domestic refuse and sewage.[57]

Zooarchaeology – or the study of animal bones – has for long been used primarily to analyse food subsistence patterns on medieval sites, with detailed reports on bird, fish and mammal bones traditionally tucked away in the back of excavation reports. But while, from a traditional archaeological perspective, animal bones are waste – exhausted resources – at another level, their analysis has enormous potential to inform us about cultural preferences, choices, fashions and aspirations. The visual impact of these animals – many of which were hunted or 'farmed' within elite settings – was of the utmost importance at the banqueting table, with the increasingly ceremonial feasting rituals of the late medieval period meaning that conspicuous consumption was demonstrated not simply by the bulk of food and the length of the feasting process, but also the variety of species on offer.[58] Rigorous sampling and analysis of animal bones sampled from excavated domestic contexts can shed light on the species that inhabited designed landscapes, with a notable trend towards an increase in numbers of exotic species from the twelfth century onwards.[59] The changing composition of deer bone assemblages from castles and palaces tells us about elite dietary preferences but also about the practice of hunting itself and its often under-estimated ritual and ceremonial meanings.[60] It is often the bones of species that are recovered in very small numbers that have most to tell us about the roles of animals as features of display, in the grounds of residences as well as on the feasting table. The rising number of swan and pheasant bones on elite sites from the fourteenth century is a good case in point (see also p. 103–6).[61]

Artefacts recovered through excavation can occasionally shed light on the appearance and functions of garden spaces as well as on their dating. For example, a polyhedral sundial recovered from Acton Court (Gloucestershire), designed by Nicholas Kratzer and inscribed with the date 1520, not only provides a likely *terminus ante quem* for the creation of the walled garden, but is substantially earlier than those known from Henry VIII's palaces at Hampton Court and Whitehall and the college gardens at Oxford.[62] A particular category of archaeological evidence for medieval gardens and gardening frequently over-looked altogether is the remains of ceramic artefacts. While there has been something of a tendency to dismiss pottery from garden contexts – in particular flowerpots – as evidence for relatively recent artefacts, the study of these assemblages has great potential to show how garden spaces were used.[63] Perhaps the most diagnostic medieval vessels are watering pots. Found in association with a wide variety of sites, including town houses, manorial sites, castles, monasteries and palaces, these fall into two main types: jug-type vessels with pierced 'roses' through which water was distributed, closely resembling modern watering cans; and flask-shaped forms with narrow necks just wide enough for a thumb to be stuck into, allowing the flow of water from holes in the bottom of

the vessel to be regulated. Plant pots are less readily identifiable in the archaeological record, although there is good evidence that some were ornamental.
Some particularly interesting late medieval handled vessels from north-east
Yorkshire have been identified as ornamental plant-holders for the garden;
especially notable is the fact that decoration appears on one face of the vessels
only, confirming a display function.[64] Other clear early evidence for ceramic
plant holders comes from the Carthusian monastery of Mount Grace (Yorkshire,
North Riding), where the gardens of cells six and seven have yielded pottery
forms best interpreted as flower pots, including jug-like vessels without necks
or handles that seem to have been sunk into the ground.[65] Rather more
obscure types of medieval ceramic garden furniture include beehives and animal
traps.

ARCHAEOLOGICAL SURVEY
If there is one method or technique that has impacted most on our understanding of medieval gardens and designed landscapes since the 1970s it is analytical
field archaeology – the branch of the subject concerned with the recognition,
recording and interpretation of 'upstanding' archaeological remains such as
earthworks and other landscape features.[66] The British landscape contains the
physical vestiges of abandoned gardens in far greater numbers than was envisaged twenty years ago. In particular, the work of the Royal Commission on the
Historical Monuments of England, through systematic recognition and mapping
of earthworks, has revealed large numbers of hitherto unrecognised gardens.[67]
By far the best studied areas are the counties of England with published
RCHME inventories, most notably Northamptonshire but also Cambridgeshire
and parts of Lincolnshire, where particularly widespread evidence of abandoned
gardens of the sixteenth and seventeenth centuries has been found.[68]
Regularity is one of the prime indicators of garden features – the grammar of,
in particular, sixteenth-and seventeenth-century garden design frequently
ensures neat, structured and identifiable remains. For example, a seventeenth-
century designed landscape at Babraham (Cambridgeshire) included a canalised
section of a branch of the River Cam that ran 'ruler straight' for nearly 500
metres, with a cut some 15 metres across.[69] We can only question whether more
informal designs, if they existed, would be so recognisable. Some of the most
important evidence exists where houses were abandoned at a relatively early
stage and the gardens were left as fossilised remains under pasture, thus
being unchanged by fashion. The phenomenon is, again, particularly well represented for the immediate post-medieval period, an excellent example being
the fantastically preserved early-seventeenth-century gardens at Campden
House (Gloucestershire).[70]
    The challenges facing field archaeologists surveying medieval gardens and
designed landscapes relate not only to their complex and interconnected nature
but also sometimes their sheer scale: the massive extent of landscape manipulation at places such as Kenilworth (Warwickshire) actually presented a barrier

to their recognition.[71] Another issue is that features of medieval and early post-medieval designed landscapes have often been misidentified in the past.[72] It is thus not that many of these sites have been 'discovered' for the first time in the last twenty years; rather, it has taken a change of perspective to interpret them as designed landscapes or garden features. In numerous cases watery appurtenances to sites formerly designated as 'fishponds' are on a sufficient scale to be relabelled as designed landscapes, as at Alvechurch (Worcestershire) *(Figure 3)*. At Higham Ferrers (Northamptonshire) earthworks long regarded as part of the medieval castle's defences were reinterpreted on the basis of documents, maps and field observation as the remains of an L-shaped fishpond and a rabbit warren.[73] The actual site of the demolished castle was far smaller than envisaged and was clearly accompanied by a designed aristocratic landscape, of which only the dovecote survives.

Field survey also has particular value for exposing the time-depth of designed landscapes. For example, it can reveal evidence for the earthworks of relict medieval settlements within later landscape parks, as at Dyrham (Gloucestershire).[74] Even the supposedly better-known parks and gardens of the post-medieval period can reveal unexpected medieval ancestry, as at Highclere (Hampshire), for example.[75] The famous parkland landscape of Stonor (Oxfordshire), which was laid out in the eighteenth century, was preceded by a larger medieval park with a fishery and rabbit warren; the setting of the house preserves a buried sixteenth-century formal garden, reconstructable from parch marks mapped during the hot summer of 1989.[76] In other cases field survey has corrected misinterpretation of medieval features as relatively modern landscape elements. Hylton castle near Sunderland, a castellated residence constructed for Sir William Hylton between 1395 and 1410, provides an illustrative example. The documentary record provides no indication of gardens at the site prior to the eighteenth century, and a complex suite of terraced earthworks east and south of the site had been interpreted traditionally as the remains of 'tidying up' operations following the cessation of mining operations in the vicinity early in the twentieth century. Geophysical and earthwork surveys in the early 1990s, however, reinterpreted these features as the remains of a late medieval ornamental garden, the earliest phase comprising an intimate arrangement of hedged or fenced enclosures that accompanied the first castle.[77]

Geophysical survey has been used increasingly in garden archaeology since the 1980s.[78] As with excavated data, most published case studies relate to post-medieval sites, however. The technique has demonstrated considerable potential to reveal the traces of buildings, walkways, walls, borders and beds, and occasionally to show that designed landscapes have greater time-depth than might be assumed.[79] The technique has particular potential to identify the regularity of formal gardens. At Acton Court (Gloucestershire), for example, geophysical survey revealed a symmetrical arrangement of rectangular units within a late medieval walled garden court that was clearly intended to be viewed across a moat from the galleries of the house and the terraces in front of it.[80] At

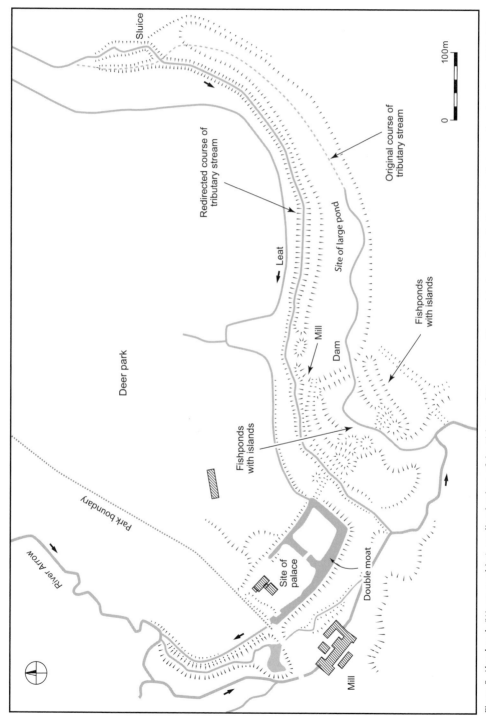

Figure 3. Alvechurch (Worcestershire): medieval palace of the Bishops of Worcester, with associated ponds and other water features. Based on Aston 1970–72, with additions.

Barrington House (Somerset), a rectilinear sixteenth- or seventeenth-century garden layout was, similarly, on the same alignment as the house.[81] The reuse of relict sites as gardens can also sometimes be demonstrated by geophysics, as at the Carthusian house of Witham (Somerset), where a rectilinear subdivision within the main cloister marks a probable post-monastic garden,[82] and at Stafford castle, where resistivity survey has clarified the layout of an early- to mid-sixteenth-century formal garden within the earthworks of the abandoned bailey.[83] Other key examples of later medieval gardens illuminated by geophysical survey include Whittington (see p. 68–9) and the moated garden at Shelley Hall (Cambridgeshire) (see p. 107–8).

The great benefit of studying gardens and designed landscapes through aerial photography, meanwhile, is the wider context that vertical or oblique views can provide, not only identifying new features but also showing the configuration of residence and garden.[84] Other aerial photographs have value as historical documents in the own right, especially those from the 1940s and 50s that depict garden features since destroyed or obscured.[85] Aerial photography can also illuminate how designed landscapes found new uses for existing landscape features. At Burton Lazars (Leicestershire), for example, analysis of oblique aerial photographs of medieval Britain's largest medieval leper colony has revealed the superimposed formal garden earthworks of a (now lost) post-Dissolution country house.[86] But we must remember that these images provide an ultimately false perspective on landscape design. Even if there is compelling evidence that medieval gardens and parks were viewed and appreciated from towers and other elevated structures (see p. 168–75), oblique views from altitude would have been entirely alien to the medieval mindset, with idealised images of country houses and their settings from this perspective being an entirely post-medieval phenomenon.

HISTORICAL, LITERARY AND PICTORIAL SOURCES
The simple fact is that the written record relating specifically to gardens and elite landscapes is generally weak before the fourteenth century and virtually non-existent before the middle of the thirteenth. Snippets of documentary data provide only the most tantalising glimpses of how these landscape elements were used and maintained: for instance, recipe books tell us about the medicinal herbs grown in enclosed gardens, while household accounts detail payments to gardeners. On the broader European front, medieval horticultural literature becomes available from the twelfth century onwards and informs us about quite different aspects of gardens and gardening. Important here are works on garden theory such as *De vegetabilibus* by the German friar Albertus Magnus (*c*.1260) and the largely derivative treatise by the retired Italian lawyer Piero de' Crescenzi (*c*.1305), while this body of source material extends to include more practically based guides such as the *Ménagier de Paris* (*c*.1393) and Jon Gardener's *Feate of Gardeninge* (*c*.1450).[87]

There is, however, very little evidence that relates to the processes by which designed landscapes were actually created in the medieval period, and maps specifically associated with episodes of estate redesign only really become available from the seventeenth century onwards. The medieval gardens that we know most about from documents were the property of the Crown of England. But even in these cases, while we have considerable knowledge of the materials used in their construction and the costs of maintaining, stocking and tending them, we remain remarkably ignorant of how they were actually used and enjoyed. Documentary sources might also disguise from us that gardens were used simultaneously for different purposes. Financial accounts, for example, are strong on anecdotal information such as types of seeds purchased or gardening tasks performed, but can be difficult sources from which to reconstruct the appearance and plans of the gardens themselves. Frequently, documentary sources will confirm the existence of a feature such as a herb garden or a fishpond in association with a manor house, palace, castle or monastery, but will furnish us with little detail about its location, use or appearance, or about how it related to a wider designed setting. The names attributed to garden features within these sources can also cause problems of interpretation, and words such as belvedere, gazebo, banqueting house, summerhouse and pavilion have been used imprecisely and interchangeably in modern scholarship.[88]

Landscape description did not emerge as an independent literary form in its own right until the very end of the period, as represented by the work of the early-sixteenth-century Scottish poet Gavin Douglas, for instance, whose rich and naturalistic descriptions of the seasons mirror the achievements of the first Flemish landscape painters.[89] Only very occasionally do documentary sources allow us to glimpse that medieval minds could look on the countryside in a purely aesthetic sense; it is this that is apparent in St Bruno's eulogy of the Calabrian countryside in the eleventh century, which was free of allegory and included appreciation of the beauty of man-made gardens as well as naturally stunning scenery.[90]

In a British context, particularly relevant are the writings of *Giraldus Cambrensis* (Gerald of Wales) in the late twelfth century. His vivid and lovingly detailed description of his family seat and birthplace of Manorbier, nestled in the coastline of Pembrokeshire in South Wales (*Colour Plate 2*), famously shows that nostalgic appreciation of beauty in the landscape was alive in the period:

> It is excellently well defended by turrets and bulwarks, and is
> situated on the summit of a hill extending on the western side
> towards the sea-port, having on the northern and southern sides
> a fine fish-pond under its walls, as conspicuous for its grand
> appearance as for the depth of its waters, and a beautiful
> orchard on the same side, inclosed on one part by a vineyard,
> and on the other by a wood, remarkable for the projection of
> its rocks, and the height of its hazel trees. On the right hand of
> the promontory, between the castle and the church, near the

site of a very large lake and mill, a rivulet of never-failing water
flows through a valley, rendered sandy by the violence of the
winds. Towards the west, the Severn sea, bending its course to
Ireland, enters a hollow bay at some distance from the castle;
and the southern rocks, if extended a little further towards the
north, would render it a most excellent harbour for shipping.[91]

Gerald's *Journey through Wales* contains other reflections on the aesthetic
qualities of elite sites, including Llanthony Priory (Monmouthshire), whose site
was blessed with rich natural resources, and Cenarth (Carmarthenshire), where
he painted an idealised scene of rural life comprising a church dedicated to
Saint Llawddog, a mill, a bridge and a fishing station accompanied by 'a most
attractive garden'.[92] Elsewhere in Britain, Gerald's description of St Hugh of
Lincoln's first visit to the episcopal palace and park at Stow Park, near Lincoln,
characterised the site as being 'delightfully surrounded with woods and ponds'
(see also p. 64).[93] Such accounts should not always be taken at face value as
resources for reconstructing the physical configuration of a site's setting: they
may exaggerate – for instance to please a patron or demonstrate a family's
power – as well as being selective in coverage, singling out tangible high-status
landscape elements.

Medieval poetry can sometimes illuminate the roles of gardens in the lives
of the medieval nobility more generally. Again, we should be careful not to take
these always at face value: for example, James Stewart's vivid description of the
enclosed garden beneath the tower in which he was imprisoned at Windsor
owes much to models provided in *The Parlement of Foules* and *La Roman de la
Rose*.[94] Medieval poems frequently identify particular features within gardens
but afford little insight into the spatial relationships between them. The portrayal of gardens in these sources is of course predominantly allegorical but an
intriguing interrelationship nonetheless exists between the medieval literary
garden and its physical manifestation in the grounds of palaces, castles and
manor houses. Crucially, this was a two-way process: medieval literary sources
inevitably drew on real-life examples, but so too did gardens make conscious
literary references within their designs, as the earlier example of Tintagel
(Cornwall) has shown (see p. 31–3).

Personal and place-names provide other under-used sources of evidence for
reconstructing aristocratic attitudes towards place and landscape, especially in
the period before *c*.1250, when documentary sources are lacking. While the
English landscape features relatively few place-names of Norman-French origin,
the tendency for names given to new Norman *capita* in the eleventh and twelfth
centuries to feature aesthetic commentary on the countryside is notable.[95] In
particular, compounds of *bel* or *beu* ('fine, beautiful'), such as Belper (Derbyshire)
(meaning 'fine retreat', and associated with a medieval deer park), confirm that
aesthetic considerations were not out of the equation; other examples, all of
which are associated with Norman centres of lordship, include Beaudesert,

Beaufront, Beaumanoir, Beaumont, Beauregard and Belvoir.[96] Toponyms that referenced elite features of the landscape featured prominently in the titles of Norman aristocrats and provide another window into aristocratic self-identity. Those names associated with English and French castles are particularly instructive. They include aristocrats whose names remembered castles that their families were never actually lords of: for example, Hugh d'Ivry (Ivry, France, where the castle was instead the possession of the duke).[97] This invention of tradition – giving the impression that a family's association with a certain place was longer-lived than it really was – is not unusual, and recurs as a theme within medieval elite attitudes to landscape.

Antique maps provide a crucial source for understanding the layout of 'lost' designed landscapes, while art-historical and literary evidence provide rare insight into how they were enjoyed and valued by contemporaries. Moreover, as socially constructed forms of knowledge, medieval maps also have under-valued potential for helping us to understand past perceptions of the landscapes they depict. In the medieval mind, features of the 'real world' depicted in cartographical forms ranging from *mappae mundi* to early estate plans were underlain by ideology and references to the spiritual world as well as holding messages about the locus of power in contemporary society.[98] It would be wrong to think of any medieval map depicting a 'designed landscape' in the same way as a post-medieval estate plan, but, nonetheless, hierarchies of representation are sometimes visible on picture maps of medieval estates: for example, where castles are shown as far larger features than the villages attached to them, while 'silences' might marginalise landscape features seen as less important in the social order.[99] The famous and much-reproduced map of Boarstall (Buckinghamshire) drawn up in 1444 and commonly held to be the earliest plan of an English village, is a case in point, with its prominent depiction of the proudly gated and moated mansion of Edmund Rede (who had the document created) at the centre of an ordered village plan surrounded by seven named woods in which lie the characteristic beasts of the chase.[100] As well as showcasing the *symbols* of power, medieval maps such as these functioned in the *exercise* of power: the massive increase in the number of private estate maps for the period *c.*1500–50 is not simply an index of an increasing survival rate for these documents, but demonstrates that new symbolic values were becoming attached to an increasingly commodified landscape.[101] As well as depicting newly privatised landscapes they could also express the need to protect them: in an estate plan of 1587 the newly emparked landscape of Holdenby (Northamptonshire) contained keepers armed with poleaxes.[102]

Other pictorial sources have a complementary role to play in exploring the medieval aristocratic landscape. In reconstructing the physical appearance of gardens, scholars have often turned to the anecdotal evidence of European manuscript illustrations that beautify textbooks, particularly the miniatures (often Flemish in origin) that become common after *c.*1400.[103] These draw primarily on the Burgundian garden style for influence, so we should question how representative these would have been of the British medieval scene and remember that many are idealised and at least semi-allegorical. The medieval 'fantasy garden' tradition, drawing inspiration from contemporary romances, reminds us of the dangers of taking these sources literally, whether for garden restoration or scholarship.[104]

In addition, the landscape was brought into the living interiors of buildings in a variety of ways: tapestries depicted parkland scenery, and sumptuous wall hangings in female lodgings in particular often displayed hunting scenes as well as gardens and exotic animals.[105] Woodland and forest imagery might be featured in domestic settings in other ways, as at Clarendon Palace (Wiltshire), where glazed floor tiles and sculptural motifs reflected these themes.[106] We should be careful, however, not to reject such sources in studies of the physical medieval landscape on the basis that they distort contemporary experience; rather, ideal and reality were blurred and the interplay between the pictorial and 'real' landscape is important.

Chapter Two Notes

[1] Hooke 2000.

[2] Hoskins 1955, 163–9.

[3] Crawford 1953, 123–31, 188–97.

[4] English Heritage Register of Parks and Gardens, No. GD1484.

[5] Taylor 200, 42; Johnson 2002, 35–6.

[6] Leslie 1993.

[7] See, for example, Barnwell and Everson 2004.

[8] Hare 1988, 226; 1990, 18–21.

[9] Taylor 1974, 136.

[10] Brown 1991; Miller and Gleason 1994; for a case study of the complementary use of different survey techniques, see Keevill and Linford 1998.

[11] See Currie 2005.

[12] Dix *et al*. 1995.

[13] MacDougall 1987; Farrar 1998.

[14] Ciarallo 2001.

[15] Cunliffe 1971; 1998; see also Manley and Rudkin 2003.

[16] Cunliffe 1998, 104.

[17] Gracie and Price 1979.

[18] Leach and Bevan 1998, 129.

[19] Williams and Zeepvat 1994; Jennings 2006, 52–3; see also Frere and St Joseph 1983, 187–200.

[20] Wacher 1974, 277, 374; Taylor 1998b, 14.

[21] Detsicas 1972; Zeepvat 1988, 18.

[22] Esmonde Cleary 1998, 424–5; Wiltshire Archaeological and Natural History Society 1998, 153.

[23] Currie and Locock 1991; Currie 2005, 58–72.

[24] Conway and Reeves-Smyth 1999.

[25] Le Patourel 1973.

[26] Christie and Coad 1980, 189.

[27] James and Robinson 1988, 22; James and Gerrard 2007, 70–3.

[28] Jacques 1997; Dix 2003.

[29] Cruft 1991, 176.

[30] Sales 1995, 6.

[31] Whittle 1988; 1991; Whittle and Robinson 1991.

[32] Landsberg 1987.

[33] Brown 2005b; see also Woodhouse 1999, 141 on the original reconstruction.

[34] Rees 1996; 1999a.

[35] Briggs 1998, 66.

[36] See Moorhouse 1989, 62–3 on the archaeology of monastic gardens in general.

[37] See Gilchrist 1995, 199–201.

[38] Coppack and Aston 2002, 89–92.

[39] Coppack 1990, 79–80.

[40] Armitage and West 1985; Greene 1992, 153.

[41] Radford 1935, 404.

[42] Rose 1994; see also Hartgroves and Walker 1988.

[43] Rose 1994, 179.

[44] Padel 1988.

[45] Padel 1981; 1989.

[46] Reeves-Smyth 2004, 104–5.

[47] Woolgar 2006, 68, 128.

[48] Taylor 1983a, 40; see also Fish 1994 on the evidence of pollen from gardens.

[49] Crackles 1986.

[50] Moffat *et al.* 1989.

[51] James 1990, 57; Harvey 1989.

[52] Robinson and Wilson 1987, 63.

[53] Bond 2004, 159.

[54] MSRG 1995, 37.

[55] Giorgi 1997, 209.

[56] Hynd and Ewart 1983, 105–6.

[57] Murphy and Scaife 1991, 95–6.

[58] Woolgar 1999, 19–25.

[59] Liddiard 2007b, 6.

[60] Sykes 2004b; 2005.

[61] Albarella and Thomas 2002, 24–32.

[62] Rodwell and Bell 2005, 104–5, 260–1.

[63] Moorhouse 1991; see also Currie 1993 on post-medieval material.

[64] Moorhouse 1984.

[65] Coppack and Aston 2002, 89.

[66] Taylor 1996; Pattison 1998a; Wilson-North 2003.

[67] Everson *et al.* 1991, 54.

[68] See Taylor 1991.

[69] Taylor 2004a, 143.

[70] Everson 1989b.

[71] Johnson 2002, 139.

[72] See Taylor 1991, 2.

[73] Brown 1974; see also Taylor 1974, 120.

[74] Smith 2002, 12.

[75] Brown 1998.

[76] Steane 1995, 467–8.

[77] Morley and Speak 2002, 263–4.

[78] Bevan 1994.

[79] Aspinall and Pocock 1995; Cole *et al.* 1997.

[80] Rodwell and Bell 2004, 102–3.

[81] Papworth 2003, 12–14.

[82] Bond 2003, 87.

[83] Darlington 2001, 88–91, 129–34.

[84] See Taylor 1998b for commentary on oblique photographs of parks and gardens generally; for examples of castles in designed settings, see Brown 1989.

[85] Taylor 1998a, 1–2.

[86] Wilson 1991, 26.

[87] Thacker 1979, 83–6; J.H. Harvey 1985; Calkins 1986, 157–9.

[88] Woodfield 1991, 128.

[89] Pearsall and Salter 1973, 200–5.

[90] Webb 2007, 180–3.

[91] Quoted in Rhys 1908, 85.

[92] Thorpe 1978, 173.

[93] Everson 1998, 32.

[94] McDiarmid 1973, 122.

[95] Creighton 2005b, 69; Reaney 1960, 193–4.

[96] Cameron 1961, 88; Steane 1999, 84.

[97] Green 1997, 343.

[98] Hoogvliet 2000, 30.

[99] Harley 1988, 292–4; 1992.

[100] Beresford and St Joseph 1979, 110, 112–13; P.D.A. Harvey 1985, 41–4.

[101] Kain and Baigent 1992, 3–8.

[102] Partida 2007, 50.

[103] Henisch 2002, 151.

[104] Thacker 1979, 89.

[105] Gilchrist 1999, 125.

[106] James and Gerrard 2007, 197.

The Inner Core:
House, Garden and Setting

Documents make abundantly clear that gardens – or *herbers* – were found in close association with most major medieval residences. A fundamental challenge in exploring the interrelationships between medieval house and garden is, quite simply, that no garden from the period survives intact. From one point of view we have the evidence of earthworks, bare, denuded and lacking colour and context, and a very limited sample of excavated sites; from another we have pseudo-medieval gardens that, however well researched, are ultimately recreated for the modern imagination and heritage industry.[1] This chapter demonstrates how gardens typically formed part of an 'inner core' of aristocratic space that linked buildings to their environs. It is crucial, of course, to get behind the simple physical relationship between buildings and gardens and consider how they were or were not linked in terms of access. In a wider sense, medieval gardens often extended to embrace pleasure grounds that could feature orchards, vineyards, groves, walkways, areas dedicated to sporting activities, terraces, mounds, trees, ponds and fountains. Following a preliminary look at the complex interplay between the garden of the medieval imagination and its reality on the ground, this chapter looks in turn at the immediate designed settings of monasteries, manorial sites, royal and episcopal palaces, and castles. It concludes by examining in a little more detail three particularly diagnostic features of the aristocratic setting: orchards and similar garden areas, watery gardens and moats.

The medieval garden: idea and reality

As the subject of a considerable body of scholarship in their own right, medieval gardens have traditionally been viewed as small-scale enclosed spaces.[2] The 'classic' image of the medieval garden, derived largely from manuscript illustrations and texts on medieval gardening theory and practice, is that of a small square or rectangular area delimited by walls, hedges or wooden palings, perhaps interspersed with semi-decorative trelliswork. The spaces they enclosed were given over to similarly square or rectangular expanses of grass or 'flowery medes', whereby green lawns were punctuated with splashes of colour, as well as gridded arrangements of raised beds and perhaps turf benches that provided places to rest and contemplate the whole ensemble.[3] In terms of its role within elite cultural practice, the garden was many things: in a day-to-day sense it was a repository of herbs for medicinal and culinary uses and a private arena for enacting the theatre of courtly ritual, as well as being celebrated as a venue for lovers' trysts.

Medieval people had a clear idea of the place of gardens within the social hierarchy, with individuals of different rank having access to gardens of different character and sophistication. Piero de' Crescenzi's early-fourteenth-century treatise on gardening drew heavily on the earlier work of Albertus Magnus in his description of the small enclosed garden, but also added two further, larger, types of garden that were linked explicitly to social status. The medium-sized garden for individuals of moderate wealth was of two to four *jugers* (approximately 0.5–1.8 hectares), surrounded by a ditch or hedge and full of vines, trees and trellises, while the largest type of garden was reserved for royalty, being larger than twenty *jugers* (5 hectares) and having the qualities of a small park (see also p. 134).[4]

Unlike many of the other components of elite landscapes, however, gardens were not the exclusive preserve of the aristocracy, but were owned and worked by other social ranks.[5] From complex professionally staffed gardens attached to palaces and mansion houses to embanked peasant plots, gardens were integral to the workings of the medieval economy and to household diet across the social spectrum. Vegetables such as leeks, cabbage and turnips would have lent variety to medieval pottage while potherbs might enhance its flavour; from the fourteenth century onwards, meanwhile, the increased commercialisation of the countryside increasingly saw garden crops such as flax and hemp yield cash.[6] In the towns, gardens ranged from large ornamental precincts associated with elite residences, such as the Archbishop of Canterbury's town house at Lambeth, to tiny plots squeezed between tenements. The symbolic associations of gardens were not restricted to those of the highest status: medieval Nottingham had a garden called 'paradise', for example, which was reflected in a street name.[7] Nor were all urban gardens private in character. Fraternities and livery companies were proud of their gardens: that of the Clothworkers' Hall at Mincing Lane, London, was designed as a series of knots.[8] Gardens were also often integral components within the planning of vicars' colleges within towns, as at Vicars' Close, Wells.[9] The inmates of urban hospitals dug, weeded and occasionally 'dressed' the gardens that were attached to these institutions.[10]

Medieval gardens were, as the previous comments indicate, far more than purely utilitarian facilities. By the later medieval period pleasure gardens and the buildings within them were complex spaces graded along social lines, some areas being more public and others more private. Different areas appealed to different senses, including smell as well as vision, and conveyed different messages, including symbolic and religious ones, to the visitor. The plants they accommodated similarly served a blend of aesthetic, medicinal and culinary purposes. It is a striking feature of medieval texts on the subject that species primarily known in the modern world for their perfume or appearance, such as the lily or rose, also served myriad practical uses.[11] In a figurative sense the garden was symbolic of virginity and was prominently associated in art with the Virgin Mary. The bible is of course full of gardens, and the medieval symbolic-allegorical tradition associated the enclosed garden with the Garden of Eden as well as Paradise.[12]

The internalisation of nature was also central to the medieval idea of a garden. The polarisation of a cultivated and controlled interior with an untamed wilderness beyond is exemplified by the case of Tintagel (Cornwall), where residence and garden stood separately in the late thirteenth century (see p. 32). In literary and poetic descriptions, the garden was cut off from the outside world: *hortus conclusus* means, literally, 'closed-off garden'. Arguably the essential defining characteristic of the garden in the medieval mind was not its internal arrangement but its physical definition. In perhaps the most famous medieval literary garden of all, Guillaume's garden in the *Roman da la Rose*, the means of enclosure is singled out as of particular importance, with other physical characteristics omitted:

> *si vi un vergier grant et lé,*
> *tot clos de haut mur bataillié*
>
> (I saw a large and roomy garden,
> entirely enclosed by a high crenellated wall)[13]

This essential characteristic of the garden as an enclosed space is reflected in other words used to describe it, such as yard, garth or curtilage; the term *vividarium*, in contrast, is more usually associated with larger pleasure gardens, and has a Classical ancestry.[14] This reminds us that the distinction between parks and gardens is a blurred one: some of the smallest parks were effectively pleasure grounds, while gardens could themselves be embedded within parkland, either in isolation or attached to lodges or occasional residences (as at Odiham, Hampshire: see p. 178).

Just as the planning of medieval domestic buildings displayed a 'grammar' that embodied social values and meanings, so the arrangement of garden spaces reflected hierarchy. Medieval gardens were in some senses like outdoor rooms, complete with their own furniture, fixtures and fittings, which were designed to be accessed from – and often to be viewed and appreciated from – surrounding buildings (*Figure 4*). But studies of the social use of space within buildings have rarely extended to embrace these designed spaces. An attractive way to understand these gardens is as extensions of domestic living space into the realm of nature. Gardens were, in a sense, transformative, mediating domestic spaces – carefully managed points of interface between the household and the natural world beyond.[15] That this was deeply ingrained within the medieval mindset is made clear in contemporary art – for example, in fifteenth-century Flemish

Figure 4. Medieval manuscript illustration of a *hortus conclusus* type garden with associated buildings, from the *Roman d'Alexandre.* Source: Parker 1853.

paintings, where the window of a domestic apartment frames a view of an ordered and enclosed garden below, beyond which the 'natural' landscape studded with hills and trees can be glimpsed, stretching away into the distance.[16] A similar mediating role is apparent in the use of the medieval garden as a literary device. Chaucer's gardens have been interpreted as 'narrative thresholds', for example, as their presence often signalled a transformation of the storyline.[17]

Monastic gardens

Virtually all monasteries possessed gardens: they were specified as an essential feature of the precinct in the Rule of St Benedict, are displayed in the famous plan of St Gall, and most establishments had more than one. The number of these garden spaces varied depending on the size, status and religious affiliation of the house, and their varied character reflected the twin needs of produce and pleasure in different ways.[18] With such a variety of evidence for gardens within and around monastic houses few generalisations are apparent; what is clear, however, is that the significance of gardens to monastic existence must have extended beyond the utilitarian. Far from being simply component parts of the monastic life-support system, gardens were also spiritual metaphors. There was no simple dichotomy between the monastic garden of recreation and pleasure and the garden of labour, nor between the garden of health and the garden of utility.[19]

While the gardens and elite landscapes of the secular medieval world are the focus of this study, it is important to establish the basic character of monastic gardens. It has been long established that monastic communities, with their well stocked libraries, were clearly key agents in the practice of medieval gardening; some of the earliest medieval texts on the subject are from monastic sources, as exemplified by Walafrid Strabo's famous early ninth-century poem *Hortulus*, and they clearly served as networks for the distribution of seeds and plants.[20] Accordingly, religious houses have been seen to play a pivotal role in the diffusion of gardening techniques to the secular world.

A critical difference exists between the designed spaces associated with monastic sites and the majority of secular examples discussed in this book, however: there is very little evidence that monastic gardens were objects of display in the same sense as the designed setting of a castle or palace. Rather, these were primarily inward-looking designed spaces, which were accessed and experienced almost exclusively by monastic communities. This is not to say that the gardens of monastic communities and of the nobility were completely separate entities, however. Religious houses might be visible from the designed settings of residences, often for reasons of quite conscious design, especially if there was a link of patronage. The location of monasteries founded in the eleventh and twelfth centuries on the edges of deer parks attached to baronial centres is particularly notable, illustrative examples including Hinckley (Leicestershire) and Pontefract (Yorkshire, West Riding), where seigneurial boroughs are another component of lordly landscapes.[21] The twinning of castle and monastery is usually late eleventh century in date. In East Anglia, for example, of 10 examples where the founder's castle stood near to the monastic site, in seven cases the arrangement dates from before 1107, with powerful families such as the Warennes and Albinis using priories to mark out their lordships early on.[22] Lordly residence, monastery and deer park could be planned in unison, as demonstrated by Geoffrey de Clinton's foundation charter for the priory at Kenilworth (Warwickshire) in *c*.1125, which explicitly reserved space for his castle and its accompanying deer park.[23] Visitors, guests and other privileged secular individuals might also occasionally enjoy the garden spaces of monasteries. For example, at Gloucester by royal request Henry III's queen, Eleanor of Provence, was permitted exclusive access to the gardens and grounds of Llanthony Priory from the adjacent castle via a specially built bridge.[24] The Scottish royal family certainly used the monastic gardens within the abbey precinct of Holyrood in the fifteenth century, where their guest house was also accompanied by a deer park.[25]

Our understanding of monastic gardens is sometimes enhanced by detailed documentary sources. Something of the potential of financial accounts to illuminate the minutiae of garden management is provided by documents left by the gardener of Glastonbury Abbey for 1333–4, Thomas of Keynesham, who, aided by four *famuli*, painstakingly accounted for expenditure and revenue with an attention to detail which included the recording of the purchase of four pairs of gardening gloves for 6d and the receipt of 3d for 10 trapped moles.[26] The infirmarer's garden of Westminster Abbey is another particularly well-documented case in point.[27] Some of the fullest records pertaining to any non-royal medieval garden in Britain relate to the monastic gardens of Norwich Cathedral Priory, where 33 rolls survive, detailing expenditure over 32 years.[28] Yet such sources might not reflect the full array of gardening activities within precincts, as individual monks in all probability maintained their own gardens, which remain invisible in the documentary record. Reconstruction of the layout of Norwich Cathedral's gardens from post-medieval ledger books and surveys reveals an intricate and hierarchical arrangement: gardens for religious contemplation and those privately maintained by the sacrist, infirmarer, almoner and cellarer lay within the inner court, while the more utilitarian 'great garden' tended by the gardener was delimited by fencing and formed part of a patchwork of orchards, meadows, vineyards and ponds within the large outer court.[29]

In contrast, studies of the archaeological evidence for monastic gardening are few, with a clear bias towards the Carthusian order, where individual garden units appended to monks' cells stand out within plans (see p. 30). Generally, the physical reality of garden planning within precincts remains obscure, while post-medieval changes to sites after the Dissolution ensure that surviving remains are exceptionally rare. In England and Wales at least, garden features that survive as earthworks on medieval monastic sites date primarily to the sixteenth or seventeenth centuries, when these properties were often rebuilt as mansion houses complete with formal gardens (see also p. 203–4). At a site such as Barlings Abbey (Lincolnshire), for instance, an arrangement of elongated canal-like ponds and garden terraces are clearly part of a post-medieval garden rather than any evidence of medieval landscape design.[30]

At their most ambitious, monastic gardens were among the most lavish found in any context, as those of Peterborough Abbey, complete with elaborate water gardens, exemplify (*Figure 5*). The abbey was, by the twelfth century, embedded in a matrix of designed spaces including a vineyard, multiple garden compartments and a relict castle mound that formed some sort of viewing platform.[31] The reality of garden planning rarely achieved this scale or sophistication, however. Precincts were busy crowded spaces, a world away from the neatly mown lawns favoured by the modern heritage industry. The mid-fourteenth-century Register of the Hospitaller Priory at Kilmainham (Co. Dublin) records an abundance of gardens – including those of the kitchen, hostiliar and obediantary, and others attached to lodgings for guests – squeezed somewhat haphazardly into spaces between working buildings in the precinct.[32] Usually divided between an inner court and a less exclusive outer court, gardens were shoehorned into all areas of the precinct, not in a formally planned manner. The enclosure of such monastic gardens, whether with wattling or paling fences, earthen banks, masonry walls or even moats, would have been a visually striking feature of the precinct.

The medieval cloister garth itself could be a grassy garden, sometimes sub-divided and provided with semi-ornamental features such as cisterns or fountains. In the twelfth century Hugh of St Victor remarked on the sensory pleasures as well as the spiritual meanings of the colour green, commenting that the grass refreshed encloistered eyes.[33] Cloistered gardens are also found at residential

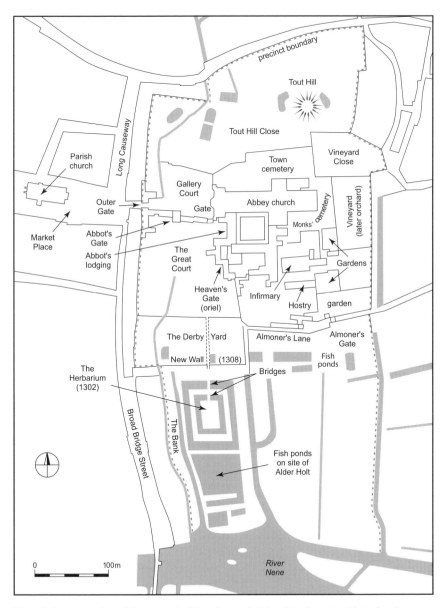

Figure 5. Reconstruction of the precinct of Peterborough Abbey (Northamptonshire), showing medieval garden features and pleasure grounds. Based on Harvey 1981, with additions.

complexes of all the main religious orders as well as larger houses of the military orders, a good example being the quadrangular garden at the heart of the preceptory at Denny (Cambridgeshire), which is known from excavation.[34] Among the more prominent of the other garden spaces around the precinct were kitchen gardens, which were inevitably the largest and usually the best documented. Medicinal or infirmary gardens contained poisons, one of the reasons they were gridded and compartmentalised; they could also be extensive – those at Westminster covered two acres (0.8 hectares).[35] The medieval mind was quite capable of laying out regular and geometric forms in gardens: at Winchester College in 1394 staff used chords and lines to measure walks.[36] Orchards can be considered a separate type of monastic garden, and 'cemetery orchards' are well attested, being sometimes used as pleasure grounds and provided with garden paraphernalia, including paths and arbours.[37] In the early fourteenth century the abbot of St Albans commented that the cemetery had been improved for the benefit of monks and visitors who liked to stroll within it.[38]

Often known as 'paradises', monastic pleasure gardens are particularly important here for their aesthetic significance.[39] Monastic communities could be censured for the misuse of pleasure gardens, including their over-use and the admission of women into them.[40] These were sometimes clearly the private gardens of monks and monastic officials. The garden known as Longnor's Garden at Haughmond Abbey (Shropshire) occupied a walled enclosure adjacent to the dormitory; created in the mid fourteenth century, it contained a dovecote and was quite separate from the private gardens of the abbot, which were overlooked by a great south-facing bay window added to the abbot's hall in the late fifteenth century.[41] According to Gerald of Wales, in the early years of the thirteenth century prior Geoffrey of Llanthony enjoyed amenities at his Gloucester house which included vineyards, orchards and pleasure gardens.[42] A tantalising glimpse of a very late 'private' monastic garden of similar character is provided by a 1539 description of Richard Whiting, the elderly last Abbot of Glastonbury, who sat in an 'arbour of bay' within his garden on a summer morning while the monks sang mass in the abbey church.[43]

The gardens of urban religious communities were usually more compact, although monastic authorities sometimes petitioned to breach defences in order to access garden spaces that provided escape as well as food: at Chester, for instance, 'Kaleyard Gate' was a postern built near the abbey by the monks in 1275 so that they could reach their extra-mural garden, while in 1335 the prior of Winchester sought a licence to construct some form of gallery over the wall so that the brethren could reach their pleasure garden.[44] Finally, properties subsidiary to the main monastic establishment also had gardens of their own, with some of our best field evidence for medieval monastic gardens coming from such sites that saw no significant post-Dissolution reuse. Particularly relevant here are the gardens of 'seyney houses' or detached infirmary retreats,[45] and those of granges, as at Monknash (Glamorgan) (*Black and White Plate 8*).

Plate 8. Aerial photograph of Monknash Grange (Glamorgan). Within the polygonal precinct of the grange earthwork remains including fishponds, garden enclosures and the base of a dovecote can be identified. (© Crown copyright: Royal Commission on the Ancient and Historical Monuments of Wales)

Manors and mansions

Pleasure gardens were among the more tangible of the features created to form the grounds of great houses, showcasing the wealth and social exclusivity of their owners. Another reason why any portrayal of *the* medieval garden is false is the fact that many elite sites had access to several, with specialised functions, while the wealthier households maintained gardens at more than one residence. The size of seigneurial gardens differed depending on the status of the estate centre they served, but in England at least were typically in the region of two acres (0.8 hectares).[46]

The distinctive grammar of aristocratic garden design extended down the social hierarchy to embrace the settings of smaller as well as larger residences. The notion of the *curia* is particularly important here – an enclosure that demarcated the manorial complex and marked the privacy of the seigneurial zone. The classic medieval manorial complex exhibited a tripartite structure, with separate domestic, agricultural and horticultural zones. Manorial court rolls can provide not only details of structures within these complexes, but also clues regarding how they physically arranged the apparatus of rural lordship.[47] Fourteenth-century sources of this type show the complexity of a typical manorial *curia* such as Rothwell (Yorkshire, West Riding) (*Figure 6:* top). It embraced features of lordship, such as dovecotes, that had connotations of status as well as practical

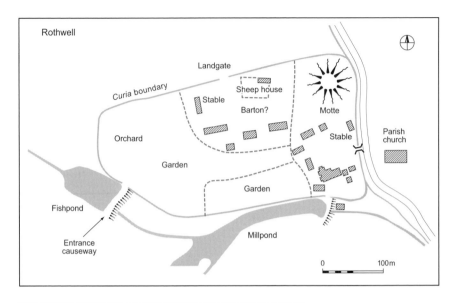

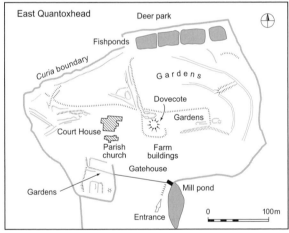

Figure 6. Examples of manorial *curiae* (or enclosures), at Rothwell (Yorkshire, West Riding), based on fourteenth-century manorial account rolls, and East Quantoxhead (Somerset), reconstructed from surviving earthworks. Based on Moorhouse 2003b and Riley 2006, with additions.

functions, and gardens that contained herbers and vineyards as well as plots for vegetables.[48] Earthworks defining enclosures around manorial sites, typically sub-divided into closes or paddocks and containing suites of fishponds, are particularly well preserved in the counties of midland England; systematic survey of sites in West Lindsey (Lincolnshire), for instance, has recorded several such complexes at places such as Buslingthorpe and Rand, which clearly equate to manorial *curiae*.[49] The construction of such boundary earthworks around gardens could entail considerable effort and expense. A lucky documentary survival from the thirteenth-century account rolls of the bishopric of Winchester affords a snapshot of the costs involved in creating and planting a new garden on one of the bishop's manors at Rimpton (Somerset) in 1264–6. Of the itemised costs, which included purchasing and planting vegetables, vines and fruit trees, by far the most expensive item was the construction of a surrounding bank and ditch, said to be 113 perches in length, four feet in depth and seven in width, and planted on top: the total cost was £1 5s 10¾d[50] At his manor house of Rochford (Essex) in 1440–3, John Grey and his three fellows worked to construct another such earthwork around the 'Wortgardyn' (or kaleyard) adjoining the manorial precinct, which also had a separate 'Great Garden'.[51]

An illustrative example of how high-status landscape 'design' was expressed at the level of a manorial site is Court House, East Quantoxhead (Somerset) (*Figure 6*: bottom). Previously recognised primarily as a Jacobean mansion house, intensive archaeological survey has revealed an underlying elite medieval landscape relating to the Luttrell family's possession of the manor. Exactly when it was laid out is unclear, but the late fourteenth or early fifteenth century, when the family's status was at its peak, is the most likely period.[52] The manor house was set prominently on a natural knoll at a central position within an oval enclosure, or *curia*, defined by earthworks and a complex system of water management that showcased the symbols and machinery of rural lordship. Standing no more than 10 metres to the south of the manor house, the parish church – almost certainly a proprietary foundation – symbolised not only the lord's patronage but the dependence of a community that had to enter the lordly enclosure to worship; that the house's medieval porch tower was given a similar crenellated parapet to the church was a further visual cue to the link between lordship and church (*Black and White Plate 9*). The 'public' route of approach from

Plate 9. East Quantoxhead (Somerset), showing the medieval manor house and adjacent parish church, both of which lay within a manorial *curia* defined by earthworks, ponds and other water features. (Photograph: Oliver Creighton)

the south guided a visitor around the millpond and through a gatehouse that provided a portal to a visibly seigneurial sphere; as well as a dovecote (later converted into a banqueting house), the *curia* contained gardens recorded in 1272, orchards and paddocks.[53] To the north, a line of four medieval fishponds of identical size and shape formed a partly ornamental boundary between the *curia* and deer park, which provided the middle ground for exquisite views to the coast, enveloped the manorial complex on three sides and contained rabbit warrens and a further pond. The complex was one of several along the rich coastal strip of the Quantocks, all featuring a similar juxtapositioning of residences with symbols of rural lordship: the manorial *curia* and landscape at nearby Kilve is also particularly well preserved.[54]

The juxtapositioning of church and manorial centre is a reoccurring feature of the British landscape more generally. Private seigneurial foundation of estate churches was one of the key motors behind the construction of parish churches, and occasional architectural parallels between the church and manorial residence further accentuate a link of patronage made apparent by the close physical proximity of the buildings. The link is especially strong where the church stands not simply adjacent to the manorial site but is somehow physically annexed to it by the earthwork of a *curia*, a moat, or the defences of a bailey. A well-known exemplar demonstrating the potential early medieval origins of church–manor complexes is Barton-upon-Humber (Lincolnshire).[55] At Linton (Lincolnshire), a boundary earthwork linked to a moated manor site seems to have embraced the church and formed part of a *curia*.[56] At Raunds (Northamptonshire), where the relationship between manorial site and adjacent church has been clarified by excavation, the two sites lay perpendicular to one another within linked embanked and ditched enclosures on ground that overlooked the settlement.[57] The number of examples probably runs into the thousands and is equally strong for sites with and without defences. In the Yorkshire Wolds, for example, 57 per cent of medieval manor houses stand adjacent to churches, while across the east midlands of England the proportion of early castles in similar positions exceeds 60 per cent.[58] What is crucial here is how these arrangements influenced the access of communities to places of worship, obliging them to cross from the public sphere into what was tangibly the seigneurial sphere, where they were often surrounded by other emblems of lordship. In some senses the association between parish church and manorial site is one manifestation of the elite patronage of religious sites that is also apparent in the foundation of monasteries. For major magnates or the super-wealthy the foundation of a grand college of clergy adjacent to their seat of lordship could be an alternative option, as in the case of the Percies at Warkworth (Northumberland) and Ralph, Lord Cromwell, at Tattershall (Lincolnshire) in the fifteenth century.

Seigneurial fishponds and demesne mills were also often found in association, typically located on the edges of manorial *curiae*, where they represented an efficient combination of water management features but also another twinning of two emblems of rural lordship. The status of the mill as a symbol of lordly authority has long been recognised. Seigneurial agency was a powerful force in the spread of milling, which demonstrated the coercive powers of the elite.[59] While the seigneurial grip on milling has probably been overstated (mills were also operated by tenants and boroughs), the link between milling and the demesne sector – expressed spatially in the juxtapositioning of watermill and manorial site – was strong, reaching its peak in England and Wales in the early fourteenth century.[60] The value of these demesne mills was dependent upon the ability of the lord to enforce a monopoly on milling amongst tenants, but they proved consistently far more profitable than horse-driven or wind-powered mills.[61] Watermills demonstrated control over the production of an agricultural surplus and constituted a minor source of income, while the obligation of tenants to use the lord's mill and pay a fee in the form of multure was another way in which the access of peasant communities to the seigneurial sphere was controlled and regulated.[62] It is in this sense that watermills have been described as one prong of a seigneurial 'triad', comprising church, manor house and mill.[63] Records of expenditure show that stew ponds and mills were often maintained in tandem, while other mill races were integrated with the moats that encircled residences. Millponds could also be, in effect, components within designed landscapes: at Nappa Hall (Yorkshire, North Riding) the pond was at least partly ornamental and designed to be seen from the hall, while the mill was tucked away out of sight downslope.[64]

Watermills were certainly the favoured form of milling in the manorialised landscape of Anglo-Norman Ireland, where they were generally located adjacent to newly established manorial capita in lowland riverine areas.[65] Manorial extents provide one of the very few sources of evidence for the existence of other appurtenances of lordship, such as dovecotes and gardens, at Anglo-Norman manorial centres in twelfth- and thirteenth-century Ireland, given the almost total non-survival of such features in the landscape and their neglect by medieval archaeologists.[66] For example, an extent of the Anglo-Norman manor of Nyncheaunlet (Inch) in 1303 lists, alongside residential buildings and agricultural facilities, the classic appurtenances of English lordship, including fishponds, a dovecote and a garden that was already a relict feature, let out to pasture.[67]

Royal gardens

We have a better understanding of the gardens that surrounded royal palaces than those associated with other types of medieval residence, largely because of the wealth of documentary material concerning their upkeep. Medieval royal financial accounts provide insight into the everyday expenses of maintaining gardens as well as the costs of employing gardening staff. Costs extended to include the procurement and transport of seeds, plants, saplings, compost, turf and wooden fencing.[68] We sometimes have remarkable insight into the minutiae of their management: one of the lawns at Westminster Palace was rolled in 1259, for example.[69] Addressed to those familiar with these designed spaces, such documents sometimes do not provide us with information on the location or physical appearance of gardens, however, so that their reconstruction is not always straightforward. If anything, gardens are recorded more frequently in royal accounts relating to non-defended houses and palaces, including properties such as Burstwick (Yorkshire, East Riding), Havering (Essex), Henley (Surrey) and Kempton (Middlesex), as well as better-known residences such as Clarendon (Wiltshire) and Greenwich (Kent).[70] This is not all: royal hunting lodges frequently had their own attached gardens, as at Birdsnest Lodge (Leicestershire) and Radmore (Staffordshire), as might detached lodges or pavilions secluded in royal parks, as at Guildford (Surrey) and Odiham (Hampshire). An extremely rare example of a royal building project of the period that provided gardens for the consumption of those outside the social elite is Henry VII's Savoy Hospital, which provided a Thames-side garden for the city's 'poer nedie people' next to the dormitory and accessible from the Poor Men's Hall via a stair.[71]

The materials used to enclose royal gardens are often recorded in particular detail: at Windsor in the 1250s, for instance, gardens were enclosed with 'walls' of earth but also wood from the royal forest in the form of thorns and switches of alder.[72] The enclosure of the royal garden at Guildford Palace (Surrey) was particularly elaborate; here, gardens next to the royal manor house were provided with a paved cloister built in the late 1260s and featuring marble columns.[73] A garden bench at Clarendon (Wiltshire) in 1250 was described as lying below a whitewashed wall, creating an image of the royal household relaxing in the summer months.[74] Changes to the ways in which gardens were enclosed might reflect a perceived need for increased privacy. For example, Henry VI's marriage to Margaret of Anjou in 1445 precipitated changes to royal accommodation that show a desire for more secluded gardens in residences around London. At Sheen her garden was enclosed within a brick-built wall, while at Greenwich extensive work for the queen was carried out at the 'Manor of Plesaunce', including brick and timber buildings in a separate garden 'ward' (the king had his own, separate enclosure), complete with an overlooking gallery and an arbour in which she could sit.[75]

Gardens and palace buildings were clearly planned as integrated designed spaces, and it is perfectly natural that the designs of gardens reflect concepts of hierarchy and privacy in the same way as did domestic accommodation. Garden spaces were always secluded: medieval palace sites such as Clarendon (Wiltshire) and Kennington (Surrey) were typical in the provision of enclosed gardens around the separate chamber blocks of the king and queen, amounting to rudimentary privy courtyards pre-dating the more formalised arrangements seen in Tudor palaces.[76] The positioning and spatial planning of cloistered spaces created in palaces of the twelfth and thirteenth centuries at sites such as Guildford (Surrey), King's Langley (Hertfordshire) and Windsor (Berkshire), many of which focused on central gardens, were primarily places for private retreat – adjuncts to the chamber rather than being intended for business or display.[77] The grounds of Langley, for example, were used extensively for bringing up royal children in the fourteenth century, when it was known as *Childre Langele*.[78] In the late fourteenth century, Kennington Palace (Surrey) had an inner garden that comprised a separate 'Privy Garden' around the queen's chamber, as well as a larger 'Great Garden' occupying a separate compartment close to the royal apartments, and a more utilitarian outer garden beyond the enclosure, north of Black Prince Road.[79] This location of private gardens directly beneath high-status apartments is reflected particularly well in calendared documents relating to royal houses. At Marlborough (Wiltshire), for example, a 'great lawn' beneath the king's chamber is recorded, as are gardens at Feckenham (Worcestershire), both examples dating to the middle of the thirteenth century.[80] Gardens such as these, intended to be seen from above, may well have displayed complex patterns of plants and other features – later styled as knots – that made full sense when seen from an elevated position (see also p. 174–5).

An outstanding example of an early garden earthwork intended to be experienced in exactly this way is preserved in excellent condition under pasture beneath Stirling castle. It is known as the 'King's Knot' (or locally as the 'Cup and Saucer') (*Colour Plate 3*). A garden here existed from at least 1502, when work on the new garden below the castle (as distinct from an earlier garden within the royal fortress) is recorded, although it was remodelled in the second quarter of the seventeenth century and 'straightened up' in the nineteenth century.[81] The centrepiece is an octagonal stepped mound known as the knot, lying within a ditched enclosure with a canalised surrounding watercourse (now dry). What is particularly significant here, however, is the feature's position within the north-east part of the royal hunting park that existed from the late twelfth century; a ditch running along one side of the knot – some 8 metres wide and at an angle to the rectilinear features of the garden – is demonstrably an early feature.[82] While this has sometimes been interpreted as a Roman earthwork, it seems far more likely to be a medieval feature serving to sub-divide an earlier garden enclosure from the park, and to keep livestock and deer out of pleasure grounds beneath the chambers of the Scottish royal family. The distinction between a royal park and garden could be subtle. The small ditched and palisaded 'park' attached to the royal house of Kennington (Surrey) was styled as a 'grove' in 1388–9, when one of the private bridges crossing the moat to link it to the manor complex was rebuilt; the seventeenth-century field name 'Prince's Walk' describes one of its functions.[83]

Perhaps the most intriguing medieval royal garden of all is that of Woodstock (Oxfordshire), its site obliterated by post-medieval landscaping in the grounds of Blenheim Palace (*Figure 7*). Secluded within parkland, the palace was not just a favoured royal retreat but also a venue for a variety of prestigious events: in the reign of Henry II it was the place where the rulers

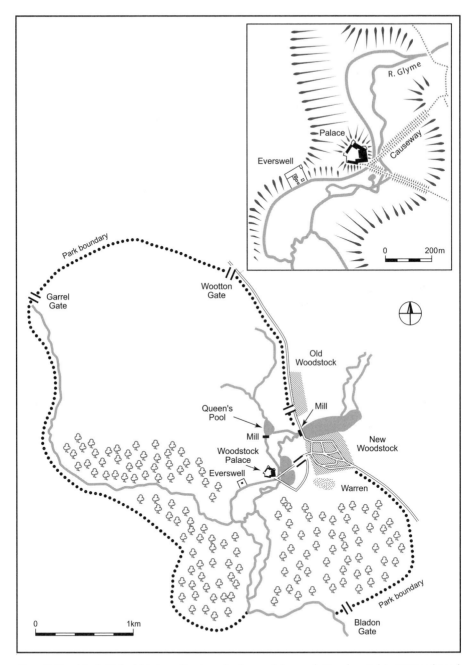

Figure 7. Woodstock (Oxfordshire): medieval royal palace and deer park. Based on Colvin 1963 and Bond and Tiller 1997, with additions.

of Scotland and Wales paid homage in 1163, and also accommodated ecclesi-astical councils and a royal wedding.[84] The complex was approached from the east by two converging causeways that crossed a suite of fishponds set within the valley of the Glyme. Of these, the northern one led directly from the town that lay beyond the park pale, and was presumably the more 'public' route of access, while the separate southern causeway linked to the park interior. Set around two courtyards and enclosed within a crenellated wall, the palace build-ings included a number of chapels, including one with an unusual circular ground plan. The bailiff was instructed in the 1240s to 'make two good high walls round the queen's garden so that no one can get in, with a suitable and pleasant herb garden by the king's stew, in which she can walk, and with a gate to the garden from the herb garden which adjoins the chapel of Edward the King's son'.[85] The gate to one of these gardens had no fewer than five locks.[86] Uniquely, the palace was associated with a separate group of buildings set around the site of a spring downslope to the south-west, recorded from the twelfth century as Everswell but associated in memory with the mistress of Henry II and hence known as Rosamund's well or bower. Separately enclosed within its own cloister and provided with a gatehouse and gardens, the centrepiece of this retreat was an elaborate arrangement of rectangular ornamental pools arranged *en echelon* between a natural spring and the river; this may betray oriental influence (see also p. 141).[87]

Detached garden buildings such as these, while rare, have outstanding importance. While the moated banqueting house attached to Kenilworth (Warwickshire) survives as a series of marshy earthworks (see p. 93), Richard II's mysterious island residence attached to the royal palace of Sheen, on the banks of the Thames on the fringes of London, is unknown archaeologically. Constructed in 1384–8, the new lodging lay on an island called 'la Nayght' and comprised a timber-framed lodging containing royal chambers and a kitchen. Additional expenditure on paling around the island, a new barge and steps for the 'king's way' down to the water give the impression of a secluded summer-house or banqueting pavilion used by the royal household.[88] An identically named but earlier royal island retreat ('Naight') existed at Gloucester, located in the Severn by the royal castle and priory.[89] Royal water gardens existed elsewhere in Britain. At Westminster, Edward I's queen, Eleanor of Castile, possessed a garden that featured an ornamental pond fed by pipes from the river, and accounts relating to the garden she had made at King's Langley (Hertfordshire) following acquisition of the manor in 1275 included work on wells and ditches, again suggesting ornamental water features.[90] The new garden created for Edward I's queen at Winchester in 1306 had water run-ning through the middle of it, but further details are not known.[91] For the construction of James I's gardens at Edinburgh castle in 1435, a certain Nicolao 'Plummar' was employed, a person evidently involved in engineering ornamental water features.[92]

Episcopal settings

The classic appurtenances and symbols of rural lordship were again clearly displayed at episcopal manor houses and palaces.[93] Secluded locations, sometimes engineered by settlement replanning, are common, as are manipulated routes of approach, often involving strings of ornamental ponds. The bishop of Ely's palace at Somersham, embedded in a designed landscape probably created in the thirteenth or fourteenth century, is the classic case study.[94] Another clear example is provided by the gardens attached to the Archbishop of York's palace at Cawood (Yorkshire, North Riding). The centrepiece of these was a rectangular moated garden enclosure of *c.*1.6 hectares, whose inner perimeter was marked by a raised walkway and interior by an axial pathway between a symmetrical arrangement of two rectangular fishponds and a series of staggered cultivation terraces marking the site of an orchard.[95] The management of water for mills and moats is another recurring theme, and medieval bishops were clearly leaders in the large-scale exploitation of fish at their residences, as detailed study of the properties of the bishop of Winchester has shown.[96] The extensive appurtenances to the bishop of St David's palace at Lamphey (Pembrokeshire) can be reconstructed in great detail from the Black Book of St David's, a fourteenth-century survey, which mentions four *vivaria*, two watermills, one windmill, fruit and vegetable gardens, three orchards and a dovecote within an extensive deer park.[97] Geophysical survey has revealed the paths of a formal garden within the courtyard, while elements of a major scheme of medieval landscaping still survive as earthworks, including evidence for a grand water-flanked approach (*Black and White Plate 10*).[98] Far more often, however, evidence on the ground is lacking. For example, at Whitbourne Court (Herefordshire), a deer park for Bishop Orleton was licensed in 1319; a garden containing fruit trees as well as vegetables and pasture, a vineyard and a rabbit warren are also recorded, but nothing remains on the ground other than the moat that enclosed the residence.[99]

Even the urban properties of ecclesiastical magnates were provided with extensive gardens from an early date. At the Southwark residence of the bishops of Winchester, for instance, the gardens took up far more space than the area occupied by the building complex, occupying the entire western portion of the palace enclosure and being divided into a more utilitarian space to the north and a smaller pleasure garden to the south. In the thirteenth century the northern kitchen garden grew saffron, grapes and hemp, alongside more 'standard' produce, and was screened from view in 1220–1 by an earthen 'wall' topped with a hedge of thorns, while extensive fishponds and 'pike-yards' are also recorded; the pleasure grounds contained at least five separate lawns as well as a summerhouse recorded in the early fifteenth century.[100]

Terraced and raised gardens are also known, providing early indications that gardens could be designed to provide viewing opportunities. At the bishop of Winchester's palace of Wolvesey a walled garden ran along one side of Bishop

Plate 10. Aerial view of Lamphey Palace (Pembrokeshire). To the south of the palace complex (towards the bottom of the photograph) are the earthworks of a large fishpond and other ornamental water features. (© Crown copyright: Royal Commission on the Ancient and Historical Monuments of Wales)

Giffard's early-twelfth-century domestic range, covering a rectangular area of *c*.38 x 7 metres.[101] Raised to first-floor level on a massive terrace of packed chalk, the garden was contemporary with the hall and built in an imposing fashion that also provided an elevated view over the cathedral to the west. Similarly careful integration of palace buildings of the period into their immediate landscape settings by means of terraces and gardens can be seen at Henry of Blois's site at Troyes and the bishop's palace at Beauvais.[102] In contrast, the fortified palace at Old Sarum featured a raised courtyard garden, although this was a cloistered space without views.[103] The construction of a small raised rectangular garden *c*.8 x 10 metres next to the solar tower of the bishop of Winchester's manor house at Witney (Oxfordshire) in the twelfth century entailed infilling the courtyard area with clay to a depth of over 2 metres and the demolition of an earlier chapel, part of which was used as a retaining wall.[104] As well as playing on the symbolic and religious role of the medieval garden, this raised feature also provided views over the curtain wall towards the meadows and fishponds (see also p. 175). The pleasure gardens of bishops' residences were used by members of the upper nobility and royal households as well as by their owners, and some had gardens designated for visiting female households, located typically away from the more public areas of the palace complex: for example, the mid-fifteenth-century bishop's palace of Knole (Kent) had a garden known as 'Queen's Court' on its north side.[105] Other palace sites had several specialised gardens: the medieval bishop's residence at Wookey (Somerset) featured a crocus garden, for example.[106]

Bishops maintained networks of palaces, and their designed settings may again have been specialised. Those of the bishops of Lincoln provide a particularly good example. A critically important site here is the bishop of Lincoln's palace at Nettleham (Lincolnshire), as archaeological and earthwork evidence points towards the palace buildings, gardens and courtyard being a unified creation of the mid fourteenth century.[107] Earthworks of well-preserved terraces, paths and the beds of the bishop's private walled garden are appended to the site of the palace buildings in a coherent arrangement, while excavation has demonstrated a well within the garden area to have been filled in during the early to mid fourteenth century, making it tempting to think of a building project coinciding with the grant of Bishop Burghersh's licence to crenellate in 1336, although the site had a longer history, with palace buildings from the twelfth century and an earlier manorial complex.[108] A further intriguing element to the palace's setting was the almost perfectly symmetrical placement of identical barn-like buildings either side of the gatehouse, which was approached along an axial pathway indicative of an access route designed to impress.[109] Entirely enveloped within its own deer park, the bishop of Lincoln's palace at Stow (Lincolnshire) was clearly a secluded, recreational seat that was complementary to Nettleham. Like its counterpart, it was provided with a dramatic and staged route of approach across a causeway between two flanking lines of ponds.[110] The palace at Spaldwick (Lincolnshire) lay within a large D-shaped earthwork enclosure at the western terminus of the village that contained ponds, closes, terraces and a circular mound indicative of gardens.[111] At Buckden (Huntingdonshire) large areas of the palace's two courts were full of gardens,[112] while the setting of Lyddington (Rutland) contains important garden features including an early walled garden with a surrounding raised walkway and an octagonal lookout tower or pavilion.[113]

Castle gardens

Surviving physical evidence for castle gardens in their medieval phases is, like those at secular sites generally, minimal. Multifaceted studies that bring together non-intrusive earthwork analysis and geophysical survey, combined with limited excavation and thorough documentary analysis, hold particular potential to understand the plans and functions of these designed spaces, as at Weobley castle.[114] A transformation of our understanding of the gardens attached to medieval fortified sites has been a direct and welcome consequence of the general shift within castle studies away from militaristic modes of interpretation towards greater understanding of the social and symbolic roles of these sites.[115] We now have a relatively sophisticated idea of the various scales at which castles were embedded within designed settings more generally, although quite how widespread this phenomenon was remains unclear.

In higher-status castles, multiple gardens are again found. A basic differentiation can be made between gardens beyond the walls – typically vineyards, orchards and vegetable gardens – and those more secluded gardens within the defences, in most cases serving as direct adjuncts to high-status residential structures, although more open garden spaces within baileys are also known. For example, at Cardiff castle the development of a new residential range for Richard, Earl of Warwick, in the second quarter of the fifteenth century included the construction of an adjoining 'plaisance' or ornamental garden to the south.[116] A hierarchy was apparent, with gardens more or less secluded from view and more and less private. At Windsor, however, the King's Garden outside the walls of the Upper Ward, and opening into what became the Little Park, could only be accessed by crossing a pathway into Windsor town, which remained a public right of way separating the royal family from their gardens and parks until the 1820s.[117] The sophisticated *gardyn* at Windsor described by James Stewart in *The Kingis Quair* in the early fifteenth century was clearly an area of parkland or pleasure grounds (see also p. 169–70). This designed space, which lay beneath the tower in which he was imprisoned, contained in one of its corners a separate wooded *herbere* enclosed with a fence and hawthorn hedge.[118] It was not unusual for high-status domestic chambers in castles to directly overlook gardens. A calendar miniature for June in the *Très Riches Heures du Duc de Berry* provides a glimpse of the king's garden in the Palais de la Cité, which was accessed from the chambers above via a covered and decorated stair.[119] At Rockingham castle (Northamptonshire) walls were built to enclose a plot of grass (*viridarium*) next to the queen's chamber.[120] At Chepstow a small projecting area of cliff-edge immediately below the late-thirteenth-century 'Gloriette' probably functioned as a small and very private garden, forming as it did a 'natural balcony' that provided dramatic views of river-valley scenery.[121] Another castle site where a likely garden enclosure survives as an earthwork below high-status chambers is Framlingham (Suffolk). Here the 'Lower Court' seems likely to have contained the documented gardens, being surrounded by a broad flat-topped terrace, suggesting that it was built or at least adapted as a walkway at some stage.[122]

We should also not overlook that castles might, in effect, form miniaturised designed landscapes in their own right. Castle gates could resemble garden gates and curtain walls were also walkways ('allures'), from which gardens could be appreciated.[123] Pontefract castle preserves a particularly well-preserved late medieval garden seat recessed into a revetment wall in the inner bailey (*Black and White Plate 11*). Constructed in the fourteenth or fifteenth century, largely from reused masonry but featuring a fine purpose-made decorative moulded lintel, the seat lay directly opposite the oriel window of the Great Hall.[124] This unusual feature demonstrates not only the recreational aspect of this part of the castle but also presumably that a direct and uncluttered line of sight existed between these two elements.

The potential for the aesthetic and other advantages of castle gardens to

Plate 11. Medieval garden seat within the bailey of Pontefract castle (Yorkshire, West Riding). (Photograph: Oliver Creighton)

conflict with military functionality is shown by Frederick II's hanging gardens of Nuremberg, built on the buttresses of his castle in the mid thirteenth century and forming the centrepiece of an oriental-style park.[125] Tensions between the need for gardens and the need for defence were more apparent at Balinghem castle, a fortress located in northern France between Guines and Ardres that was in English hands early in the fifteenth century. In 1428–9 gardens immediately outside the defences were removed for the safety of the sentries patrolling the walls.[126] In England, the gardens of Carlisle castle lay in the space between the south curtain wall of the fortress and the city; they were damaged in the Scottish siege of 1173–4 and later maintained as part of the castle's outer defences.[127] Containing a fishpond and fruit trees as well as beds, the gardens featured a watchtower to the east and a postern gate blocked in 1384; it is unclear whether a mound within the garden documented in the 1380s was a defensive or ornamental feature, this being heightened and reinforced with piles and surrounded with a hedge.[128]

The landscape of Godolphin (Cornwall) is exceptionally important in this context (*Figure 8*). The standing fifteenth-century mansion known as Godolphin House was preceded by an early-fourteenth-century defended house built for Sir Alexander de Godolgham that stood on a slightly different site. Excavation and survey has shown that this lay within a rectangular walled and embanked precinct that was divided into nine separate compartments laid out in groups of three, the total covering an area of *c.*100 x 130 metres; the building was located centrally, the eastern units were occupied by gardens and orchards, and there were estate and other agricultural buildings to the west.[129] While other elements

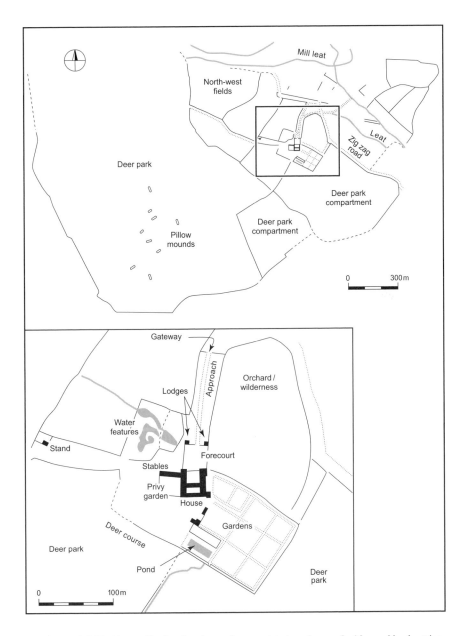

Figure 8. Godolphin (Cornwall), showing the castle, associated gardens and wider parkland setting. Based on Herring 1997, with additions.

of the surrounding landscape relate to a redesign that accompanied the later house, including a deer course (see p. 152), the axial route of approach from the south, oriented towards a deer park on top of Goldolphin hill, represents another medieval element.[130]

Another means by which gardens might be enclosed was within a bailey or outer court linked to a fortified building. Tully castle (Co. Fermanagh) is a Plantation-period tower-house with an attendant 'bawn' or walled enclosure with flanking towers at the corners.[131] While these features are commonly thought to have housed ancillary buildings, representing the agricultural part of the lordship complex, here excavation has shown that paths lie inside the lines of all four walls, with another down the middle linking the bawn entrance to the tower door in a symmetrical manner that must indicate a garden, which has been reinstated (*Colour Plate 4*).[132] There is no denying the place's violent history – it was built *c*.1610–18 and ruined after a bloody siege in 1641, never to be reoccupied – but there is also no denying that what outwardly appears to be a fortified complex contained a pleasure ground in miniature. In other cases it is clear that castle baileys were not intended initially to house gardens but were remodelled for such a purpose. A clear case in point is Whittington castle (Shropshire), where the site was transformed from a border stronghold into an elite residence at the heart of a designed watery landscape (*Figure 9*). A reference of 1413 to a garden on the north side of the castle ditched around with water can be reconciled with developments to the site's moated outer bailey.[133] Perhaps originating as a prehistoric enclosure, the bailey was sub-divided into two halves by a broad water-filled ditch at a late stage of the castle's life: a working area to the east containing stables and service buildings; and there was a garden to the west.[134] Geophysical survey within the western part of the bailey has revealed a series of rectangular features reminiscent of a garden-like arrangement of paths and beds which, while not aligned with the perimeter of the bailey, have a formal spatial relationship with a 5-metre-high artificial mound, a feature easily taken for a motte but more appropriately interpreted as an elevated island or early prospect mound for viewing an ornamental arrangement beneath it.[135] While these changes are not closely documented, the circumstances of the site's ownership history point towards a major change in its role in the first half of the fourteenth century, in the wake of the Edwardian subjugation of North Wales.[136] Other castle gardens within or attached to baileys and known through survey or excavation include examples at Ludgershall (Wiltshire), Stafford and Tintagel (Cornwall) (see p. 160, 39 and 32–3).

Examples of castle earthworks adapted as garden features in the post-medieval period are well understood: mottes at Dunham Massey (Cheshire) and Marlborough (Wiltshire) were adapted as viewing mounts, for instance.[137] We are less aware that similar processes were at work in the medieval centuries, where remodelling of sites with tangibly high-status associations shows an interest in manipulating the imagery of the past as much as in pragmatic reuse. The earthworks of a motte and bailey castle at Shotwick (Cheshire) were transformed into a remarkable late medieval water garden: the bailey was divided up into a series of sunken rectangular compartments with a central eminence reminiscent of a viewing mound, while its moat was widened and turned

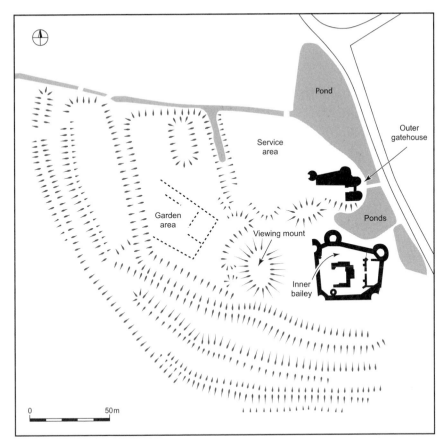

Figure 9. Whittington (Shropshire): earthwork plan of a medieval castle preserving a likely viewing mound and other garden features. Based on Terra Nova 2002, with additions.

into one of a suite of ornamental ponds, complete with walkways.[138] Like Whittington, adaptation of the site in this way represents a new life for a border castle, and must post-date the Welsh Wars of the late thirteenth century; a likely historical context is provided by the emparkment of the manor for Edward III in 1327.[139]

Another important site for understanding medieval designed settings on the Anglo-Welsh Marches is Castell Blaenllynfi (Brecknockshire), a quadrilateral, stone-built and moated castle to the north of the Usk valley. Here the date range for the construction of a designed landscape can be relatively tightly defined. Established as the _caput_ of a lordship in the period 1208–15, the site was largely ruinous by the second quarter of the fourteenth century, with no evidence of later reuse.[140] A flat terrace at the base of the castle platform was part of a garden arrangement including a rectangular ornamental pool _c._100 x 20 metres, probably one in a series of other more vestigial linked pond-bays. These were fronted, in turn, by a broad bank that acted as a dam but also as a garden walk-way, with a mound at each end, the eastern one of which is recorded as a dovecote in the early nineteenth century. Place-names indicate the presence of a park on the rising ground above the site. The castle's lifetime was violent as well as short, being sacked or taken at least three times, but it is highly relevant that the designed setting would have positively weakened the site's defensive capabilities.

The fortified manor house of Stokesay (Shropshire) is hugely important as here the designed setting was the creation of a member of the urban classes, the wool merchant Lawrence de Ludlow.[141] The residence was upgraded from an earlier manorial house to a pseudo-fortified site in the 1280s, with de Ludlow receiving licence to crenellate from Edward I in 1291. The ornamental setting included a shallow lake to the south-west and a series of ponds to the south, both seemingly intended to be seen from the south tower (*Black and White Plate 12*); a narrow moat around the 'castle' and an orchard completed the arrangement.[142] Lying adjacent to a much earlier parish church, the site was lent something of the spirit of an established seigneurial centre despite the 'new wealth' of its owner. What is crucial is that despite his urban roots in Shrewsbury and his European business interests, de Ludlow's social aspirations were expressed through the development of a quintessentially English rural seat of lordship. To a visitor approaching the 'castle' along the main road from Ludlow, the building's appearance was enhanced not only by these water features, and the causeway-like earthwork that navigated a path across

Plate 12. View of Stokesay castle (Shropshire), showing the solar tower overlooking a designed landscape probably created in the late thirteenth century. (Photograph: Oliver Creighton)

them, but also by the fact that from this direction the building proclaimed its martial credentials in the form of the south tower, serving to disguise what was in essence a manor house.[143] A comparable site in some ways is Hopton (Shropshire), built in anachronistic form by an active locally based family and accompanied by a suite of water and garden features.[144]

In physical terms the remains of castle gardens could resemble fortifications in microcosm. At Wallingford (Oxfordshire) the royal gardens were hedged and ditched and their security was ensured with complex arrangements of gates; at least one garden had an outer door and separate wicket gates, for which the constable of the castle purchased keys, locks, latches, hasps, screws and hinges.[145] Today, the gardens are difficult to differentiate from the earthwork fortifications of the site's outer bailey. One of the most remarkable suite of castle gardens surviving as earthworks can be found at Sheriff Hutton (Yorkshire, North Riding), a fortified palatial residence of the Neville family dating to the 1380s.[146] The gardens occupy an extensive area sandwiched between the complex of lordly buildings to the north and the great expanse of the deer park to the south. Immediately beneath the inner court, pathways lead from a broad garden terrace down to a rectangular formal garden enclosure, leading the visitor between two ponds, one of which was slightly higher and probably flowed into the other. This area was delimited to the south by two parallel canals, each of them over 10 metres wide, with a flat-topped bank between them. This feature marked the transition between the seigneurial complex and the park beyond, with the bank forming a walkway that provided an ornamental route of approach into and out of the park via the 'Lady Bridge'. To the west further subsidiary garden enclosures and a rectangular space that may have been an orchard completed the ensemble. The dating of the garden complex is uncertain and may relate to more than one phase; the date bracket is between *c*.1400, when the castle was finished, and the early seventeenth century, when Ingram's New Lodge replaced the castle as the focus of garden activity. One possibility is that the canals are additions of the early sixteenth century to an existing arrangement of early formal castle gardens, although their line would have perpetuated an existing division between the domestic and emparked zones.[147] The location of castle gardens at the point of interface between the residential complex and a zone of parkland beyond is a recurring theme, exemplified by a site such as Oakham (Rutland). Here the perimeter of a large embanked rectangular garden of *c*.200 x 60 metres, recorded in the first half of the fourteenth century and now known as 'Cutts Close', was formerly flanked on two sides by broad fishponds and projected into the castle park known as 'Flitteris Park'.[148]

If any image or notion of the 'ideal' castle existed in the Middle Ages, it is quite clear that a garden was an integral component of it. Several of Edward I's famous royal fortresses in north Wales, traditionally viewed as the 'apogee' of medieval castle building, featured gardens.[149] Thus even fortifications built in explicitly martial circumstances to sophisticated designs at the cutting edge of military architecture were afforded pleasure grounds of their own. Royal expenditure on the king's garden at Caernarfon is recorded in 1295, a year after it had been damaged in the disastrous Welsh attack; newly ditched and hedged, it evidently lay outside the walls.[150] The garden at Harlech, in existence by 1343, lay near the south-east corner of the site, near the Mortimer Tower that was known as the 'Garden' Tower, presumably within the line of the castle's immense rock-cut ditch.[151] This was not only the most sheltered position around the site but also the sunniest; the 'Prince's Garden' at Caernarfon was located in in a similar position in the former bailey of the first castle on the site.[152] Caernarfon was also provided from the start with a garden for the queen and, after Queen Eleanor's death, a separate ditched and hedged garden for the king; a further ornamental component of the castle was the swan's nest created in the centre of the 'King's Pool' to the east of the site.[153] The garden at Conwy occupied the area known as the East Barbican, a levelled court at the western extremity of the site enclosed within a wall with three towers. The garden enclosure was appended to the Inner Ward, from which the three large windows of the king's great chamber looked down upon it and beyond over the river, while a path linking the garden directly to a fortified dock allowed exclusive private access to the area.[154] Named as the *herbarium* in an account of 1316, the garden was clearly an original feature, intended at least partly for the queen, and survived into the seventeenth century, when it is depicted on a map, laid out with trees and formal beds.[155] Nor were gardens neglected at other long-established royal castles and palaces during Edward's reign; a garden of 9,000 turfs was laid at the Tower of London, for example, while a new herber was built at the palace of Westminster, where royal accounts detail the purchase of extensive stocks of vines.[156]

Edward's queen, Eleanor of Castile, was clearly a key influence. A celebrated gardener, she is known to have imported gardeners from Spain and perhaps Italy and in several cases the gardens were effectively hers.[157] This is confirmed at Rhuddlan (Flintshire), where the castle garden again lay in the south-east part of the castle complex. Expenditure on this garden was listed under the 'queen's work' in 1282–3 and it was clearly a gendered space; the works comprised a little fishpond near the castle well, lined with four cartloads of clay, surrounded by seats and a courtyard planted with 6,000 turves and fenced off with staves.[158] Royal building accounts also make clear that at a very early stage in the development of Conwy castle and town a garden was created in front of the queen's temporary chamber in the spring of 1283. This was a timber building near the site of the Cistercian abbey of St Mary and away from the area occupied by the castle. Some measure of the importance of gardens to the royal household is provided by the fact that even in the case of what was intended from the start as an impermanent building, the queen's *camera* was fronted with a lawn laid with turf transported to the site via river and watered for the first time one July evening by Roger le Fykeys at a cost of 3d.[159]

The designed settings of castles occasionally provided backdrops for displays of chivalry involving tournaments. The miniature for September in the *Très*

Riches Heures du Duc de Berry shows an open jousting list awaiting competitors at the foot of the towering château of Saumur, with the harvest being gathered in the ordered estate landscape in the foreground.[160] Drawing on the mythical imagery of chivalric literature, especially from the late thirteenth century onwards, Arthurian-style round-table festivals were hosted in and around castles. Among the earliest in Britain were held by Roger Mortimer at Kenilworth (1279 and 1282) and Warwick (1279), although the most celebrated was held by Edward III at Windsor in January 1344, when an enormous round-table building was erected in the upper bailey, transforming this part of the castle into a literary landscape in miniature.[161] The Round Tables held by Roger Mortimer to celebrate his elevation to the earldom of March in 1328 included the transportation of an enormous canvas castle, complete with poles and pegs, from Wigmore to Woodstock – evidently a piece of tournament scenery.[162] These were relatively private and exclusive occasions compared to the fully-fledged medieval tournaments that as well as being occasions for aristocratic display also attracted members of the lower social groups in large numbers. The geography of these 'public' medieval tournaments shows a strong preference for liminal sites: twelfth-century tournaments at Chester, Northampton and York took place just outside city walls, while locations near political or other geographical boundaries such as watersheds were also common.[163]

Orchards, vineyards and mazes

Orchards and vineyards comprise a distinctive type of garden in their own right, both being commonly integrated into the immediate settings of noble buildings. Vineyards were not an introduction of the post-Conquest period, although the policies of new Norman landlords towards their estates ensured that their distribution widened and the scale of their exploitation expanded. They are recorded at something in the region of 45 places in Domesday Book and, critically, most lay within estates under the direct lordship of Norman tenants in chief. Their extent was frequently measured in the French unit of measurement 'arpents', especially in the south-east of England. Rayleigh in Rochford (Essex) is an illustrative case in point, where a park and six arpents of vineyard are recorded in the same manor where Suen had built his castle.[164] On the Anglo-Welsh Marches, documentary and place-name evidence shows that vineyards were generally small, being mostly less than two acres (0.8 hectares), and found close to estate centres, particularly those of ecclesiastical magnates.[165] Vineyards contained within monastic precincts are particularly well documented, with important examples known from Beaulieu (Hampshire), Bury St Edmunds (Suffolk) and Abingdon (Oxfordshire), and despite later medieval decline some examples survived until the Dissolution.[166] The walled vineyard created to the north of St Augustine's Abbey in Canterbury in 1320 involved the clearance not only of the land but of a small resident population and the closure of a public road by royal licence.[167] A particularly early example is the 'little plot' conferred by King Eadwig to Glastonbury Abbey in AD 956. Located on an 'earthen hill' that almost certainly equates to the local landmark Barrow Hill, where earthwork terraces can be identified, the vineyard continued in use through the medieval period and is particularly well documented in the thirteenth century, when tenants of Glastonbury provided labour services on it.[168]

In contrast, evidence for vineyards in medieval Ireland is extremely limited, where they are one element of the characteristic Norman package of estate management that is usually missing. Gerald of Wales commented on their absence in the late twelfth century, although they were not unknown in the early medieval period, Bede commenting in the eighth century that the country was not lacking vines.[169]

It is clear that vineyards were admired for their visual qualities as well as for their produce. One was incorporated into the King's Garden at Windsor, which existed outside the walls of the Upper Ward from the twelfth century and was restored by Henry III, having been destroyed in the siege of 1216; terraces for vines also lay outside the Tower of London.[170] Those depicted in front of the Château de Lusignan in the scene for March in the *Très Riches Heures du Duc de Berry* are enclosed with walls of stone and have an almost fortified appearance, one having a corner tower; the scene for April shows another type of walled vineyard overlooked by a multi-windowed belvedere-like structure.[171] Another measure of the elite status of grapevines is the prestige associated with the post of Master of the King's Vines (or King's Vinedresser), which was a highly paid position quite separate from that of the gardeners, whose payments even at royal palaces could be modest, as was the case at Windsor in the late medieval period.[172]

Climatic deterioration from the fourteenth century had a major impact on the viability of large-scale vineyard production, while English consumers were increasingly turning to the wines of Gascony and the Mediterranean world.[173] Suburban vineyards are well known from twelfth- and thirteenth-century London, for example, but after *c.*1300 vines are primarily recorded in decorative contexts: for example, growing on trellises in the gardens of the city's livery companies.[174] Late medieval household accounts frequently show that demesne vineyards supplied only a small fraction of the needs of a great household, and the product was markedly inferior to imports from the continent.[175] The status of vineyards as specialist gardens available only to the elite was if anything enhanced in the later medieval period, when it is clear that vines were often grown for ornamental purposes, sometimes being trained on trellises to create shaded garden walks.[176] Typical is the case of Kennington Palace (Surrey), where the gardener purchased small quantities of timber and poles for supporting vines in the 'inner garden' in 1362.[177] Other specific expenditure on vineyards at the king's houses is recorded widely across the south of England, at Beckley (Oxfordshire), Eltham (Kent), Langley Marish (Buckinghamshire), King's Langley (Hertfordshire), Rotherhithe (Surrey) and Sheen (Surrey), while vineyards are found as far north as the royal house at Burstwick, on Holderness, in the fourteenth century.[178] They also occasionally lay within parks: a vineyard belonging to the bishop of Winchester is recorded in Bishopstoke Park in 1477–8,[179] while the vineyard mentioned at Rockingham (Northamptonshire) in 1130 and 1440 lay on the edge of the oval castle park.[180]

Archaeological evidence for vineyards has been detected for the Roman period in the form of parallel trenches for vines, with the side of each ditch flanked by postholes for supporting timber structures, as at Wollaston (Northamptonshire).[181] Comparable evidence from the medieval period is rare, but a sample excavation on one of over 200 rock-cut rectangular features revealed as parch marks in a field near Longtown (Herefordshire) has raised the possibility that they represent part of a medieval vineyard associated with the nearby Norman estate centre.[182] Archaeological remains of medieval viticulture have also been identified in the form of earthworks, as at Donnington (Herefordshire) and Milton Abbas (Dorset), where sinuous terraces run in pairs.[183]

Orchards represent another type of resource with connotations of status. As well as providing fruit they offered peace, shade, beauty and interest, medieval gardening books showing a fascination with grafting together different species.[184] Orchards also reflect changing patterns of elite consumption. The fruit course was common amongst French nobility by the end of the fourteenth century and had an increasingly important place at the high-status table in Britain. As well as apples and pears, household accounts show that cherries, quinces, plums and damsons were obtained from orchards, while the king's fruiterers were responsible for gathering supplies for the royal household.[185]

Compartments in medieval pleasure gardens given over to orchards are well known, and the status of the orchard was particularly clear where it was enclosed. Moated orchards are also not unknown (see p. 90–2). A detached moated orchard complete with an entranceway embellished with military architecture was an appurtenance to the bishop of Durham's manor house at Howden (Yorkshire, East Riding). In a survey of 1561 it was described as lying in pasture to the south of the moated residence, in 'the myddest of which ground, enclosed by a great ditch, was an orchard with a fruit house sett on to the north side of the same, over a draw-bridge at the entry into the same orchard'.[186] Rare archaeological evidence for a medieval orchard has been identified at the bishop's palace of Cawood (Yorkshire, West Riding), where a series of cultivation ridges either side of an axial garden path, deliberately staggered so they did not align with one another, mark the site of the orchard recorded as Apulgarth Flatte in 1515.[187] Other evidence comes from Oxford: regular rows of tree holes indicating the likely site of a small orchard have been excavated at the site of Beaumont Palace, a royal house outside the city's north gate.[188]

We should also remember that in medieval elite landscapes more generally trees had had significance beyond the functional. The appeal of trees lay not only in their physical appearance but also in their metaphorical capacity to represent ideas in the human mind. Moreover, the fact that the lifetimes of trees

visibly spanned many generations ensured that they had significance as historical markers.[189] From at least the sixteenth century the owners of later designed
landscapes incorporated 'ancient' trees to lend the settings of their houses a
certain maturity – creating the illusion of greater antiquity than was the case in
an effort to display permanence and social stability.[190] In the designed landscapes of Georgian England, planting trees showed control over an estate and
emphasised its size and unity, while old oaks were appropriated and showcased
in views and portraits.[191] Medieval oak trees certainly had a particularly strong
association with the monarchy in folk memory, although we remain rather
unsure as to whether medieval designed landscapes included deliberately
planted trees of other types.[192] At his manor house of Easthampstead (Berkshire)
Henry IV had carpenters construct a wooden bench around the great oak in
front of the king's chamber.[193] Also in this context we might note how the
'tremendous trunks' and massive boughs that appeared to hem in and visually
frame the Green Knight's vision of Bertilak's castle sound very much like ancient
parkland oaks (see also p. 150).[194] On several of the famous late medieval tapestries designed to commemorate Emperor Maximilian's hunting activities,
arrangements of thickets and managed woodland frame hunting scenes; in one,
an open glade where a boar is hunted has been cleared artificially, as tree
stumps are visible.[195]

Designed landscapes in miniature are found in the form of medieval mazes,
although the likelihood that many were, in effect, public monuments (see
below) makes them rather different in character to the other settings described
in this book. Some mazes were certainly of the highest status, however. The
hedged maze that lay within the elaborate gardens of Henry VIII's palace of
Nonsuch is well documented, while in August 1533 a 'watermace' (water maze)
is recorded in the king's garden at Greenwich.[196] Genuinely antique mazes in
Britain that survive as field monuments number no more than a dozen located
mostly in midland and southern England, although many more have been
obliterated in the nineteenth and twentieth centuries.[197] Most were turf
mazes, where tortuous routes of twists and turns are formed by raised pathways created by the excavation of ditches to either side.[198] Far more than
leisure facilities, mazes seem to have had ritual religious significance.[199]
Although they are notoriously difficult to date and frequently shrouded in mytho-
logical folk history, a strong likelihood nonetheless exists that some have
medieval origins. The most well known, on Saffron Walden common, is traditionally asserted to be medieval in date, although the earliest documentary reference is to a recutting in the late seventeenth century.[200] More likely is the example at Leigh (Dorset), which survives on open ground as a relict hexagonal
enclosing earthwork with slight evidence of a central mound; potential
medieval origins are indicated by its depiction on a sixteenth-century map.[201]
Other indications of potential medieval origins include plan-forms: the turf
maze at Wing (Rutland) displays a design closely resembling the well-documented 'mosaic mazes' of French cathedrals such as Chartres, Poitiers and Saint-

Quentin.[202] Among the most plausible other extant mazes with possible medieval origins are examples at Asenby (Yorkshire, North Riding), Boughton (Northamptonshire), Breamore (Hampshire) and Somerton (Oxfordshire). What is indisputable is the locations of historic turf mazes in relatively 'public' positions, such as commons, hilltops and in open ground near churches, which is in sharp contrast to the 'private' contexts of other late medieval garden features.

Watery gardens and settings

The properties of water, in particular its reflective qualities, ensured that it had a unique ability to transform the human experience of landscape.[203] Large-scale ornamental lakes are a famous hallmark of the eighteenth-century English landscape park, typically serving to link the immediate setting of the country house to the wider rural background, yet the concept well established by the eighteenth century had a medieval ancestry.[204] Where the circumstances of the site allowed, ornamental water features were common within the medieval designed landscape, both in reality and in pictorial depictions. In several of the famous calendar miniatures in the *Très Riches Heures du Duc de Berry*, for instance, lakes form visual links between palatial residences in the background and ordered estate landscapes in the foreground.[205]

Most research on water management within the medieval landscape has taken a functionalist perspective.[206] But water was often crucial not only to the structuring but also the very meanings of medieval designed landscapes: expanses of water – whether artificial, natural or somewhere in between – often served to seclude the spaces within which buildings stood (*Figure 10*). We almost certainly also underestimate the number of palaces, castles and other elite medieval dwellings that were designed to be accessible from waterways. In reflecting the structure above, water magnified the visual impact of noble architecture, which could appear to float above a shimmering pool, and could give the optical illusion that buildings were larger and further away than they actually were, as at a site such as Caerlaverock (Dumfriesshire) (*Black and White Plate 13*). The perception of buildings across water was also a recurring theme in medieval Arthurian literature, for example. Water lent special significance to the journey into such a structure, which would be especially marked at sites with double moats (see p. 93–5). A broad moat provided an environment for animals such as swans that carried elite symbolism of their own, while the artificial dams that held lakes and meres back were sometimes used as walkways and vantage points.

On a far smaller scale, wells and well-heads in gardens and courtyards could have decorative functions. For example, the enormous ornamental fountain built in the courtyard of Linlithgow palace for James V in the 1530s was ostentatiously Gothic in inspiration despite the king's patronage of classical styles elsewhere, representing a consciously anachronistic celebration of Scottish origin myths.[207] 'Fontaines' or springs feature in the early-thirteenth-century

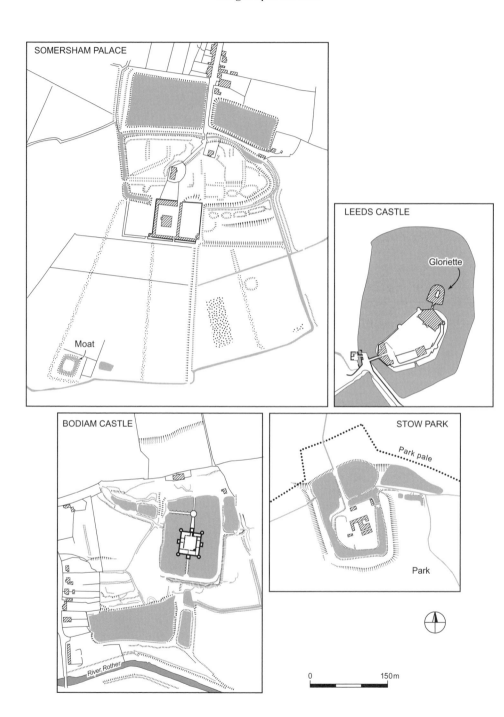

Figure 10. Comparative plans of medieval elite residences associated with ponds, meres and other water features. Based on Taylor 1989, Everson 1996a and Everson 1998, with additions.

Plate 13. Caerlaverock (Dumfriesshire): a late-thirteenth-century castle in its watery setting. (Photograph: Oliver Creighton)

Roman de la Rose, and are represented in later manuscript illustrations as elaborate features.[208] They were also present in pictorial representations of hunting landscapes: in fifteenth-century illustrations of the *Livre de Chasse*, for example, springs come forth from artificial masonry structures.[209]

The relationship between residence and water might work two ways: very often, ponds or moats served to influence the way in which a residential site was experienced and approached by outsiders, while a watery backdrop might structure the landscape setting as viewed from within the building. There are two basic categories of site here: places where water swept right up to the walls of a building, and others where water features were self-contained and peripheral to the residential complex. We should also add that the seascape was a water feature in its own right, while in certain areas of Britain lakes were essential components of lordly landscapes. Water features were not universal, of course, as their creation was ruled out in certain places by natural topography.

The most celebrated example of a large-scale watery elite landscape is Kenilworth (Warwickshire), where in the fourteenth century the great artificial mere could be seen and appreciated from John of Gaunt's enormous first-floor hall (*Black and White Plate 14*).[210] The mere at Framlingham (Suffolk) was formed by enlarging a natural glacial lake and damming a small stream. While its creation is not dated, this may have occurred in the early thirteenth century when the castle was enlarged by Roger Bigod, and by the fourteenth century it was referred to as the 'Great Lake beneath the castle'.[211] As well as functioning as a

Plate 14. Kenilworth (Warwickshire), showing a view towards John of Gaunt's Great Hall across the area formerly occupied by the medieval mere. (Photograph: Oliver Creighton)

fishery, it was at least partly an ornamental feature, visually enhancing the castle's imposing appearance from the north and west. From this perspective, the mere filled a valley between the castle and rising ground, with a great deer park enveloping the whole ensemble, effectively privatising its immediate setting. The castles of Leeds (Kent) and Bodiam (East Sussex) supply us with other clear examples, but represent an extreme manifestation of a much wider phenomenon. We should be careful not to create a false class of 'water castle' or 'fantasy castle', however, as the terms carry something of an implication of folly.[212] In some contexts water features doubtless had serious military purpose, as at Roscommon castle (*Black and White Plate 15*), where the thirteenth-century castle occupies a flat site with the shallow waters of Lochnaneane ('lake of the wildfowl') running up to its walls: a bloody history and powerful concentric defences make any aesthetic setting unlikely.[213]

That many artificial water features have been drained or are else shadows of their former selves is one barrier to their recognition. At places such as Bodiam (East Sussex) and Caerphilly (Glamorgan), the watery surroundings of elite medieval buildings have been re-created; at many others physical traces of moats or meres that have been drained or disrupted through agricultural clearance are unimpressive and indistinct muddy hollows that are difficult to reconcile with any image of a shimmering sheet of water. In other cases post-medieval landscaping has obscured their medieval form. At a place such as Scotney 'Old Castle' (Kent), the romantic aesthetic of a ruinous late-fourteenth-century castle, set gloriously within a broad moat in a wooded valley bottom, is

Plate 15. Roscommon castle (Co. Roscommon), showing the site's watery setting. (Photograph: Oliver Creighton)

the result of eighteenth- and nineteenth-century remodelling; a medieval designed context is a tantalising possibility but ultimately impossible to prove.[214] In addition, terminology is something of a barrier to our appreciation of the importance of water in elite settings. 'Water features' is a peculiarly archaeological term that fails to do justice to the extent and impressiveness of many lakes and ponds, while 'fishpond' and 'moat' do not reflect the variety of uses these features might have had beyond subsistence and defence. Like their post-medieval counterparts, medieval lakes around elite residences were multifunctional and had a variety of origins, from entirely artificial creations with dams and feeder systems to landscaped meres. At one level, of course, these features indeed had utilitarian functions: moats, meres and ponds could contain fish, help the drainage of a site and add to its defences.

The present-day settings of monuments can be extremely misleading. For example, the fourteenth-century castle at Nunney (Somerset) now resembles a rather dinky tower-house in a small pond. The small island that the site presently stands on is a post-medieval creation and the castle originally rose directly out of the water, partially concealed by a wall that survived on all but the moat's east side when visited by John Leland in the sixteenth century.[215] This would have made the castle suddenly come into the view of visitors.[216] The castle was only one component within a broader designed watery landscape including a more extensive artificial mere in the valley bottom of Nunney Brook. It is surely beyond coincidence that the castle's founder was named Sir John de la Mare (Mere) after he received licence to crenellate in 1373, and the place was known as Nunney Delamare when Leland visited it.[217] That is not all: the approach route to the site was from ground that overlooked it to the north. Here, on the slopes above, earthworks previously thought to represent the remains of a service area are now thought to be ornamental; they include a level platform that may well be a viewing terrace.[218] Like many ostentatious castles resulting from licences to crenellate in this period, Nunney was the product of new wealth.

The palace of the bishops of Salisbury at Sherborne (Dorset), built by Roger, Bishop of Salisbury, in the 1120s and 30s, is another clear example of an elite residence surrounded by a low wide lake whose purpose was as much ornamental as defensive.[219] A naturally sloping site was skilfully adapted to create a level platform enclosed within a stone wall that rose above its flooded surrounds with a deer park on the opposite side of the lake. While the lake in its present form is a mid-eighteenth-century creation, the area was previously occupied by a string of marshes and lakes,[220] and an antecedent medieval landscaped water feature seems distinctly likely. The provision of three separate gates – the grand south-west gatehouse, for high-status visitors; the north-east gatehouse, comprising a smaller-scale version facing the route from the nearby village of Castleton; and the more functional North Gate with its lakeside wharf through which the site was supplied by boat – tells us much about the sophisticated arrangements designed to ensure strict differentiation of access routes and, vitally, different views of the site, for different groups of visitor.

In other contexts, pathways alongside elongated ponds and causeways between separate water features were commonly used to structure approach routes, as at Ravensworth (Yorkshire, North Riding) (*Black and White Plate 16*). Here, an earthen causeway linking castle and village crosses a marshy depression representing the vestiges of a shallow mere, and is flanked by the terraces of a formal garden.[221] Equally dramatic are cases where elongated strings of ponds were created around a site. The mid-fifteenth-century fortified manor house of Baconsthorpe 'castle' in Norfolk had such a series of ponds created in front of it, forming a vista beneath one of its towers.[222] The bishop's palace at Cawood (Yorkshire, North Riding) is another good example, where three long parallel ponds form part of a remarkably formal arrangement that must be medieval in date, as the palace was abandoned in the sixteenth century.[223] At the mid-fifteenth-century castle of Herstmonceux (East Sussex), a northward extension from the corner of the formerly square moat that encompassed the site marks the position of a broad mere along the valley that would have confronted anybody approaching from the east.[224] At Castle Bolton (Yorkshire, North Riding) a series of canalised watercourses carried water from springs on the slopes, via header tanks, to feed an extensive series of gardens that contain rare evidence for a fountain base.[225]

We sometimes have clear evidence of the relocation of a seigneurial site to a lower-lying position complete with a watery setting, as at Bolingbroke (Lincolnshire). Constructed in the 1220s by Ranulph de Blundevill, Earl of

Plate 16. Ravensworth (Yorkshire, North Riding): masonry remains of a castle, set within a former mere, surrounded by the gardens and parkland of a fourteenth-century designed setting. (Photograph: Oliver Creighton)

Chester, in a new position in the base of a valley below an earlier Norman site, the castle was embedded within a watery landscape, although it is unclear whether this was created from the outset.[226] The large rectangular lake south of the castle was a more artificial creation than we see elsewhere, skilfully engineered so that the water within actually lay at a higher level than the surrounding land. Even unfinished residences could have designed watery landscapes realised in part, as exemplified by William Lord Hastings' moated house of brick at Kirby Muxloe (Leicestershire). Set back from the village in open space with a symmetrical front designed to be admired, work began in October 1480 but came to an abrupt halt in the summer of 1483 following the execution of its owner. While only the gatehouse and a single corner tower were built in anything like their intended form, the site was set within a broad and majestic moat and was accompanied by a suite of fishponds, a garden, an orchard and an enormous new park that could be reached across a bridge.[227] A probable Irish equivalent of an unfinished masonry castle (here of the fourteenth century) within a watery setting is Ballymoon (Co. Carlow) (*Black and White Plate 17*).[228] While lacking serious defences and designed as a formal square, the plan and display qualities of Ballymoon have been likened to Bodiam (East Sussex) (see also p. 5), and a context within a watery landscape may be another area of similarity.[229]

These watery landscapes have an underestimated European dimension. Examples in Scandinavia include the fifteenth-century tower-house at

Plate 17. The unfinished castle at Ballymoon (Co. Carlow). Surrounding earthworks suggest an ornamental setting, including an artificial mere. (Photograph: Oliver Creighton)

Bergkvara, Småland, and the late medieval residence at Glimmingehus, Scania.[230] Among the most spectacular anywhere in northern Europe was the 'House of the Marshes' (*Maison du Marais*) that lay within the duke of Burgundy's pleasure park of Hesdin, Artois (France). This ostentatious building, depicted in a late medieval Flemish painting rising above shimmering watery surrounds supporting swans, was a focal point for activities of the Burgundian court, including the fêtes champêtres or rural feasts.[231] Something of the potential effect of such an ensemble can be glimpsed in pictorial sources. For example, in the famous early-sixteenth-century hunting tapestry representing September made for Emperor Maximilian, a large artificial lake, apparently in the Forest of Soignes, is depicted as the last refuge of a hunted stag, the scene being penned in by sylvan scenery on either side, with the hunting party on the water's edge and a grand residence in the background.[232] In the depiction of April in the *Très Riches Heures du Duc de Berry* a naturalistic lake with boats upon it forms the middle ground and visual link between the gleaming walls of the fortress behind it and the scene in the foreground, comprising a party next to a lodge-like building with its own enclosed garden, all set in parkland.[233]

In certain geographical contexts the view of an elite residence from the sea could be as important as the view from the land, and perhaps even more so. It could be argued that Gerald of Wales' reference to the harbour in his description of the family seat at Manorbier is because of its intervisibility with the castle, which could be seen by the frequent traffic along the Bristol Channel (see p. 40–1). As a visual statement, Henry I's donjon at Orford (Suffolk) was clearly positioned with reference to those approaching the site by sea, inland views being blocked by slightly rising ground.[234] Dunstanburgh (Northumberland) presents another important case study in this regard (*Colour Plate 5*). Built for Thomas, Earl of Lancaster, from 1313, the castle's setting offers considerable problems of interpretation that can only convincingly be addressed by considering the site and its environs as an elite ensemble designed with an eye for visibility and impact upon the senses, in particular for those approaching it by sea.[235] Here, perhaps more than anywhere else covered in this book, the experience of approaching this site can still be understood on the ground – the castle, set in splendid isolation on its bare promontory, and its picturesque silhouette from the south, is an endlessly reproduced icon of Britain's medieval heritage.

Located on a remote, rugged and open headland setting unencumbered by any earlier structures, the castle's positioning is strategically meaningless, like that of Tintagel (Cornwall) (see p. 33). While it is usually axiomatic that castles were symbols of territorial control, here the site did not exist at the hub of a lordship as such, nor did its builder make any attempt to build up an effective lordship of any size.[236] As a building, Dunstanburgh presents something of an optical illusion, its impressive silhouette and magnificent double-towered gatehouse masking what was largely an open site (*Figure 11*). It is also not coincidental that the royal castle of Bamburgh, a few miles along the Northumbrian coast, was intervisible with the earl of Lancaster's hugely impressive masonry

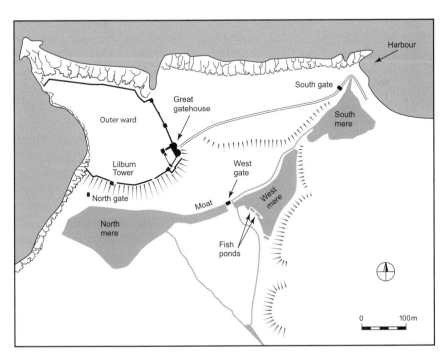

Figure 11. Dunstanburgh (Northumberland): reconstruction of the medieval landscape, showing the string of meres that formerly flanked the castle. Based on Oswald *et al.* 2006, with additions.

Plate 18. Castle Tioram (Argyllshire), showing the castle's setting on a tidal island. A site of lordship such as this commanded a 'seascape' as much as the landscape. (Photograph: Oliver Creighton)

edifice, which provided a visual counterpoint to the royal fortress. Analytical field survey of the site and its immediate setting, meanwhile, has thrown new light on its contemporary landscape and routes of approach to the site. The key to the castle's designed setting was a series of linked meres around the base of the castle on its landward side. The gatehouse looked not towards Embleton, the settlement from which the castle's lordship was named, but across an open expanse, apparently out to the open sea. The realisation that the castle's harbour was in a different position to that traditionally accepted, being in fact directly aligned with the gatehouse so that a visitor travelling by boat would appreciate its remarkable symmetry and brooding majesty, gives the castle's setting additional coherence.[237] This theatrical route of approach was enhanced by John of Gaunt's rebuilding of the system of gateways and addition of a barbican in the 1360s.[238]

The link between elite residences and views over or control of large expanses of water was stronger still in areas of northern and western Britain, especially in regions with a strong Gaelic influence that saw lordship expressed in quite different ways to the feudal norm.[239] Castle Tioram (Argyllshire) (*Black and White Plate 18*), is a prime example of a medieval seat of lordship whose hinterland was a seascape rather than a landscape, being a stronghold of the Clan Ranald, senior cadets of the Lords of the Isles.[240] Here, a castle established in the thirteenth or fourteenth centuries had access to poor agricultural resources but excellent maritime linkages and access to seaways, and it is in this sense that we should try and understand how contemporaries approached it and valued its visual qualities. Lakes formed stunning visual backgrounds for other noble residences, as at Linlithgow palace (West Lothian), where galleries and first-floor windows overlooked the loch, while earthwork terraces between the palace and the water's edge perhaps mark early gardens (*Colour Plate 6*).[241] The likelihood that inland lakes in Ireland could have been perceived as elite spaces in the later Middle Ages has been highlighted by a ground-breaking programme of research around Lough Gara, on the borders of Counties Roscommon and Sligo (*Figure 12*).[242] This part of medieval Ireland was not atypical in the fact that watery landscapes played critical symbolic roles in the control of territory. It is quite clear that elite families exploited and drew upon the mythical pasts of these environments, as expressed for instance in poems, to both legitimate and express their power. A spatial link between the waters of the lake and sites of lordship is clear in the construction of later medieval tower-houses and substantial moated residences, while there are also indications that at the same time lakes were becoming more exclusive resources, with families bringing entire lakes into their control.[243]

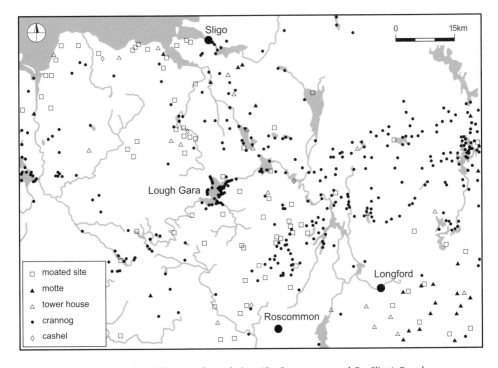

Figure 12. Medieval sites of lordship around Lough Gara (Co. Roscommon and Co. Sligo). Based on Fredengren 2002, with additions.

Moated sites

The many thousand medieval moated sites of various size, shape and date that dot the British landscape hold a great deal of potential for the understanding of gardens and designed settings of the period. For example, Le Patourel's pioneering study of moated sites in Yorkshire found evidence for gardens attached to all four of the principal case study sites, at East Haddlesey, Rest Park, Newstead and Methley.[244] Many moated sites possessed more than one garden, especially those of higher status, as revealed by documentary sources.[245] For example, the moated mansion of Mannington Hall (Norfolk), built in the 1460s, possessed extensive multiple gardens both within and beyond the moat, as well as fishponds, although they have been remodelled up to the twentieth century.[246] Such evidence is particularly important as it can tell us something of the gardens in the possession of the middle classes, at least in England, where moated sites (comprising water-filled ditches surrounding central islands that were often raised) proliferated as the seats of minor gentry, especially in the thirteenth and fourteenth centuries. In other cases, however, formal enclosed gardens of the sixteenth and seventeenth centuries have been erroneously identified as moated sites, as at Childerley (Cambridgeshire).[247] Nonetheless, there is good reason to suppose that many genuine examples of medieval moated sites would have been accompanied by gardens, while others may well have functioned at least partly as garden features in their own right.

Traditional explanations for the phenomenon of moated sites, involving the need for defence and drainage at the homes of lesser lords, can only take us so far. That the builders of these sites were emulating social superiors who used large-scale water features to enhance the magnificence of their homes is another attractive scenario.[248] There is certainly a fine line between such sites and the larger-scale manipulation of watery landscapes – involving lakes, meres and ponds – for dramatic effect (see p. 77). Moats have significant potential as ornamental sites, and four particular arrangements can be defined: moated platforms that contained gardens as well as a principal residence; small moats that are clearly subsidiary to a major residential site; paired moats; and sites with double (i.e. concentric) moats. We should remember that many such sites were surveyed and recorded several decades ago, and that it is only in retrospect that we can recognise that they had 'designed' elements. For example, close scrutiny of Allcroft's chapter 'The Moated Homestead', in his seminal study of earthworks in the English landscape (1908), shows that it contains examples of all of these possibilities: for example, Little Kimble and Saunderton (Buckinghamshire) (*Figure 13*).[249] Only with the benefit of recent studies can it be seen that the line of fishponds at the former and the arrangement of multiple islands (one containing the church) in a shallow artificial lake at the latter make these places excellent candidates as designed landscapes. In other cases, shallow depressions traditionally identified as horse-ponds at moated sites may well be ornamental.

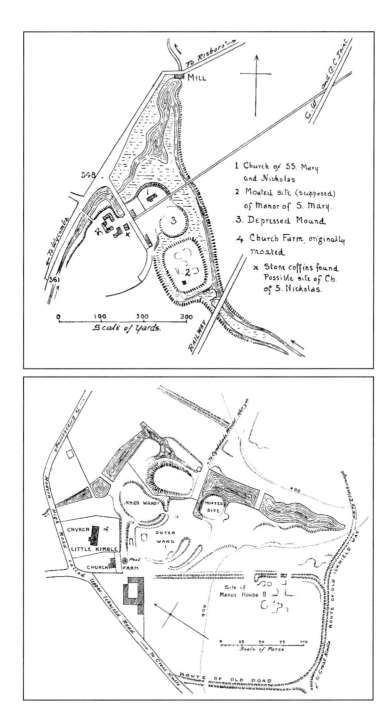

Figure 13. Medieval earthworks at Saunderton and Little Kimble (Buckinghamshire).
Source: Allcroft 1908.

MOATED GARDENS

Moated sites are frequently associated with the same appurtenances of lordship as other manorial centres and, because of their low-lying positions, frequently have particularly impressive fishpond complexes. Garden compartments attached to moats are also well known. Systematic study of documentary references to moated sites within the Lancashire hundred of West Derby has shown gardens and dovecotes to have been relatively commonplace additions to even relatively minor moated sites of lordship, even if virtually no physical evidence for them survives.[250] Archaeological fieldwork in Suffolk has suggested that moats ancillary to both medieval manorial sites and gentry houses of the early Tudor period contained detached gardens, orchards, dovecotes and banqueting houses, as at sites such as Rishangles Lodge and Helmingham Hall.[251] Another excellent example is the castle of Bredwardine (Herefordshire), where a series of fishponds and mounds stretching in a line south of the site represent a probable ornamental watery landscape alongside the River Wye.[252] A late twelfth-century charter of the castle lords, the de Baskervilles, mentions an orchard, gardens and a separate kitchen garden, all tended by Semert the gardener, as well as vineyards, fishponds and a deer park.

The large moated site known as The Belgrave Moat, just south of Chester, is particularly important in this context, not only as it preserves the earthwork remains of a medieval garden surrounding the moated platform, but also because the date and status of the site are known. The moat was an estate centre built for Richard the Engineer (or Lenginour), a leading servant of Edward I, by *c*.1300, and abandoned by the end of the fourteenth century. Excavation and survey have revealed a complex of garden features including a broad terrace-like walkway around three sides of the island and a pair of separate moated mounds at the north-west corner of the site, at least one of which was topped by a flower bed (*Figure 14*).[253] The construction of a garden on a non-

Figure 14. The Belgrave Moat (Cheshire), showing medieval garden features. Based on Turner *et al.* 1988, with additions.

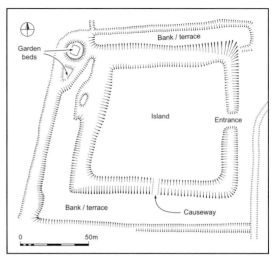

defended site by a royal servant known to have been heavily involved with the labour force in Chester mirrors the proliferation of garden building associated with Edward I's castles in North Wales, seemingly indicating an aping of elite design further down the social scale. The couple of hundred medieval moated sites in Wales show a higher concentration in the more manorialised 'English' districts and it is unsurprising that here too there are sites which may have associated enclosed gardens. A clear case in point is Horseland Moat (Glamorgan), a manorial site probably of the thirteenth century, where an attached ditched enclosure contains six irregular islands; an interpretation as a fishpond is out of the question and a function as a water garden seems likely.[254] This example is from the Welsh county with probably the highest intensity of archaeological survey, and countless other examples doubtless remain to be identified.

SUBSIDIARY MOATS

While medieval moated sites are generally assumed to have enclosed manorial buildings, the fact that archaeological excavation and fieldwork has often failed to recover occupation evidence opens up possibilities for other interpretations.[255] One of these is that 'empty' moated islands could have contained gardens or orchards.[256] We may well be underestimating the number of medieval moated sites across the British landscape that did not contain high-status residential complexes but, rather, functioned as garden features, perhaps with small buildings such as pavilions or gazebos that afforded seclusion. Such features are best known from continental pictorial sources: for example, the *Book of Hours of Isabella of Portugal* (1480) depicts King René d'Anjou sitting in a brick building that is set within a garden that is clearly moated and accessed from the principal residence via a tree-lined avenue that leads to a wooden bridge.[257] It is a measure of the status of such a garden that it was furnished with its own water-filled moat, serving as a marker of rank and social separateness. Abandoned medieval moated sites also have particularly rich potential for the preservation of buried garden soils and waterlogged deposits containing pollen and seeds. For example, excavation on the moated platform of Wood Hall, Womersley (Yorkshire, North Riding) has revealed an arrangement of linear planting trenches that was part of a late medieval garden, with a masonry feature to the south being identified as a possible bench and an area of dense organic soil as a lawn.[258]

Not all moated gardens are necessarily late, however. Such an appurtenance apparently existed at Hereford by the late twelfth century; this was located on the opposite bank of the Wye to the castle in the area of the Bishop's Meadows and was later referred to as the *Kingsorchard*.[259] Another potential example is the square moated platform, *c.*60 metres across, adjacent to Wattlesborough castle (Shropshire) and linked to the castle's wet outer defences. The feature is recorded as a moat in 1379 and, while it has now been demolished by agricultural clearance, it is recorded on aerial photographs and maps and is another potential enclosed orchard or garden, perhaps contemporary with the thirteenth- or fourteenth-century tower-house on the site.[260] The important castle of the Fitz Alan family, earls of Arundel, at Clun (Shropshire) seems to have been redesigned *c*.1300 with a designed setting that included a lake and moated water garden or 'pleasance' below a new residential block; a 'little park' was a further component of this ornamental landscape.[261] Here, as elsewhere on the Anglo-Welsh Marches, attention was devoted to the design of castle surroundings at the end of the thirteenth century, when the military significance of these places was in decline and their administrative and amenity roles, in particular as hunting lodges, increased in importance. A miniature moated site (now ploughed into oblivion) within the grounds of the bishop of Ely's palace at Somersham (Cambridgeshire) also seems likely to have functioned as a 'pleasance' supporting a summerhouse or pavilion, perhaps dating to the fourteenth century judging by materials recovered from its interior.[262] Other relevant sites include the moats in medieval designed landscapes at Ballyloughan and Ballymoon (Co. Carlow), which both lay within a couple of hundred metres of masonry castles.[263]

PAIRED MOATS

Classifications of moated sites on the basis of their plans have recognised the complex relationships between principal units and subsidiary enclosures.[264] While an obvious explanation is that the pairing of moats in this way demonstrates a replacement of one site with another, it is worth considering whether in some cases one of the enclosures is in fact a garden or orchard. The likelihood of a medieval moat being a garden feature is heightened where it is sited in the immediate vicinity of what was clearly a primary manorial site. Such a moat is recorded at Wressle (Yorkshire, East Riding). The substantial moat surrounding the Percy family's elegant quadrangular castle of the late fourteenth century was accompanied to the north by a second, slightly smaller, squarish moat, now vanished but recorded in a map of 1610 and visible in aerial photographs.[265] It was probably in this area that John Leland observed two ornamental viewing mounds decorated with topiary hedges, into which spiral pathways had been cut.[266]

The island of a moated site in Bassingbourn (Cambridgeshire) measured little more than *c*.30 x 15 metres, and may have had a garden function, as it was attached to a manorial site converted to a garden by Richard Lynne in the late fifteenth or early sixteenth century.[267] The 'twinned' moated sites at Linwood (Lincolnshire), recorded on early Ordnance Survey plans and aerial photographs before being destroyed by agriculture in the 1960s, offer another obvious possible candidate; standing little more than 30 metres apart, a successive relationship seems inherently unlikely and one may well have been an orchard.[268] Another likely candidate is the medieval moats north of Grimston Garth on the Holderness coast (Yorkshire, East Riding). Little more than 30 metres separates a quadrangular homestead moat on the site of medieval Grimston Hall from a subsidiary moated enclosure of *c*.15 x 37 metres known as 'The Mount', too small to have contained residential buildings and too close to suggest an antecedent site. It lies in an area known as 'Great Parks' and near other features including fishponds, and a function as an orchard or pleasure garden is highly likely.[269]

Excavation within such an ancillary enclosure adjacent to the principal moated residence at Swannington Hall (Norfolk) has revealed garden features of twelfth- to fourteenth-century date. These, which comprise a series of slight parallel linear features less than 50 centimetres wide and little more than 6 centimetres deep, remind us of how fragile and unobtrusive medieval garden archaeology can be.[270] In the absence of such excavation it is difficult, of course, to prove that such garden features were not post-medieval additions; after all, the modification of moats in the sixteenth and seventeenth centuries in line with contemporary gardening fashions is well known.[271]

Paired moats are rare in Ireland, but the possibility that some of these which do exist represent a combination of manor house and enclosed garden or orchard cannot be ruled out. Potential examples include the site at Longford Pass North (Co. Tipperary), although the fact that in most such cases both moats contain platforms – suggesting that they were not open – raises the possibility of other origins, such as enclosures for agricultural buildings.[272]

DOUBLE MOATS

Double moats – ones which are planned concentrically, one inside the other – provides perhaps even more compelling evidence for a diagnostic type of medieval garden feature (*Figure 15*). The new 'herbarium' made at Peterborough Abbey (Northamptonshire) in 1302 was of this form (see p. 51). Double moats could certainly indicate status: the author of *Sir Gawain and the Green Knight* took care to describe that Sir Bertalik's castle was surrounded by two moats, for instance.[273] In terms of actual sites, the royal pleasance at Kenilworth is the most prominent example known to us. The word 'pleasance' or 'pleasuance' is most commonly associated with garden features of the nineteenth century, usually a secluded garden within a garden, but the word and concept has medieval origins. That at Kenilworth, the *Plesauns en Marys*, was constructed between 1414 and 1417 for Henry V on the opposite side of the lake from the castle, and comprised a four-acre island surrounded by concentric wet moats.[274] Internal features identified in aerial photographs indicate the positions of stone buildings within their own enclosure and traces of garden beds.[275] John Leland described the site as having been an 'attractive wooden banqueting house known as the pleasuance which stood next to the lake' prior to its dismantlement by Henry VIII,[276] and a raised strip of ground between the two moats formed a walkway. Notably, the position of the pleasance, secluded from the castle around a bend of the mere, behind a low rise in the ground, must have ensured that it was suddenly revealed to approaching visitors.

Examples of other water gardens of this status are few, although a potential candidate is a square feature to the south of Raglan castle, visible as a vestigial

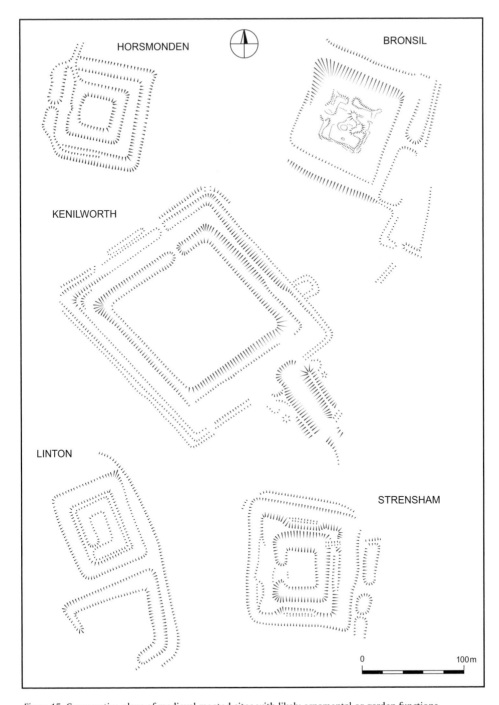

HORSMONDEN

BRONSIL

KENILWORTH

LINTON

STRENSHAM

0   100m

Figure 15. Comparative plans of medieval moated sites with likely ornamental or garden functions.

earthwork and depicted on a map of 1652 as being divided into four squares and surrounded by water. It is quite separate from, and apparently antedates, the elaborate sixteenth- and seventeenth-century gardens at the site, although its precise context is obscure.[277] But archaeology is revealing other evidence relating to sites further down the social hierarchy, as at Linton (Cambridgeshire) (*Figure 16*). Here, a garden site with two concentric water-filled moats has been surveyed; the central island was *c*.24 x 10 metres and accessed by three causeways.[278] The moated mansion of Bronsil (Herefordshire) is another prime example. Remodelled as a mansion house in the fifteenth century by Richard Beauchamp, who had received a licence to crenellate and empark, the site comprises an earlier medieval moat to which an outer moat has been added, leaving a broad flat area between which functioned as a kind of walkway; a further element in the site's designed setting was a line of five linked ponds descending down the valley side, creating a cascading effect.[279] Other sites bearing comparison include Strensham (Worcestershire), a concentrically moated site crenellated in the mid fourteenth century, and Horsmonden (Kent), where two concentric moats are set at the confluence of two streams forming, in effect, a third moat.

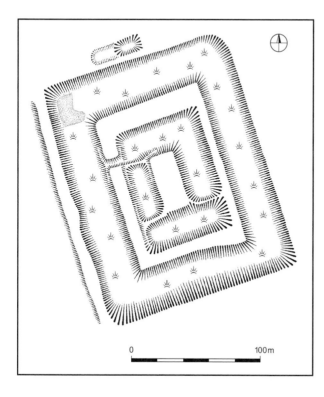

Figure 16. Linton (Cambridgeshire): a medieval moated garden. Source: Brown and Taylor 1993.

0   100m

Chapter Three Notes

[1] Landsberg 1996, 101–39.

[2] See Everson and Williamson 1998 on the problems and possibilities of medieval garden archaeology.

[3] Thacker 1979, 84–6.

[4] Calkins 1986, 165–6.

[5] Dyer 2006a, 40.

[6] Dyer 1997, 62.

[7] Foulds 1997.

[8] Schofield 1994, 89–90.

[9] Quiney 2003, 232–3; Rodwell 2005, 122.

[10] Orme and Webster 1995, 92, 122.

[11] Thacker 1979, 82.

[12] Comito 1971, 494–7.

[13] Quoted in Fleming 1986, 201.

[14] Webb 2007, 185.

[15] Alexander 2002, 858.

[16] MacDougall 1986a, 5.

[17] Howes 1997, 1–10.

[18] Moorhouse 1989, 62.

[19] Webb 2007, 175.

[20] Thacker 1979, 81–2; Hobhouse 1992, 74–5.

[21] Creighton 2005b, 127–31.

[22] Pestell 2004, 175–82.

[23] Page 1908b, 129.

[24] James 1990, 84.

[25] Jamieson 1994, 18.

[26] Keil 1959–60.

[27] Harvey 1992.

[28] Noble 1997.

[29] Gilchrist 2005, 60–3.

[30] Everson *et al.* 1991, 68–9.

[31] English Heritage Register of Parks and Gardens, No. DG2824.

[32] Reeves-Smyth 2004, 114–15.

[33] Eco 1986, 46, 57–8.

[34] Christie and Coad 1980, 189.

[35] Harvey 1992.

[36] Harvey 1981, 109–10.

[37] Reeves-Smyth 2004, 117.

[38] Webb 2007, 173.

[39] Reeves-Smyth 2004, 117.

[40] Webb 2007, 173.

[41] Taylor 1998b, 26.

[42] Thorpe 1978, 163–4; Webb 2007, 183.

[43] Bettey 1993, 47; Aston and Bettey 1998, 121.

[44] Creighton and Higham 2005, 171–2; Goodman 1927, 123.

[45] Moorhouse 1989, 62.

[46] Dyer 2000a, 114–16.

[47] See, for example, Harvey 1985, 37–41 for the reconstruction of a medieval *curia* at Cuxham (Oxfordshire) on the basis of surveys and court rolls.

[48] Moorhouse 2003a, 192–4.

[49] Everson *et al.* 1991.

[50] Hunt 1959–60, 92.

[51] Harvey 1984, 99, n. 43.

[52] Jamieson and Jones 2004.

[53] Jamieson and Jones 2004, 12, 24–35.

[54] Riley 2006, 102–4.

[55] Morris 1989, 253.

[56] Everson *et al.* 1991, 127–8.

[57] Saunders 1990, 187–8.

[58] McDonagh 2007, 187; Creighton 1998, 147–56.

[59] Bloch 1967; see also Langdon 1994.

[60] Holt 1988, 39–40; see also Watts 2002, 83.

[61] Treen and Atkin 2005, 20.

[62] Holt 1988, 36–53.

[63] Langdon 2004, 108.

[64] Moorhouse 2003b, 330.

[65] O'Conor 1998, 33–4; Rynne 2004, 76–9.

[66] O'Conor and Murphy 2006.

[67] O'Conor 2004, 235.

[68] Colvin 1986.

[69] James 1990, 84.

[70] Colvin 1963.

[71] Colvin 1975, 196–9.

[72] Steane 1999, 118.

[73] Colvin 1963, 951.

[74] James and Robinson 1988, 22; this was not unknown elsehere: work at Stonor (Oxfordshire) *c.*1480 included whitewashing of the garden walls and daubing and pargetting those of the orchard: Steane 1995, 464.

[75] Colvin 1963, 949, 1001.

[76] Dawson 1976.

[77] Ashbee 2006, 87–8.

[78] Woolgar 2006, 224.

[79] Dawson 1976, 187.

[80] Steane 1999, 117.

[81] RCHAMS 1963, 187, 219–20.

[82] RCHAMS 1963, 112, fig. 113.

[83] Dawson 1976, 54.

[84] Elrington 1990, 431–48.

[85] Steane 1999, 117–18.

[86] Steane 1999, 118.

[87] Colvin 1963, 1009–17; Elrington 1990, 431–48; Ashbee 2006, 78–81.

[88] Colvin 1963, 997–8.

[89] James 1990, 134.

[90] Parsons 1995, 53; Tolley 1991, 176.

[91] Colvin 1963, 862–3.

[92] Cooper 1999, 819, 832 n. 25.

[93] Thompson 1998, 150–4.

[94] Taylor 1989a.

[95] Oswald 2005, 2–6.

[96] Roberts 1986.

[97] Willis-Bund 1902, 168–71; Turner 1991, 8.

[98] Emery 2000, 691.

[99] Whitehead and Patton 2001.

[100] Steane 2001, 65; Seeley and Phillpotts 2006, 54, 74, 94–5.

[101] Biddle 1969; Biddle 1986, 24–30; Thompson 1998, 46.

[102] Biddle 1986, 30.

[103] Shortt 1965, 37.

[104] Allen and Hiller 2002, 215–16.

[105] Faulkner 1970, 141.

[106] Payne 2003, 219–20.

[107] Taylor 1998b, 22.

[108] Everson *et al.* 1991, 129.

[109] Everson *et al.* 1991, 130.

[110] Everson 1991, 185.

[111] Taylor 1989b, 72–4.

[112] RCHME 1926, 34–8.

[113] Woodfield and Woodfield 1988, 3; Emery 2000, 276.

[114] Nash and Redwood 2006.

[115] Johnson 2002; Creighton 2005b; Liddiard 2005a.

[116] Whittle 1992, 12; Emery 2000, 690.

[117] Roberts 1997.

[118] McDiarmid 1973, 84, 122.

[119] Cazelles and Rathofer 1988, 34–7.

[120] English Heritage Register of Parks and Gardens, No. GD2040.

[121] Turner 2006a, 43.

[122] Brown 2002, 30–1.

[123] Brown 1984, 443.

[124] Roberts 2002, 121, 409.

[125] Hobhouse 1992, 75.

[126] Colvin 1963, 450–1.

[127] McLean 1981, 92.

[128] McCarthy *et al.* 1990, 150–3.

[129] See Cooper and Fletcher 1995; Herring 1997.

[130] English Heritage Register of Parks and Gardens, No. GD4198.

[131] Waterman 1959.

[132] Meek 1984; Mallory and McNeill 1991, 312–13.

[133] James 2004, 287–8.

[134] Brown *et al.* 2004, 114–15.

[135] Terra Nova 2002.

[136] Brown *et al.* 2004, 115.

[137] Bowden 1998.

[138] Everson 1998, 77; CBA 1997.

[139] Stewart-Brown 1912.

[140] Silvester *et al.* 2004.

[141] Creighton 2005a, 282–3.

[142] Taylor 1998a, 5; Emery 2000, 576.

[143] Liddiard 2005a, 44–6.

[144] Bowden 2005, 8.

[145] Steane 1999, 118.

[146] Foreman and Dennison 2005.

[147] Dennison 2005, 122–6; 212–13.

[148] Hartley 1983, 30–2.

[149] Brown 1976, 95.

[150] Colvin 1963, 381.

[151] Peers 1921–22, 72–3.

[152] Colvin 1963, 380.

[153] Whittle 1992, 10.

[154] See Ashbee 2004a, 53.

[155] Taylor 1998b, 24; Taylor 2003, 35–6.

[156] James 1990, 96.

[157] Tolley 1991, 175–6; Parsons 1995, 53.

[158] Colvin 1963, 324.

[159] Colvin 1963, 338; Brown 1976, 210.

[160] Cazelles and Rathofer 1988, 46–7.

[161] Barber 2007, 95.

[162] Barker 1986, 89–90.

[163] Crouch 2005, 49–55.

[164] Darby and Terrett 1957, 259.

[165] Homes 1973, 9–13.

[166] Gilchrist 2005, 62.

[167] Gem 1997, 130.

[168] Hudson and Neale 1983, 66.

[169] Kelly 1997, 262–3.

[170] Steane 1999, 118; Roberts 1997.

[171] Cazelles and Rathofer 1988, 22, 26.

[172] Roberts 1997.

[173] Carus Wilson 1947, 146–7.

[174] Schofield 1994, 89.

[175] Woolgar 2001, 131.

[176] Steane 1999, 118–19.

[177] Dawson 1976, 187.

[178] Colvin 1963; Steane 1999, 118.

[179] Roberts 1988, 75.

[180] English Heritage Register of Parks and Gardens, No. GD2040.

[181] Meadows 1996, 213–15.

[182] Van Laun 1981, 355–6.

[183] RCHME Herefordshire 1932, 69–70; RCHME Dorset 1970, 199; other good candidates for medieval vineyards leaving similar evidence of terracing include Vineyards Brake, Thornbury and Wearyall Hill, Glastonbury.

[184] Thacker 1979, 85.

[185] Woolgar 2001, 130–1.

[186] Le Patourel 1973, 113.

[187] Blood and Taylor 1992, 97–8; Oswald 2005, 4.

[188] Poore and Wilkinson 2001.

[189] Davies 1988, 32–3.

[190] Rackham 2004, 5–9.

[191] Daniels 1988, 43.

[192] Harris *et al.* 2003, 139–42.

[193] Colvin 1963, 927.

[194] See Elliott 1997, 107.

[195] Cummins 2002, 50.

[196] Colvin 1982, 106.

[197] Russell and Russell 1991, 72; see also Trollope 1858.

[198] Fisher 2004, 9–12.

[199] Doob 1990.

[200] RCHME Essex 1916, 260; English Heritage Register of Parks and Gardens, No. GD1733.

[201] Trollope 1858, 80; RCHME Dorset 1952, 132.

[202] Hartley 1983, 48; Pevsner and Williamson 1984, 522.

[203] Gandy 2006.

[204] Roberts 2001, 12.

[205] Cazelles and Rathofer 1988.

[206] See, for example, Cook and Williamson 1999.

[207] Cooper 1999, 821–5.

[208] Thacker 1979, 90–1.

[209] Cummins 2002, 47.

[210] Drew 1963; Thompson 1965; Johnson 2002, 139–42.

[211] Brown and Pattison 1997; Brown 2002, 31.

[212] Everson and Williamson 1998, 144.

[213] McNeill 1997, 96–9.

[214] Leslie 1993, 4–5.

[215] Chandler 1993, 428.

[216] Emery 2006, 606–7.

[217] Toulmin-Smith 1910, 97; Rigold 1957, 3–4; Everson 2003, 30–2.

[218] Somerset Historic Environment Record PRN 23897; for an interpretation of the feature as a bailey see, for instance, Rigold 1957, 9.

[219] Davison 2001.

[220] Waymark 2001, 64; Payne 2003, 190–2.

[221] Ryder 1979; Dennison *et al.* 2006.

[222] Dallas and Sherlock 2002, 32–5.

[223] Taylor 1998b, 28.

[224] English Heritage Register of Parks and Gardens, No. GD1139.

[225] Moorhouse 2003a, 206; 2003b, 329.

[226] Taylor 1998b, 38.

[227] Peers 1986; Beresford and St Joseph 1979, 55–6.

[228] O'Keeffe 2004, 59–63.

[229] See McNeill 1997, 110–13.

[230] Hansson 2006, 156–9.

[231] de Winter 1983, 115–16; see also Beck *et al.* 2001 on the parks and gardens of the dukes of Burgundy more generally.

[232] Cummins 2002, 50.

[233] While traditionally identified as the Château de Dourdan, the scene is more likely to represent the residence of the Orléans family at Pierrefonds, which stood next to a lake and a subsidiary residence known as the Parcq: Cazelles and Rathofer 1988, 26–7.

[234] Barker 2004, 44.

[235] See Oswald et al. 2006; Oswald and Ashbee 2006; this re-evaluation was anticipated by Shanks 1992, 148–57, in a phenomenologically inspired account of walking to and around Dunstanburgh.

[236] King 2001, 230.

[237] Oswald and Ashbee 2006, 96–7.

[238] King 2001, 228.

[239] McNeill 2002.

[240] Fisher 2005, 85–91.

[241] Hynd 1984, 270.

[242] Fredengren 2002.

[243] Fredrengren 2002, 271, 276–8, 283.

[244] Le Patourel 1973.

[245] Le Patourel 1978a, 23.

[246] English Heritage Register of Parks and Gardens, No. GD2010.

[247] Taylor 1974, 62, 93.

[248] See Aberg 1978; Le Patourel 1981; see also Taylor 1972, 246–8, for a regional case study.

[249] Allcroft 1908, 453–93.

[250] Lewis 2000, 119.

[251] Booth 2005, 241.

[252] Whitehead 1995, 199.

[253] Turner et al. 1988, 68–73.

[254] RCAHMW 1982, 96–101.

[255] Johnson 2007, 109.

[256] Le Patourel 1978b, 40–1.

[257] Harvey 1981, 111.

[258] MSRG 1995, 37; Nenk et al. 1995, 261–3.

[259] Whitehead 1995, 198.

[260] Gaydon 1968, 198.

[261] Stamper 1996.

[262] Taylor 1998b, 30.

[263] O'Keeffe 2000a, 172.

[264] For instance, see Le Patourel 1973, 4.

[265] Le Patourel 1973, 6, 117.

[266] Chandler 1993, 538–9.

[267] Oosthuizen and Taylor 2000, 65.

[268] Everson et al. 1991, 49, 127.

[269] English Heritage National Monuments Record, No. TA 23 NE 2.

[270] Whitmore and Robertson 2002, 101.

[271] Le Patourel 1973, 5–7.

[272] Barry 1977, 71.

[273] Barron 1974, 69; an alternative explanation is that the 'double ditch' is one that required a double throw of spoil to excavate, see Thompson 1997, 125.

[274] Thompson 1964.

[275] Taylor 1998b, 34.

[276] Chandler 1993, 475.

[277] Whittle 1989, 90.

[278] Brown and Taylor 1991.

[279] Smith 2000; Emery 2000, 523–5; see also Whitehead 1995, 201–2.

LEEDS TRINITY UNIVERSITY

—— *Chapter Four* ——

Shaping Nature:
Animals and Estates

In trying to grasp something of the meanings of aristocratic landscapes it is important also to consider the animals that inhabited and moved within them. Across the demesne estates that served the residences with which the previous chapter was concerned, the display and management as well as the hunting and consumption of species that carried connotations of social status came to represent a defining hallmark of the later medieval elite landscape. There existed by the late Middle Ages an established hierarchy of birds and fish for the table, while the hunting opportunities available to any individual depended, similarly, on social rank. A clear hierarchy was again in operation, with the hunting of deer and boar somewhere near the top and fowling and ferreting towards the lower end of this spectrum of activities. Whether displayed on the feasting table or encountered on the hunt, animals therefore clearly played an important role in marking distinctions within the social elite, while the ways in which they were managed constituted conspicuous statements of privilege to wider communities.

In addition, we should not overlook the fact that the symbolism of animals was integral to the medieval experience of elite landscape. A culture of 'animal vocabulary', whereby certain species were thought to symbolise particular human characteristics or carried specific religious meanings, is prominently displayed in medieval literature and public ritual, for instance.[1] There are good reasons to think that animals within parks, forests and gardens also conveyed their own messages and meanings to contemporaries. Representing far more than naturally occurring resources, these fauna were often actively introduced, nurtured and managed in ways that have left physical traces in the historic landscape. Fieldwork and documentary study reveals that features such as dovecotes, fishponds, swanneries and rabbit warrens were tangible symbols of elite status that could be structured and located to impress as well as to provide foodstuffs.

The Welsh court poet Iolo Goch presents a poetic description of an idealised demesne landscape packed with elite animals in a particularly vivid image that focuses on Owain Glyn Dŵr's *llys* (estate center) of Sycharth (near Llansilin, Denbigh) in the late fourteenth century (*Colour Plate 7*):

> *Each side full, each house at court,*
> *Orchard, vineyard and white fortress;*
> *The master's rabbit warren;*
> *Ploughs and strong steeds of great frame;*
> *Near the court, even finer,*
> *The deer park within that field;*
> *Fresh green meadows and hayfields;*
> *Neatly enclosed rows of grain;*
> *Fine mill on a smooth-flowing stream;*
> *Dovecot a bright stone tower;*
> *A fish-pond, enclosed and deep,*
> *Where nets are cast when need be,*
> *Abounding, no argument,*
> *In pike and splendid whiting;*
> *His land a board where birds dwell,*
> *Peacocks, high-stepping herons.*[2]

While individually the features listed (orchard, vineyard, rabbit warren, deer park, dovecote, fishpond and perhaps a heronry) represent the minutiae of demesne farming, they clearly also formed visual foci within elite landscapes and were essential to how these settings were experienced and valued. Collectively, they not only resulted in profound physical changes to the countryside but also came to symbolise a new level of human control over nature, and it is these building blocks of elite landscape design that are the subject of this section of the book. This chapter explores the place of birds, rabbits and fish in the elite landscape, while deer, and the parks in which they were bred, hunted and displayed, are covered in the following chapter.

Noble game reserves

Collections of exotic animals were kept by many of the courts of later medieval Europe. Gifts of unusual specimens were a means of expressing status and favour, while their presence could add mystique to the rituals of courtly life.[3] The tradition of the Roman *vivaria*, whereby noblemen and senators possessed elite game reserves that sometimes contained aviaries and large fishponds as well as walled game parks, drew on the 'paradises' of earlier Persian rulers.[4] Exotic animals also played important roles in royal ceremony in the Byzantine world; as well as collections of live beasts, mechanical devices in palace contexts are known from tenth-century sources, as in the well-known case of the animatronic birds and other animals described by Liudprand of Cremona.[5]

In medieval Britain, the notion of the noble menagerie seems to have drawn its inspiration from early medieval continental European influences. Charlemagne's zoo set within a park at Aachen is well known from poetic descriptions; he was given monkeys, a lion and a bear during his reign and famously requested and received an elephant from the Sultan of Baghdad.[6] It is not until the thirteenth and fourteenth century, however, that the fashion for elite menageries really took off. In his *c.*1305 description of a model medieval park stocked with rare and elegant fauna, Piero de' Crescenzi specified that rows of trees planted around the setting of a noble residence 'should run from the palace to the grove but not crosswise, so that one can see easily from the palace whatever the animals do in the garden'.[7] Something of how such an arrangement might look is hinted at in the depiction of the Château de Dourdan in the *Très Riches Heures du Duc de Berry*, where trees in the parkland scene that occupies the foreground are clearly planted in straight lines oriented towards the fortress in the background, while others form more naturalistic clumps.[8] Despite this, images of larger beasts confined within the gardens that are sometimes found on later medieval paintings and tapestries have religious significance and should not be interpreted literally.[9]

However, we know that Frederick II, emperor of Germany and king of Sicily, maintained a zoo that included lions, leopards, panthers, elephants, dromedaries, camels and exotic birds in the first half of the thirteenth century,[10] while Philip the Bold, Duke of Burgundy, possessed a 'Jardin de Monseigneur' in his castle of Rouvres that housed a small menagerie including two swans, a deer, a small bear and, from 1375, a leopard; it was quite distinct from the 'Jardin de Madame' renowned for its lavender and rose bushes.[11] In England, Henry I first established a royal collection of exotic animals within his deer park at Woodstock, near Oxford (see p. 147). The menagerie was maintained at the Tower of London from the early years of the thirteenth century until its removal to Regent's Park in 1831.[12] Archaeology has added to our understanding of the composition of this famous collection. Excavations within the late-thirteenth-century Lion Tower, which housed part of the menagerie, have recovered evidence of the earliest big cats in post-Pleistocene Britain, including two medieval lion skulls and the remains of a leopard.[13] The notion of keeping exotic animals for display purposes was not limited to the Crown, however. The Archbishop of Canterbury's residence at West Tarring (Sussex) reputedly contained a menagerie building that housed monkeys.[14] Bears were kept by households including that of the Countess of Warwick in the early 1420s, when a beast formed a living heraldic device for the Beauchamp family.[15] Keeping and giving exotic species was also not unknown in Western Britain: the Annals of Inisfallen record that the king of Scotland sent a camel as a gift to Muirchertach Ua Briain, King of Munster, in 1105.[16] It is quite clear that these collections of animals were maintained for reasons of status and symbolism rather than any fondness for the creatures *per se*. Indeed, the indulgence or pampering of pets could be frowned upon in elite society, their ownership by religious orders being suppressed from the thirteenth century.[17]

Birds

When falconry and hawking can be glimpsed in the material culture of authority, the evidence relates to the very highest echelons of medieval society. The use of birds of prey is sometimes represented in emblematic form on the badges and seals of the higher nobility, while something of the practice itself can be illuminated by rare surviving examples of hawk hoods, rings and gloves, which are derived largely from royal contexts.[18] It is therefore interesting that skeletal remains of birds of prey recovered from archaeological contexts within medieval sites show that falconry was actually practised within a rather wider sector of society and among an 'elite' less exclusive than the limited sector who hunted deer, at least legally. Bones of hunting falcons are not unknown in urban contexts, for example.[19] Also, as a less public sport than the chase, falconry played a prominent role in the distinctive hunting activities of the female elite; in the fourteenth-century Queen Mary's Psalter, for instance, women are shown casting hawks as well as netting, ferreting and clubbing rabbits.[20] Birds of prey also featured on the seals of noblewomen, while parks provided a favoured but also secluded venue for the activity.[21]

Falconry was a sport that entailed a very real need to control nature, and medieval texts contain telling observations on the human–animal relationships it embodied. The list at the end of the fifteenth-century *Boke of St Albans*, for instance, lists the hierarchies of medieval society and the avian world in parallel.[22] While twelfth-century treatises on falconry are essentially practical works, from the thirteenth century onwards writers develop sophisticated observation of birds as part of the natural world, as exemplified by Frederick II of Hohenstaufen's *De arte venandi cum avibus*.[23] In terms of elite display, birds of prey were effectively forms of material culture in their own right. An acknowledged hierarchy of species reflected the social positions of the practitioners of hawking, with the peregrine falcon at the top and goshawk and sparrowhawk nearer the bottom.[24] Rather less is known about the physical appearance of the mews in which falcons were housed, other than those of the very highest status. The structure built for Edward I's falconers at Charing Cross adjoined an enclosed garden that contained a birdbath supplied with fresh water via what sounds like a miniature aqueduct.[25] Robert the Bruce's aviary for falcons at Cardross, Dumbarton, was similarly set within a royal garden and surrounded by a hedge when it was repaired in the 1320s, suggesting at least a degree of aesthetic value.[26] In contrast, a chamber made at Windsor in 1287 for the royal falcons kept by John of Brabant was a more utilitarian building, with walls of wood and daub and a thatched roof.[27]

It was often the physical appearance or rarity of birds, as opposed to their nutritional value or taste, that accounted for their increasingly prominent role on the feasting table. Analyses of bird bone assemblages from elite medieval sites in England show that pheasants, for example, were exploited increasingly from the fourteenth century onwards.[28] The crane meanwhile, was bony, awkward to eat and certainly not valued for its taste, but was difficult to obtain and prized at the late medieval feasting table.[29] Household accounts sometimes show how 'wild' birds could be effectively stored in the parks next to great residences until they were netted or caught with hawks: in 1501, for example, the duke of Buckingham obtained 25 herons (17 of them alive) in this way from his private park at Newton Blossomville (Buckinghamshire).[30] The social significance of species of birds such as teal, woodcock, pheasant, heron and swan certainly extended far beyond their role at the table: the means of their exploitation in parks and other exclusive spaces arguably became recognised as a badge of social status in its own right. This rise in wild bird exploitation, which involved an intensification of hawking as well as netting and other hunting methods, was arguably part of a broader process by which lords were making extra efforts to distance themselves from a society that was eating more and more meat, given the social transformations of the post-Black Death period.[31]

The consumption of exotic, colourful or unusual birds at banquets could carry social messages, but so too could their presence as captive specimens in and around residences. A royal aviary existed in Winchester castle in the twelfth century and another, at Westminster Palace, was made for Eleanor of Castile in the 1270s, whose accounts include references to swans, Sicilian parrots and nightingales.[32] The pursuit of solace through bird song was a recurring motif in medieval literature, while swans were reputed to have sweet voices.[33] Peacocks strutted around the grounds of medieval greater houses. On the Bayeux Tapestry one of William I's palaces is depicted with an adjacent peacock, while the earliest known bone in England, dating to the eleventh or twelfth century, comes from Carisbrooke castle (Isle of Wight).[34] The species is recorded relatively commonly on Anglo-Norman manors in thirteenth-century Ireland; here their introduction may not entirely have been a post-Conquest phenomenon, however, as there is some anecdotal written evidence that peacocks were kept in early Irish monasteries, the species being symbolic of immortality.[35] Swans and pheasants were among the other lesser-known exports to Ireland in the Anglo-Norman period, alongside fallow deer and rabbits.[36]

Swans had special status as the animal species with perhaps the highest-status connotations of all, and had particularly strong associations with the monarchy. While zooarchaeological evidence suggests that elite consumption of swans can be traced back into the early medieval period, it is quite clear that their exploitation and consumption rose dramatically from the middle of the fourteenth century.[37] The rise to prominence of swan breeding might also mirror the representation of the species in romances (including that of the Swan Knight) and manuscript illustrations, and at the highpoint of chivalric culture these species featured prominently in heraldry. The swan was one of the personal emblems of Jean de Berry, for example, and was depicted in his famous fifteenth-century Book of Hours as an heraldic symbol as well as swimming in the moats of his residences, for instance at the Château du Clain in Poitiers, in the depiction for July.[38] Swans also played a prominent role in Christian theology for their purity and associations with Christ.[39] It is perhaps partly because of this religious significance that swanneries featured prominently in the landscapes around bishops' palaces. It was within the setting of the bishop of Lincoln's palace at Stow (Lincolnshire) that Gerald of Wales vividly described the enormous pet swan of St Hugh in 1186 (which became his emblem), in what was clearly a designed setting.[40]

By the later medieval period the Crown, through a licensing system enforced by an appointed official and his regional deputies, regulated the breeding of swans. The first recorded Master of the King's Game of Swans was Thomas de Russham, appointed in 1361.[41] Unlike other key species of 'wild' bird, such as the teal and woodcock, that found their way on to the late medieval feasting table with increasing frequency, however, swans were semi-domesticated, being actively introduced, bred and of course displayed around the settings of great residential buildings. It is to the period between the thirteenth and fifteenth centuries that we can probably date the construction of most artificial estate swanneries, although the king's swan master was largely responsible for protecting swans on the waterways. Several crimes involving the theft of swans are recorded by c.1250, many relating to the removal of birds from private pools and fisheries on demesne estates.[42] At the very summit of the social spectrum, swanneries had particular associations with royal castles and residences: the 'King's Pool' that flanked the iconic royal castle and walled town of Caernarfon (Caernarfonshire), for instance, contained an elaborate swan's nest constructed on the orders of Edward I in 1304–5, as well as being stocked with fish.[43] In Scotland, within the area of the important royal park at Falkland (Fife), special laws protected swans as well as boar.[44] The construction of swanneries as islands within artificial fishponds was the usual practice. This was the case at several of the bishop of Winchester's houses in the southern counties of England. His residences at Bittern and Bishop's Sutton (both Hampshire), for instance, featured swanneries by the mid thirteenth century, located within fishponds and built on raised islands that acted as nesting sites.[45] One of Britain's largest swanneries was next to the bishop of Winchester's residence at Downton (Wiltshire), which had up to 200 birds by the late fourteenth century.[46] As archaeological sites, the surviving field remains of swanneries are problematic, however. Very few sites are identified with certainty. Unexplained 'islands' within fishponds can be one indicator of their presence, although similar earthworks were associated with the practise of fish breeding. What seems clear is that they were more common in southern England and, apparently without exception, were appendages to high-status sites. The best-known is the monastic example at Abbotsbury (Dorset), an appurtenance to the Benedictine house there from at least the late fourteenth century and the site of a duck decoy from the seventeenth century.[47] The swannery at Stow (Lincolnshire) was a component within the designed landscape around one of the bishop of Lincoln's palaces, where a system of moats and ponds clearly in existence by the late twelfth century has been mapped.[48] Other likely medieval swanneries identified on the basis of field evidence were similarly embedded in elite contexts: an example at Chelvey Court (Somerset) was set within a seigneurial deer park alongside a warren, while at Taynton Parva (Gloucestershire) the site of a swannery is associated with medieval earthworks of a motte ('Swan Tump'), a moated site and a suite of fishponds.

DOVECOTES

In England the right to build dovecotes was a privilege of manorial lordship from the Norman period onwards and, prior to the seventeenth century, they are virtually without exception found in immediate proximity to high-status sites, both secular and ecclesiastical.[49] Unrecorded in Domesday Book, dovecotes were built in large numbers in the twelfth and thirteenth centuries, so that by the middle of the fourteenth century most important residences possessed one and many manors had several, these highly visible structures becoming standard appurtenances to elite households in Britain as they were in north-west Europe more generally.[50] The relaxation of laws concerning the possession of dovecotes in the seventeenth century ensured their subsequent spread further down the social hierarchy. The small number of recognised medieval examples that lay within peasant crofts presents something of an anomaly, but probably shows that some were leased out in the later Middle Ages.[51]

Alongside the utility value of doves as providers of rich manure and as rapid breeders that provided food for the table in the form of squabs (unfledged birds), dovecotes had an aesthetic appeal and symbolic significance in aristocratic culture that can be easily underestimated. Indeed, we should not overstress the importance of squabs to the aristocratic diet. There is surprisingly little evidence for their consumption in high-status households on the basis of animal bone assemblages from excavated sites, where pigeon and dove bones usually occur far more infrequently than those of popular species of wild bird.[52] Manorial accounts show that the supply of squabs could fluctuate dramatically during the year; few were available in the winter months and supplies could be affected by climate and disease as well as economic fortunes.[53] Rather, the beauty and emblematic importance of the bird was crucial to its aristocratic exploitation. The medieval dove was the pure white *Columba livia*, and this species, perhaps more so than any other creature, was extraordinarily rich in symbolism, as expressed in manuscript illustrations, bestiaries, religious texts and poems.[54] The Christian associations of the dove are made clear in texts such as Hugh of Fouilloy's twelfth-century *Aviarum*, where its attributes and their religious meanings received much more attention than any other wild or domestic bird.[55] Saint Columba took his name from a species that was an evocative symbol of peace.[56] A single dove bird was also a symbol of the Holy Spirit and a bird landing on the head or shoulder stood for religious perfection; a pair of birds stood for loyalty, marriage and courtly love; a flock, meanwhile, represented preachers.[57]

Known in Latin as *columbaria* (but frequently recorded in English as 'culver-houses' and in Scots as 'doocots'), most medieval dovecotes were freestanding structures built in stone, cob, brick and, occasionally, ostentatious timber-framing. High-status imagery and a degree of elaboration were present in early dovecotes, which were unmistakable features of the landscape. One of the earliest excavated examples, in the precinct of Thornholme Priory (Lincolnshire), was a rectangular building dating to the mid twelfth century with plastered walls painted in imitation of ashlar, capped with a decorative tiled roof.[58] Perhaps the finest dovecote surviving in Britain is the circular example attached to the Hospitaller commandery at Garway (Herefordshire), complete with an inscription on the tympanum over the door dating its construction to 1326.[59] Architectural and archaeological evidence shows that they became increasingly impressive and decorative from the fourteenth century onwards. By the later medieval period roofs were often tiled rather than thatched, architectural trappings such as stepped gables and well-fashioned doorways were not uncommon and multi-storeyed polygonal forms were adopted, so that by the sixteenth century their ornamental and recreational significance had clearly eclipsed any utility value.[60] It is from this period that dovecotes are more commonly found in garden contexts, illustrative cases in point being the doocot built within the terraced garden created in the middle of the sixteenth century for the earl of Morton at Aberdour castle (Fife),[61] and the example that formed the centrepiece of an enclosed formal garden created in front of Acton Court (Gloucestershire) for Sir Robert Poyntz in the very early years of the same century.[62]

The association between a high-status household and the 'farming' of doves was made especially clear to the wider world where nesting holes were built into the upper storeys of prominent residential buildings. The earliest and most remarkable example is the twelfth-century Norman donjon at Rochester (Kent), which incorporated a double row of purpose-built nest-boxes at the top of its north wall, just above the roofline.[63] Conisbrough (Yorkshire, West Riding) is another great tower with an integral dovecote, here built into one of the six massive buttresses surrounding the cylindrical donjon of the late twelfth century.[64] The practice of positioning dovecotes within mural or corner towers would have created a similar effect. Of the many 'dovecote towers' in later medieval castles and fortified manor houses, good examples preserving nest holes include Bodiam (East Sussex), Hemyock (Devon), Markenfield Hall (Yorkshire, North Riding), Usk (Monmouthshire) and Westenhanger (Kent). It is not difficult to imagine a flock of doves, swirling high in the air around such lofty and impressive structures, adding to their visual roles as icons of authority.

Most dovecotes were, however, freestanding buildings constructed on the demesne, very often in deliberately obvious and visible positions. If not standing prominently in outer courtyards or enclosures attached to the residence, as was the general rule,[65] dovecotes were built on approach roads or immediately outside gatehouses, where visitors could easily see them; still others were embedded within designed spaces such as gardens, parks and orchards.[66] At Shelley Hall (Cambridgeshire) geophysical survey and trial trenching has revealed the principal structure within a moated island adjacent to the late medieval manor house to have been a dovecote that stood centrally within its own small cruciform garden.[67] It was one component within a structured arrangement of garden features clearly intended to impress visitors approaching the site via an entrance causeway. At Cosmeston (Glamorgan) a circular medieval dovecote has been excavated within the earthwork of a four-sided enclosed garden attached to the small manor and its castle in the fifteenth century.[68] Another good example in Wales is Castell Blaenllynfi (Brecknockshire), where a circular mound directly facing the castle entrance across a series of ponds and a garden terrace can be interpreted as a dovecote (*Figure 17*), the feature being surmounted by a circular structure topped with a conical roof in an eighteenth-century depiction by the Buck brothers.[69] The site's heyday was in the middle of the thirteenth century, when it was the centre of a local barony, and it is to this period that the arrangement can most probably be dated. Elsewhere, the fifteenth-century dovecote of Caister (Norfolk) stood proudly in the field adjacent to the castle, alongside the Norwich–Yarmouth road, where it signalled a lordly presence to travellers against a backdrop of ostentatious water features.[70] In contrast, it was those approaching Castle Rising (Norfolk) by river that would have seen the seigneurial dovecote here.[71] Perhaps most famously, at Manorbier (Pembrokeshire) the site of the dovecote described by Gerald of Wales is now marked by a domed structure, conspicuously positioned on the slopes above the manorial fishponds and adjacent to the castle orchard, where it was a landmark to those on the road between the castle and the bay (see p. 40).

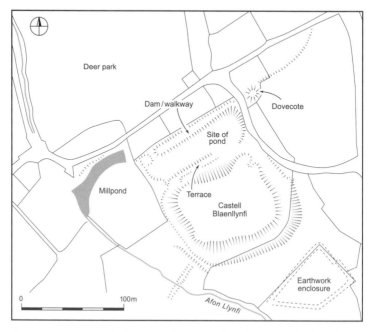

Figure 17. Castell Blaenllynfi (Brecknockshire): earthworks of a medieval castle with associated ponds and the site of a former dovecote. Based on Silvester *et al.* 2004, with additions.

Dovecotes could also make statements of lordly privilege to communities: at Rand (Lincolnshire) the dovecote was positioned at the south-east corner of the manorial *curia*, facing the village, with the substantial moated complex with which it was associated lying just out of view over a slight slope.[72]

While the exploitation of fish and rabbits on manorial centres in medieval Ireland was apparently rare, evidence for dovecots is, by comparison, plentiful.[73] They were introduced by Norman landlords to the manorialised landscape of eastern and south-east Ireland, and documentary sources confirm that they were typical appurtenances to elite residences although few survive as standing structures, perhaps as most were built with timber or clay walls. No examples have been excavated.[74] Monastic accounts show that there were sometimes several dovecotes in the settings of abbeys and priories and that orchards were favoured locations; the best-surviving stone-built examples are the thirteenth-century structures at the Augustinian priory of Ballybeg (Co. Cork) and the Cistercian site of Kilcooly (Co. Tipperary).[75] Seigneurial examples sometimes clearly stood within deer parks, as was the case with the example at Dunganstown (Co. Wicklow) described in an inquisition of 1333.[76] By the late medieval period the construction of dovecotes extended beyond those areas with a strong Anglo-Norman heritage to include Gaelic centres of lordship: Aughnanure castle (Co. Galway), for example, preserves a sixteenth-century mural tower converted into a dovecote (*Black and White Plate 19*).[77] A comparable Scottish example is Craigmillar castle (Midlothian), where a flanking dovecote tower was constructed as part of the site's sixteenth-century outer enclosure. Housing the bird of peace, it was also equipped with gunloops.[78]

Plate 19. Aughnanure castle (Co. Galway), showing a late medieval dovecote tower. (Photograph: Oliver Creighton)

RABBITS

There is little reason to question the orthodoxy that in the British Isles the rabbit (*Oryctolagus cuniculus* – known until the eighteenth century as the 'coney') was a Norman reintroduction.[79] Their spread across north-west Europe was not natural, but encouraged through human agency, in particular by the construction of artificial warrens.[80] In England, archaeological, art-historical and documentary sources are all in broad agreement about the introduction of rabbits: the first evidence dates to the mid to late twelfth century.[81] The single mention of a warren in Domesday Book is in Gelston (Lincolnshire), and this (*warenna leporum*) was almost certainly intended for the exploitation of hares.[82] Rabbit farming was introduced into Wales by new Norman landlords primarily in the thirteenth century, but had a limited distribution; it was exported on a smaller scale still into the manorialised landscape of Ireland in the late twelfth century.[83] In Scotland, rabbits remained relatively rare prior to the nineteenth century; in the medieval period their exploitation was restricted to the king and occasionally the higher nobility, and rabbit farming in general had less of an impact on the landscape.[84] The earliest rabbit warrens recorded in Scotland, at Crail (Fife) in 1264–6, were under royal ownership, and the Crown led the way with other early examples at Cramond (Midlothian) and Perth (Perthshire).[85]

Rabbits were thus first introduced to Britain from northern Europe or the western Mediterranean not, it seems, with the initial wave of new Norman aristocrats, but within a couple of generations of the Conquest. Their exploitation was initially confined to island or coastal locations, especially where controlled by powerful monastic landlords,[86] before spreading inland, through the medieval period and beyond, to make England probably the most intensively rabbit-farming area in Europe. Given the lack of any clear chronological development in the form of the artificial warrens, buries and pillow mounds that constitute the key physical evidence of rabbit exploitation (*Figure 18*), it can be difficult to distinguish medieval from post-medieval sites. That said, there is a growing realisation that across much of the British Isles the peak of intensity was reached in the post-medieval period. Rabbit farming seems to have spread down the social scale from the sixteenth and seventeenth centuries particularly, and it is to this period or later that much of the

Figure 18. Women catching rabbits emerging from an artificial rabbit warren, as depicted in the fourteenth-century Queen Mary's Psalter. Source: Green 1892.

field evidence relates, especially in high moorland and other inhospitable locations, as exemplified by the vast post-medieval warren complexes found on Dartmoor, for instance.[87] Medieval rabbit warrens were far less widespread and of much higher status compared to their post-medieval successors, and it is highly likely that many of those found in close proximity to medieval elite residences and monastic sites are relatively early examples. Deer parks were particularly favoured locations for early rabbit warrens, with a significant number established by *c*.1250.[88]

Live rabbits were used as high-status gifts to those setting up warrens in the vicinity of their residences: the Despencers gave Henry III 10 in order to set one up at Guildford in 1235, for example, where it lay on the edge of the park, while gifts in the opposite direction – from king to favoured nobleman – are also well documented.[89] Most medieval royal and episcopal palaces had access to a warren; Clarendon (Wiltshire) was typical in that the warren was incorporated into the royal park, located prominently but rather impractically on the same north-facing scarp as the palace, hinting that it was meant to be seen.[90] In contrast, the royal palace at Kennington (Surrey) contained a warren at the heart of the building complex. In use by 1408, this was the responsibility of the palace gardener (styled as 'keeper of the garden and warren') and was clearly located in the inner garden that surrounded the chamber blocks of the king and queen; another, perhaps later, warren lay near the small grove or park attached to the site.[91] Parallels can be found in pictorial sources: an illumination from the man-uscript *Songe du Vergier* (*c*.1378) shows an enthroned Charles V of France within a garden enclosed with interlocking trees and containing a flower meadow, a spring and pool, and an orchard full of burrowing rabbits.[92] The medieval royal association with rabbit farming was long-lived: Henry VIII's palace at Hampton Court featured a warren, apparently containing pillow mounds, within its grounds, as a smith named Robert Bing was employed specifically to manufac-ture an iron auger for boring holes in the king's 'beries'.[93] Animal bones from Henry's banqueting house at Nonsuch show that rabbits were still in demand at the royal table in the sixteenth century,[94] while rabbit warrens continued to play a prominent role in designed landscapes of this period, as at Ascott House (Buckinghamshire), where one formed part of a contrived 'natural' setting that could be observed from a viewing mount.[95]

Rabbits were sometimes required at the table in enormous numbers: in 1386 a warren within the deer park at Lopham (Norfolk) provided 300 rabbits for the Countess of Norfolk's table.[96] They were also valuable. In thirteenth-century England a rabbit sold for perhaps 3½d and the fur for another 1d, far more than a craftsman's daily wage, maybe five times the price of a chicken and the equiv-alent of a suckling pig, another prized delicacy.[97] Besides the monetary value of rabbit fur and meat, the volume of offences committed against warrens in the possession of wealthy landlords is another reliable indicator of this species' elite status. Enclosures around warrens were as much to keep malefactors out as to keep rabbits in and were occasionally semi-fortified, comprising hedges, walls and banks but also sometimes palisades, lockable gates and water-filled moats.[98] In the mid fourteenth century, for example, the warren in the medieval park at Petworth (Sussex) was hedged, fenced and entered via three gates, two with padlocks and one with a mortice.[99] The bishop of Ely's warren at Lakenheath (Suffolk), probably originating in the twelfth century, enclosed a vast area of the common heath embraced within a substantial perimeter bank that was doubled and even tripled in places.[100] Warren lodges, meanwhile, could be impressive structures whose architectural qualities extended beyond the functional; often resembling tower-houses in miniature, they prominently stamped lordly author-ity on the landscape and may also have been designed with surveillance in mind.[101] The most remarkable upstanding remains are the Warren Lodge at Thetford (Norfolk), comprising a two-storey building that resembles a minia-ture tower-house, with walls a metre thick.[102] Dating to the early fifteenth century but incorporating much earlier masonry, the building was a possession of the Cluniac Prior of St Mary's, Thetford; its architectural qualities suggest it was far more than a gamekeeper's residence and may have accommodated hunting parties in the heated upper level. Another good example is Norton Tower (Yorkshire, North Riding), a semi-fortified structure of *c.*1540 with walls more than 1.2 metres thick, which overlooks a late medieval enclosed warren near Rylstone in the Yorkshire Dales.[103]

The social value of rabbit exploitation in the medieval period is reflected further in the way that grants of free warren – whereby the recipient was given the sole right to kill beasts of the warren (small game: primarily hare, rabbit, pheasant and partridge but also badger, otter, squirrel and marten) – were jealously guarded symbols of privilege and status.[104] Legislation to protect warrens as well as the employment of warreners again demonstrates that these features were sometimes resented and potentially the focus for expressions of discontent: during the Peasants' Revolt of 1381 Wat Tyler demanded that war-rens were among the resources of the countryside that should be made common to all.[105] We should be careful here to differentiate the warren as a legal concept from the physical reality of the rabbit warren, the locations of which are some-times but not always indicated by the telltale earthworks of pillow mounds.[106] A 'warren' might thus not be manifested in the historic landscape in a simple way; it is quite clear in court rolls, for instance, that offences 'within the lord's war-ren' were transgressions of legal rather than physical boundaries.[107] In the English and Welsh landscapes the locations of 'lost' medieval warrens might be indicated by field names, *Coniger* or *Coneygarth* being classic examples. Besides its significance as a marker of elite exploitation, the broader symbolic and, indeed, theological significance of rabbit farming is easily overlooked. The inherent vulnerability of medieval rabbits and the necessity of nurturing and shepherding them in communities ensured that they were viewed in religious teachings as emblems for the salvation of mankind.[108] In monastic contexts the meanings of rabbit warrens on the precinct boundary might be especially clear, while in manorial contexts they symbolised seigneurial munificence.

Early rabbit farming in Wales was, similarly, a high-status activity. Rabbits are first recorded here in 1282, when Richard le Forester was paid 3s 6d for catching them on behalf of the king and for keeping royal ferrets at Rhuddlan castle (Flintshire); the earliest known rabbit warren lay in the dunefields next to the castle and borough of Kenfig (Glamorgan), being first recorded in 1316 when it was partly inundated by the sea.[109] While rabbit warrens are, of course, difficult to date it is again beyond coincidence that many are found in prominent association with manorial centres and castles, especially in the heavily Normanised coastal strip of south Wales and in Pembrokeshire. Good examples of medieval pillow mounds in such contexts that have been surveyed in Glamorgan include those at Cefn Hirgoed, Dunraven and Penmaen.[110] In contrast, while rabbit farming in medieval Ireland is occasionally recorded in documents it has left little or no tangible traces on the landscape. The first reference to rabbits in Ireland is in *c*.1185, a mere 16 years after the Norman invasion,[111] but it was not until the early thirteenth century that rabbit farming was carried out on Anglo-Norman lordships on any scale, when it is referred to in rentals and manorial extents. A warren is recorded on the Anglo-Norman manor of 'Dunfert' (Danesfort, Co. Kerry) in 1307, for instance, and others are attested at the manors of Forth (Co. Carlow) and Dunamase (Co. Laois). To date, however, field archaeology has recovered no positively identified examples of artificial warrens or pillow mounds, although the earthworks of relict ringforts may well have been adapted for the purpose.[112] Medieval rabbit farming was, at least initially, also an elite pursuit more generally within north-west Europe: Flanders and the North Sea coast of Holland in particular experienced an upsurge in warren exploitation on great estates from the twelfth century, although the activity is less well attested in France.[113] Rare archaeological insight into this activity has come from the castle of Laarne, in East Flanders, Belgium, where rabbit and ferret bones have been recovered from late-thirteenth-century excavated contexts and clearly relate to the management of a large warren prominently located on a hillside between the centre of lordship and its attendant village.[114]

Excavation of features associated with medieval rabbit warrens is generally very rare, however. A late-fourteenth-century date has been obtained for a pillow mound that formed part of an extensive warren complex at Bryn Cysegrfan (Cardiganshire), on a spur of the Cambrian Mountains in west Wales.[115] It lay within an upland area enclosed from common pasture lands and consolidated into an area of demesne; here, as elsewhere, pillow mounds were also markers of zones bought under direct seigneurial control. In the dry soils of East Anglia that were particularly suited to rabbit farming, warrens were prominent components of the landscapes around Norman castles at places such as Castle Acre, Castle Rising and New Buckenham (all Norfolk) where they invariably lay on the edges of parks.[116] At Hopton (Shropshire), the rabbit warren lay immediately beyond a late medieval ornamental garden laid out around a castle.[117] Another good example is the Ellerlands warren, complete with pillow mounds, that was created in the late-fourteenth-century parkland landscape around Castle Bolton

(Yorkshire, North Riding).[118] One of the most intact and closely dateable medieval rabbit-farming landscapes anywhere in Britain is that created around Barden Tower, in the mid Wharfe valley (Yorkshire, North Riding). It was part of a late medieval reorganisation of the central part of the Forest of Barden, involving the creation of a Little Park, Great Park and Cony Warren that together occupied the slopes rising east of the tower and formed a designed landscape intended to be viewed from it (see p. 186–7). What is particularly remarkable is that this coherent exercise in landscape planning can be dated to within a 50-year time bracket, occurring shortly after 1485 but before the decline of the estate in the 1520s.[119]

A final, rather unanswerable, question concerns why rabbit warrens such as these were positioned in such prominent locations. A utilitarian explanation is plausible: the health of rabbits demanded that sites should be well-drained with dry, loose soils, while the volume of crimes committed against warrens suggests that their visibility could be a deterrent. In some cases, however, the location of warrens must have been more deliberate, with social messages in mind: most obviously, the prominence of warrens would have demonstrated not only ownership over or privatisation of a tract of landscape, but also proclaimed in a conspicuous way a universally recognised symbol of privilege. At Godolphin (Cornwall), for instance, four large late medieval pillow mounds were positioned, silhouetted proudly against the skyline, along the crest of a dome-like hilltop in parkland from which tenants had been evicted.[120] Other good examples can be found in the deer parks along the west Somerset coast and Quantock Hills, where rabbit warrens set within deer parks were positioned on the edges of commons, on sloping land above the manorial enclosures to which they relate, with pillow mounds forming highly visible landmarks.[121] Another scenario is present at Lockington (Yorkshire, East Riding), where the earthwork of an early castle – comprising either a low motte or a raised ringwork – was clearly reused as a pillow mound, hence the name 'Coney Hill'.[122] What makes this example particularly interesting is that the manorial complex (now known as 'Hall Garth') that succeeded the castle site, perhaps in the thirteenth or fourteenth century, stood immediately adjacent. Embraced within a moat and including a suite of fish-ponds, this remodelled seigneurial site incorporated the rabbit warren as a particularly prominent feature (in an otherwise featureless area) that proclaimed the status of the place and the long-term continuity of lordship.

FISH

There was no such thing as a 'village pond' in medieval Britain; rather, ponds for freshwater fish were privately owned and jealously guarded resources. Many – perhaps the majority – were the possessions of manorial lords and lay within the demesne, while countless others were under royal or monastic ownership.[123] The shape of ponds owed much to the practicalities of fish keeping, of course. A useful physical distinction can be made between the remains of the *vivarium* (larger ponds for breeding fish) and the *servatorium* (smaller ponds where stock was held prior to delivery to the table and therefore usually immediately adjacent to the residence), although the sharp differentiation apparent in documents is not always apparent on the ground.[124] Of course fish could also be kept in other water-filled features: medieval representations of conspicuously fish-filled moats around manor sites and castles are well known.[125] The locations and shapes of smaller seigneurial ponds were dictated by the micro-topography of their settings, without embodying any conscious 'design'.[126] But larger-scale fish farming could transform the appearance of the landscape. Documents detailing expenditure on the construction and maintenance of fishponds show that their costliness alone ensured that their possession was restricted to the upper echelons of medieval society, while the ways in which they were positioned to complement the visual appearance of elite sites highlights that they too were cultivated as an insignia of rank. Gerald of Wales commented that the fishpond at his old family home at Manorbier was particularly impressive on account of its great depth.[127] That 'ponds' and 'fishponds' are distinguished from one another in fifteenth-century records for the gardens of the Neville family at Middleham castle (Yorkshire, North Riding) suggests different types of water feature, the former presumably being ornamental.[128] It is certainly over-simplistic to think of medieval fishponds as *either* utilitarian *or* ornamental features, however; they were often both.

Frequently forming the barriers of manorial *curiae* or secluded behind park pales, fishponds 'were associated with the physical barriers that helped to separate the aristocracy from the rest of society'.[129] Artificial water features not only changed the configuration of tracts of landscape but also had a profound impact on how it was seen, its reflective qualities sometimes transforming the visual appearance of buildings and influencing how they were approached and where they were experienced from (see also p. 77). A raised linear earthwork between two ponds providing a causeway-like entrance is a familiar layout; at the courtyard house of Keynedon Barton (Devon), for instance, a dam between two ponds was built on an axial alignment with the gatehouse, providing a dramatic and staged approach.[130] The *curia* at Rothwell (Yorkshire, West Riding) (see *Figure 6*: top) was similarly accessed via a causeway across the manorial fishponds,[131] while other illustrative examples known through archaeological survey are the bishops of Lincolns' palaces at Somersham (Cambridgeshire)[132] and Stow (Lincolnshire).[133] Another site at which multiple ponds were apparently designed in an ornamental manner is Hopton castle (Shropshire). Here, a series of at least three ponds immediately south of the late-thirteenth- or early-fourteenth-century tower show evidence of surrounding walkways, and the entire arrangement is indicative of a contrived setting that visually complemented the tower.[134]

Major questions remain concerning the chronology of fishpond construction in medieval England and Wales, as these features are extremely difficult to date archaeologically. Across western Europe as a whole the great expansion in fishpond construction seems to have occurred in the twelfth and thirteenth centuries.[135] This process is increasingly seen as seigneurially driven, with monastic landlords being less innovative in water management than was previously assumed.[136] In particular, the boom in pond building in the period after the Norman Conquest seems to have everything to do with social display associated with the arrival of a new social order and little to do with the concept spreading from the monastic to the secular sphere. The fourteenth century saw something of a decline in the construction and farming of fishponds by the social elite because of the increasing trend towards the leasing out of demesne for money rents.[137]

The freshwater fish that filled these ponds were not kept simply to provide food during Lent, but also to provide a prestige foodstuff to special guests and at important feasts.[138] Animal bone evidence suggests that even for high-status secular sites with good access to fishponds, however, fish still made a relatively small contribution to diet.[139] The key species kept within medieval fishponds were bream and roach; it was not until the sixteenth century that the carp was introduced.[140] The pike, however, seems always to have been perceived as a fish of superior standing and had special status in the medieval mind as well as at the banquet. The predatory and fearsome 'water wolf' was sometimes afforded its own, discrete, ponds, as at Lyddington (Rutland) (*Figure 19*), where the bishop's 'Little Park' preserves a suite of fourteenth-century ponds which are among the most sophisticated found anywhere in medieval Britain.[141] Pike could be stocked in large numbers and were especially favoured by the Crown as well as episcopal lords. For example, at Woodstock (Oxfordshire) in 1241 the bailiff was ordered to stock the ponds with 1,000 pike.[142] In north-west Europe more generally, pike had Christian associations: in one widespread tale, markings on the fish's head were seen to represent symbols of Christ's passion, including the cross, ladder, nails, whip, sponge and thorns.[143]

While the earthworks of drained medieval fishponds can be barely perceptible hollows, living and working ponds could comprise vast sheets of water that altered their surroundings and might even impact on wider populations. This was certainly the case with the 'King's Pool' at York, created in the Foss in 1069 and representing the earliest known fishpond in post-Conquest Britain.[144] Its construction resulted in severe disruption of the townscape, including the inundation of property and agricultural land, the clearance of mills and rerouting of roads.[145] Fishponds could occasionally pose unforeseen hazards to communities: the first reference to the fishponds around Raglan castle (Monmouthshire), in 1465, was in an inquest held into the drowning of an infant in the 'Fysshe Pole' next to the lord's manor.[146] Some of the most important royal fishponds in southern Britain were at Marlborough (Wiltshire), standing at the junction of the Rivers Og and Kennet.[147] Extending over six hectares, they were used as a store of food for the itinerant royal court, for the supply of large consignments of live fish as gifts to favoured nobles, and to stock a network of other royal ponds, as is well documented in the twelfth and thirteenth centuries.[148] Only very exceptionally do we find straightforward evidence that these ponds were there to be enjoyed

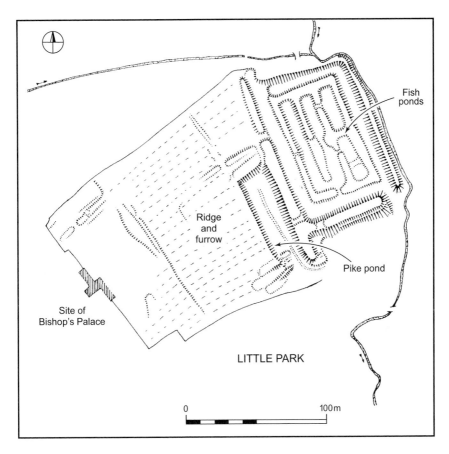

Figure 19. Medieval fishponds associated with the Bishop of Lincoln's palace at Lyddington (Rutland). Based on Hartley 1983, with additions.

as well as to provide food for the table. Quite unsurprisingly, household accounts are concerned with the stocking and maintenance of ponds rather than how they were appreciated. Occasionally, however, fishponds were clearly garden features. At Rhuddlan (Flintshire), one of Edward I's great fortresses in north Wales, a series of improvements in the late fourteenth century included the creation of a small fishpond around the head of the castle well, which was lined with clay and surrounded by newly built seats.[149] This seems to have been a specifically gendered space: its construction is listed under the 'queen's work' of 1382–3, which included the construction of an adjacent courtyard, in the same corner of the castle's inner ward, that was turfed and fenced in.

Bishops were also energetic builders of fishponds. Those built on the estates of the bishops of Winchester are especially well understood, their management being finely detailed in the bishopric pipe rolls, which indicate an explosion of activity in the period 1150–1220; the episcopal *magnum vivaria* at Alresford

Plate 20. Leamanagh (Co. Clare), showing the late medieval tower-house with later additions; in the foreground can be identified a string of ornamental ponds with accompanying terraced walkways. (Photograph: Oliver Creighton)

(Hampshire) and Frensham (Surrey) were extraordinarily large, occupying 24 and 40 hectares respectively.[150] It is quite clear that these resources were not managed commercially or used for sport in any sense, but supplied the bishop's table directly. Most episcopal fishponds were, again, located on demesne estates, although there are interesting exceptions, such as in Surrey, where an intriguing tradition of fishpond construction by the social elite on commons can be observed. Here, ponds such as those on Chobham and Epsom Commons, constructed for the abbot of Chertsey, were maintained in areas that would have attracted conflict with the grazing rights of commoners.[151] Other areas of contrast await explanation, however. For instance, while the bishops of Winchester maintained a network of fishponds at the principal residences, such facilities were uncommon or absent on properties of the bishops of Salisbury and Bath and Wells.[152]

That fishponds were appurtenances to Anglo-Norman manors in Ireland is clear from documentary references, but field evidence for these features is somewhat lacking.[153] Expenditure on what appears to have been a new purpose-built fishpond at Limerick castle is recorded in 1211–12; it cost the substantial sum of £33 6s 8d.[154] The high-status connotations of 'farmed' fish were not restricted to Anglo-Norman Ireland: in 1061 the Annals of Clonmacnoise describe the theft of two salmon from the 'fountain or fishpond' of the king, which lay near his fort at Kincora (Cenn Corad).[155] A problem with the interpretation of such references (and those in later, Anglo-Norman, manorial documentation) is that it is difficult to distinguish artificial ponds from fisheries in rivers and lakes that were also under seigneurial control, such as the extensive suite of fish traps known from archaeological survey in the Shannon estuary, within the Anglo-Norman lordship of Bunratty established in the late thirteenth century.[156] A scattering of surviving examples of medieval fishponds has been identified at monastic sites and occasionally also masonry castles and tower-houses. Most are late in date, however, as with the string of ponds laid out in the base of a valley stretching away from the tower-house of Leamanagh (Co. Clare), a building reused as a service tower for a later fortified house (*Black and White Plate 20*). Accompanied by a terraced walkway and other garden features, the ponds are probably creations of the seventeenth century, as are the pair at Loughmoe (Co. Tipperary).[157] The relative proximity of so many lordship sites to inland lakes and (as in Devon and Cornwall) the coast may have contributed to the fact that fishponds are not the common appurtenances to medieval sites of lordship here as they are over much of lowland England.

Chapter Four Notes

[1] Cohen 1994, 60; see also Salisbury 1993.

[2] Quoted in Breeze 1997, 137–9.

[3] Thomas 1983, 277.

[4] Donald Hughes 2003, 22–3.

[5] James 1990, 26–7, 94; Ševčenko 2002, 72.

[6] Gautier 2006, 55–6.

[7] Calkins 1986, 166; see also Ševčenko 2002, 83.

[8] Longnon and Cazelles 1969, f.4v.

[9] Pearsall and Salter 1973, 111–13.

[10] Benton 1992, 15, 95–6.

[11] de Winter 1983, 104.

[12] Thomas 1996; Kisling 2001, 49–55.

[13] O'Regan *et al*. 2005, 49–55.

[14] Payne 2003, 219, citing Johnson 1996, 131.

[15] Woolgar 1999, 195.

[16] Kelly 1997, 124.

[17] Serpell and Paul 1994, 132–4.

[18] Steane 1999, 152–5.

[19] Grant 1988, 180.

[20] Warner 1912, 31.

[21] Steane 2001, 274; Pluskowski 2007, 77.

[22] Reeves 1995, 113–14.

[23] Oggins 1993, 50–4.

[24] Prummel 1997; Cherryson 2002.

[25] Reeves 1995, 112.

[26] Cooper 1999, 819.

[27] Woolgar 1999, 195.

[28] Pluskowski 2007, 68.

[29] Albarella and Thomas 2002, 23.

[30] Woolgar 2001, 114.

[31] Thomas 2005; Albarella and Thomas 2002, 29.

[32] Colvin 1986, 16; Parsons 1995, 53.

[33] Woolgar 2006, 68.

[34] Serjeantson 2006, 142.

[35] Kelly 1997, 108; Hicks 1993, 253.

[36] Kelly 1997, 299–300.

[37] Albarella and Thomas 2002, 14–16, 33–4.

[38] Yapp 1981, 24; Cazelles and Rathofer 1988, 14.

[39] Sykes 2004a, 91–2.

[40] Gransden 1972, 50; Everson *et al*. 1991, 185.

[41] Ticehurst 1957, 54; see also MacGregor 1996.

[42] Ticehurst 1957, 4–5.

[43] Carter 1969, 4.

[44] Gilbert 1979, 220.

[45] Roberts 1986, 135–6.

[46] Stone 2006, 157–8.

[47] Prendegast 1984.

[48] Everson 1998, 32–3; Everson *et al.* 1991, 129–31.

[49] Hansell and Hansell 1988; McCann 2000; Stone 2006, 151.

[50] Beacham 1990, 88; Hansson 2006, 131.

[51] Le Patourel 1991, 883.

[52] Serjeantson 2006, 141–2, 147.

[53] Dyer 2006b, 206; Stone 2006, 151, 156.

[54] Scheibe 1997, 107.

[55] Clark 1992, 121–37.

[56] Kelly 1997, 107.

[57] White 1954, 144–5; Scheibe 1997, 107–22.

[58] Coppack 2006, 125–6.

[59] RCHME Herefordshire 1931, 72.

[60] Henderson 2005, 14; Stone 2006, 156.

[61] Hynd and Ewart 1983, 106.

[62] Rodwell and Bell 2005, 103–4.

[63] Port 1987, 12; Spandl 1998.

[64] Whitworth 1993, 75.

[65] Gardiner 2007, 172.

[66] Le Patourel 1991, 883.

[67] Booth 2005, 241.

[68] RCAHMW 2000, 476–7.

[69] Silvester *et al.* 2004, 96.

[70] Liddiard 2000b, 113.

[71] Liddiard 2000a, 181, 184.

[72] Hansson 2006, 139–41; see also Everson *et al.* 1991, 153–5.

[73] Kelly 1997, 107; O'Keeffe 2000b, 70.

[74] O'Conor 2004, 235.

[75] Stalley 1987, 175; Reeves-Smyth 2004, 117, 138–9.

[76] O'Conor 2004.

[77] See Sweetman 1999, 166, 169.

[78] Douglas Simpson 1954, 10.

[79] Veale 1957; Bond 1988b; Callou 2003; Williamson 2007; see Warry 1988 for a discredited alternative argument hinging on the ambiguous Latin term *Lepus*.

[80] Van Dam 2001; 2002, 59–62.

[81] Williamson 1997, 96; Sykes 2004b, 191.

[82] Darby 1977, 9.

[83] O'Conor 2004, 237–8.

[84] Thompson 1994, 64.

[85] Gilbert 1979, 211–12.

[86] Bond 2004, 180.

[87] Williamson and Loveday 1988, 299; Williamson 1997, 100.

[88] Stamper 1988, 145; see also Williamson 2007, 14–15.

[89] Bailey 1988, 5.

[90] James and Gerrard 2007, 197–8.

[91] Dawson 1976, 187.

[92] British Library Royal MS 19.C.IV, f.1v; see also Thacker 1979, 88–9.

[93] Sheail 1971, 43.

[94] Biddle 2005, 465.

[95] Everson and Williamson 1998, 147.

[96] Bailey 1988, 4.

[97] Veale 1957, 89; Bond 1988b, 55; Thompson 1994, 64.

[98] Williamson 2007, 14, 65–70.

[99] Moorhouse 1989, 65.

[100] Rackham 1986, 292–3.

[101] Williamson 2007, 82–3.

[102] Bond 2004, 181–2.

[103] Moorhouse 2007, 118–19.

[104] Bailey 1988, 2.

[105] Almond 1993, 151.

[106] Cantor 1982, 82–3.

[107] Sheail 1971; Bailey 1988, 17.

[108] Stocker and Stocker 1996, 267–8; see also Williamson 2007, 164–7.

[109] RCHAMW 1982, 315, 321–3.

[110] RCAHMW 1982, 321, 335–7, 338–40.

[111] Kelly 1997, 131–3.

[112] O'Conor 1998, 34–5; 2004, 237–8.

[113] Van Dam 2002, 59–60.

[114] Van Damme and Ervynck 1988, 282.

[115] Austin 1988.

[116] Liddiard 2000a, 180; 2000b, 58–9.

[117] Bowden 2005, 4.

[118] Yorkshire Dales Historic Environment Record No. MYD36704.

[119] Moorhouse 2003b, 345–8; see also Beaumont 1996.

[120] Herring 2003, 44.

[121] Riley 2006, 98–9.

[122] Loughlin and Miller 1979, 31.

[123] Dyer 2000b, 101–2.

[124] Roberts 1993, 229.

[125] Barry 1977, 79.

[126] Cantor 1982, 78.

[127] Thorpe 1978, 150.

[128] See Moorhouse 2003b, 329–30.

[129] Dyer 2000b, 110.

[130] Waterhouse 2003, 67–8.

[131] Moorhouse 2003a, 193.

[132] Taylor 1998b, 30.

[133] Everson *et al.* 1991, 185.

[134] Bowden 2005, 8–10.

[135] Querrien 2003.

[136] Currie 1989, 147–50; Hoffman 1996, 659–60.

[137] Currie 1991, 106–7.

[138] Currie 1990, 23.

[139] Serjeantson and Woolgar 2006, 125.

[140] Serjeantson and Woolgar 2006, 125–6.

[141] Woodfield and Woodfield 1988, 12–13.

[142] Elrington 1990, 445.

[143] Hoffman 1993, 63.

[144] Currie 1989, 147.

[145] Creighton 2005b, 145.

[146] Taylor 1950, 12; Whittle 1989, 83.

[147] Steane 1988.

[148] Currie 1994, 100–1; Clarendon, Winchester, Windsor and Westminster were among the royal ponds supplied.

[149] Colvin 1963, 324.

[150] Roberts 1985; 1986, 136.

[151] Currie 2003b, 287–91.

[152] Payne 2003, 221.

[153] Kelly 1997, 133; O'Conor 2004, 230.

[154] O'Conor and Murphy 2006.

[155] Kelly 1997, 132–4.

[156] O'Conor 1998, 34; Van de Noort and O'Sullivan 2006, 83–5.

[157] O'Conor 2004, 230.

—— *Chapter Five* ——

Parkscapes and Communities

The ritualised display of violence through hunting was an essential element of elite identity across medieval Europe. Occupying the minds as well as the bodies of the nobility, hunting had a wider impact on society out of all proportion to the relatively small area of the landscape over which it was actually practised. Essentially new modes of environmental management were developed in the form of parkland and forest to serve, among other things, the elite passion for the chase. The most tangible impact of hunting on the countryside came in the form of deer parks, although as we shall see, it is over simplistic to view these features simply as hunting reserves or, indeed, that they were intended purely to contain stocks of deer. Most of the components of the aristocratic settings discussed so far were discrete features, taking up relatively limited areas of the demesne. Parks, in contrast, constituted elite landscapes in their own right, often forming stunning visual backdrops for palaces, manor houses, monasteries and castles, as exemplified by the famous view of Windsor's Great Park (*Colour Plate 8*). They often provided physical contexts for fishponds and warrens and sometimes contained their own occasional residences as well as lodges for park-keepers. Their creation and management went hand-in-hand with the introduction of new species – most notably fallow deer, but also birds and wildfowl, while rabbits and fish had their own important place within the parkscape, as the previous chapter has shown. Parks were also carefully controlled environments, where the species they contained were dependent upon active management to survive. In these senses they embodied a fundamentally new type of human–animal relationship and a different level of human control over nature.

Hunting was also expressed in the imagery of kingship and nobility, for instance through the selection of harts and boars as emblems, while the landscape features constructed to maintain these species have their own place in the material culture of elite identity. For instance, the early-fourteenth-century seal of John de Warenne, eighth Earl of Surrey, shows rabbits emerging from artificial burrows.[1] That of George Douglas, fourth Earl of Angus in the middle of the fifteenth century, displayed a park pale, apparently built of wattle and with an entrance bent back, probably representing a deer trap.[2] The imagery of hunting could also be incorporated into other symbols of rural lordship. Hunting scenes are well represented on the lintels and tympana of

Norman parish churches, although the tradition declined after the middle of the twelfth century and seems to represent the culmination of an early medieval tradition rather than a Norman import.[3] A visitor to the manor house of Essendine (Rutland) could not help but admire the elaborate hunting scenes on the twelfth-century south door of the church, which lay within a moated enclosure and directly faced anybody entering the site across its entrance cause-way.[4] The site's moated defences incorporated a mill race and were linked to extensive suites of fish stews, while a deer park was in existence by the thirteenth century.[5] Anybody approaching the manor house at Faccombe Nethercombe (Hampshire) would have seen a vivid hunting scene expressed in a rather different way, in the form of decorated tile finials on the building's roof.[6]

The medieval deer park has attracted a larger body of scholarship than any of the other landscape features and forms of animal exploitation covered in this book. In addition to a wealth of information on the distribution and chronology of deer parks at a national scale,[7] there exist numerous detailed county-based and regional studies, especially on midland and southern England,[8] while fresh approaches have emphasised the social side of empark-ment and the roles of parks as ecosystems.[9] The intention here is not to repeat this work, but to draw out from a complex body of scholarship a sense of how deer parks articulated as features of elite design that provided settings for the buildings, activities and other means of high-status exploitation covered in this book.

Parks: character, chronology and owners

At its very essence a medieval park had a dual purpose: it kept game in and peo-ple out. It is also important to stress that there was no standard medieval deer park, nor a model to which lords aspired; rather, a high level of regional varia-tion existed, with different systems of lordship and land tenure exerting influ-ences on the ability of the elite to empark, while parks also evolved through the Middle Ages. Medieval parks were actually very diverse, the larger examples embracing differing landscape types in their own right, and the variety is more apparent still when we consider those in Scotland and Ireland. As physical enti-ties, deer parks ranged from tens to thousands of hectares in extent, and impacted on different landscape types in myriad ways. The park provided a remarkably flexible template, adaptable in different social contexts and ranging from glorified demesne pastures to vast pleasure parks containing their own set-tlements. All they had in common was the notion of a bounded and controlled space given over to specialised activity.

In addition to some 70 royal forests and a similar number of chases in the possession of major magnates, England had well over 3,000 of these deer parks.[10] The term 'emparkment', however, simplifies what was often a gradual and piecemeal process, as exemplified by the complex evolving parkscape around Windsor (Berkshire), which grew from the mid thirteenth century by a process of accretion and acquisition; by the end of the Middle Ages it encompassed three separate main parks with quite different functions (Great Park, Little Park and Moat Park).[11] There is some correspondence between the status of residence and the number of parks attached to them, although the possession of deer parks in general extended much further down the medieval social hierarchy than some other appurtenances of lordship and authority. Where noble families maintained multiple parks at separate residences it is quite possible that these served specialised functions – for pleasure and utility, but also perhaps for their seasonal qualities.

Some scholars have stressed the utilitarian roles of parks as enclosing food resources: they have been described as 'enclosures for storing live meat'[12] and 'live larders',[13] while the social status of the deer park has frequently seen them portrayed as symbols of 'conspicuous consumption'.[14] At the most basic level, parks ensured ready access to a foodstuff whose high-status connotations were universally known – venison. The festive consumption of venison, in particular, has special significance, representing a type of hospitality universally recognised as elite, while live deer as well as their meat were prized as prestigious gifts in the same way as were rabbits and freshwater fish. Venison could not be obtained on the open market (at least, not legally, although a niche illegal trade grew up from the Norman period onwards[15]), and was available only from the lord's own demesne or through a privileged social network.[16] Other scholars have focused on the roles of parks as hunting preserves, although the terms 'deer park' and 'hunting landscape' both give an over-simplistic view of features that were exploited day-to-day for a huge variety of specialist reasons.[17] Their more mundane uses included pannage (grazing of pigs), herbage (grazing of livestock) and the exploitation of various types of timber and underwood. It is also instructive that, while these features of the landscape are commonly labelled 'deer' parks, medieval documents usually refer to them with the single word *parcus*.

The right to empark was a jealously guarded privilege and badge of lordly authority, while another type of social statement was implicit in the very act of enclosing, quite tangibly and visibly, a large tract of landscape, and sometimes taking it out of agricultural production. A close look at financial accounts can sometimes show that parks were not profitable at all, something which was certainly true of the Duchy of Cornwall's parks in the fourteenth century, where the substantial initial costs of emparkment, the running costs of park maintenance and the loss of rents contrasted with pitifully small income. The huge outlay involved in the creation of parks and the challenges of maintaining them, combined with the minimal financial returns that accrued, shows that they were not geared to maximise profit by cold, hard businesslike patrons. The motives of emparking lords – in these cases at least – must have been largely non-economic,[18] and the everyday functions of parks thus cannot be separated from their deep-seated conceptual place in elite ideology and role as venues for aristocratic discourse.[19] Crucially, we should not see hunting as their 'primary' role and other activities and uses as somehow 'secondary'; rather, the economic, amenity and symbolic values and meanings were unseverable and entwined.

The role of Norman lords in introducing deer parks to England has probably been over-stated; Anglo-Saxon antecedents are certainly represented by the *haiae* or hays recorded in Domesday Book.[20] However, hunting was an essential part of the Normans' developing sense of self-identity in the late eleventh century. It was expressed not only through physical alteration of the landscape and changes to its accessibility, but also through a new ritual dimension to the practice of hunting, as manifested in the process of breaking (*défaire*) the deer carcass, which was sub-divided with parts distributed to esteemed individuals involved in the hunt.[21] The hunt and the stag were also popular motifs in medieval literature,[22] while in visual culture deer had strong Christian associations and ritual significance, with the hunting of a solitary stag representing the crucified Christ.[23] An association between the consumption of red deer and the expression of medieval social status is reflected in the Scottish Isles as early as the eighth century, when engravings of red deer and other hunting motifs on Pictish inscribed stones demonstrate the definition of ecclesiastical and aristocratic territorial rights and symbolic control over a mystical animal; the phenomenon is also observed on late medieval highland tombstones.[24] In medieval Ireland, too, hunting scenes featuring red deer are represented on high crosses, often below scenes of the crucifixion and last judgement, sometimes marking significant points within monastic enclosures, as at Clonmacnoise (Co. Offaly).[25]

The great surge in emparkment occurred several generations after the Norman settlement, and was part of an upsurge in park creation more generally within north-west Europe. Deer parks appended to noble residences are well attested in northern France by the twelfth and thirteenth centuries,[26] and Sicily was doubtless another important source of inspiration. Here the Norman kings created extensive pleasure parks and gardens and it is clear that Anglo-Norman aristocrats travelled frequently between Sicily and England and emulated the achievements of their contemporaries overseas.[27] It now seems likely that the introduction of fallow deer to Britain in the late eleventh century followed a tradition established in Sicily (where they are known to have been kept within elaborate pleasure parks) rather than one from Normandy, where zooarchaeological evidence shows the species to have been absent.[28] The royal park at Palermo was particularly magnificent, being provided with decorative springs and ornamental ponds and punctuated with three important buildings: the Ziza (a hunting lodge), the Cuba and the Cubala. In the late twelfth century, Archbishop Romuald of Salerno described it thus:

> And on certain hills and forests around Palermo he likewise
> enclosed with walls, and there he [Roger] made the Parco – a
> pleasant and delightful spot, shaded with various trees and
> abounding with deer and goats and wild boar. And here he also
> raised a palace, to which the water was led in underground
> pipes from springs whence it flowed ever sweet and clear. And

thus the king, being a wise and prudent man, took his pleasure from these places according to the season. In the winter and in Lent he would reside at the Favara, by reason of the great quantity of fish that were to be had there; while in the heat of the summer he would find solace at the Parco where, with a little hunting, he would relieve his mind from the cares and worries of state.[29]

Building up a chronology of medieval emparkment is not straightforward. One of the key problems in dating medieval deer parks is that while we may suppose that many pre-dated their earliest reference in documentary sources, this is impossible to prove. On the basis of available evidence, in lowland England at least the high point of emparkment was clearly in the late thirteenth and early fourteenth centuries, coinciding with a high point in pressure on the land.[30] The effective privatisation of busy landscapes already under considerable demand would have sent out important messages to wider communities, of course. Across Britain, the rise of the park mirrored both the decline of the forest and the spread of fallow deer, which were more suited to confinement, while red deer are more territorial and have a more extensive home range.[31] Changing emphasis from roe and red to more park-friendly fallow deer can be traced in animal bone assemblages from elite medieval residences, for instance at Okehampton (Devon)[32] and Barnard Castle (Co. Durham),[33] although the transition may not have been as pronounced in northern and western parts of the British Isles.

In Anglo-Norman Ireland the introduction of fallow deer mirrored the spread of hunting preserves at newly established power centres. The first reference is in 1213, when the archbishop of Dublin received fallow deer from Coventry, and the earliest bones are found at Norman castles.[34] Trim castle has produced examples, but skeletal remains from Carlow dated to c.1200–10 are the earliest of all.[35] The growth of deer parks in Ireland is hard to gauge because of the lack of a formalised system of licensing. Among the handful known from documentary references, most date to the thirteenth century and were restricted to Anglo-Norman centres. Good examples include those appended to castles at Dunamase in the late thirteenth century and Maynooth (Co. Kildare) and Trim (Co. Meath) in the fourteenth.[36] Physical evidence for pales is almost totally lacking, although vestigial traces have been identified at Curtlestown (Co. Wicklow) of a park carved out of the royal forest of Glencree.[37] In the north of Ireland later deer parks at places such as Massareene, near Antrim, and Kiltierney (Co. Fermanagh) date to the Plantation period and represent one way in which newly acquired estates were modified, at least in part for leisure.[38] Fallow deer are first recorded in Scotland in the late 1280s in the context of royal parks.[39] The number of deer parks here is, again, hard to judge. Fewer than one hundred are recorded under royal or baronial ownership in the Middle Ages and they emerged onto the scene often later than in England, with numbers multiplying in the fourteenth and fifteenth centuries as parkland reserves were favoured as more easily managed resources than the forests and warrens created by royal grant.[40]

In the later medieval period in England, licences to empark frequently coincided with major phases of building or refurbishment to residences and were not unusually combined with grants of other seigneurial rights. None, however, exceeded the enormous 4,600-acre (1,862 hectare) park created in 1449 for Robert Botyll, Prior of the Hospital of St John of Jerusalem, at Eagle (Lincolnshire), which, characteristically for the period, formed part of a package of privilege including grants of market rights and a licence to crenellate.[41] The creation or extension of a park in this period was thus often only one element in a broader and co-ordinated scheme of aggrandisement that might also include, for instance, the foundation or extension of a borough. In the fifteenth century, in particular, there is also a notable tendency for parks to be created by those who had recently arrived or had risen rapidly within elite society. It is paradoxical, however, that while the period after *c*.1350 saw many parks progressively opened up to grazing and other less visibly elite land uses, those entirely new parks that were laid out were often more consciously designed for aesthetic reasons. At Herstmonceux (East Sussex), for example, the extravagant brick-built castle constructed for Sir Roger Fiennes in the 1440s lay in a vast park that was formed by twice enlarging an earlier deer park on the site; other 'improvements' included the closure and diversion of a road, while a survey of 1570 described extensive areas of lawn, great oaks and beech trees, a herony, a rabbit warren and a thatched park lodge, as well as a chain of ponds that swept in front of the castle on a series of descending levels.[42] The parks created for Lord Hastings in Leicestershire in the late fifteenth century present other good examples of later medieval pleasure parks, while several others of the period resulted in depopulations (see p. 217).

Ecclesiastical parks

While hunting was strictly forbidden by canon law many monastic houses possessed a park and some maintained several (Glastonbury Abbey had at least seven across three counties, for example),[43] and zooarchaeological evidence shows that venison played a small role in the monastic diet.[44] Deer parks were virtually mandatory at bishop's houses and palaces of any significance. In Britain as a whole, among the most impressive still surviving as landscape features is that associated with the residence of the bishops of Durham at Bishop Auckland (Co. Durham), which was extant in the late twelfth century and substantially enlarged *c*.1350 to comprise a small 'Near Park' around the bishops' castle defined by a loop of the River Gaunless and the more open, wild, 'High Park' to the east.[45] Peripatetic bishops maintained extensive networks of palaces and had a wide choice of parks, which might have had subtly different purposes: the abbots of Bury St Edmunds possessed eight or nine, for example.[46] To take the south-west of England as a further case study, the medieval bishops of

Salisbury had 5 deer parks; the bishops of Bath and Wells 13 or more; and the bishops of Winchester no fewer than 23.[47] More deer parks belonged to the bishop of Winchester than to any other see: by the mid thirteenth century virtually every palace on the bishop's estates had a deer park, with houses such as Ramsbury (Wiltshire) and Dogmersfield (Hampshire) buried deep within parkland; the urban property of Wolvesey, hemmed in by Winchester's ancient Roman walls, was the sole exception.[48] This situation was not unusual, in that the development of demesne parks by ecclesiastical magnates occurred early and actually anticipated the rise in seigneurial deer parks, which was a generally later phenomenon. The broader impacts of these schemes of emparkment could be particularly profound: studies of deer parks in Cambridgeshire and Hampshire have raised the possibility that episcopal parks were built on prime agricultural land more often than those developed by other lords.[49]

Parks attached to episcopal residences seem to have been intended primarily for the enjoyment of visitors, although hunting was never entirely excluded from religious life. The chronicler Jocelin of Brakelond commented on the activities of Abbot Samson of Bury St Edmunds, *c*.1200, who, as well as reorganising the abbey's estates,

> ... also made a number of parks which he filled with beasts,
> and kept a huntsman and hounds; and when any distinguished
> guest came to him, he would sit at times with his monks in
> some woodland glade and watch the hounds run; but I never
> saw him taste venison.[50]

Critics of medieval abbots and archbishops sometimes alleged their passion for hunting, and laws could be stretched; in 1408 Archbishop Arundel prohibited hunting at Glastonbury Abbey but permitted the abbot hounds for use in the parks and warrens of surrounding estates, for example.[51] And senior clergy took part in poaching expeditions, as witnessed by thirteenth-century forest eyres.[52] Direct evidence for the involvement of ecclesiastics in hunting is on the whole sparse, however, and does not compare to the incident in 1621 when George Abbot, Archbishop of Canterbury, shot a gamekeeper with a crossbow while aiming at a buck.[53]

Park pales and landscapes within parks

While the spatial extent of a royal forest was defined in a legal sense, serving to give it imaginary boundaries, the limits of a medieval park were real and visible. Whether marked in the form of a pale, a hedge or a wall of masonry, park boundaries acted as physical statements to those outside their bounds. Unless the park lay on rising ground, park pales could conceal what went on within, adding to their mystique. The boundaries of parks frequently coincided with those of parishes, and it was not unknown for tenants to owe obligations of service related to the park, such as the repair of pales.[54] For example, the pale around the royal park of Moulton, attached to Northampton castle, was maintained by tenants in the thirteenth and fourteenth centuries; by the sixteenth century it had been built as a wall with the names of the townships owing service inscribed upon stones along its length.[55] In twelfth- and thirteenth-century Scotland, similarly, the king was able to extract from tenants not only bridge-building services but also service on the pales of royal parks.[56]

While very few archaeological excavations across medieval park pales are known and none has provided fresh dating evidence, the sectioning of these earthworks can remind us of their physical magnitude and impact on the landscape. Earthworks surrounding two of the bishop of Winchester's parks have been sampled archaeologically and probably represent well the 'typical' pale: at Bishop's Waltham (Hampshire), the bank was *c.*5 metres across and survived to almost 2 metres in height; that of Poundisford Park, Pitminster (Somerset), was 6–8 metres wide and 0.8–1.2 metres high; both represent truncated vestiges of once much larger embankments that ran for several kilometres.[57] Britain's largest medieval park, accompanying the royal palace at Clarendon (Wiltshire), was defined by a bank and ditch 16.5 kilometres in length, representing a huge undertaking, probably of the twelfth century.[58] Flitteris Park, adjoining Oakham castle (Rutland) and enclosed by Richard, Earl of Cornwall, in the 1250s, was unusual in having a pale earthwork comprising double banks separated by a ditch.[59] Most parks had more than one gate, and these were not always simple utilitarian structures. Some displayed features of military architecture, with towers and bridges, and resembled castle gates. The main gate of Woodstock Park (Oxfordshire), facing the town, was substantial enough to accommodate a chamber above it, and the pale of this large royal park was pierced by at least five others.[60] The limits of parks could also coincide with rivers and other water features, and at the royal manor of Kennington (Surrey) financial accounts make it clear that there was one bridge at the entrance to the park and another between the park and the manor house.[61] Coastal parks are also not unknown: along the west Somerset coast a number of medieval parks ran right up to the cliff edges, effectively privatising access to the sea, as at East Quantoxhead and Kilve.[62]

The curving pales of medieval parks ensure that, on maps and aerial photographs, they often have the appearance of lobe-like features. As well as ensuring the maximum enclosed area with the minimum effort and expenditure and perhaps holding advantages for hunting where this was carried out within the park, this ensured that they also tended to cut across the grain of the landscape. Enclosure with a broad bank and accompanying ditch and a timber pale was most common, but in places local vernacular traditions were followed and stone used: drystone walls marking park boundaries are known in Scotland at Linlithgow (West Lothian) and Stirling (Stirlingshire), for example. In lowland England, walling a park was generally indicative of special status: the royal park at Woodstock (Oxfordshire) had a wall of stone by the early twelfth century.[63] Enclosed initially by Henry I, the original park was over 11 kilometres in circumference, and this was extended later in the twelfth century to take in a lobe of land to the south-east so as to leave the palace entirely enveloped and hence secluded.[64]

There is no simple correlation between the size of a park and the status of its owners, however: while the royal park at Clarendon (Wiltshire) embraced over 1,700 hectares (*Figure 20*), that associated with the nearby royal house at Ludgershall (Wiltshire) was a modest landscape feature of no more than 100 hectares.[65] Deer parks were frequently maintained in groups of more than one, of course, whose functions could be complementary. The phenomenon of multiple parks, closely juxtaposed and under the same lordship, has been noted but not adequately explained.[66] Quite often, the pattern is for the smaller unit to have been enclosed directly adjacent to the residence, with more extensive deer parks built at greater distances. The topographies of these parks often resemble 'nested' spaces, whereby a smaller unit was set within or was linked to a larger one, the innermost being the most private and the outermost the more public. 'Little parks' adjoining residences and linking them to larger parks are the most obvious manifestation of this (see below, p. 134–8), while other parks were themselves set within larger, elite hunting spaces such as forests and chases.

Understanding the place of deer parks within elite landscape design can be difficult given the long-held belief that they were essentially functional entities. Scholars have traditionally neglected their symbolic and visual qualities to the extent that '… they [deer parks] did not indicate that medieval lords had even the slightest interest in the appearance of the countryside'.[67] Parks that secluded residential sites by enclosing an envelope of space immediately adjacent to them are particularly important here; countless examples directly append medieval residences and others were expanded to do so. If anything, the relationship between park and great house became closer through the medieval period, with the fourteenth and fifteenth centuries in particular seeing residences secluded deep within parkland. The aesthetic roles of medieval parks were multiple: they formed backcloths to great houses viewed from the outside as well as dominating views from towers, windows and sometimes gardens within; yet hunting parties would also look inwards at the castle itself. Parks on even gently rising ground above lowland sites could provide spectacular views, as with the bishop of Ely's 250-hectare park at Somersham (Cambridgeshire), from which the palace site and its water gardens were showcased.[68]

At Castle Rising (Norfolk) it has been noted that the park pale was situated immediately beyond the viewshed from the high-status upper rooms within the donjon, giving the appearance that it extended far further than it really did – an effect magnified by the 'natural amphitheatre' of the castle's topographical setting.[69] A later site bearing comparison is Okehampton (Devon), whose setting and views from lodgings were again dominated by a huge seigneurial deer park

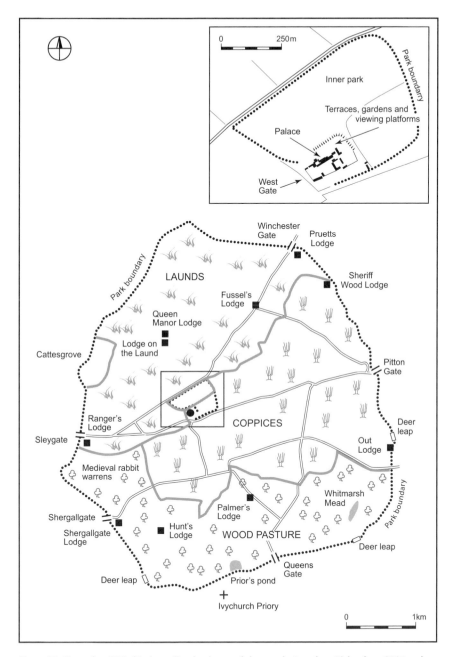

Figure 20. Clarendon (Wiltshire): medieval palace and deer park. Based on Richardson 2005 and James and Gerrard 2007, with additions.

(*Figure 21*) (see also p. 186). Again, the park pale lies beyond the tract of landscape that could be seen from the highest points within the site, so that the park took up virtually the entire view, although the park lodge and keep seem to have

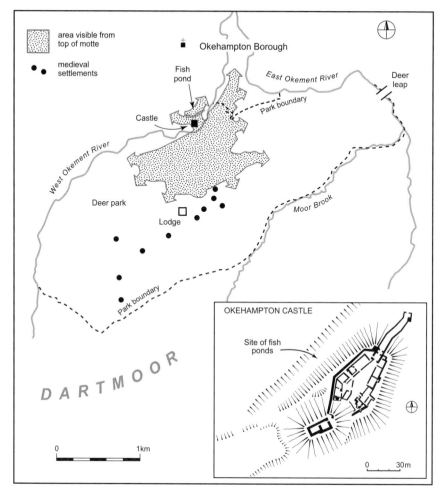

Figure 21. The medieval deer park at Okehampton (Devon), showing the location of medieval set-tlements and the 'viewshed', or area intervisible with the donjon. Based on Probert 2004 and Higham *et al.* 1982 with additions.

been just intervisible.[70] It is, again, surely not coincidental that the great four-teenth-century quadrangular castle of Sheriff Hutton (Yorkshire, North Riding) was visible from everywhere within the great park that was attached to it. The site's position at the end of a ridge ensured that it was visible from even the remote southern and eastern limits of the park, forming a constant point of ref-erence during hunting and other leisure activities and the visual centrepiece of what was a vast designed landscape.[71]

But parkland landscapes were more complex entities than simple enclosed spaces. That scholarship has focused on the act of emparkment and the topographies of enclosure should not deflect our attention from the fact that park interiors were landscaped in intricate ways. That so many medieval deer parks have been later landscaped means that their medieval appearance can be difficult to visualise, and only in very exceptional cases do parkscapes retain an authentically medieval flavour: Bradgate Park (Leicestershire), for example, was enclosed before 1241 and enlarged before the Hall was constructed within it in the early sixteenth century, but escaped any significant landscaping.[72] The classic medieval park was not one landscape but several, and the 'design' of deer parks also extended far beyond the physical act of enclosure to embrace the active management of their interior habitats and the provision of elite facilities, buildings and gardens, while lines of sight were carefully managed to create miniaturised landscapes of exclusion as well as display. That so many medieval parks were carved out of woodland meant that the trees they contained could be visibly ancient, although the grazing of deer ensured rapid transformation of the park's appearance, with grass replacing other ground vegetation.[73] More deliberate landscaping within parks might include the addition of hedgerows and fences and the creation of mosaic-like arrangements of woodland through artificial plantations and the carving out of grassy open spaces (or 'launds') in other areas. Natural topography ensured other variations in scenery within these parkscapes, with valleys and sloping ground providing different visual opportunities and experiences. Marshy areas and expanses of water provided an idea environment for the cranes and herons that were taken by trained hawks, while open spaces were created for sporting reasons as well as for deer grazing: in 1535 a series of hedgerows in parkland near The More (Hertfordshire) was removed to make a 'lawnde' for the 'kyng's course'.[74] 'Design' might also describe those parkscapes that grew by accretion – the case of Windsor in the fourteenth century being a particularly clear example (see p. 142) – not necessarily to accommodate more deer, but to visually isolate residences and lodges, to incorporate areas intervisible with buildings, and to embrace landscapes of varied texture. This privatisation of land should not be seen in isolation, however: royal park extensions occurred as areas under forest law were diminishing. The century after 1250 saw the area under forest law decrease sharply; some royal forests vanished entirely while others were diminished in the wake of disputes.[75] Tightening royal control over parkland was in one sense, therefore, a response to a loss of control in other areas.

In the wider medieval landscape the deer park constituted a unique type of semi-designed environment – an enclosed space that was neither natural nor artificial in physical appearance and neither public nor private in terms of its social functions. This liminal status was sometimes manifested physically where the park occupied a position between the 'managed' environment of house and garden, which visually embodied anthropogenic control over nature, and the 'unmanaged' forest, wildwood or wilderness beyond, where nature challenged human authority. The arrangement of gardens lying at the junction between residences and their attached deer parks occurs time and again, as at Hopton (Shropshire), for example, where a garden compartment forms a zone of transition between the residence and hunting park.[76] Other parks sat at the junction of landscapes of different appearance and texture. This was most obvious on the edges of upland zones. In medieval Cumbria, for instance, typical baronial deer parks such as Cockermouth or Kendal were set within a more extensive licensed zone known as a 'hay' (equating to a wider hunting area, itself probably enclosed), which in turn was set within a private forest with its own legally defined boundaries.[77] Barnard Castle in Teesdale (Co. Durham) is another case in point: a survey of 1539, describing the parks in detail, shows that the 'Little Park', stretching away from castle and borough, was sub-divided into closes for orchards and the exploitation of wood, horses and minerals, while the 'Great Park' was a much larger and more open space, with the Forest of Marwood beyond forming the main medieval hunting grounds.[78] Also potentially relevant were more distant views towards more rugged 'undesigned' scenery. At Raglan (Monmouthshire), for example, the terraced castle gardens looked towards the Black Mountains across an ornamental mere; at Ludgershall (Wiltshire), Salisbury Plain could be glimpsed from the royal hunting lodge's designed setting; while at Sanquhar (Dumfriesshire), the rugged mountains above Nithsdale formed the backdrop for the familiar castle–garden–park arrangement.

The Italian authority on agriculture Piero de' Crescenzi, writing in *On the gardens of Kings and other illustrious and rich lords* in the early years of the fourteenth century, argued that the largest type of garden should be twenty *jugers* (approximately five hectares) or more, with the palace located on its edge.[79] His description of an area enclosed within a high wall and featuring a spring, fishponds, pavilion and a grove stocked with birds and beasts is mid-way between a park and a garden, and, while clearly an idealised parkland image, it gives colour to the numerous medieval 'little parks' that served as the pleasure grounds of noble residences. Far smaller than most parks, usually measuring in the tens of hectares, these were characterised by their intimate association with residential sites, which they directly adjoined and partly enveloped.

The exemplar is Windsor's 'Little Park' (known from the nineteenth century as 'Home Park') (*Figure 22*), which is depicted in vivid detail by John Norden in 1607 as a lobe of enclosed ground stretching away from the castle. The park enclosed an envelope of space immediately around the Upper Ward (or Inner Bailey) that was the focus of the later medieval palace complex, while the Lower Bailey projected into the 'public' sphere of the town. It gained its form in the reign of Edward III, who enclosed private ground north and east of the castle in 1368 and 1375 respectively, compensating tenants including the abbot of Reading and appointing a dedicated keeper for the 'Little Park under the Castle'.[80] This was a much smaller and more intimate space than the park depicted by Norden, being originally around twenty hectares in area, and was massively expanded by Edward IV in the middle of the fifteenth century. Crucially, the Little Park's origins follow Edward III's inordinately expensive renewal of the Upper Ward's domestic accommodation between 1357 and 1368, in what amounted to among the greatest secular building projects of the Middle Ages in Britain.[81] If the upper court created a grand setting for royal ceremony and entertainment, then the

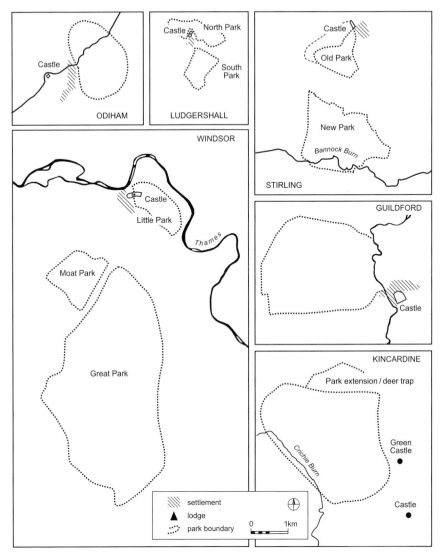

Figure 22. Plans of medieval royal deer parks in England and Scotland. Based on Creighton 2005b, Poulton 2005 and Roberts 1997, with additions.

Little Park was complementary to it visually as well as functionally.[82] In addition to its amenity value, the Little Park served to seclude from the outside world the most private area of the castle, which, with its characteristic flat-topped towers, provided opportunities for taking in the newly designed surrounds.

The combination of towered development within an intimate parkland setting at Windsor may have been influential among the nobility of north-west Europe more generally (see p. 185), but it was certainly not the first little park in England. An equivalent at Clarendon (Wiltshire) was the park 'under the king's court' recorded in 1265, for example.[83] Ludgershall (Wiltshire) is a local parallel, where the royal hunting lodge was associated in the thirteenth century with the small 'North Park' which was the home park of the castle, as well as a larger 'South Park' which extended over the county boundary into Hampshire and constituted the site's outpark; further-flung hunting opportunities were available in the royal forests of Collingbourne and Chute.[84] Characteristically, the little park at Ludgershall was designed to almost entirely envelop the residence, which contained provision for viewing activities within it. As seen from the royal residence, the home park appeared to disappear into the distance, while the larger park was a detached feature, the site of 'Warren Hill' marking its medieval rabbit warren.[85] Ravensworth (Yorkshire, North Riding) bears comparison (*Figure 23*). Here, a fourteenth-century designed landscape around the castle of the Fitzhugh family included a small pleasure park containing gardens, accessed from the village via a causeway across an ornamental mere.[86]

Usually, the little park was a secondary addition or late arrival to the landscape. Farnham's (Surrey) 800-acre (324 hectare) Great Park was in place by the early thirteenth century; the 300-acre (121 hectare) Little Park was a later addition of the 1370s.[87] Late medieval examples are inevitably better documented. The Percy family's castle at Wressle (Yorkshire, East Riding) is an illustrative example. Attached to the castle were three parks: a 'Little Park' immediately north of the castle, which contained a moated garden and viewing mounts and was measured in 1512 as 11 acres (4.5 hectares) in extent; a slightly larger park ('Wressle Park') a little further to the north; and a further detached hunting park ('Great Park' or 'Newsholme Park').[88] On the Welsh Marches, the 'Little Park' at Bronsil (Herefordshire) was apparently created by John Beauchamp, Justice of South Wales, Knight of the Garter and ultimately Lord Treasurer, shortly after he received licence to empark 300-acres (121 hectares) in 1447.[89] Fotheringhay's (Northamptonshire) Little Park, one of two attached to the castle, was established in 1464 on part of the village's open fields.[90] Stafford's Little Park was first mentioned in the mid fifteenth century, post-dating the twelfth- or thirteenth-century Great Park.[91] That at Barden Tower (Yorkshire, North Riding) was a creation of the late fifteenth or early sixteenth century.[92] Episcopal examples are also known: the bishop of Salisbury's residence at Ramsbury (Wiltshire), for example, was another accompanied by separate 'Great' and 'Little' Parks, the latter, enclosed by the fourteenth century, complete with mill and fishponds.[93] The bishop of Winchester's 'Inner' and 'Outer' parks at Merdon (Hampshire), meanwhile, were in place by the late twelfth or early thirteenth century and the bishop of Lincoln's 'Great' and 'Little' Parks at Lyddington (Rutland) by the early fourteenth.[94]

Little parks sometimes went by other names. Helmsley castle (Yorkshire, North Riding) has the 'Old Park' to the east and a smaller emparked unit ('La Haye') forming its immediate setting to the west.[95] Brancepeth castle, extensively rebuilt *c*.1398, stood between two parks – an east park and a west park.[96] In other cases the existence of a little park is confirmed by evidence in the field rather than documents or field names. A boundary earthwork to the south of

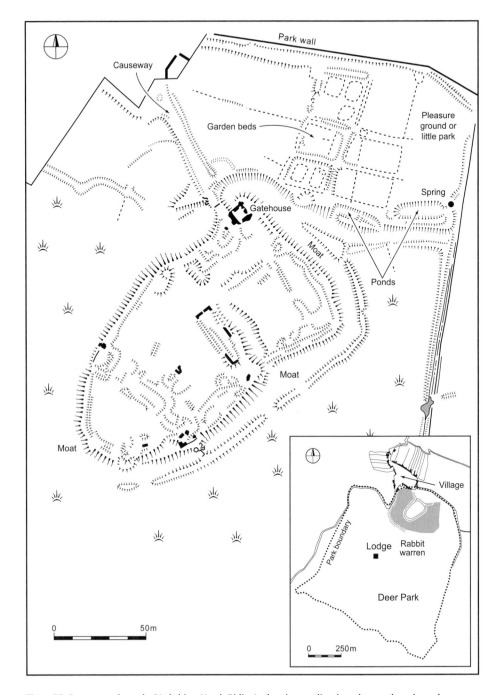

Figure 23. Ravensworth castle (Yorkshire, North Riding), showing medieval garden earthworks and the site's parkland setting. Based on Liddiard 2005a, with additions.

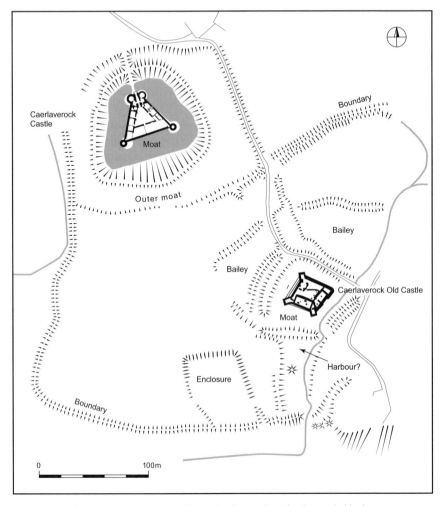

Figure 24. Caerlaverock castle (Dumfriesshire), showing earthworks that probably demarcate a small park. Based on Brann 2004, with additions.

Caerlaverock castle (Dumfriesshire) (*Figure 24*), double-banked in places, with an internal ditch and incorporating the defences of the 'Old Castle' (an earlier seat of lordship established in the 1220s), defines an area of approximately six hectares.[97] It is tempting to see this area, which directly appends the spectacular late-thirteenth-century triangular castle of the Maxwell family, as another small pleasure park; other possible Scottish examples can be identified at the Peel of Lochmaben and Auchencass (both Dumfriesshire).[98] The distinctive topography and character of the medieval 'little park' has also been recognised in northern France,[99] while a direct equivalent is found in the 'petit paradis' at Hesdin (see p. 148–9).

Twin parks might be created for reasons other than amenity, isolation and aesthetics. In the seventeenth century Gervase Markham, writing on deer management, specified that the aggressive tendencies of red deer ensured that they should be kept separately from fallow deer.[100] Medieval equivalents can be found: in 1244 Henry III ordered both fallow and roe deer to be kept in the park at Freemantle, Kings Somborne (Hampshire), suggesting that the two species were kept segregated in what was effectively two units.[101] In the late medieval period Wardour castle in Wiltshire, similarly, had separate parks: the one for red deer was located at a distance from that for more domesticated fallow deer, while a separate Rayles Park (the name denoting the railings that surrounded the park) and grassy expanse known as 'The Lawn' lay next to the residence.[102] Red as well as fallow deer were found in the Scottish royal parks of Falkland (Fife) and Stirling in the early sixteenth century, and were again presumably kept in separate compartments.[103]

Buildings in the park: hermitages, banqueting houses, lodges and standings

Rather less obvious features of the hunting landscape were hermits, whose solitary needs were well served by locations within forested or wilderness environments. In the twelfth and thirteenth centuries in particular, hermits sponsored by the king lived within royal forests such as Neroche and Sherwood, as they did in private chases such as Charnwood in Leicestershire.[104] We know that a hermitage lay on the edge of the hunting chase attached to the Norman earth-and-timber castle of Old Montgomery because the rocky bluff on which it perched was given up shortly after the borough of New Montgomery was founded on its site in 1223.[105] Attached to Chirbury Priory, the hermitage was a foundation of one of the de Bouler lords of Hen Domen in the early years of the twelfth century.[106]

Seigneurial parks accommodated hermitages too, although we should be careful not to confuse medieval examples with those built during the eighteenth-century craze for mock-Gothic hermitages, some of which were constructed in former medieval deer parks redesigned as landscape parks.[107] One of the very few medieval hermitages to have been excavated, at Grafton Regis (Northamptonshire), occupied a secluded grove within a medieval hunting park that was attached to a mansion house and contains the earthworks of warrens, fishponds and house platforms suggestive of seigneurially forced depopulation.[108] The medieval hermitage at Warkworth (Northumberland), meanwhile, arguably the most fully preserved in Britain, was built by the lords of the castle in Sunderland Park, within which the resident hermit grazed his cattle.[109] Probably founded in the fourteenth century, this rock-cut building featured a separate sacristy, chapel and solar and had attached to it an orchard and garden, forming an important, if secluded, feature of the castle's medieval setting.[110] Comparable rock-cut chapels of the early fifteenth century at Knaresborough (Yorkshire, West Riding) and Warwick also occupied emparked settings near important baronial castles.[111] Other sites are known from documentary evidence: the resident hermit in the castle park of Restormel (Cornwall) was paid an annual fee in the fourteenth century, and two bells removed from the hermitage to the castle chapel are recorded in a survey of 1337 (see also p. 19),[112] while at Fotheringhay (Northamptonshire) a hermitage on the edge of the castle park is recorded in 1176, when it was confirmed to the abbey of Sawtrey.[113]

Medieval romances and saints' lives provided one source of inspiration for the association between hermits and hunting landscapes. The popular medieval saint St Gilles was a hermit accidentally injured by an arrow from a hunting party,[114] while Eustace and Hubert were among several hermit saints converted while engaged in hunting.[115] In addition, hermits were encountered by hunting parties in contemporary romances. In the early-thirteenth-century *Morte D'Arthur*, for instance, Sir Lancelot visited hermitages on his journeys through forests and stayed with a hermit having sustained an injury caused by a huntsman.[116] As well as translating the eremitical tradition of the desert fathers to the designer wildernesses of medieval parks, hermitages were presumably built and sponsored by wealthy patrons in order to add to the mystique of the hunting landscape. The isolated locations of these sites also reflect the liminal status of medieval solitaries within society more generally.[117] It is quite clear that even if hermitages were less publicly visible than other lordly expressions of piety, to the medieval mind they were no less important and evocative features of the elite landscape.

Of the many other types of standing structure built within medieval parks, some were undeniably more utilitarian in function. The position of kennels might be indicated by place-name evidence, as on the west side of the medieval park at Sherborne (Dorset), for example, while deer houses and hay racks are known from documentary references.[118] In other cases buildings within the park were of higher status and show evidence of positioning in the landscape to provide certain types of view or experience. Construction of parkland pavilions and banqueting houses, as distinct from the lodges of park-keepers, were restricted to the very highest ranks of the medieval nobility. Such facilities were venues for secluded courtly entertainment, and in medieval romances the activities of the hunt and events in the bedchamber were often parallel narratives.[119] The phrase 'banqueting house' is something of a misnomer, as these were primarily private venues rather than ones which hosted grand feasts.[120] Animal bones from the occupation phases of the banqueting house at Nonsuch (Surrey) confirm exactly this: the assemblage was characterised by a limited range of species (including rabbit, mutton chops and chicken drumsticks), indicating the consumption of nibbles and light refreshments rather than formal dining.[121]

Examples from royal contexts are, unsurprisingly, the best documented. Relevant here is the moated banqueting pavilion built for Henry V near Kenilworth castle (Warwickshire) early in the fifteenth century (*Black and White*

Plate 21. Kenilworth (Warwickshire): wet moat surrounding the site of a medieval banqueting house attached to the castle. (Photograph: Oliver Creighton)

Plate 21) (see also p. 93), but by far the most celebrated example is 'Everswell', which Henry II had constructed, reputedly for his mistress, within the royal park of Woodstock (Oxfordshire) in the twelfth century.[122] Located less than 100 metres from the manor house but just out of sight from it within a deep hollow, this can be best interpreted as a secluded pleasure-palace, complete with an elaborate cloistered water garden (see p. 61). Now almost entirely destroyed or obscured by later landscaping, including a large ornamental lake that occupies much of the site, in the grounds of Blenheim palace, the only tangible field evidence is a single stone-lined pool, interpreted as one of a series of three set within a double cloister (the inner provided with niches or seats) arranged in line, as depicted on an imperfect map by the seventeenth-century antiquary John Aubrey and labelled 'three baths in trayne'.[123] As well as mentioning these ornamental pools, thirteenth-century writs for building works in the period *c.*1220–50 furnish additional details, including covered walkways around a cloister (*claustrum*), an overlooking chamber, and the existence of accompanying gardens and an orchard of pear trees.[124] Given the wider contacts of the Angevins, a Sicilian influence can be expected, and while the sites of *la Zisa* and *la Cuba* can be rejected as prototypes on the grounds of their dating, an overall argument for the transmission of the idea of the cloistered water garden from North Africa to England, via Norman Sicily, seems secure given other sites from twelfth-century Palermo and the links between the two courts. The 'twinning' of the principal palace complex with a more secluded pavilion, complete with gardens, can also potentially be interpreted as a stage set on which contemporary romance could be acted out – in particular the twelfth-century legend of *Tristan and Isolde*, as the configuration of a palisaded orchard, a spring, channel and pool seems more than a coincidental combination.[125]

A ring of parkland retreats surrounded Windsor castle by the late fourteenth century.[126] Edward III's extensive remodelling of the estates around his principal residence ensured that by the end of his reign the Great Park was circled by some five royal houses which were effectively detached palatial complexes in their own right, mostly set within their own parks and provided with moats and fishponds.[127] Five miles to the south of Windsor castle the place-name Manor Hill remembers a favoured occasional retreat and resting place known as Manor Lodge. Built in the 1240s and favoured in particular by Edward I, who used it immediately after his coronation, the site, secluded within the Great Park, featured a hall and chamber and was set within a rectangular moat.[128] By the late fourteenth century the great chapel at the site was embellished with the iconography of hunting in the form of harts and gilded horns.[129] A site in a similar mould that has been investigated archaeologically is the moated 'hunting lodge' at Writtle (Essex). Here, a sequence of domestic structures, including a great chamber used extensively by the king in the thirteenth century, has been revealed by detailed excavation.[130] It is important to note, however, that in contemporary documents the site was consistently styled not as a lodge but as one of the king's 'houses'.[131]

In the late thirteenth century the royal park at King's Langley (Hertfordshire) featured a lodge called 'Little London' which was, again, a place of retreat.[132] Archaeobotanical remains of exotics such as fig and grape from the moat of the king's house within Cowick Park (Yorkshire, East Riding) afford a glimpse of luxurious living in a site of similar function buried deep in the countryside of Holderness.[133] Clarendon's (Wiltshire) lodge 'on the Laund' was a stone-built structure with multiple chambers constructed or completely rebuilt in the 1340s in an open space opposite the main palace buildings, from which it was clearly visible.[134] While these sites have vanished, in other cases they might outlive the 'principal' residences, as at Guildford (Surrey), where a moated residence was located centrally within the park. First documented in 1318, and by the end of the century eclipsing Guildford castle and palace as the principal residence in the locality, this featured four chambers and a chapel and was clearly able to accommodate a sophisticated household.[135] The king's house in Beckley Park (Oxfordshire) had no fewer than three concentric quadrangular moats, good earthwork traces of which survive on the site of Lower Park Farm. When the site was rebuilt for Edward III in 1375 an outer ditch (*le utmest dych*) was excavated and provided with a two-storey timber gatehouse and porter's lodge, while in the following year a hedge was planted on an outer bank, forming yet another secluding layer.[136]

It is oversimplistic to see such structures as features of the 'hunting landscape'. While some such buildings were undoubtedly the residences of park-keepers and periodically accommodated hunting parties, others were used as sanctuaries for private courtly entertainment, as household accounts sometimes reveal. For example, in 1465 Anne Stafford's household paid for a substantial lunch to be transported from the hunting lodge at Writtle (Essex) to a separate, more secluded retreat in Horsefrithpark.[137] Certainly, the labelling of subsidiary elite residential sites located in and around forests and parks as 'hunting lodges' can be misleading.[138] In documentary sources such as the Pipe Rolls the word 'lodge' is reserved almost exclusively for the houses of park-keepers. A rare exception is Edward III's property of Hatheburgh in Hampshire: one of several houses in the New Forest, tucked away in Lyndhurst (Old) Park, this was evidently a substantial and high-status complex with a great gate, chamber, hall and chapel, but it was styled as a *logea* when constructed in 1358–61.[139]

There are occasional glimpses that the higher nobility possessed essentially similar buildings. The Neville family had a lavish summerhouse in the West Park at Middleham (Yorkshire, West Riding) in the late medieval period, for instance. Known as *Conyesmirehouse*, this had its own garden, with walls repaired in 1483–4, while the remains of enclosures and raised walkways survive as earthworks.[140] Detached from the main residence and located within parkland, such buildings may also have functioned occasionally as the 'secret houses' that feature in late medieval household accounts. These show that lords withdrew, sometimes clearly as an annual ritual, to a specified retreat accompanied by a restricted household while the accounts were worked on.[141] An element of theatre was integral to the popular fêtes champêtres (outdoor festivals or picnics) of the later Middle Ages that utilised these retreats against parkland backdrops.[142] It is this type of parkland lodging that is depicted in castellated form, complete with its own enclosed garden, in the calendar miniature for April in the *Très Riches Heures du Duc de Berry*.[143] Featuring substantial domestic comforts, these were elite residences in microcosm; as such, they are in a sense the forerunners for the explosion of lodge building after *c*.1540 exemplified by sites such as Claverdon (Warwickshire) and Beckley Park (Oxfordshire).[144]

Where built in towered form, as at Berkeley castle (Gloucestershire) in the early fourteenth century, and in brick, as at Leconfield (Yorkshire, East Riding), the upper rooms or roofs of parkland residences could be used for observing hunting activities, effectively doubling their uses as standings.[145] The circular moated site known as The Old Lodge in Chepstow Park Wood (Monmouthshire) bears comparison. Positioned on a gentle slope within the thirteenth-century hunting park, probably to be intervisible with the castle, and encircled with a flat outer bank very much like a walkway or viewing platform, the lodge buildings here featured a vaulted chamber over a natural spring, interpreted as a facility for a post-hunt cold plunge.[146] Also on the Welsh Marches, the huge and ruinous site of Llangibby (Monmouthshire), a fourteenth-century castle and hunting lodge of the Clare family between their residences of Usk and Caerleon,

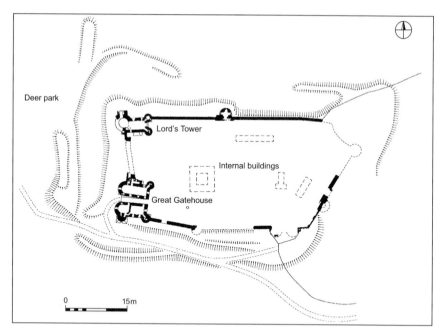

Figure 25. Llangibby castle (Monmouthshire): fourteenth-century castle or hunting lodge closely associated with a park of the Clare family. Based on Priestley and Turner 2003, with additions.

seems to have 'looked out' onto its accompanying deer park (*Figure 25*). At the west end of the site the immense Lord's Tower and Great Gatehouse formed a magnificent façade fronting an enormous but weakly defended castle facing on to an open area of the adjacent deer park. Recorded in the mid eighteenth century as covering 23 acres (9.5 hectares), this laund was a space where deer would have grazed and, perhaps more importantly, would have been driven for staged hunting spectacles. As so often, accompanying fishponds either side of the castle and a rabbit warren completed the ensemble.[147]

The residences of park-keepers were of rather lower status. According to Gervase Markham, an authority on country pursuits writing in the early seventeenth century, these buildings should be positioned at the highest points within parks. This is true of, for instance, the seven medieval parks that form the core of an extensive hunting landscape within the lordship of Middleham (Yorkshire, North Riding).[148] In medieval Wessex, those lodges not positioned centrally on the highest points within parks stood next to park gates.[149] Park lodges represent the archaeology of surveillance. Reconstruction of individual park topographies from cartographic sources and the present-day landscape can reveal similar arrangements: the park at Ongar (Essex) – one of very few to have demonstrably pre-Conquest origins – also has the lodge at its very centre,[150] while the lodge within the thirteenth-century park at Willey (Shropshire) was set in a central open gated enclosure.[151] The only known parker's lodge that survives as a standing building is at Odiham (Hampshire), and is located centrally within the royal park next to a bridge over the river no more than a mile from the castle. Comprising a timber-framed hall with cross-wing (*Figure 26*), this was a relatively modest structure without architectural embellishment, and, while it was built for Edward III in the period 1368–75 (replacing an earlier structure in existence in the late thirteenth century), it was clearly a parker's residence rather than a place where hunting parties stayed.[152]

Again, fishponds and other appurtenances might accompany such sites: the park lodge within the deer park attached to Framlingham (Suffolk) had its own

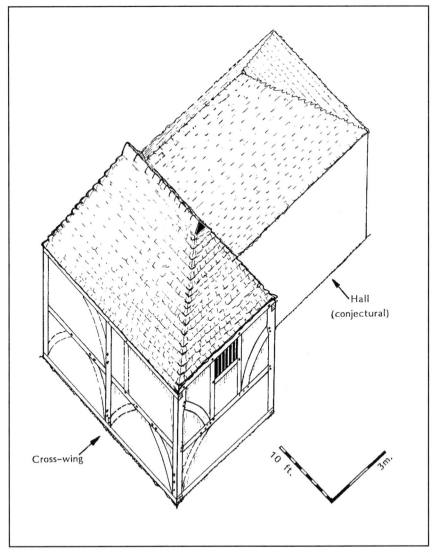

Figure 26. Hunting lodge at Odiham (Hampshire). Source: Roberts 1995.

gardens by the sixteenth century, for example.[153] A striking number of keepers' lodges were also provided with moats, partly no doubt to give the impression of seclusion and status, although we should not underestimate the mythical imagery that the use of water embodied (see p. 77). But moats around buildings within parks might not be purely for show. Acts of park breaking and poaching could endanger park-keepers: one was killed in an incident at Haughley (Suffolk) in 1316–17.[154] The largest poaching operations resembled warfare in microcosm, while parks could be the focus for other forms of social discontent. During the 'Northern Rebellion' of the late 1380s, Sir William Beckwith's local rebels attacked foresters and their property, targeting parks within the Duchy of Lancaster's free chase. In November 1388, a band laid siege to Robert the Forester's lodge of *Haywrocastell* in Haverah Park (Yorkshire, West Riding), while in August 1389 the rebels broke into the chamber at the same lodge and stole a silver-mounted horn and a bow and arrows – artefacts symbolic of the forester's authority.[155] Known as 'John of Gaunt's Castle', the site survives as an earthwork complex positioned at the end of the ridge prominently within the park, a central earthwork platform *c*.12 metres square showing the position of a tower that would have overlooked a substantial tract of the chase.[156]

Of rather more transient character were the stands or standings built for the practice and observation of hunting. They have particular importance for this study as they provide direct evidence that activities within elite landscapes were intended to be experienced as grandstand views from pre-positioned facilities. Park standings are well known from Tudor-period England, as at Chatsworth (Derbyshire) and Nonsuch (Surrey).[157] Many were clearly temporary structures: those depicted in the *Noble Art of Venerie* (*c*.1575), for example, are simple raised timber platforms surrounded by balustrades, which would have left no physical trace. On John Norden's vivid depiction of Windsor in 1607 a feature of precisely this type in the Little Park labelled as 'The Standing' overlooks a sinuous deer course running away to the east of the castle.[158] An identical feature is depicted by Norden in the southern part of the royal park at Guildford (Surrey), near a 'dove hows'.[159] Some were clearly more substantial multi-storey features: the stand erected for Henry VIII at Egham (Berkshire) in 1539 was 26 feet high, while at Ampthill (Bedfordshire) 19 feet and 3 inches of new glass were needed to glaze the queen's standing in the Great Park.[160] Two such structures of the period survive in good condition. A three-storey timber-framed building in Chingford (Essex) known as Queen Elizabeth's Hunting Lodge was, despite its name, built in the 1540s for Henry VIII. Originally known as the 'Great Standing' or 'High Standing', it was positioned, lying within a series of paddocks laid out for coursing, to provide excellent views over Fairmead Park and was the largest and most important of a number of grandstand-like buildings from which hunts were watched and deer shot with bows.[161] Positioned just to the north-west of Chatsworth House (Derbyshire), the stone-built platform known as Queen Mary's Bower is another sixteenth-century hunting stand that, with its moat, doubled as a feature within a contemporary water garden and was retained as a picturesque element within Lancelot Brown's landscaping of the site in the middle years of the eighteenth century.[162] Evidence for similar activities before the sixteenth century is more problematic. A fifteenth-century depiction of an idealised medieval park in *The Master of Game* depicts four elaborate tower-like buildings punctuating the battlemented park wall.[163] Evidence for what may have been temporary structures on the ground is, unsurprisingly, difficult to locate. The 'King's Standing' in the area of Lancaster Great Park, near Crowborough (East Sussex), comprising a slight quadrangular earthwork set on a natural ridge-end viewpoint, is one probable example of a late medieval standing.[164] What has been interpreted as a 'hunting tower' dating to *c*.1500 has been identified within Ripley Park (Yorkshire, West Riding). Set on an artificial mound on high ground, this small rectangular stone structure seems likely to have been a point from which deer were shot, with a funnel-like configuration of boundary earthworks and a moat presumably acting to direct the deer accordingly.[165] The medieval parkland landscape developed around Castle Bolton (Yorkshire, North Riding) by the end of the fourteenth century contained two tower-like buildings: one apparently a banqueting pavilion, of which elements remain built into seventeenth-century field walls (high-quality tablewares have also been found in the vicinity); and the other the probable residence of a parker.[166] The deer park at Harringworth (Northamptonshire) contained a central stone building with a first-floor viewing platform, while another potential candidate is the 'Newground' in the hunting park at Dartington (Devon), where a rectangular stone building is set within a circular earthwork and walled enclosure.[167]

Hunting landscapes

The private nature of parkland spaces was essential to preserving and enhancing the mystique of hunting, which came to symbolise the superpredatorial role of man.[168] In a sense, parks were early forms of nature conservation – but conservation for a reason. The animals these parks contained have been curiously neglected in historical studies, not least as deer are mentioned infrequently in documentary sources, and estimates of their populations are necessarily vague.[169] Deer parks accommodated far more than deer, as the example of Woodstock (Oxfordshire) famously shows.[170] It was within this park that Henry I kept the royal menagerie, comprising exotic species given as gifts by foreign rulers and dignitaries; William of Malmesbury specifically mentioned a porcupine given by William of Montpellier and listed other animals obtained from foreign rulers, including lions, lynxes, camels and leopards. The park also accommodated an eyrie of falcons in the thirteenth century as well as containing a rabbit warren, a dovecote and part of the royal stud; it was stocked with boar in the mid fourteenth century and both partridge and deer were hunted from the sixteenth; finally, pigs and cattle grazed on enclosed spaces within the pale.[171] Horse studs are known from parks of the Crown (e.g. Guildford (Surrey) and Woodstock (Oxfordshire)) and the higher nobility (e.g. Haverah (Yorkshire), West Riding, and Mere (Wiltshire)). At Stirling an equestrian display involving Spanish horsemen took place in 1505 within the park,[172] while Edward I's extravagant tournament was staged in the park at Windsor in 1277.[173] Parks could also contain species with less obvious elite connotations, including cattle (which could be wild, as with the herd that grazed in Windsor Great Park until the animals were caught and sold in the 1270s), sheep, which grazed on open lawns, and pigs, which foraged within wooded areas.[174] Alongside the exploitation of a miscellany of woodland resources, arable cultivation and vineyards were not unknown within parks (see p. 75), while mineral exploitation, peat cutting, charcoal burning and pottery production are also well attested.[175]

In a wider European context, one medieval pleasure park that we can understand in particularly vivid detail was at Hesdin, in north-west France.[176] Encompassing a vast area of over 800 hectares and emparked for Count Robert II of Artois in the late thirteenth century, this park was described in a famous poem. The park boundary was over 4 kilometres in length, punctuated by no fewer than 11 gates and walled in stone (*Figure 27*). The park afforded guests a variety of experiences through an intricately compartmentalised

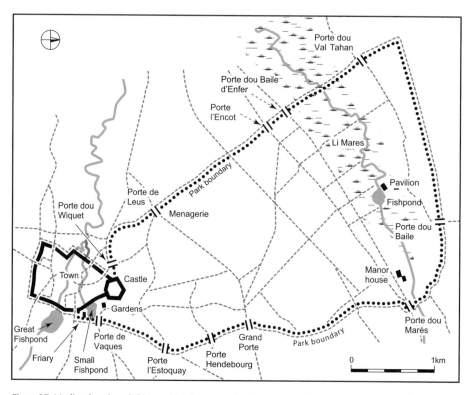

Figure 27. Medieval park and designed landscape at Hesdin, northern France. Based on Hagopian van Buren 1986, with additions.

design based around three distinct types of terrain: an explicitly 'designed' series of garden spaces immediately below the castle that included orchards, stables, a menagerie and a small fishpond; a wilderness-like zone of hills and woods in the centre of the park that was crossed by roads; and, at the far (northern) end, a watery landscape (*li Marés*) moulded in the valley of the Ternoise River that featured marshes, ponds, rivers and fountains, and focused on a large pavilion accessed via a bridge. As well as different types of orchard, it accommodated various types of animals in their own microenvironments through the provision of a menagerie, aviaries and fishponds. Other parkland animals were not real at all: rather bizarrely, a bridge supported animatronic monkeys, dressed in badger fur, which waved at visitors. A comparable case is the parkland setting around the palace of Kaiserslautern (Germany) created for Frederick I Barbarossa by 1158, and described by the chronicler and biographer Rahewin thus:

> On one side he surrounded it by a strong wall; the other side
> was washed by a fish pond like a lake, supporting all kinds of
> fish and game birds, to feast the eye as well as the taste. It also
> has adjacent to it a park (*[h]ortus*) that affords pasture to a large
> herd of deer and wild goats. The royal splendour of all these
> things and their abundance (which precludes enumeration) are
> well worth the spectator's effort.[177]

The deer with which parks were stocked occupied a somewhat hazy area between 'wild' and 'domesticated'.[178] They feature only rarely in medieval agricultural treatises and frequently appear in manorial documents as 'wild' (*ferae*) beasts when clearly stocked within parks.[179] Their 'wild' status is also celebrated in hunting literature. Yet the practice of deer management was well developed by the late medieval period, extending far beyond the creation of agreeable microhabitats to include the provision of shelters and artificial fodder, including hay and oats, while it was not unknown for cows to suckle deer calves.[180] This is important: parks, rather paradoxically, constituted artificial wildernesses, where the hunting experience could be carefully controlled.

To understand something of the medieval hunting experience to which parks were crucial, we have to turn to pictorial and literary sources. From the second half of the thirteenth century onwards, hunting handbooks show that hunting etiquette was becoming increasingly complex, providing evidence of an ever more theatrical and ceremonial discourse.[181] Hunting scenes also feature prominently in later medieval illuminated manuscripts. Given the symbolic and religious allegories associated with these activities it is no surprise to find hunting, coursing and hawking vignettes in sources such as the *Queen Mary's Psalter* and *Gorleston Psalter*.[182] These sources, with their highly stylised depictions, generally tell us little about the environments in which these activities were pursued. It is only in more complex depictions within medieval hunting books, such as the *Livre de Chasse* of the late fourteenth or early fifteenth century, that the wider landscape context of hunting is represented. Equally rich hunting compositions are found on later medieval tapestries, some showing features such as woodland pavilions.[183]

In the world of medieval literature the forest was a quintessential romance landscape that was not only a place of danger, but of mystery and perhaps love, as manifested by the Grail and Tristan romances, for instance, or Sir Thomas Malory's *Morte D'Arthur*.[184] The 'soundscape' of the hunt – the hue and cry dominated by the echoing sounds of horns – would also have been important to the sensory experience,[185] as would the event of returning to the residence at the end of a day's sport, the sight of a fortress such as Peveril (Derbyshire) presenting an image of civility unexpectedly revealed, contrasting with the wild scenery and perhaps generating its own sense of mystery.[186] Accounts of hunting in romances emphasise that movement between landscapes of different texture, giving different experiences, was important, and pictorial sources show us the same. Miniatures in the *Livre de Chasse*, for instance, show that expanses of grassland interspersed with woodland were integral to the hunting experience.[187] In romances, images of hunting parties crossing water via bridges and fords or traversing moats were recurring motifs that signified movement into deeper and more mystical hunting landscapes.[188] In Chrétien de Troyes' late-twelfth-century *Le Chevalier de la Charrete*, for example, the episode of the castle of the flaming lance involves the hunting party processing from managed meadowland immediately around the castle into a park provided with a metalled road before plunging into the forest, which sees a transformation from the social spaces of a managed world to the realm of the supernatural.[189] Similar movements between the civilised and magical spheres are represented by journeys between castle and rugged wild hunting landscapes in the Gawain poem.[190]

In the medieval mind, parks might therefore be perceived as liminal spaces, located between the known and inhabited world and the wildwood or forest, with its own distinctive folklore. William Shakespeare's *Merry Wives of Windsor* provides vivid insight into the character of Windsor's Little Park, which provides one of the settings for the punishment of the poacher, Falstaff. Lying on the margins of the town and under the shadow of the castle, the Little Park is depicted as a space that was neither private nor public – between court and countryside – and thus a fitting venue for correction.[191] The park in *Sir Gawain and the Green Knight* lay close to the castle, which was: 'erected in a meadow surrounded by a park, set about by a palisade of close-set spikes, which enclosed its circuit of more than two miles'.[192] Maybe this too was an allusion to a form of 'little park', whose scenery contrasted with the wild forest in which the events of the hunt dramatically unfold. If so, it is not inconsistent with the landscape setting of Beeston castle (Cheshire), sometimes suggested as a source of inspiration for the poem, where the fortress, perched high on a rocky eminence above the Cheshire plain, was accompanied from the mid fourteenth century by a palisaded park carved out of the wooded area of Peckforton.[193]

But how did 'real' parks fit into the hunting experience? One reason that these were not 'hunting parks' in the strict sense is that many were far too small. *Sir Gawain and the Green Knight* provides the most vivid depiction of a hunting scene available in Middle English, but this did not occur within the palisade park next to the castle that so impressed Gawain when he came upon the site for the first time.[194] In fact, there is surprisingly little direct documentary evidence for seigneurial hunting within parks;[195] for instance, there is only a single reference to a king hunting in a royal park in medieval Scotland: James IV at Falkland (Fife) in 1508.[196] The traditional pursuit of the stag *à force*, usually involving a large party hunting and taking place over an extensive tract of landscape, was out of the question within the confines of any but the largest of parks.[197] However, less prestigious 'bow and stable' hunting, where deer were driven towards pre-positioned archers, clearly took place, providing evidence that hunting could be carefully choreographed to provide a spectacle for observers. The theatre of the deer drive is attested in medieval courtly literature, with the alliterative poems *Sir Gawain and the Green Knight* and *Awntyrs off Arthure* providing vivid accounts.[198]

The drive was always more favoured than the *par force* chase as a method of hunting in medieval Scotland, perhaps a Gaelic legacy.[199] This sort of hunting was certainly practised at the parks of Linrathen (Angus) and Kincardine (Kincardineshire), where pale 'extensions' served to funnel deer towards a gap in the boundary where they could be shot, although these were located some distance from the castles to which the parks were attached (see p. 135). The deer trap at Kincardine (*Black and White Plate 22*), which is probably dateable to

Plate 22. Kincardine (Kincardineshire): view of part of the pale surrounding the royal park; the deer trap lay in the steep-sided valley to the left. (Photograph: Oliver Creighton)

1266, when the park was rearranged, is particularly well preserved and is focused on a steep-sided valley running in towards the park boundary.[200] A further intriguing example is Hermitage castle (Roxburghshire), rebuilt as an austere and imposing masonry edifice in the fourteenth century to replace Liddel castle as the primary estate centre in Liddesdale. This site was conveniently located for the area's extensive hunting lands and lay at the heart of a remarkably preserved landscape of reorganisation, including enclosed assarts along the river embracing fields, settlements and the Hermitage chapel, as well as a deer dyke that arcs away from the castle up the slopes to the north (*Colour Plate 9*). The fact that this 'park' was clearly open on one side, and the manner in which its earthworks define a 'funnel' of ground open to the hills with a gap at the narrow end less than 10 metres wide focused on an overlooked gully, suggests a deer trap into which deer were driven, with a killing ground adjacent to the castle as its focal point.[201] This example further demonstrates that not all deer parks were necessarily enclosed reserves, but could have more active roles in aristocratic hunting culture.

Medieval coursing – whereby small numbers of deer (or occasionally hare) were released along a pre-prepared route to be chased by hounds – is well known from documentary and literary sources in Britain.[202] It was clearly a visual spectacle, with courses being provided with artificial standings or located so that they could be seen from residential buildings (see also p. 146). At Godolphin (Cornwall) (see *Figure 8*), for example, a square masonry standing still overlooks an early post-medieval course of *c.*400 metres, while an elevated garden walk of the 'Side Garden' adjacent to the house provided another vantage point.[203] The plan of the course itself, which was usually set within or on the edge of a park, was marked by boundaries. As well as being long strips of land, courses were sometimes sinuous and wider at one end than the other: seventeenth-century accounts describe the funnelling effect created by a progressively narrowing enclosure, with a ditch that prevented deer being pursued beyond the terminus.[204] Coursing was popularised if not invented in the sixteenth century: a particularly elaborate walled course, a mile long with a stand at one end, was built east of Henry VIII's Hampton Court Palace in 1537, although it was swept away at the end of the seventeenth century.[205] Identifiable physical traces of this activity within the landscape are few and far between, however, and those examples with surviving vestiges in the form of boundaries or related buildings are mainly post-medieval in date.[206]

Four good candidates for medieval courses within deer parks are Clarendon (Wiltshire), Ravensdale (Derbyshire), Stafford, and Windsor (Berkshire).[207] The royal course at Clarendon was known as the 'Pady' (or 'Paddock') course.[208] Depicted on an estate map of *c.*1640 and described in a survey of 1651 when clearly derelict, this narrow strip of land was enclosed with a paling fence and featured a 'standing' at its widest (western) end.[209] Valued at £30 and described as a turreted structure, this was clearly more impressive and permanent than a simple timber grandstand and was located on the edge of the 'Little Park' that

Plate 1. Aerial view of Haverfordwest Priory (Pembrokeshire), showing the excavated remains of a monastic garden below the site of a lodging.
(© Crown copyright: Royal Commission on the Ancient and Historical Monuments of Wales)

Plate 2. Manorbier (Pembrokeshire) from the air, showing the area of landscape described by Gerald of Wales in the late twelfth century, including the castle, church and fishponds.
(© Crown copyright: Royal Commission on the Ancient and Historical Monuments of Wales)

Plate 3. View from the walls of Stirling castle (Stirlingshire), showing the King's Knot garden and part of the area taken up by the medieval royal park. (Photograph: Oliver Creighton)

Plate 4. Recreated medieval garden within the enclosure (or 'bawn') of Tully castle (Co. Fermanagh). (Photograph: Oliver Creighton)

Plate 5. Dunstanburgh castle (Northumberland), showing the former route of approach to the main gatehouse from the site of the medieval harbour. (Photograph: Oliver Creighton)

Plate 6. Linlithgow (West Lothian) from the air, showing the royal palace and its lakeside setting. (© Crown copyright: Royal Commission on the Ancient and Historical Monuments of Scotland)

Plate 7. Aerial photograph of Sycharth (Denbighshire): a lordly site set within an elite landscape described by the poet Iolo Goch in the late fourteenth century. (© Crown copyright: Royal Commission on the Ancient and Historical Monuments of Wales)

Plate 8. Windsor Great Park (Berkshire), showing grazing fallow deer and the medieval shell keep in the background. (Photograph: Lee Andrews)

Plate 9. Hermitage castle
(Roxburghshire) from the air,
showing the area occupied by the
medieval deer park and part of the
earthwork pale.
 (© Crown copyright: Royal
Commission on the Ancient and
Historical Monuments of Scotland)

Top right: *Plate 10.* Ashby-de-la-Zouch
(Leicestershire) from the air, showing the
late-fifteenth-century tower built for William,
Lord Hastings, and associated gardens.
(© Crown copyright: English Heritage)

Right: *Plate 11.* Halesowen (Worcestershire)
from the air, showing the site of a
Premonstratensian monastic house and
surrounding earthworks. Did the complex
series of ponds and causeways surrounding
this site amount to a 'designed landscape'?
(© Crown copyright: English Heritage)

Plate 12. Aerial view of Thornbury
(Gloucestershire), showing the 'castle' built
for Edward, third Duke of Buckingham, in
the early years of the sixteenth century,
and its associated walled gardens.
(© Crown copyright: English Heritage)

formed an inner sanctum dedicated to pleasure and leisure at the heart of the enormous park attached to the palace (see p. 192). While there are no direct medieval references to coursing at Clarendon, the course seems most likely to have been laid out before the end of the fifteenth century, after which the site went into decline, and would have been visible from the royal apartments, as it lay beneath a steep natural scarp with the appearance of a natural grand-stand.[210] At Windsor – where Edward IV is known to have enjoyed coursing[211] – the banana-shaped course depicted by Norden on his detailed map of 1607, complete with a course in progress, matches the angled plan of the feature at Clarendon and was clearly intended to be viewed, similarly, from the royal resi-dence (in both cases it is the start rather the end of the course which was clos-est to the palace). A baronial equivalent is a short deer course within Stafford Great Park.[212] Terminating near the castle donjon, the layout of the course can be reconstructed on the basis of eighteenth-century cartographic evidence, and while it could feasibly have been laid out as late as the early sixteenth century, after which the castle was disued, a reference in 1433–4 to a chase within the park provides a hint that its origins are medieval.[213] An exceptionally rare exam-ple of a surviving medieval course – its topography reconstructable from earth-works and field boundaries – has been identified at Ravensdale.[214] Apparently a late medieval feature, it again ran on a sinuous course through the centre of the deer park, its start marked by kennels, its terminus by a lodge and hunting stand, and its wider setting visually enhanced by a series of lakes.

The impacts of emparkment

While deer parks cumulatively took up a tiny proportion of the total surface area of the medieval landscape, their social impacts were felt much more widely. The creation or extension of parks could result in the constriction of settlement growth or the desertion of places entirely (see p. 156). More commonly, they impacted upon traditional common rights such as the pasturing of animals, the collection of wood and the digging of turf, as well as affecting access to hunting and game. An illuminating parallel is the impact of the imposition of Norman Forest Law. The creation of the *Nova Foresta* impacted on communities not sim-ply by removing lands or obliterating settlements outright, but by usurping the customary rights of individuals who continued life but with the rhythms of daily existence altered by officialdom.[215]

An attractive way to think of parks is as seigneurially regulated 'taskscapes':[216] the rhythms of use were not only seasonal but closely regu-lated by the lord, and extended beyond access to grazing resources to encom-pass service work on pales and lodges (see p. 21). The rights of peasants might be extinguished altogether or be forcibly altered, being restricted to certain zones of the parkscape or timed so that access did not disrupt the sea-sonal rhythms of deer management. In all cases the vernacular experience of parkland was controlled, including the ways in which it was viewed and accessed via gates and prescribed routeways. Lords could not empark without impunity, however. In the later medieval period park creation was challenged in the central and assize courts.[217] Compensation or exchange usually accompanied the taking in of agricultural land. At Okehampton (Devon), for example, an agreement of 1292 between Hugh de Courtenay, lord of the honour and castle of Okehampton, and the burgesses detailed how common rights to pasture in woods to the south of the castle would be transferred to a new location where they would be guaranteed, prior to the creation of an enormous park in existence by 1306.[218] Similar conditions extended to the highest authorities, as with Edward IV's proposal to extend the park at Windsor (Berkshire), for which the townspeople were compensated.[219] Other agricultural resources could also be affected. The outline of a medieval watermill complex lying within the royal parkland at Woodstock (Oxfordshire), revealed as parch marks in the hot summer of 1976, represents the mill that Edward III ordered to be dismantled and re-erected outside the park.[220] While elsewhere the physical juxtaposition of manorial residence and mill side by side was an evocative symbol of rural lordship (see p. 57), mills might not be wanted within a park of this status.

The traditional explanation is that medieval parks made maximum use out of poor-quality land; they often lay on the edges of parishes, their pales cutting off corners, and are thought to have enclosed uncultivated or waste ground.[221] Such positions could provide parks with particular visual opportunities. In Hertfordshire, for example, the location of many parks on the edges of parishes and watersheds ensured that they commanded spectacular views.[222] Other regional differences are apparent, however, showing that parks were not necessarily relegated to areas of marginal agricultural quality. In Cornwall, for instance, deer parks occupy areas of the agricultural heartland rather than the uplands or terrain that was in any way poor or secondary.[223] In central-southern England, similarly, several of the parks of the bishops of Winchester and Bath took in prime agricultural land.[224]

The plan of the classic medieval park, with its oval or lobe-like appearance and rounded corners, may have originated as an 'economical' measure due to the expense of paling,[225] but this had the knock-on effect of cutting across the grain of the landscape. Many of the key case studies of parkland landscapes contained within this book, such as Windsor (Berkshire) and Woodstock (Oxfordshire), show that farmland was appropriated during emparkment. If not necessarily ousting commoners outright, emparkment might simply result in inconvenience for tenants. Communication patterns could be disrupted, as when the earl of Cornwall's emparkment of Cippenham (Buckinghamshire) blocked a road in the 1250s.[226] The bishop of Exeter was accused in 1283 of blocking two public highways: his emparkment of Lanner (Cornwall) was said to disrupt access to the market at Truro, while Pawton blocked the route to Bodmin, although he was found to have provided new roads and retained these parks.[227] Other sites at which there are good examples of clearly dated road diversions due to park creation in England include Little Bolton in Wensleydale (1314), Hodnet (Shropshire, 1256), Hunsdon

(Hertfordshire, 1445), Tusmore (Oxfordshire, 1357) and Whichford (Warwickshire, 1252).[228] It is precisely this sort of development that must explain the countless existing roads and tracks that sweep on curving lines around former park boundaries, indicating diverted road systems.[229] Such topographies are one of the key ways that we can trace the outlines of parks, but must also have served to condition the vernacular experience of the park. The pale provided a visual reminder of why a road had been moved – and one that would have carried signals of status where this was a substantial feature of stone, as at Lamphey (Pembrokeshire), Lyddington (Rutland), Moulton (Northamptonshire), Ravensworth (Yorkshire, North Riding) and Woodstock (Oxfordshire), for example. In Scotland, the royal park at Kincardine (Kincardineshire) contains former pre-park roadways fossilised as earthworks, while a road following part of the park perimeter represents a diverted communications route.[230] In Anglo-Norman Ireland lords sometimes also had to petition the king in order to undertake such acts: in 1228, for instance, Walter de Riddelsford asked permission to divert a road that ran through the middle of his park of Garnenan (probably Co. Wicklow).[231]

Evidence for the removal of villages in advance of emparkment is of course well attested in post-medieval contexts and exemplified by places such as Milton Abbas (Dorset) and Nuneham Courtenay (Oxfordshire).[232] For the medieval period the clearest evidence for the forcible removal of populations by powerful landlords is associated not with schemes of polite landscape redesign but with the establishment of monastic houses whose rules stipulated isolation, or the clearance of settlements from royal forests, as well as the widespread late medieval conversion of arable to pasture. Parks newly created in the later medieval period tended to be large; they invariably took in areas of arable and occasionally settlements, and their impacts on settlements are better documented.[233] It also became relatively commonplace for park extensions to take in areas of ridge and furrow cultivation, which may still survive where earthwork preservation is good, as at the Northamptonshire parks of King's Cliffe and Wadenhoe.[234] In certain cases the sites of former villages were incorporated within new designed settings. At Whorlton (Yorkshire, North Riding), for example, the earthworks of a deserted village were transformed into a designed landscape created in front of a castle, probably in the late fourteenth century when the site was rebuilt by the Meynell family.[235] The twelfth-century church of the Holy Cross, directly aligned with the castle's new gatehouse, was incorporated as an antique point of reference into a new setting that featured formal gardens and ornate water features, all enveloped within Whorlton 'Great Park', which may have been extended at the same time.[236] There is, however, little to suggest that depopulation associated with emparkment was motivated primarily by aesthetic concerns; rather, it appears to have been a by-product of a change in land use.

The examples that we have are mainly late and affected small or weakened communities. But it was certainly not unusual for late medieval parks to result in depopulations, as at Easton Neston (Northamptonshire).[237] Among the most celebrated cases, from the mid to late fifteenth century, is the Hertfordshire village of Pendley:[238] the park, which was developed by the Whittingham family near Tring in Hertfordshire in the 1440s, initially infringed on grazing rights before affecting the settlement.[239] Another classic case is the palace-like mid-fifteenth-century residence of Wingfield (Derbyshire), constructed in the middle of the fifteenth century for Ralph Lord Cromwell, which was isolated within a parkland setting.[240] The village of Kirby, within this park, was certainly deserted by the seventeenth century but the depopulation may well be associated with the hall's construction.[241] In the later medieval period rural depopulation in the face of emparkment was not an isolated phenomenon, but part and parcel of a wider pattern of desertions attributable to the enclosure of open fields and engrossment of farms, especially in midland England.[242]

But could similar ideas – of removing populations to create space and seclusion – have been expressed further down the social hierarchy? Detailed plan analysis of a series of villages in south Cambridgeshire has raised the possibility that as early as the twelfth century lords were involved in schemes of estate improvement entailing the removal of village properties and their relocation to nearby 'model' medieval villages.[243] What is relevant here is that these changes to settlements such as Harston, Little Shelford and Whittlesford had in common the creation of closes around manor–church complexes that, as well as indicating agricultural improvement, consistently ensured the seclusion of lordship sites and sometimes involving road closures.[244] Even if these relatively minor rural landlords were not creating elaborate routes of approach to their residences or did not have the wealth and status to create formal deer parks, an element of 'design' is still apparent in their actions.

The well attested phenomenon of seigneurial village planning, which in many cases extended to embrace field systems, can be taken as further evidence for the expression of lordly authority, in which ordered landscapes of production were created in microcosm, often on the edges of parks.[245] There are two fundamental problems with this approach, however. First, peasant communities could themselves have played a role in settlement planning.[246] Second, huge swathes of the medieval landscape were characterised by non-nucleated forms of rural settlement, although this need not rule out the possibility of lordly intervention entirely.[247] Overall, while lordly authority was clearly a key motor in the planning of settlements, a kaleidoscopic array of regional and sub-regional patterns can be observed. We should also remember that settlements existed *within* some parks. That the deer park at Okehampton (Devon) preserves evidence of medieval settlements in the form of several clusters of longhouses represents an intriguing case. One interpretation has envisaged these settlements as having been deserted upon the enlargement of the park in a case of forced seigneurial depopulation.[248] Reinterpretation suggests, however, that they may represent a short-lived venture sponsored by the earls of Devon and are actually contemporary with the park.[249] Crucially, however, they lay just beyond the area intervisible with the castle (see p. 131–2). Other late medieval parks saw encroachment by settlements, signalling a downturn in their elite status: it was in the first decades of the fifteenth century that the first settlements appeared in Stanhope Park in Weardale, for example.[250]

Seigneurially planned urban settlements arguably represent the most 'designed' medieval landscape features of all, and their plan-forms could have important symbolism of their own.[251] It may not be accidental that the site of Clarendon Palace (Wiltshire) loomed large over the bishop's 'new town' of Salisbury; the city's establishment in 1226–7 coincided with the declaration of Henry III's majority and the reconstitution of Clarendon Forest.[252] Set almost centrally within its huge accompanying park, standing proudly on the crest of a ridge visible across open downland, the palace would have been unmistakable to travellers from Salisbury or Winchester, while an alternative route of approach provided a more secluded wooded experience.[253] Beyond park pales, settlements could sometimes effectively form adjuncts to the medieval parkscape, their topographies moulded to ensure the exclusivity of the aristocratic sphere (*Figure 28*). One of the clearest examples is Devizes (Wiltshire),

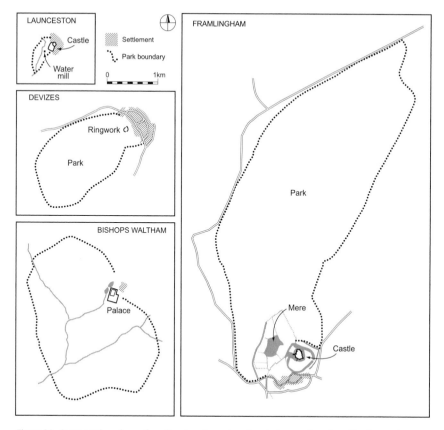

Figure 28. Comparative plans of medieval parks and park-gate towns. Based on Hewlett and Hassell 1971, Hare 1988, Brown 2002, Herring 2003 and Creighton 2005b, with additions.

where castle, deer park and borough represent a unified exercise in medieval town and country planning carried out by Bishop Roger of Salisbury in the early years of the twelfth century.[254] A comparable case is Launceston (Cornwall), where funnelled routes of approach to the town showcased symbols of lordship by providing contrived views of castle, park and the walls that embraced the seigneurial borough.[255] Castle Acre (Norfolk) shows that views towards castle–borough units could be manipulated for dramatic effect (*Figure 29*). Here, the former Roman road known as the Peddars Way was diverted in the Norman period, probably to create a vista for approaching travelers that showcased the planted town, priory and castle.[256]

At Bishop's Waltham (Hampshire) the palace of the bishops of Winchester was bracketed between a gridded planted town to the east and an enormous deer park to the south. While a large walled outer court, complete with gatehouse and lined with barns and apartments, marked the point of interface between the residential core of the palace and the borough, a planned arrangement of walled garden and fishponds marked the zone of transition between the inner court and the parkland beyond.[257] The desire to seclude palaces from busy urban environments was not simply a phenomenon of the twelfth and thirteenth centuries, however. It is displayed well in Henry VIII's development of the area around Whitehall Palace (formerly York Place), following its appropriation in the wake of Cardinal Wolsey's fall in 1529.[258] A complex series of land transactions in the 1530s and 1540s ensured that the riverside palace precinct was flanked by a vast green belt of newly acquired land, including Hyde Park, St James's Park and Marylebone Park, over which the king enjoyed exclusive access and hunting rights.

Ecclesiastical magnates were also involved in settlement planning. The village of Spalding (Lincolnshire) is a prime example: it was planned, probably in the twelfth century when the bishops of Lincoln were especially active in estate reorganisation, with its green butted against the enclosure of the bishop's palace, which lay secluded in its own gardens.[259] The designed surrounds of the bishop of Ely's palace at Somersham (Cambridgeshire) were created by the removal and replanning of the village of that name over its own field system,[260] while at Cawood (Yorkshire, West Riding), the ornamental setting of the Archbishop of York's palace was also closely related to a contemporary scheme of settlement planning.[261]

In many cases medieval deer parks on the urban fringe influenced the direction of subsequent expansion, as at Coventry (Warwickshire) and Sheffield (Yorkshire, West Riding), where seigneurial parks formed in effect great suburban green belts. Moreover, there is good reason to think that emparkment could actually disadvantage urban communities or arrest their growth. Windsor (Berkshire) is perhaps the most striking example. While the nucleation of New Windsor at the castle gate from the eleventh or twelfth century might outwardly seem to indicate a privileged community that benefited from its association with a major royal residence, the community's subsequent development shows something rather different. A series of disputes between representatives of the king and the town in the thirteenth and fourteenth centuries

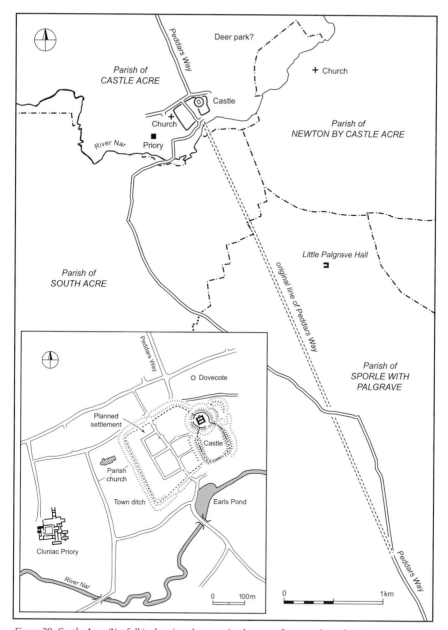

Figure 29. Castle Acre (Norfolk), showing the contrived route of approach to the Norman castle–borough complex. Based on Liddiard 200b, with additions.

show the royal arrogation of areas of common pasture into the castle parks; other disputes related to unpaid pontage by the royal purveyors, and interference over water and fishery rights.[262] The net result was that Windsor did not exhibit the intensively developed street frontages of otherwise comparable towns. Its failure to develop walls – a characteristic otherwise common to medieval castle-gate towns – was another symbol of its far from mutually beneficial relationship with the great royal castle.[263] At Ludgershall (Wiltshire), replanning of the castle gardens also infringed on the town plan, while the royal parks strangulated its growth.[264] The same was true of Helmsley (Yorkshire, North Riding), where an expansion of the castle precinct to the north in the thirteenth century which entailed the creation of a large enclosed garden, complete with a raised walkway still preserved as an earthwork, infringed on the main route west out of the town.[265]

Resistance and dissatisfaction

Most studies of parks have, unsurprisingly, examined these landscapes from the point of view of the emparkers. However, for the post-medieval period records of vandalism against features such as belts of trees and plantations provide one index of disaffection with polite landscapes,[266] and although direct written evidence for the attitudes of medieval peasants to elite landscapes is difficult to find before the very end of the period, there is still good reason to think of medieval parks, warrens and gardens as contested spaces. Many parks were recorded for the first time not when they were licenced or created, but when they were first broken into.[267] As well as rigidly enforced game laws, the abrogation of rights represented by emparkment may have generated resentment and invited resistance.[268] Transgressions against parks could reflect more than simple criminality; seigneurial exploitation of the landscape could breed social discontent. Elite game reserves were certainly the target of discontent during the Peasants' Revolt. According to the chronicler Henry Knighton, among the demands presented by Wat Tyler at Smithfield in June 1381 was the call that 'all game, whether in waters or in parks and woods should become common to all, so that everywhere in the realm, in rivers and fishponds, and woods and forests, they might take the wild beasts, and hunt the hare in the fields.'[269] Resistance to emparkment might also be expressed through legal challenges. For example, in 1299 the Anglo-Norman lord Theobald le Butler petitioned the king in order to divert a road at Nenagh (Co. Tipperary) so that he might enclose a park next to his castle; among the objections raised by tenants was the fact that it would oblige some of them to make a circuit of four furlongs in order to reach their lands.[270]

Direct incidences of park-breaking can be glimpsed through the Patent Rolls, where details of stolen animals are sometimes recorded.[271] Evidence of poaching is also found in the form of the tightening legislation to counter it, particularly from the late fourteenth century onwards, with increasingly repressive measures targeting not only the act of poaching but restricting access to the material culture of hunting such as nets and dogs.[272] Medieval treatises on estate management, meanwhile, remind us that vandalism directed at recognisably elite features of the landscape was commonplace. Writing in the late thirteenth century, Walter of Henley listed among the duties of the steward the inspection of parks, fishponds and cony-garths (rabbit warrens) for signs of tres-pass.[273] Allusions to peasant dissatisfaction might even be found in medieval pictorial sources. In the famous calendar pictures of the early fifteenth-century *Très Riches Heures du Duc de Berry*, images of aristocratic material culture and elite recreation contrast with images of the peasant not only at work, but also as a figure of disobedience and laziness.[274]

Poaching from royal forests, which is readily visible in the documentary record, can be understood in more detail. Rolls drawn up at eyres (special forest courts) in the thirteenth century detail large numbers of offences, although the triumph of officialdom that these documents represent must grossly underestimate the overall scale of poaching.[275] Rockingham (Northamptonshire) had more than 230 offenders in 1272 and 1286, for example, while peaks in offences that coincide with Christmas, Easter and Whitsuntide show that poaching intensified on a seasonal basis, no doubt to provide venison for these festive occasions.[276] Numbers of offences within seigneurial parks are much harder to quantify, however, with our understanding based on occasional, anecdotal information. For example, in 1441 the lord of Okeover park (Staffordshire) reported a loss of some 100 deer from a total of 125 – an attrition rate through poaching of 80%.[277] The targeting of seigneurial parks might be symbolic and attributable to wider discontent felt locally: in the late 1480s and 90s actions against the parks and warren of the Wilstrop family near York sometimes involved several hundred malefactors disaffected by the alleged enclosure of arable and village property, which fermented a family feud.[278] Attacks on rabbit warrens could be ferocious and sustained as peasants took direct action against a type of exploitation that often appropriated their commons and competed with their agricultural practices, especially in the fourteenth and fifteenth centuries.[279] Escaped rabbits and deer as well as doves from manorial dovecotes presented a pest to peasant cultivators. Theft from dovecotes was not unknown; a particularly elaborate attempt at Walsham-le-Willows (Suffolk) in 1398 involved the placement of snares around the lord's dovecote at High Hall.[280]

Far from being merely a subsistence strategy, poaching could also function as a display of male gender identity.[281] It could extend to quite conscious displays of impudence and deliberate challenges to authority, as in the case of the poaching group that set up a deer head with a spindle in its mouth on a stake within the Forest of Rockingham in August 1272.[282] Furthermore, the licensing system ensured that parks were symbols of favour, and so were attacked by rival members of the social elite more often than we might imagine: Richard Stafford, Sussex knight and serial park-breaker, active in the south-east of England in the early fifteenth century, is a good example.[283] Activities in Knaresborough Chase during the 'Northern Rebellion' of the late 1380s extended beyond park-breaking to involve the systematic slaughter of stock within parks, attacks on foresters and vandalism and theft directed at their lodges.[284]

Poaching was not simple class war; it was frequently a noble- or gentry-led activity and a social networking opportunity whereby elites, supported by their own tenants, settled private scores of their own.[285] Archbishops and barons feature alongside peasants in thirteenth-century forest eyres:[286] thus in 1413 the scholars of Oxford were prohibited from entering the king's park at Woodstock (Oxfordshire) because of an established track record of poaching game there.[287] Poaching parties targeting private parks could be socially diverse. Details of prosecutions against individuals who had illegally entered parks at Thornbury (Gloucestershire) in the 1320s show that poaching parties contained burgesses, villeins and freeman as well as members of the ruling classes.[288] These operations sometimes resulted in symbolic acts of defacement rather than attacks on the economic base of parks. As recounted by Matthew Paris, the illegal activities carried out by William de Valence in the Middle Park of the bishop of Ely at Hatfield (Hertfordshire) in 1252 extended beyond 'token' poaching to include pulling down the park pale and vandalism of the house there.[289] In the early-fifteenth-century poem *Sir Degrevent*, the hero is wronged by a feudal superior, the earl, who despoils his lands by park-breaking and vandalism of his fishponds.[290] Gamekeeper could become poacher: foresters themselves were enthusiastic poachers, according to thirteenth-century forest records, while in 1301 the bishop of Exeter's park at Pawton (Cornwall) was broken into by members of the local clergy, who removed two fallow deer.[291]

But can we find resistance to seigneurial authority of this sort expressed in physical terms in the archaeological record? Material evidence of poaching might be apparent in the recovery of deer bones in certain contexts, as venison was not available on the open market. A near-complete red deer skeleton shoved into a well in the peasant potters' site of Lyveden (Northamptonshire) in the fourteenth century might be a case in point.[292] Late medieval red deer antler and bone from North Petherton (Somerset) might tell a similar story.[293] 'Suit of mill', whereby peasants were compelled to grind their corn at the lord's mill, could not always be enforced: Ralph Mortiga of Aldborough (Yorkshire, West Riding) was accused of using his own millstones (presumably for hand-milling) rather than the lord's demesne mill.[294] The recovery of hand querns from excavated settlements might be another indication of peasant resistance, therefore.[295] Continuity in customary practices or conservatism in the use of traditional technology could be another indicator of intransigence in the face of seigneurial control; this has been suggested at Bunratty (Co. Clare), for example, where the same techniques of fish-trapping were practiced in the Shannon before and after the establishment of the new Anglo-Norman lordship in the late thirteenth century.[296] We should also remember that while rural settlements might outwardly display regularity in their plan forms, many of which can be attributed to seigneurially led schemes (or at least estate improvements brokered by lords), this can disguise peasant individualism. Decades of excavation and fieldwork focused on medieval rural settlements reminds us of this, as exemplified by two of the best-understood villages of all – Shapwick (Somerset) and Wharram Percy (Yorkshire, East Riding) – both of which are clearly 'planned' villages but whose plots display individualistic biographies of peasant occupation.[297]

Chapter Five Notes

[1] Pluskowski 2007, 69–71.

[2] Gilbert 1979, 219.

[3] Hicks 1993, 260–70.

[4] Page 1908a, 251–3; Hartley 1983, 15, 18.

[5] Creighton 1999, 25–6.

[6] Hansson 2006, 145.

[7] For England see Cantor and Hatherly 1979; Cantor 1983; for Scotland, see Gilbert 1979, 215–24.

[8] See, for example, Cantor 1970–71 on Leicestershire; Steane 1975 on Northamptonshire; Bond 1994 on Wessex.

[9] Liddiard 2007b.

[10] Stamper 1988, 140.

[11] Roberts 1997.

[12] Crawford 1953, 189.

[13] Partida 2007, 59.

[14] Stamper 1988, 146.

[15] Birrell 1992, 114–15.

[16] Rackham 1986, 126.

[17] e.g. Birrell 1992.

[18] See Hatcher 1970, 170–83.

[19] Liddiard 2007b, 1–4.

[20] Hooke 1989, 123–5; Liddiard 2003.

[21] Thiébaux 1974, 36–8; Sykes 2005, 74.

[22] Thiébaux 1974.

[23] Payne 1990, 38; see also Soderberg 2004, 174.

[24] Gilbert 1979, 75–6; Morris 2005, 13–15.

[25] Soderberg 2004, 173–7.

[26] Whitely 1999; Beck and Casset 2004; Gautier 2006, 56.

[27] Jamison 1938.

[28] Sykes 2004b; 2005.

[29] Quoted in Rowley 1999, 181.

[30] Cantor 1982, 76–7; Hoppitt 2007, 154; Way 1997, 87.

[31] Astill and Grant 1988, 165; Stamper 1988, 140; Soderberg 2004, 172.

[32] Maltby 1982.

[33] Austin 2007, 673.

[34] Soderberg 2004, 171–2.

[35] O'Conor 2004, 238–9.

[36] O'Conor 2004, 238–9; O'Conor and Murphy 2006.

[37] O'Conor and Murphy 2006.

[38] Mallory and McNeill 1991, 305.

[39] Gilbert 1979, 219.

[40] Gilbert 1979, 221–2, 356–9.

[41] Mileson 2005, 19–20, 35; see also Page 1906, 211.

[42] Salzman 1937, 132–4.

[43] Bond 1998, 25–6.

[44] Bond 2001, 82; see also Moorhouse 1989, 64.

[45] English Heritage Register of Parks and Gardens, No. GD1718.

[46] Hoppitt 2007, 157.

[47] Payne 2003, 220.

[48] Roberts 1988, 67–9; Payne 2003, 219–20.

[49] Roberts 1988, 76; Way 1997, 59.

[50] Butler 1949, 28.

[51] Orme 1992, 135.

[52] Birrell 1982, 11, 17.

[53] Roberts 1988, 70–1.

[54] Cantor 1982, 77.

[55] Steane 1974, 176; 1975, 213.

[56] Gilbert 1979, 219.

[57] Hewlett and Hassell 1971, 36–9; Hawkes 1991.

[58] James and Gerrard 2007, 47.

[59] Hartley 1983, 32.

[60] Elrington 1990, 444.

[61] Colvin 1963, 967–8.

[62] Riley 2006, 95–7, 99.

[63] Stamper 1988, 141.

[64] Elrington 1990, 439–48.

[65] Richardson 2007, 34.

[66] Cantor and Hatherly 1979, 74.

[67] Williamson and Bellamy 1987, 71.

[68] Taylor 1998b, 30.

[69] Liddiard 2005b, 40.

[70] Probert 2004, 94–5.

[71] Dennison 2005, 96.

[72] Emery 2000, 225–7.

[73] Rackham 1986, 122–9; 2001, 153–4; 2004, 2–3.

[74] Colvin 1982, 168.

[75] Cantor 1982, 66–9.

[76] Bowden 2005, 4.

[77] Winchester 2007, 171–2.

[78] Austin 2007, 107–10.

[79] Calkins 1986, 165–6; Ševčenko 2002, 83.

[80] Roberts 1997.

[81] Wilson 2002.

[82] Emery 2005, 146.

[83] Richardson 2007, 39.

[84] Watts 1998, 94–6.

[85] Everson *et al.* 2000, 104–6.

[86] Liddiard 2005a, 98–9.

[87] Roberts 1988, 82; English Heritage Register of Parks and Gardens, No. GD4724.

[88] Neave and Turnbull 1992, 54–5.

[89] Smith 2000.

[90] Page 1906, 572; Partida 2007, 49.

[91] Darlington 2001, 15.

[92] Moorhouse 2003b, 345–8.

[93] Payne 2003, 178–9.

[94] Roberts 1988, 77, 83; Woodfield and Woodfield 1988, 12–13.

[95] Barnwell and Everson 2004.

[96] English Heritage Register of Parks and Gardens, No. GD1720.

[97] MacIvor and Gallagher 1999, 143–4; Brann 2004.

[98] Brann 2004, 18–19.

[99] Beck *et al.* 2001; Casset 2003.

[100] Markham 1616, 670.

[101] Roberts 1988, 77; other examples where twin medieval parks reflect the two species are those of the Clare family at Thornbury, Gloucestershire: Franklin 1989, 156, and the pair at Nether Stowey, Somerset: Riley 2006, 97.

[102] Watts 1998, 100–3.

[103] Gilbert 1979, 219.

[104] Clay 1914, 17–31.

[105] Beresford 1967, 564.

[106] Barker and Higham 1982, 13; Higham and Barker 2000, 142–3.

[107] Coffin 1994, 87–126.

[108] Parker 1981–2, 252; Fletcher 2002, 144, 147–8.

[109] Goodall 2006, 28–31.

[110] Gilchrist 1995, 170.

[111] Goodall 2006, 28.

[112] Hull 1971.

[113] Page 1906, 574.

[114] Gilbert 1979, 76.

[115] Saunders 1993, 120.

[116] Cable 1971, 84–96; see also Saunders 1993, 70–1, 121–2, 182–5.

[117] Gilchrist 1995, 162.

[118] Payne 2003, 190–2.

[119] Saunders 1993, 27–8; Rooney 1997, 158–60.

[120] See Woodfield 1991, 124–5.

[121] Biddle 2005, 465.

[122] Colvin 1986; Ashbee 2006, 78–82.

[123] Ashbee 2006, 78–9.

[124] Ashbee 2006, 79–80.

[125] Colvin 1963, 1014–15.

[126] Roberts 1988, 100.

[127] Astill 2002, 11.

[128] Colvin 1963, 1007–9.

[129] Roberts 1997.

[130] Rahtz 1969.

[131] See Colvin 1963, 1019.

[132] Tolley 1991, 176.

[133] Greig 1986.

[134] Richardson 2007, 35; James and Gerrard 2007, 65.

[135] Poulton 2005, 150; Richardson 2007, 34–5.

[136] Lobel 1957, 57; Colvin 1963, 898–9.

[137] Woolgar 1999, 165.

[138] See Steane 2001, 274–5.

[139] Colvin 1963, 984–5.

[140] Moorhouse 2003b, 332.

[141] Girouard 1978, 76.

[142] Woolgar 1999, 165.

[143] Cazelles and Rathofer 1988, 27.

[144] Cooper 1999, 109–128; see also Henderson 1999, 59.

[145] Girouard 1978, 77.

[146] Turner and Priestley 2006, 194–7.

[147] Priestley and Turner 2003, 37–9.

[148] Moorhouse 2003a, 332.

[149] Bond 1994, 150–1.

[150] Liddiard 2003, 5.

[151] Stamper 1988, 142.

[152] Roberts 1995.

[153] Taylor 1998b, 40.

[154] Hoppitt 2007, 149.

[155] Marvin 1999, 232.

[156] Grainge 1871, 345–7; Dennison *et al.* 2007–8, 158–9.

[157] Woodfield 1991, 131.

[158] Roberts 1997.

[159] Crocker 2005, 192.

[160] Colvin 1982, 16, 40.

[161] Powell 1966, 108.

[162] Brighton 1995, 41–3; Williamson 2001, 85.

[163] Pluskowski 2007, 71–3.

[164] Tebbutt 1974.

[165] Muir 2001, 94–6.

[166] Moorhouse 2003b, 350, 353.

[167] Pluskowski 2007, 76; Taylor 2000, 42; Waterhouse 2003, 77–8.

[168] Pluskowski 2002.

[169] Birrell 1992, 112.

[170] Elrington 1990, 439–48.

[171] Bond and Tiller 1997.

[172] Gilbert 1979, 221.

[173] Roberts 1997.

[174] Roberts 1997.

[175] Cantor and Hatherly 1979, 80–1; Birrell 1992.

[176] Charageat 1951; Hagopian van Buren 1986.

[177] Quoted in Sevcenko 2002, 82.

[178] Salisbury 1994, 50.

[179] Mileson 2005, 25–6.

[180] Birrell 1992, 116–19; Salisbury 1994, 51.

[181] Thiébaux 1974, 26–7.

[182] Pearsall 1977.

[183] Grönwoldt 1977.

[184] Saunders 1993, 2–3.

[185] Woolgar 2006, 74.

[186] Barnwell 2007, 30–1.

[187] Cummins 2002, 44.

[188] Saunders 1993, 73–4.

[189] Saunders 1993, 155–7.

[190] Elliott 1997; Howes 2002, 204.

[191] Theis 2001, 59–61.

[192] Barron 1974, 69.

[193] Thompson 1989; 1997, 122–5.

[194] Barron 1974, 88–9.

[195] Birrell 1992, 113.

[196] Gilbert 1979, 221.

[197] Thiébaux 1974, 28–36; Cummins 2002, 39–40.

[198] Rooney 1997, 159.

[199] Gilbert 1979, 52–6.

[200] Gilbert 1979, 24, 54.

[201] Dixon 1997, 352–4.

[202] Taylor 2004b, 47–53.

[203] Herring 1997; English Heritage Register of Parks and Gardens, No. GD4198.

[204] Musty 1986, 132.

[205] Fretwell 1995, 136.

[206] See, for example, Fretwell 1995 on an early seventeenth-century example on the Sherborne estate in Gloucestershire, which incorporated an ornate lodge as a viewing stand; coursing could be watched from the roof and balcony.

[207] Other plausible candidates include Breedon (Leicestershire), Filleigh (Devon), Harringworth (Northamptonshire), Helmdon (Northamptonshire), Odiham (Hampshire) and Rothwell Haigh (Yorkshire, West Riding); see Taylor 2004b, 48–50.

[208] Richardson 2005, 80–2; James and Gerrard 2007, 65, 110–13.

[209] Musty 1986, 131.

[210] Richardson 2005, 72, 80–2; 2007, 39–40.

[211] Roberts 1997, 137.

[212] Milln 1993, 2–4.

[213] Darlington 2001, 5, 15–16.

[214] Taylor 2004b, 37–43.

[215] Mew 2000, 160–2.

[216] See Ingold 1993.

[217] Beresford 1971, 194.

[218] Austin 1978, 195–6; Austin *et al.* 1980, 41.

[219] Beresford 1971, 195.

[220] Watts 2002, 84–6.

[221] Cantor 1982, 75.

[222] Rowe 2007, 144.

[223] Herring 2003, 37.

[224] Payne 2003.

[225] Rackham 1976, 144; Cantor 1982, 75.

[226] Cantor and Hatherly 1979, 81.

[227] Henderson 1935, 159.

[228] Beresford 1971, 87–8, 193.

[229] Beresford 1971, 193; for specific examples see Franklin 1989, 165, on the Clare parks at Thornbury, Gloucestershire.

[230] Gilbert 1979, 85.

[231] O'Conor 2004, 238.

[232] Taylor 1983b, 209–13.

[233] Mileson 2005, 21.

[234] Cantor and Hatherly 1979, 79; Stamper 1988, 146.

[235] Creighton 2005b, 217–18.

[236] Page 1923, 309–19; RCHME 1990.

[237] Emparked for Richard Empson in *c.*1499: Fletcher 2002, 102–3.

[238] Beresford 1954, 147–8.

[239] Munby 1977, 133–4.

[240] Emery 2000, 449–59.

[241] Stocker 2006, 144; in the same county Haddon Hall bears comparison, see Emery 2000, 383–91.

[242] Fryde 1996, 185–203.

[243] Taylor 2006.

[244] Taylor 2006, 121–6.

[245] See Saunders 1990, 187–94.

[246] Dyer 1985; see also P.D.A. Harvey 1989 for an opposing view.

[247] See Creighton 2005b, 195–8.

[248] See Austin 1978; Austin *et al.* 1980.

[249] Probert 2004, 93.

[250] Drury 1976, 143–4.

[251] Lilley 2004.

[252] Richardson 2005, 87; James and Gerrard 2007, 53.

[253] James and Gerrard 2007, 49–54.

[254] Taylor 1998b, 32; Creighton 2005b, 193.

[255] Herring 2003, 47–8.

[256] Liddiard 2000b, 60–2; 2005a, 134–9.

[257] Hewlett and Hassell 1971, 29–32; Lewis 1985, 122–3.

[258] Thurley 1997, 98–101.

[259] Taylor 1989b, 74.

[260] Taylor 1998b, 30.

[261] Blood and Taylor 1992.

[262] Astill 2002, 8–9.

[263] Creighton and Higham 2005, 216.

[264] Ellis 2002.

[265] Barnwell and Everson 2004.

[266] Williamson 1998, 176; 1999.

[267] See, for example, Liddiard 2000a, on the park at Castle Rising first broken in 1325; many of the Duchy of Cornwall's medieval parks are first documented for similar reasons: see Hatcher 1970.

[268] Marvin 1999, 225.

[269] Martin 1995, 219; see also Hilton 2003, 230.

[270] O'Conor and Murphy 2006.

[271] For example, for evidence from Suffolk see Hoppitt 2007, 149–51.

[272] Mileson 2005, 37.

[273] Oschinsky 1971, 269.

[274] Alexander 1990.

[275] See Young 1974.

[276] Birrell 1982, 9–10, 19; see also Hanawalt 1988.

[277] Birrell 1992, 115.

[278] Beresford 1954, 303–4; 1971, 205–6.

[279] Williamson 2007, 161–2.

[280] Stone 2006, 159.

[281] Hanawalt 1988, 192–3.

[282] Birrell 1982, 15–16.

[283] Bellamy 1973, 80–1.

[284] Marvin 1999, 231–2.

[285] Manning 1993; see also Hanawalt 1988, 188–90.

[286] Birrell 1982, 11.

[287] Stamper 1988, 145.

[288] Franklin 1989, 157–60.

[289] Beresford 1971, 204–5.

[290] Casson 1949, 9.

[291] Henderson 1935, 159; Orme 1992, 136.

[292] Steane and Bryant 1975, 156–7.

[293] Leach 1977, 39.

[294] Holt 1988, 39–40.

[295] Treen and Atkin 2005, 20; Dyer 2007, 82.

[296] Van de Noort and O'Sullivan 2006, 83–5.

[297] Wrathmell 1989; Gerrard and Aston 2007.

Seeing and Believing: Understanding Designed Landscapes

It is now well understood that the domestic planning of castles and other high-status medieval buildings, especially those of the later medieval period, channelled movement and manipulated the experience of architectural space in sophisticated ways that reflect the social order.[1] Less clearly understood, however, is how the organisation of their wider settings did the same. Experiences of medieval landscape – like those of contemporary architecture – were, of course, not static. Encounters with the elite settings that have been described in the preceding three chapters required the active involvement of the spectator from a viewpoint that was ever-changing. The predominant way in which these gardens and designed spaces was experienced was through movement across the surface of the landscape, by foot or in the saddle. Medieval literary and art-historical sources remind us that this type of visual engagement with scenery – which was revealed step by step as the individual proceeded through it – represented a deeply ingrained way of thinking about the landscape.[2] Perhaps the most vivid medieval literary source showing exactly this is *Sir Gawain and the Green Knight*, in which, in an almost cinematic passage, the knight approaching Sir Bertalik's castle suddenly came upon and took in the fortress and its setting as one: occupying a knoll above an open glade, sylvan scenery framed a multi-towered structure that 'shimmered and shone' behind a surrounding moat.[3]

At the same time, it is also clear that views of medieval residences could be revealed to visitors in different ways: in some cases vistas were gradually and tantalisingly opened up, while elsewhere buildings providing icons of authority intended to be visible over large tracts of the landscape. The manipulation of views of buildings and landscapes in such cases was not purely for aesthetic beauty, but also for emblematic reasons, creating settings that were loaded with imagery and symbolism. As the previous chapter has shown, the grounds of great residences were also the home of species of animals of recognisably elite status, carrying symbolism of their own – not only deer, but also rabbits, doves, swans, herons and peacocks – and contributing to the image of splendour. There was also, of course, no single way that a given building or landscape was meant to be experienced. Rather, a multiplicity of views existed. The most important of these were: views *of* the elite site itself, especially as seen from a route of approach or from associated pleasure grounds; and views *from* the place of residence, through windows or from rooftops. The previous chapter has also shown how buildings within parks could provide equally spectacular views.

What makes these ideas contentious is that the notion of looking outwards, whether from a garden or building, is seen as an innovation of the Renaissance.[4] At a European scale, reawakening interest in the visual qualities of landscape as experienced from buildings is traditionally seen as a phenomenon that developed in fifteenth-century Italy. In particular, the construction of the famous Villa Medici in Fiesole, built in the 1450s and commanding hilltop views over Florence and the Arno valley, is seen as a particularly seminal moment.[5] Yet there is also compelling evidence in earlier centuries that designated viewing points – whether window seats in residential chambers, the parapets of buildings, or earthwork terraces above gardens – provided, in essence, composed views. This chapter attempts to establish a framework for their interpretation.

Room with a view: looking in on the garden

An intriguing dimension to the study of the garden spaces covered in this book that has not yet been considered in detail is the question of whether or not they were intended to be experienced from the residential buildings to which they were nearly always attached. Unfortunately, however, spatial and access analyses of medieval buildings have not usually extended to embrace gardens, and have certainly not engaged with the control of access to views over landscapes.[6] It is also instructive to remember that the perspectives from which the medieval gardens illustrated in the book have been depicted were all alien to the medieval mind: two-dimensional plans of earthworks, oblique aerial photographs and plans of excavated features are all next to meaningless in medieval terms.

One characteristic type of feature from which gardens could be viewed was the loggia – a covered walkway on the side of the building, with one or more open sides carrying an arcade or colonnade. While the 'long gallery', located at an upper level for the admiration of gardens as well as a means of intercommunicating between rooms, is characteristic of Tudor and Elizabethan houses, medieval forerunners are not unknown. In France the word 'galerie' was used as early as the early fourteenth century to describe sheltered walkways around the edges of gardens or orchards, as well as corridor-like features connecting different parts of domestic accommodation.[7] In Britain, evidence that medieval 'alures' and 'pentices' of earlier centuries fulfilled any observational functions is sparse, although references to gardens directly below chamber windows of palaces occur frequently in royal accounts.[8] The ornamental pools at the heart of Henry II's secluded pleasure-palace of Everswell (Oxfordshire) were overlooked by a two-storey chamber block, while accounts for the construction of a walkway (*alei*) between this and the queen's chamber in 1237 suggest some form of covered walkway at upper-floor level, mirroring the cloistered walkway around the central garden below.[9] In Britain, the earliest explicit references to 'long galleries' built as structures from which to view courtyard gardens date to the late fifteenth century.[10] Galleries in late medieval houses in London were certainly provided with windows that overlooked gardens, as in the Clothworkers' property in Throgmorton Street, where a long first-floor gallery terminated in a bay window that served this purpose.[11] At Herstmonceux (East Sussex), galleries over ground-floor arcades surrounded the 'Green Court' on three sides, while at Knole (Kent) timber galleries looked down on the 'Stone Court'; both these examples date to the middle of the fifteenth century.[12] The gallery built at the royal hunting lodge of Falkland (Fife) in the mid fifteenth century for Marie of Gueldres is another quite early example. That this was more than a corridor is indicated by the construction of two rooms within it in 1461, while the contemporary building of a queen's upper chamber linked to a newly laid out private pleasure garden below.[13]

Windows played an important role in framing the visual experience of elite settings in both real and imagined contexts. In north-west Europe more generally, later medieval pictorial and literary sources sometimes provide insight into the experience of looking into private gardens from above. In particular, Flemish panel paintings show how the layout of gardens could be appreciated from elevated perspectives through windows. One particularly fine late-fifteenth-century example by a student of Hans Memling shows a window framing an ordered garden that is visually linked by a pathway to meadows and parkland beyond.[14] Written descriptions of essentially similar arrangements are also known. In the late fourteenth century, for instance, Jean Froissart's *Chronicles*, celebrated as the quintessential expression of the chivalric revival, featured some vivid descriptions of high-status gardens that were viewed from above through windows.[15] In the unfinished late-twelfth-century romance the *Conte de Graal* ('Story of the Grail'), Sir Gawain first perceived the stronghold *La Roche de Sanguin* not from ground level, but framed through the 'turret windows' of his waterside lodging, seeing it rise on a rocky precipice amidst a 'vast terrain' of fields and woods.[16]

In the real world, the areas of residences that supplied these views were invariably high-status lodgings, although the genre of late medieval prison poems provides another context for views from elite buildings out on to 'designed' scenery, as in the early-fifteenth-century *The Kingis Quair*.[17] In this case a window set in the upper part of one of Windsor castle's mural towers served to frame a prospect over gardens and a small park that engaged and delighted the imprisoned Scottish king James Stewart.

> *Now was there maid fast by the touris wall*
> *A gardyn faire, and in the cornere set*
> *Ane herbere grene, with wandis long and small*
> *Railit about; and so with treis set*
> *Was all the place, and hawthorn hegis knet,*
> *That lyf was none, was walking there forby,*
> *That myght within scarce ony wight aspye.*

So thik the bewis and the leues grene
Beschadit all the aleyes that there were;
And myddis of the herber myght be sene
The scharp, grene, suetë jenipere,
Growing so faire with branchis here and there,
That, as it semyt to a lyf without,
The bewis spred the herbere all about.[18]

But does the architecture and planning of multi-storey medieval buildings provide evidence that viewing opportunities were provided by deliberate design, or is the fact that windows sometimes provided delightful prospects purely coincidental? Many of the buildings considered in this book had windows in their higher-status areas that were accompanied by stone seats. These would have provided spaces for activities needing plenty of light, such as reading and needlework, but would also have enabled and indeed encouraged occupants to contemplate the view beyond from a position of comfort. Sometimes accompanied by raised foot rests and usually situated either side of the window opening at an angle to the wall, the first known examples date to the late twelfth century and the tradition continued into the later Middle Ages. In royal accounts they are sometimes referred to as 'sitting windows', as in the case of those in the queen's apartments at Marlborough in the thirteenth century.[19] We should be careful, though: the shells of medieval buildings that survive may give the impression that windows are larger than they really were, as evidence of barring or subdivision with mullions and transoms may not survive.

A prime candidate for a major masonry building intended, at least in part, as a viewing platform is the 'High Tower' of Launceston castle, Cornwall (*Black and White Plate 23*). A prominent local landmark forming the centrepiece of a unique motte-top structure with a remarkable 'wedding cake' (or perhaps crown-like) profile, this unusual building is worth considering in detail. Inserted within and rising above an earlier shell keep, the High Tower was probably added to the castle complex by Richard, Earl of Cornwall and 'King of the Romans', in the period *c.*1272–1337.[20] The High Tower, which removed all internal rooms within this earlier structure, was a far smaller, darker, more cramped and generally less usable space than its predecessor. Despite its marked lack of utility value, it is undeniable that the resultant triple-tiered masonry ensemble served as a demonstration to the Cornish countryside of its builder's seigneurial power, perhaps as a monument to Richard's elevation to the earldom.[21] More intriguing still is the likelihood that the tower presented opportunities for looking out over the territory that it dominated visually. While the room at the base of the High Tower was unlit and featureless, its unusual height suggests a need to elevate the evidently higher-status room above it, which was positioned to provide access directly on to the wall-walk around the former shell keep across a platform decked in timber. The upper chamber itself was provided with a hooded fireplace and a single, large, window, complete with large window seats at

Plate 23. Launceston castle (Cornwall), showing the triple-tiered motte-top structure. (Photograph: Oliver Creighton)

either side.[22] What is crucial is that the embrasure faced to the west; immediately below it an awkward view into the bailey did not justify its existence, but beyond, where the castle was enveloped by the private seigneurial deer park, is an enclosed and effectively designed backdrop (*Black and White Plate 24*). It is not difficult to imagine the tower being used as a private grandstand, while the platform and parapet walk below presented opportunities for lordly display to the castle community and surrounding population. First recorded from 1282 but perhaps contemporary with the earlier walling of the town, the deer park formed one component in a classic exercise in medieval town and country planning, with the castle at the interface between planned town on one side and private hunting reserve on the other.[23] For travellers approaching the town of Launceston, meanwhile, the alignment of the road system along the edge of the park pale and town walls represented a manipulated route of approach that showcased the symbols of seigneurial authority, while the central location of the mill within the park highlights another area in which the populace engaged with this lordly landscape.[24]

An intriguing possibility is that other contrived views through windows set in elevated medieval buildings could reference symbols of past power-holders as well as contemporary features of medieval lordship. For example, the two principal windows in the great chamber at the top of the late-twelfth-century donjon at Peveril (Derbyshire) presented contrasting views. To the north-west the ancient Iron Age hillfort of Mam Tor stood out on the skyline, while the win-

Plate 24. View of the medieval deer park at Launceston (Cornwall) through the window at the top of the 'High Tower'. (Photograph: Oliver Creighton)

Plate 25. Monea (Co. Fermanagh): Plantation-period tower-house over-looking the site of an earlier crannog. (Photograph: Oliver Creighton)

dow to the north-east was aligned with the tower of the parish church in the seigneurial borough below. It is arguable that the building was built with manipulation of this visual experience in mind.[25] A far later example is the Plantation-period tower-house of Monea (Co. Fermanagh), which stands amidst bare surroundings above a drained lake containing a crannog that presumably represents the earlier Gaelic power centre in the locality.[26] Built *c.*1610–18 in alien Scottish style for the newly settled lord, Malcolm Hamilton, the building was placed close to the lake edge, its plan and architecture suggesting that it was quite deliberately intended to face the antecedent site, the large main window of the first floor hall indeed framing it (*Black and White Plate 25*).

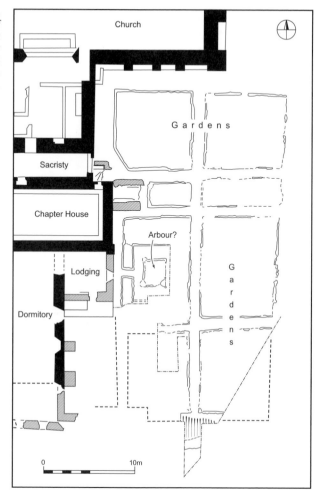

Figure 30.
Excavated evidence of
medieval gardens at
Haverfordwest Priory
(Pembrokeshire). Based
on Rees 1999b, with
additions.

It is only very infrequently that the converse argument can be made – that evidence for the arrangement of garden features suggests they were created to be seen from above. Perhaps the clearest evidence comes from Haverfordwest Priory (Pembrokeshire). Here, a medieval garden which was found quite unexpectedly during excavation comprised a gridded system of compartments bounded by low walls and occupied a zone of *c*.50 x 20 metres between the priory buildings and the precinct walls (*Figure 30*). What is especially significant is the axial arrangement of the garden, with a centrally positioned ornate bed giving the appearance of an arbour, and a two-storey residential block for guests projecting from the east wall of the dormitory. The entire arrangement seems to have been intended explicitly to have been appreciated from this raised perspective; indeed, a large Perpendicular window is

known to have been placed in the relevant position.[27] Another suggestive example from an ecclesiastical context is the bishop of Winchester's solar tower at
Mount House, Witney (Oxfordshire), which had a rectangular garden beneath it,
accessible from a small private stair identified through excavation, by the mid
twelfth century.[28] Here and elsewhere gardens could be enjoyed from two levels.
The bishop of Lincoln's gardens at the palace of Nettleham (Lincolnshire) were
similarly overlooked from the west side of the palace complex, where a large projecting earthwork aligned with the centre of the garden, suggesting a tower from
which this designed space could be appreciated.[29] Field survey of earthworks
around castles raises similar possibilities at Stafford and Hopton (Shropshire)
(see pp. 115 and 182).[30]

The gendered garden

If it is instructive to consider how certain types of designed space were
intended to be deliberately visible, then we should also consider others that
were more restricted in terms of who could see them. While traditional studies
of castles and other elite medieval buildings have depicted these sites as
emblems of a masculine culture, it is clear that the use of space within and
around them could have a gendered dimension. Medieval elite society did not
necessarily see gardening as a masculine pursuit: for example, critics of Edward
II commented that the time he spent 'hedging and ditching' compromised his
military prowess.[31] More specifically, many gardens were clearly gendered
spaces and had explicitly female associations. The involvement of queens in gardening is particularly evident in the thirteenth century. Henry II's queen,
Eleanor of Provence, seems to have been personally involved; gardeners are
mentioned frequently in royal accounts from *c*.1250 and at least one Provençal
name is known.[32] There is again direct evidence for the introduction of foreign
horticultural expertise under Eleanor of Castile, queen of Edward I. She is
known to have employed Aragonese gardeners and an Italian vineyard keeper
and to have imported French apple cuttings.[33] Whether such personnel physically altered the surrounds of buildings in a manner indicative of foreign influence is less certain. In the cases of King's Langley (Hertfordshire) and
Westminster Palace accounts indicate the presence of ornamental water features
and, while physical evidence is now lacking (see p. 61), the likelihood is that
these would have betrayed the influence of Spanish courtly gardens ultimately
of Islamic inspiration.[34] A parallel in Scotland is the investment in new royal gardens following the marriage in 1449 of James II to Marie Gueldres, a Burgundian
princess and niece of the Duc de Berry, whose parks and gardens are vividly
depicted in the *Très Riches Heures*.[35] Within four years the first works on gardens
at Stirling and Falkland (Fife) were being carried out, and at the latter an elaborate arrangement of an upper chamber and private pleasure garden for the
queen echoes contemporary practice in the Burgundian court.[36]

Medieval manuscript illustrations which depict women engaged in social rituals within gardens, such as the plucking of flowers for festive garlands, are well known.[37] Literary sources and manuscript illustrations make clear that the female imagery of the garden was deeply ingrained in elite medieval culture, but texts such as the late-fourteenth-century *Le Menagier de Paris* made explicit the expected role of women in the practicalities of garden management as well.[38] Crucially, however, this gendered aspect of medieval garden history extended to influence the ways in which these designed spaces interrelate to adjacent buildings. Again, models were widely available in literary sources. The legend of Katherine of Alexandria, a popular female noblewoman saint, featured a secluded garden beneath her chamber, to which she possessed the only key.[39] The fourteenth-century mansion house described in Chaucer's *Troilus and Criseyde* featured a private garden directly below Criseyde's first-floor chamber; it was reached by a private stair that seemingly ran up the outside of the building.[40] In Chrétien de Troyes' late twelfth-century romance *Perceval*, on approaching a fantastic palace of dark marble, Sir Gawain observed more than 500 windows along the walls, full of maids and ladies looking out onto flower-filled gardens below and fields beyond them.[41] The mid-fourteenth-century romance *William of Palerne*, meanwhile, features two lovers engaged in a tryst within a park or garden while dressed as deer; they were visible from the chamber window of the queen, which lay above.[42]

But how did the relationships between female lodgings and gardens work in 'real' buildings? Crucially, female garden spaces were virtually without exception buried deep within the spatial matrix of domestic planning so that they could not be accessed easily from other areas.[43] The gardens attached to these lodgings were more exclusive spaces than the chambers themselves, showing a need for seclusion but also, arguably, distancing women from the hub of power. At Clarendon Palace (Wiltshire), for instance, Eleanor of Provence's apartments in the 1270s were the 'deepest' within the entire site, complete with their own secluded gardens and with access to a postern gate and the site's parkland setting, all hidden away out of sight.[44] Sightlines were carefully managed for gender reasons: female gardens were carefully hidden from view, while the chambers above them enjoyed a wide but exclusive 'female gaze'.[45] For example, at the royal house of Kennington (Surrey), built for the Black Prince in the 1340s and used extensively in the reign of Richard II, the 'Privy Garden', which enveloped the detached queen's chamber, was a private space located in the northern corner of the palace complex and, characteristically, accessed via a postern gate (*Figure 31*). Attempts were made to ensure that the garden remained secluded and hidden from view: in 1441–2 a stone new wall was built between it and the more public 'Great Garden' to the south, while the queen's views over garden spaces contrasted with the king's over the hall, chapel and 'processional' route to his chambers.[46] A further improvement was made in 1472–6, when an oriel window was added to the first floor, jettied out over the walled Privy Garden below.[47]

Other examples from royal palaces span the period from the middle of the thirteenth century onwards, as detailed in surviving building accounts. Soon

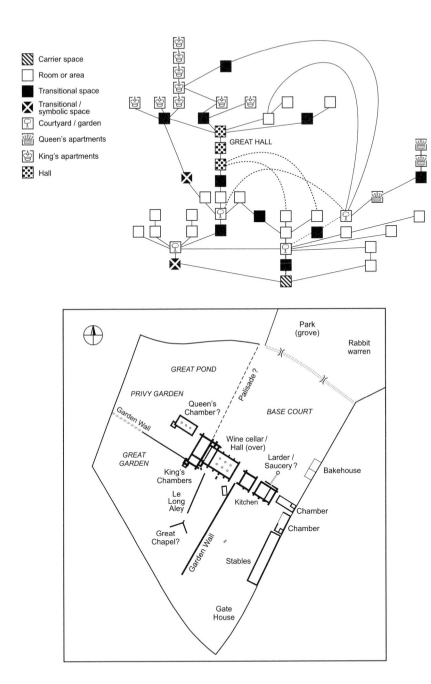

Figure 31. Kennington Palace (Surrey): plan of the palace complex showing the location of associated gardens, and access diagram. Based on Dawson 1976 and Richardson 2003b, with additions.

after Henry III's marriage to Eleanor of Provence (1236), the Queen's Chamber at Windsor was improved by the addition of two windows 'towards the king's herb garden'.[48] At Clarendon (Wiltshire), gardens lay beneath the queen's chambers that were constructed in 1247 and improved in 1252, while the king's chambers overlooked another garden on their south side. A reference to the insertion of a new window, barred with iron, in the queen's hall specified that this should look towards the garden.[49] At Easthampstead (Berkshire) carpenters were engaged in 1292–3 in constructing a timber palisade to enclose a garden beneath the queen's chamber,[50] while at King's Langley (Hertfordshire) it is clear that Eleanor of Castile's garden was directly accessible from her chamber, as the queen's garden was repositioned closer to her apartments.[51] Within the royal fortress of Portchester (Hampshire), excavation revealed that in the fourteenth century the queen's privy garden beneath her chamber was segregated from the remainder of the courtyard and was hidden from view by a fence of large timbers.[52] At Woodstock (Oxfordshire), documents make explicit that a balcony constructed in 1354 outside the window of the apartment of Edward III's daughter Isabella was intended to provide her with a view over the park.[53] In a much later context, at Nonsuch (Surrey), a modish new garden associated with the king's apartments was clearly intended to be a vehicle for exhibition and entertainment, complete with a maze, decorative water pyramid and 'wilderness'. In contrast, a rather less fashionable garden was overlooked from the queen's accommodation, being a place of retreat rather than display.[54]

Another indication that gardens were clearly essential appurtenances to the female royal household is the readiness with which they were laid out as adjuncts to temporary accommodation. When Edward I's second queen, Margaret, stayed in the bishop's palace at Wolvesey, Winchester, in 1306, the apartments in the royal castle having been destroyed by fire four years previously, £2 3s 9d was spent on creating a new garden, comprising a turf enclosure with water running through the middle, to accompany newly fitted chambers.[55] The queen's garden at Odiham (Hampshire) was secluded in a rather different way. Located deep within the deer park, probably in the vicinity of the hunting lodge, this was in existence by 1293 and rebuilt forty years later by Edward III for Queen Philippa, who stayed on a number of occasions.[56] It was enclosed by a boarded fence composed of 742 separate oak boards manufactured by four men over 24 days, had five separate doors, a garderobe screened by a hedge, and several seats with turf roofs.[57]

A probable example of a specifically female designed space at a non-royal site is the water garden created for the aristocratic widow Elizabeth de Burgh at Clare (Suffolk) in the first half of the fourteenth century; this apparently featured a fountain and was marked on nineteenth-century maps as a suite of ponds.[58] Another case in point is the thirteenth-century Countess's chamber at Chepstow (Monmouthshire), which enjoyed wide views over the castle, the beautiful gorge of the River Wye and a garden-like space in the upper bailey below.[59] Ornate painted plaster survives in the reveals of the windows, which

Plate 26. Window of a thirteenth-century chamber in the Marshal's Tower at Chepstow castle, showing the location of window seats. (Photograph: Oliver Creighton)

are provided with seats (*Black and White Plate 26*), showing this to have been a domestic area of particularly high status, secluded away but commanding an exquisite outlook.[60] In Yorkshire, meanwhile, the lady's lodgings in the upper parts of the south range of Middleham castle looked out onto a suite of private gardens, while at Castle Bolton the ornate west-facing window attached to the Great Chamber fulfilled a similar purpose.[61] Gardens created specifically for women in other contexts include those at hospital sites such as St Mary Spital, London, where the separate garden has been excavated.[62]

Looking out on to the park: towers and rooftop views

> *His host the boatman and the knight*
> *went up around the spiral stair*
> *beside the vaulted palace fair,*
> *until they reached the tower's summit*
> *and viewed the lands surrounding from it.*
> *The country round the citadael*
> *Was lovelier than one can tell.*[63]

This vivid scene from Chrétien de Troyes' *Perceval*, after which Gawain goes on to admire the river, plains and deer-filled forest below the tower, reminds us that we should consider views as important to the functions and meanings of elevated buildings. Perhaps the clearest piece of evidence supporting the notion that elite medieval buildings might purposefully provide opportunities for the structured seeing of landscapes is the case of the medieval 'gloriette'. In the context of garden history generally, this word is most commonly associated with summerhouses or pavilions, usually of post-medieval date; perhaps the most famous internationally is the Early Classicist colonnaded gloriette of the Habsburg palace of Schönbrunn in Vienna, which was set on a viewing terrace and provided a vantage point for the admiration of the surrounding parks and gardens.[64] In a medieval context the term has usually been thought of as a reference to an essentially similar feature: a type of garden pavilion, whose origins can be traced back to the Islamic world.[65] However, a detailed reappraisal of the written evidence from Britain has shown that the word *gloriette* was primarily used for upper chambers within high-status buildings.[66] Derived from the Spanish *glorieta*, it was used not so much to describe a building with a specific function as it was a space with glamorous associations from the contemporary world of literature and romance. For example, the twelfth-century French epics *La Prise d'Orange* and *Aliscons*, by Guillaume d'Orange, feature elegant tower-like buildings styled as gloriettes. Best described as a 'pleasure palace', the gloriette of the medieval romance thus has a corollary in the sumptuous and private suites of apartments identified with the same word.[67] Three surviving examples have been recognised in Britain (another, in the conventual buildings in the Cathedral Priory at Canterbury, no longer exists), and their contexts are worth considering.

The gloriette at Corfe castle (Dorset) was built by King John in *c*.1201–5 as an elegant palace-like suite of apartments with its own garden; it was located within the inner ward and separated from the rest of the complex by a gatehouse and bridge.[68] That at Leeds castle (Kent) (*Black and White Plate 27*) was created by Edward I for Queen Eleanor between 1279 and 1288 at one of their most favoured residences.[69] With its vineyard, fishponds and park, this site was particularly closely associated with medieval queens.[70] As at Corfe, the gloriette occupied the most secluded part of the castle, taking the form of an island-like

Plate 27. Leeds castle (Kent) from the air, showing the site of a detached medieval 'gloriette' within the lake. (© Crown copyright: English Heritage)

enclosure linked to the rest of the complex by a bridge. But, uniquely in England, it was entirely surrounded by water in the form of one of two adjoining artificial lakes, while strings of ponds laid out in parkland to the east and north-west, designed to be seen from the apartments, acted as medieval 'eye-catchers'.[71] The lake around Leeds castle could be appreciated not only from the high-status apartments within the gloriette, but from a terraced viewing platform on the slopes above. Unlike the previous two examples, the gloriette of Chepstow castle (Monmouthshire) was not a royal building. First mentioned in 1271, when it was repaired as part of an ambitious scheme of rebuilding for Roger Bigod, it took the form of a chamber within a new range of domestic quarters in the lower bailey, and had a small garden on a ledge over the River Wye beneath it.[72] Comprising the most private and perhaps the most lavishly decorated space within the entire site, the gloriette was built in a dramatic cliff-top position that affords stunning views over the dramatic gorge of the valley.[73]

What unites these examples is not only the exceptionally high status of the buildings and the extremely private nature of the spaces concerned, but also the drama of their settings: at Leeds the gloriette looked out on to a shimmering lake; at Chepstow it faced the striking scenery of the Wye valley; and at Corfe it afforded a dramatic view from the castle's dominant natural setting over the Purbeck Hills.

A structure that may have had a similar function to these gloriette chambers was the upper part of Windsor's belvedere-like Rose Tower, which is known to have featured ostentatious wall paintings; another is the turret above the Painted Chamber at Westminster Palace, which was provided with a window looking directly over the king's garden.[74] The imagery of the garden could also be reflected in names attached to other towered buildings: the Castle of Roses features in the *Roman de la Rose*, for example, while Sir John Putney, Mayor of London in 1336, possessed a mansion in Pountney Lane called the 'Manor of the Rose', which was depicted in later drawings with a battlemented tower.[75] Similarly, the large fourteenth-century quadrangular castle at Wressle (Yorkshire, East Riding) had a tower called 'paradise'.[76] Crucially, we are dealing here not with the provision of views for their own sake; rather, that access to an elevated gaze over the countryside was controlled.

Archaeology can sometimes illuminate the configuration of tower and garden. For example, the western gardens of Stafford castle occupy a triangular area immediately below the motte, where Ralph Stafford's tower of 1348 would have overlooked them.[77] Comprising a compartmentalised arrangement of zig-zag paths and terraces accessed via a stairwell in the north-west tower of the donjon, this was clearly a private facility, characteristically located on the side of the site that was enveloped by the seigneurial deer park. More puzzling is the case of Hopton castle (Shropshire), where a series of ornamental ponds form a coherent arrangement with the thirteenth- or fourteenth-century tower, which is aligned not with any of its faces parallel with the rectilinear arrangement of ponds and other garden features, but at a deliberate angle to it. A possible explanation is that, viewed across the water features, the tower looked more impressive, with three of its four corner towers visible, and appeared to be bigger than it really was.[78]

The late medieval passion for residential towers within parkland, especially in the English midlands, must have something to do with the provision of views from elevated, frequently ostentatious structures provided with lots of windows.[79] This tradition reached an apotheosis with the 'super towers' of the fifteenth century, Ralph Cromwell's brick-built edifice at Tattershall (Lincolnshire) (*c*.1445) being a classic example in a parkland setting.[80] Wingfield manor (Derbyshire) is another, its imposing five-storey High Tower provided with massive windows that commanded the surrounding parkland, while a belvedere-like lantern turret above the privy bedrooms provided other opportunities for viewing the countryside more privately.[81] At Ashby-de-la-Zouch (Leicestershire) the fifteenth-century refurbishments by Lord Hastings were not designed primarily to impress the adjacent town; instead, the solar tower commanded a southern prospect, over gardens, towards the private area of the site (*Colour Plate 10*).[82] There were also three parks and a water garden here too, although it is not clear which phase of the site this feature was associated with. At Sheriff Hutton (Yorkshire, North Riding) the Neville family's palatial quadrangular castle of the period preserves buttressing and machicolation on only one of its four corner towers. It was on this (south-east) side that the castle enjoyed particularly impressive views over the adjacent park and it is not at all inconceivable that the machicolations supported a parapet or viewing platform of some sort.[83] Towered hunting lodges could fulfil similar functions (see p. 143).

Evidence of gardens laid out to complement elevated residences can also be found in the late medieval tower-houses which were built in great numbers in northern and western parts of the British Isles particularly. In Ireland, where several thousand such edifices were created in the fifteenth and sixteenth centuries, the 'bawns' or fortified enclosures that often adjoined the tower sometimes contained gardens and orchards as well as ancillary buildings, as recorded in the seventeenth-century Civil Survey.[84] While the number of bawns that has been investigated archaeologically is miniscule, there are tantalising hints that these were not always simple gardens of utility. Excavation at Barryscourt (Co. Cork) has revealed remarkable evidence for the layout of a late medieval garden, probably of the early to mid sixteenth century, within the walled bawn. Raised beds were identified by the presence of shallow soil-filled trenches, carefully lined with stones to encourage drainage, with evidence of planting holes and fragments of a garden path.[85] Although the full layout was not recovered, it seems that the arrangement was not entirely symmetrical but, rather, followed the outlines of surrounding buildings, with a platform at the east end of the garden forming a likely viewing point. Tully (Co. Fermanagh) is another case in point (see p. 68). Whether these are late or unusual examples or whether other bawns could act as designed spaces remains to be seen.

Other evidence – albeit indirect – that towered residential structures provided deliberately contrived views comes in the form of the internal planning of these buildings and, more specifically, the access arrangements within them. As well as forming the visual foci of castles as viewed from outside, towers are the obvious place to look for evidence that access to viewing areas in the upper levels was intended for those of higher status. For example, at Harewood (Yorkshire, West Riding), the rooftop of a mid-fourteenth-century tower supported a walkway that provided views over the Wharfe valley and deer park, while windows in the highest-status rooms on the upper floor also command an extensive prospect.[86] There was plenty to look at: the castle was the focal point within a symmetrical arrangement of gardens and agricultural buildings laid out on terraces.[87]

McNeill has identified two types of arrangement that provide circumstantial evidence for the upper levels of towers potentially acting as viewing points.[88] At sites such as Hylton (Co. Durham) and Tattershall (Lincolnshire), access to the stair leading to the upper level is not directly from the ground floor but via a chamber or some other private space. Alternatively, in large donjons such as Trim (Co. Meath) and Warkworth (Northumberland), duplicate stairs to the roof are provided, one of them presumably for private access. Of course, only in exceptional conditions of preservation can such arrangements be discerned. For example, the top floor of Bishop Roger's twelfth-century Great Tower at Sherborne (Dorset) does not survive but, containing as it did the bishop's private suite, this seems another likely candidate for a structure with large windows overlooking the deer park.[89] Another intriguing possibility is that wall-walks could provide viewing terraces, as the example of Restormel (Cornwall) suggests (see p. 20).

The technique of access analysis – whereby the spatial relationships between rooms and other areas within a building are depicted as a matrix – can show levels of accessibility to roof-top spaces such as the tops of turrets and walkways. Frequently, it seems, these lay in relatively 'private' zones within elite buildings. At Edlingham (Northumberland), detailed mapping of access arrangements shows a clear correlation between the tops of roofs and high-status activity, with access to these points often clearly controlled or restricted (*Figure 32*).[90]

At the very top of the medieval social spectrum, there is particularly compelling evidence that Edward III's inordinately expensive remodelling of Windsor castle as a palatial complex in the middle years of the fourteenth century included provision for exactly these sorts of views. In the upper ward that was the focus of Edward's refurbishment, rectangular mural towers concealed almost flat roofs behind their crenellated parapets. The two towers containing the king's lodgings were not only differentiated by their location at the cor-

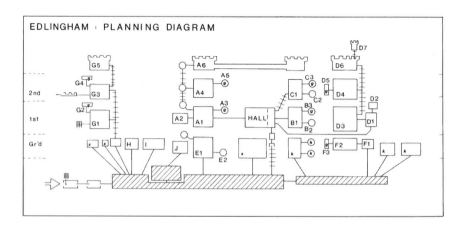

EDLINGHAM : PLANNING DIAGRAM

Figure 32. Edlingham (Northumberland): a planning diagram of the castle in period B (c.1365). The boxes represent rooms and are proportionate to the size of floor space; lines between them represent access between rooms, and ladders show stairs. Note that the turret-top spaces are among the least accessible within the building. Source: Fairclough 1992.

Plate 28. Dartington Hall (Devon): a 'trophy house' of the late fourteenth century, built on the edge of an emparked setting in rural Devon. (Photograph: Robert Higham)

ners of the complex but by their partly polygonal plans; a fact easily overlooked is that this enabled exceptionally wide views to be obtained from their upper levels. The castle's 'blocky' silhouette and rooftop views were of influence as far afield as Charles V's rebuilding of Vincennes, near Paris, in the 1370s.[91] Something of this aesthetic is encapsulated in the calendar miniature for December in the *Très Riches Heures du Duc de Berry*, which depicts Vincennes' flat-topped towers rising above dense forest.[92] Besides their status as important royal residences, both sites have in common locations within vast hunting parks, over which their towers afforded spectacular panoramic views.

Few medieval residences below the very summit of the social spectrum present better credentials for an association with a designed setting than Dartington Hall (Devon). Architecturally one of the very grandest late medieval domestic buildings in Britain (*Black and White Plate 28*), this innovative double-courtyard residence was built in the late 1380s and 90s for the leading magnate John Holand, Earl of Huntington.[93] While the hall's present-day setting owes much to an early-twentieth-century scheme of design, it also preserves traces of a designed landscape that accompanied its construction in the late fourteenth century.[94] Explicable in social terms as a 'trophy house',[95] Dartington Hall reflected Holand's social status and achievements, its construction marking his elevation to the earldom. While the lack of a conspicuous 'showfront' initially makes the notion of a contrived setting seem unlikely, it is clear that the building is keyed into its surroundings in subtle ways, intended not to serve as a display of naked power, but to provide contrasting views to and from an essentially secluded residence with a non-defended character. Located deliberately off the beaten track, this was a rural powerbase with a setting unencumbered by settlement. To the south and west, as observed from a window-lined gallery within the inner court, the site's immediate setting presented an image of seclusion, looking across a garden and orchard to a steep-sided and closed-in valley. To the north a much more expansive setting opened up, comprising views over the sylvan scenery of the Dart valley and including a walled deer park within a loop of the River Dart, enclosed by the Martin family in the fourteenth century but extended to the east and west in the early years of the fifteenth to create a suitably private setting.[96] Beyond it, the rugged scenery of Dartmoor provided a striking visual contrast to the organised estate centre landscape, complete with seigneurial church, immediately around the hall.

Dartington reminds us that noble buildings faced more than one way, their access arrangements and architecture giving quite different visual impressions to different audiences. Another exceptionally good case in point, also in Devon, this time on the northern fringes of Dartmoor, shows how this relationship could work for a fortified structure. Built along a locally prominent ridge oriented south-west–north-east along the line of the West Okemont River, Okehampton castle displayed two different faces in its developed fourteenth-century phases, when it was the seat of the Courtenay family (see *Figure 21*).[97] On the north, anybody passing or travelling to visit the site along the Old Okehampton Road would have seen an embattled building of unmistakably military appearance dominated by a curtain wall. A string of five fishponds along the base of the site enhanced the dramatic vista and a remodelling of the earthworks, including enlargement of the motte, further accentuated its imposing appearance from this perspective.[98] The southern face displayed an entirely different character. A series of generously proportioned window seats in well-appointed lodgings looked straight out onto the great seigneurial deer park, unimpeded by any curtain wall, with Dartmoor again a rugged backdrop. Other examples can be found, such as Robert de Ros I's rebuilding and landscaping of Helmsley (Yorkshire, North Riding) in the late twelfth or early thirteenth century to provide similarly contrasting 'public' and 'private' views respectively towards the town and deer park.[99] But on the whole we are only dimly aware of how such different scenery was valued by noble builders.

That more modest structures could still provide views over designed surroundings is shown by the example of Barden Tower (Yorkshire, North Riding) (*Figure 33*), a late-fifteenth-century tower-house remodelled for Sir Henry Clifford and forming the centrepiece of a designed landscape featuring surrounding garden terraces, great and little parks and a rabbit warren (see p. 114). Sir Henry's chamber windows provided views over the gardens towards the valley beyond, while the chapel built adjacent was positioned carefully on a lowered terrace so as not to disrupt the view; a slightly later addition of the

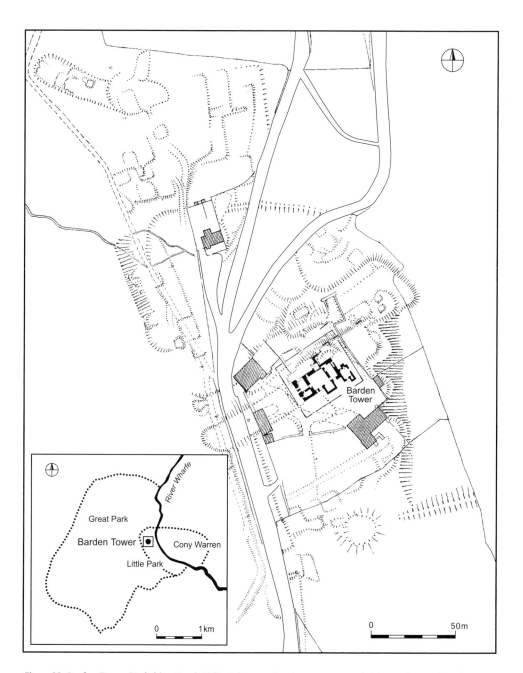

Figure 33. Barden Tower (Yorkshire, North Riding): late medieval tower surrounded by garden earthworks and with accompanying 'great' and 'little' parks. Based on Moorhouse 2003b, with additions.

early sixteenth century was a porch that doubled as a banqueting tower, carefully fenestrated to give excellent all-round views.[100]

The visual links between medieval towers and sightlines in the opposite direction leave no doubt at all that elements of buildings were meant to be seen from landscapes. An interesting site in this regard is Monkton Old Hall, a substantial stone-built medieval domestic building situated prominently above the castle and market town of Pembroke (Pembrokeshire). Built in the ostentatious style of a northern French fortified house and comprising a hall with a later cross-wing over vaulted undercrofts, the structure was part of a larger complex of some pretension which included a surviving dovecot and walled orchard.[101] Standing close to the Priory Church of St Nicholas, it was built as the *hospitium* (or guest-house) of the Benedictine Priory in the late fourteenth or early fifteenth century. Adjacent to the hall is an enclosed and compartmented garden that, despite secondary landscaping and terracing, has probable medieval origins.[102] What is most significant is the spectacular view afforded of the castle to the north-east, which is exhibited from the most complementary of angles with the circular donjon as its centrepiece and water all around (*Black and White Plate 29*). One of the secondary functions of monastic establishments closely associated with castles was to provide additional accommodation, and it is not difficult to imagine that the views from this facility were intended to give a favourable impression of the elite ensemble below.

It is well understood that castles were sometimes intended to be intervisible with extensive territories. In the south-east English midlands, for exam-

Plate 29. View of Pembroke castle and its setting from the garden of Monkton Old Hall. (Photograph: Oliver Creighton)

ple, the selection of sites with exceptional 'viewsheds' was certainly apparent in the choices made by Norman castle-builders; sites such as Great Staughton (Cambridgeshire), built shortly after the Conquest for Eustance, Sheriff of Huntingdon, were selected as estate centres partly because they were well placed to overlook land and, moreover, were visible from within the associated lordships and on routes of approach.[103] The highest points within a locality were not necessarily chosen for castles, and the siting of some important medieval buildings on 'false crests' is intriguing, and it may seem surprising to some that many medieval castles were overlooked by higher ground nearby. Guildford castle (Surrey) is a good example. While its gleaming white walls were particularly visible both from the valley floor below and the heights above, this contrasted with the convoluted and indirect route of approach to the site.[104]

Also of great importance here are changing ideas about the functions and significance of the keep, or donjon, a word derived from the Latin *dominium*, or 'lordship'.[105] Analysis of a number of great towers has revealed architectural features explicitly associated with lordly display to surrounding landscapes and populations. The Norman donjon at Richmond (Yorkshire, North Riding), built in the 1170s, features three large openings at first-floor level that provided a balcony-like feature; another case is Norwich castle, where a balcony set into the donjon overlooked the market place of the replanned town. Other relevant sites with similar features connected with display include Caldicot (Monmouthshire), Chepstow (Monmouthshire) and Corfe (Dorset). This was, of course, a two-way process: architectural elaboration ensured both that the location of the upper chambers was apparent to even distant observers, while the exceptional scope of the views obtained from within afforded a form of visual control. French donjons whose dimensions and planning suggest construction for propaganda as opposed to residential purposes have been termed 'marker towers', and include sites such as Montbrun (Haute-Vienne) and Commarque (Dordogne).[106] In an English context a clear case in point is the well-preserved Norman donjon at Hedingham (Essex). A reassessment of this site has demonstrated that the structure was an architectural showpiece dating to the second half of the twelfth century, built primarily as a symbolic and ceremonial structure to mark the elevation of the de Vere family to the status of earls of Oxford.[107] The most ostentatious architectural features were windows at the very top of the tower, in what appeared from the outside to be a fourth storey. They were actually 'dummy' features designed with an eye for the impression they would create to those looking at the donjon from the surrounding landscape, while the high-status apartments below looked out on to the 'little park' located close to the castle.[108] The Norman donjon at Rochester, where the top-floor windows most visible from the castle's surroundings are the only ones to receive external decoration, bears comparison.[109] Structures such as London's White Tower featured exterior decoration recalling *Rominitas*, creating an impression far removed from the popular view of the 'keep' as a grim stronghold of last resort.[110]

Mounts and walkways

Just as the upper portions of multi-storey medieval buildings afforded 'com-posed' prospects over designed landscapes, so there is also evidence that, con-versely, features within parks and gardens could act as viewing points. An excep-tional example is the 'Giltern Arbour', which lay within the gardens of the Dominican Priory at Perth (Perthshire). An ostentatious building with a deco-rated gilded roof, this seems to have more resembled a summerhouse than the image of a vine-clad timber structure that is usually associated with the word 'arbour', and was substantial enough to have been adapted as a grandstand when Robert III and his entourage observed the infamous 'Battle of the Clans' from its roof in 1396.[111]

The prospect mound as strictly defined – an artificial eminence intended as a viewing point from which to admire a park or garden – is essentially a post-medieval phenomenon, however. These features are also problematic from an archaeological point of view, being often difficult to discriminate from similar earthworks such as windmill mounds, prone to remodelling, and difficult to date. That said, the likelihood is that prospect mounds associated with sites of medieval high-status residences are mainly later additions. At places such as Canons Ashby Priory (Northamptonshire) and Garendon (Leicestershire), for example, prospect mounds were components within designed settings created for post-Dissolution country houses, while at Laxton (Nottinghamshire) a 'pimple' on the top of a medieval motte is a similar feature, built to view a Tudor mansion and its gardens in the bailey.[112] In contrast, the reuse of the motte of Whittington castle (Shropshire) as a viewing mount has a probable medieval context (see p. 68–9).

But good evidence exists that other forms of medieval earthwork were designed to provide contrived views of elite settings. The only widely acknowl-edged examples of medieval ornamental garden mounds are those in college gar-dens at Oxford and Cambridge, although their original context is much obscured by later reworking.[113] Archaeological investigation of the mount in the gardens of New College, Oxford, did not date the feature with any precision, although records for the large-scale movement of soil into the garden in 1529 may indi-cate its existence by then, and it was certainly being maintained by the 1590s.[114] Located immediately inside the north-east corner of the city wall, the 15-metre-high square-based mound was clearly built to provide views out beyond the city as well as over the formal garden associated with it. Medieval 'park mounts' pro-vide other examples of early garden features with some of the functions of prospect mounds. Only one is known through excavation: 'Giant's Hill' at Swine (Yorkshire, East Riding).[115] Built as a conical timber-revetted mound *c*.3.5 metres high, this feature has been dated by excavation to the fourteenth or fifteenth century – certainly too late for a motte – and it lay on the edge of a hunting park in existence by the end of the thirteenth century; it is almost certainly a viewing mount built for the admiration of surrounding parkland attached to a Cistercian nunnery.[116]

Plate 30. Framlingham castle (Suffolk), showing the mere that was an essential part of the site's setting and could be seen from chamber windows. (Photograph: Oliver Creighton)

In other cases earthwork terraces, walkways or other elevated features in the immediate settings of residences provided viewing opportunities. The garden at Framlingham (Suffolk) first recorded in 1302, almost certainly occupied the small embanked court that lay between the castle and the mere (*Black and White Plate 30*), with the great deer park stretching away beyond.[117] While this feature seems likely to have formed the bailey of Roger Bigod's early castle, it is tempting to see the flat-topped bank around its perimeter as having been later adapted as a walkway or viewing terrace. An essentially similar arrangement existed at Kilpeck (Herefordshire) by the end of the thirteenth century, where the slopes beneath the shell keep are still marked by the banks of a medieval garden or orchard enclosure, below which lay a mere crossed by an elevated walkway, with the deer park and rugged skyline of the Black Mountains beyond.[118] Other insight comes from sites that have been excavated. Remarkable evidence of an early viewing mount comes from The Belgrave Moat, on the outskirts of Chester, which was the fourteenth-century rural retreat and garden of a prominent royal servant (see p. 90–1). Archaeological investigation of garden features surrounding the site of this moated residence has revealed a sub-rectangular garden bed containing soil *c*.16 centimetres deep and four-teenth-century artefacts, which was centrally placed on the flat summit of a prominent mound *c*.16 metres in diameter. This and a separate triangular mound seem to have been moated vantage points from which the site could be viewed; the latter feature contained post-holes suggestive of a bridge between them, and both were linked to a raised walkway.[119] At Clarendon Park

Plate 31. Clarendon Palace (Wiltshire), showing the site of the great hall and other high-status domestic buildings that looked out on to a series of garden platforms. (Photograph: Oliver Creighton)

(Wiltshire), gardens on the north side of the complex included a series of terraced viewing platforms (*Black and White Plate 31*) that overlook the inner park and the 'Tilting Field' within.[120] Occupying an area of *c*.140 x 50 metres, this garden-like space was defined by a large earthwork along the edge of the hillside, demonstrated by excavation to have been built, probably in the thirteenth century, as a flint retaining wall holding back a mass of chalk rubble and creating a levelled platform in front of the domestic quarters and other buildings.[121] Alterations to the bishop of Winchester's moated manor house at Witney (Oxfordshire) in the period *c*.1140–75 included the construction of a raised terrace, retained by a low wall, alongside the east range of domestic lodgings and next to the solar tower.[122] This development, which raised the ground surface to first-floor level, can only be interpreted as the creation of a garden feature or viewing platform adjacent to, and accessible from, the highest-status and most private areas of the complex, where views had previously been obscured by the curtain wall. Orientated towards the east, the terrace provided a vantage point that afforded a contrived view over the rabbit warren, fishponds, mill and meadows along the River Windrush, while the chapel that bounded the terrace to the north blocked views of the barnyard and the working face of the site.[123] Other relevant examples covered elsewhere in this book include Bodiam (East Sussex) (see p. 5), Leeds (Kent) (see p. 180–1), Ludgershall (Wiltshire) (see p. 136), Nunney (Somerset) (see p. 81–2) and Wardour (Wiltshire) (see p. 26).

The further horizon: monastic designed landscapes?

While evidence for the design of medieval secular landscapes for structured viewing seems compelling, especially for the later period, the intriguing question remains as to whether monastic sites might also have been embedded within immediate settings 'designed' for visual impact. This book certainly does not pretend to provide the answer, but the possibility should at least be acknowledged, and the area highlighted as a fascinating avenue for potential future research. At one level, of course, monastic precincts themselves formed sacred landscapes in their own right and not necessarily landscapes in miniature, as detailed study of Norwich Cathedral Close has shown. Occupying a vast area that occupied a significant part of the entire city, the precinct can be conceptualised as a 'sacred space' comprising zones that were accessible and permeable to different degrees, and characterised by different levels of sanctity, its 'design' drawing quite deliberately on the imagery of nostalgic symbols to harness the power of the past.[124]

Other insight can come from literary sources. Idealisation of monastery and setting as *locus amoenus* (delightful place) features in literary descriptions found in hagiographies, poems and monastic chronicles.[125] The Glastonbury Chronicle, for example, in depicting the abbey's landscape setting as an 'island of apples', seeks to present an image of beauty and fertility enriched with classical and biblical references.[126] A twelfth-century poem to *Little Downham* describes what amounts to a designed setting around a monastic site deep in the Cambridgeshire Fens, including references to a 'green grove ... well suitable for frequent hunts, adorned with flowers and set about with banked-up turf'.[127] Other parts of the poem describe rivers full of fish, chattering birds, a fertile agricultural hinterland, beautiful woodland, a shining palace and a garden bearing all kinds of fruit. While this is an idealised model drawing on classical influences, it should be noted that the checklist of elite landscape features is essentially similar to that found at a high-status secular site, including what appear to be earthwork ramparts (*terrarum*), giving the beautiful island site a fortress-like character in the mind of the poet.[128]

Given the traditional view of the monastic pleasure garden as an inward-looking contemplative space exclusively reserved for the use of the community, the notion that the settings of religious houses were manipulated for effect might seem to defy reason. Yet monastic houses hold great potential for the preservation of controlled and structured approach routes. Countless sites occupy isolated, watery or hilltop positions, raising questions over whether routes of access were contrived to impress visitors – abbots, patrons and royalty.[129] Archaeological survey of superbly preserved earthworks around the Premonstratensian house of Halesowen (Worcestershire) (*Colour Plate 11*) has enabled access arrangements to be reconstructed in some detail.[130] The site was set near the end of a long spur with valleys on either side and the principal route of access was from the north, leading to a gatehouse that was clearly part of a structured approach, across an earthen causeway that provided visitors with superb views over a line of five ponds cascading into one another down the valley.[131] In many other low-lying sites in watery settings entrance causeways would have similarly structured the approach to precincts, as at Catley (Lincolnshire), where the end of a causeway was developed as a formal entrance to the Gilbertine Priory.[132] Water certainly conditioned the way other ecclesiastical sites were accessed and experienced; the location of so many minster churches near water is striking.[133] In other contexts, chapels positioned near entrance causeways and gatehouses to precincts were another important part of the experience of entering the monastic sphere.[134]

Abbeys and priories with extensive suites of fishponds, such as St Benet (Norfolk), by the River Bure, demand particular attention in this regard.[135] Debate over the purposes of monastic fishponds has centred on the relative importance of their commercial and subsistence functions, but has largely ignored the possibility of any ornamental, aesthetic or symbolic significance.[136] These were clearly important factors when monastic precincts were remoulded as garden settings for post-Dissolution country houses, but we may wonder whether this change from functionalism to ornamentation was so clear-cut. A danger for clear interpretation is that sixteenth- and seventeenth-century landscaping of precincts could create earthworks that superficially resemble the dramatic watery landscapes known to have existed at medieval secular sites.[137] At Cerne Abbas (Dorset), for instance, a series of formal gardens north-east of the former Benedictine abbey included an enclosing raised walk and canal remodelled from the precinct boundary.[138] But in other cases apparently utilitarian monastic buildings may have had unrecognised aesthetic significance: at Pilton (Somerset), for example, the great barn of Glastonbury Abbey was clearly intended to be seen from the side facing the abbot's manor house on the opposite side of the valley; it was this face of the building that displayed ornamentation, including cruciform-shaped vents, in contrast to the more functional appearance of the other side.[139] Another key area for future work will be to examine whether monastic foundation and landscaping represented a phase within a longer-term continuum of ritual activity, as seems to have been the case with the landscape of religious houses in the Witham valley of Lincolnshire.[140]

Chapter Six Notes

[1] Faulkner 1963; Fairclough 1992; King 2003.

[2] Howes 2002, 205.

[3] Barron 1974, 69; Elliott 1997, 107.

[4] Thacker 1979, 85.

[5] Ackerman 1990, 73–8.

[6] For an exception, see Richardson 2003b.

[7] Coope 1986, 45–6.

[8] James 1990, 84.

[9] Ashbee 2006, 80.

[10] Colvin 1982, 17.

[11] Schofield 1994, 84–6.

[12] Coope 1986, 44–5.

[13] Cooper 1999, 820.

[14] Henisch 2002, 154–5.

[15] For example, the gardens viewed from the apartments of the earl of Flanders in Bruges: Berners 1901–3, Book II, ch. 30.

[16] Harwood 1985, 201; see also Luttrell 1974, 142–3.

[17] Mooney and Arn 2005.

[18] McDiarmid 1973, 84.

[19] Wood 1965, 346, 351.

[20] Saunders 2006, 58.

[21] For an earlier interpretation of the tiers of motte-top masonry structures as 'fighting platforms', see Renn 1969, 11.

[22] Saunders 2006, 15–17, 230–1.

[23] Herring 2003, 47.

[24] Herring 2003, 47–8.

[25] Barnwell 2007, 32–3.

[26] Guy 2005, 16; Jope 1951, 42–3.

[27] Rees 1999b, 69–71.

[28] Allen and Hiller 2002, 196, 215.

[29] Everson *et al*. 1991, 130.

[30] Bowden 2005.

[31] Prestwich 1980, 80.

[32] James 1990, 83–4.

[33] Tolley 1991, 175–6; Parsons 1995, 53.

[34] See Parsons 1995, 53.

[35] Longnon and Cazelles 1969.

[36] Cooper 1999, 820.

[37] Power 1928, 19–30.

[38] Power 1928, 17–30, 195–204.

[39] Nevanlinna and Taavitsainen 1993.

[40] Smyser 1956, 300–1.

[41] Harwood 1985, 194; see also Luttrell 1974, 142.

[42] Richardson 2007, 39.

[43] See Gilchrist 1999, 128–36.

[44] Richardson 2003b, 140–1.

[45] Gilchrist 1999, 137; Steane 2001, 107.

[46] Dawson 1976, 52; see also Richardson 2003b, 144–6.

[47] Dawson 1976, 52.

[48] Roberts 1997.

[49] James and Robinson 1988, 22.

[50] Colvin 1963, 927.

[51] Neal 1971, 32, 118; Parsons 1995, 53; Woolgar 2006, 224.

[52] Cunliffe and Munby 1985, 20–2, 124, 142–3.

[53] Colvin 1963, 1016–17; 1986, 11.

[54] See Richardson 2003b, 148.

[55] Colvin 1963, 862–3.

[56] MacGregor 1983, 79, 102.

[57] MacGregor 1983, 102; see also Brown 2004 on the designed setting of the castle.

[58] Liddiard 2005b, 41–2.

[59] Gilchrist 1999, 133–4.

[60] Turner 2006b, 76–80.

[61] Moorhouse 2003b, 330.

[62] Gilchrist 1995, 29.

[63] Harwood 1985, 213.

[64] Rieser 1946, 152.

[65] See, for instance, James 1990, 93–4.

[66] Ashbee 2004b.

[67] Reeve and Thurlby 2005.

[68] Yarrow 2003, 12; Reeve and Thurlby 2005, 168.

[69] Colvin 1963, 695.

[70] Woolgar 2006, 224.

[71] Taylor 1998b, 36.

[72] Turner 2004, 297–8; 2006a, 42.

[73] Turner 2006a, 42.

[74] Wilson 2002, 55–9, 65.

[75] Schofield 1984, 81.

[76] Chandler 1993, 538–9.

[77] Darlington 2001, 12, 89–90, 99.

[78] Bowden 2005, 10.

[79] Mileson 2007, 24.

[80] Girouard 1978, 73–4.

[81] Emery 2000, 456–8.

[82] Emery 2000, 211–20; Stocker 2006, 143.

[83] Dennison 2005, 108.

[84] Barry 1987, 190.

[85] Pollock 2004, 167–72.

[86] Aalen 2006, 76; Dennison and Richardson 2007–8a, 170.

[87] Moorhouse 1986; see also Taylor 2000, 42–3.

[88] McNeill 2006.

[89] Davison 2001, 8–9.

[90] Fairclough 1992, 361–2; see also Emery 1996, 88–91.

[91] Chapelot 1998; Wilson 2002, 64–5.

[92] Cazelles and Rathofer 1988, 58, 224.

[93] Emery 1970; Emery 2000, 534–1.

[94] English Heritage Register of Parks and Gardens, No. GD1421.

[95] Emery 2005, 157–8.

[96] Emery 1970, 19–20; Emery forthcoming; see also Waterhouse 2003, 77–8.

[97] See Creighton and Higham 2004.

[98] Probert 2004, 22.

[99] Barnwell and Everson 2004.

[100] Moorhouse 2003b, 346–8.

[101] Cobb 1880.

[102] Cadw 2002, 272–6.

[103] Lowerre 2006, 133–5.

[104] Poulton 2005, 1.

[105] See Creighton 2005b, 66–7.

[106] Marshall 2002a; 2002b, 33.

[107] Dixon and Marshall 2003, 306.

[108] Liddiard 2005b, 39–40.

[109] Marshall 2002a, 146.

[110] Dixon 2002, 11.

[111] Cooper 1999, 819.

[112] Wright 2008, 15, 39.

[113] Thacker 1979, 85.

[114] Bell 1994, 116.

[115] Varley 1973; another good candidate is 'The Mount' at Etton (Yorkshire, East Riding): English Heritage National Monuments Record No. SE 94 SE 8.

[116] Varley 1973, 145–6; Neave 1991, 52; Moorhouse 2003a, 202.

[117] Taylor 1998b, 40.

[118] Whitehead 1995, 199–200.

[119] Turner *et al.* 1988, 61–7.

[120] Richardson 2005, 61–3; James and Gerrard 2007, 70–3.

[121] James and Robinson 1988, 79.

[122] Allen and Hiller 2002, 213–14.

[123] Allen and Hiller 2002, 194.

[124] Gilchrist 2005, 236–57.

[125] Zink 2008.

[126] Clarke 2006, 2, 72–3.

[127] Fairweather 2005, 490.

[128] Clarke 2006, 80–3.

[129] Everson and Williamson 1998, 144.

[130] Brown 2005a.

[131] Brown 2005a, 29.

[132] Hunt and Brown 2005, 24–5.

[133] Blair 2005, 193.

[134] Everson and Stocker 2007.

[135] Williamson 2006a, 132–3.

[136] Bond 1988a; 1998; Currie 1989, 151–2.

[137] Wilson 1991, 24–6; Everson 1996c.

[138] Riley and Wilson-North 2003, 104–5; see also Everson 1989a, 143–4, for Lincolnshire examples.

[139] Bond 2004, 138.

[140] Stocker and Everson 2003.

Touchstones to the Past: Legacies

Although the central aim of this book is to examine evidence for 'design' in the medieval landscape, a look forward at subsequent developments is instructive. The conventional story is that, in a British context, designed landscapes started life in the sixteenth century, growing up from the 'stiff and geometric' gardens of the Tudor and Stuart periods that contrasted so markedly with the later landscape parks that were imitated across Europe.[1] One thing that has happened in recent years to change this situation is an upsurge in archaeological evidence for gardens and designed landscapes before the Renaissance, so that the developments of the Tudor period can now be seen as less of a case of outright innovation and more of a new take on inherited practices. Sixteenth-century gardens and designed landscapes looked backwards as well as forwards.[2] Even at the very top of the social spectrum, many elite settings were essentially rearrangements of familiar elements and concepts, albeit larger in scale and at a greater level of complexity than before. The previous chapter has shown, meanwhile, that some of the supposed hallmarks of sixteenth-century polite landscaping, such as elevated views, were not unknown in the earlier period. Such is the body of scholarship that designed landscapes of this period have attracted that the following section provides a digest of the more relevant themes in their study rather than offering substantially new data.[3]

What is undeniable is that new forms of documentary and pictorial source became available for the study of elite landscapes, particularly in the form of topographical drawings and treatises, while the estate maps that multiply in number from the second half of the sixteenth century are statements of a new attitude to the control of land. Exceptionally, 'before' and 'after' estate maps showcase transformations of estate landscapes that might incorporate and reference select features of the medieval past but eliminate others, as at Holdenby (Northamptonshire), where a designed setting created around Sir Christopher Hatton's new house entailed the eradication of a village but the retention of its church.[4] Yet no sixteenth-century garden or designed landscape survives intact; as with the medieval period, we are left either with abandoned fragments or palimpsests redesigned by subsequent generations. Nonetheless, that the garden designs of the period often entailed the creation of enormous earthwork features ensures that, in general, the physical evidence has proved more resistant to destruction than that of the preceding period.

Formality was the hallmark of the sixteenth-century garden, as manifested in the interlaced knot-type arrangements of plants and neatly clipped hedges that sub-divided gardens into neat compartments. Earthwork terraces and enclosing walls followed similarly regular lines, as did the plans of artificial ponds, canals and, ultimately, 'parterres' that comprised square and rectangular plots delimited by paths and terraces. The period saw the increasing prominence of heraldry in the garden: as well as emblems of office displayed on gateways in the medieval style, knot gardens and garden mounts also drew on heraldic symbolism in their organisation. The emerging science of military engineering was another occasional influence, as expressed most obviously in Henry VIII's banqueting house at Nonsuch, but also in the angular bastion-like earthworks sometimes found at the corners of terraces and walkways.[5] Garden buildings became more diverse, permanent and elaborate, meanwhile, while lodges proliferated and were built on a far larger scale than before.[6]

Not only are the physical characteristics of sixteenth-century designed landscapes better understood, but so too are their social and intellectual contexts. It is something of a cliché that the relative internal stability of the sixteenth century provided the social elite with the opportunity of turning their attentions away from castle-building towards increasingly fashionable peaceful pursuits, of which gardening was the prime example.[7] Sixteenth-century garden design shows an intriguing intersection of prevailing concepts of taste and fashion with the idiosyncrasies and individuality of the owners, including the physical expression of religious sensibilities.[8] Furthermore, the boom in garden construction after *c*.1500 did not occur simply because design was permeating further down the social hierarchy than before. The sale and grant of monastic estates after the confiscations of the 1530s and 40s created a redistribution of land on a massive scale and a fundamental change in the size and composition of the social elite in a period that coincided with the new ideas of the Renaissance. Supported by new forms of wealth, this aspirational gentry class had different ambitions, outlooks and rivalries, for which garden design became an important means of expression.[9] This was not entirely new, as the previous chapter has shown: men on the make – socially climbing knights, courtiers and esquires – were responsible for a large proportion of new parks in the fifteenth century.[10]

Research into the gardens and designed landscapes of the period has been uneven, however, with those associated with early Tudor palaces being particularly well studied and documentary and art-historical approaches dominating the subject until relatively recently.[11] Archaeology has since played a key role in transforming studies of the Renaissance garden, with field survey in particular emphasising the status of the sixteenth century as a boom time for garden and landscape design across the gentry classes.[12] Several hundred relict examples of sixteenth-century gardens or designed landscapes have been recognised in Britain, although knowledge is greatest in the parts of England that have been systematically recorded by the Royal Commission for the Historical Monuments of England.[13] The inventories for Cambridgeshire and Northamptonshire, in particular, are packed with garden features of the period, and in England alone it is estimated that well over 5,000 formal gardens were created between the early sixteenth and early eighteenth centuries, with perhaps 20 per cent leaving tangible physical traces.[14] Archaeological survey can also show individuality in design: the circular arrangement of gardens with associated ponds adjacent to Croxton Hall (Cambridgeshire) are of sixteenth- or seventeenth-century date, for example.[15] A peculiarity of the evidence is that formal gardens are often better preserved where the house that they once accompanied has been totally demolished. Schemes of polite landscaping that were themselves unfinished and abandoned have particular importance, as at Lyveden (Northamptonshire), where an extensive complex of formal gardens partly built by Sir Thomas Tresham *c*.1597–1604 has been mapped.[16] Excavation of sixteenth-century gardens is uncommon, however, with the project at Kirby Hall (Northamptonshire) the outstanding example (see also p. 27). Here, the 'Great Garden' has been restored according to its appearance in the mid seventeenth century, although excavated evidence has also allowed reconstruction of an underlying sixteenth-century arrangement.[17] A comparable example in Scotland is Aberdour (Fife), where the layout of a terraced garden created in front of the medieval keep in the second half of the sixteenth century has been clarified by excavation.[18]

The setting of Thornbury castle (Gloucestershire) (*Colour Plate 12*) highlights many of the key characteristics of early-sixteenth-century polite landscaping. An extravagant magnate house built in castellated style for Edward, third Duke of Buckingham, following receipt of a licence to crenellate in 1510, but ultimately left unfinished, the 'castle' was accompanied by an elaborate arrangement of three enclosed gardens that gives the impression of a suite of linked outdoor rooms.[19] On the south side of the complex a quadrangular Privy Garden was surrounded on three sides by a crenellated wall that supported timber-framed galleries. Although these no longer survive, doorways in the walls show how they were accessed and lent the central space a theatre-like appearance, while oriel windows in adjacent apartments similarly afforded views down onto the garden.[20] An adjoining enclosed garden was accessible via passages and raised galleries, while beyond the residential core a suite of pleasure gardens contained an orchard planted with fruit trees and roses as well as arbours and further galleries.[21] The model seems to have been Henry VII's palace at Richmond (Surrey), where wooden garden galleries supported on posts existed (at Thornbury the outer wall was of stone), although the ultimate inspiration was probably the garden complexes of Blois and Gaillon in France.[22] The impact of Thornbury was not restricted to the upper echelons of society, however. Three parks (New, Marlwood and Eastwood Parks) embraced over 400 hectares.[23] Some thirty years

LEEDS TRINITY UNIVERSITY

after building at Thornbury had started, John Leland noted how the inhabitants cursed the duke as his 'fine park' incorporated 'a great deal of very fertile arable land, to make good glades for coursing', while its subsequent enlargement to encompass an area six miles round caused further displeasure among tenants.[24]

Royal palaces and their settings

In England, Henry VIII's reign saw extravagant expenditure not only on his famous palaces but also on their grounds. The changing use of space in gardens reflects the radically changing composition and outlook of the royal household during the period.[25] In early Tudor palace complexes the most private areas were not discrete buildings, detached from the main residence in the medieval style of Kenilworth or Sheen (see pp. 93 and 61); rather, the most exclusive spheres for the retreat of royal parties were accommodated on single sites through sophisticated spatial planning and new forms of courtly etiquette. The inspiration behind these extravagant designs was complex; the French Château de Fontainebleau is often cited as a major influence,[26] but the pleasure gardens of Hampton Court show the influence of the Burgundian court,[27] while the conspicuous display of armorial display in garden designs reflects an English contribution.[28]

The most magnificent gardens, at Hampton Court (*Figure 34*: top), rivalled the fame of the palace itself.[29] By 1547, Henrician remodelling of the grounds of Cardinal Wolsey's confiscated palace had created an integrated suite of pleasure gardens. To the south were the Privy Garden, the Pond Yard and Mount Garden, surrounded by brick walls and earthen banks that afforded views in and out of the grounds, as well as the combined boat house and grandstand that was the Thames-side Water Gallery.[30] The design of the Privy Garden is particularly well understood. Laid out in a simple geometric design resembling a chequer board, its compartments were coloured red (using brick dust), white (sand) and green (lawn), and punctuated with elaborately carved and brightly coloured heraldic posts, each of which held a vane that revolved with the wind, as famously depicted by Anthonis van Wyngaerde.[31] Some of the walls surrounding the Privy Garden contained windows, as is also clear in Wyngaerde's drawings.[32] To the north, a Privy Orchard lay within a moated enclosure and beyond it lay a tiltyard and the Great Orchard, with its centrally placed banqueting house; beyond these the palace grounds were embedded within a series of parks, resembling the compartmentalised arrangement of gardens but on a massive scale, including the House Park and Course (designed together for deer coursing), and the Hare Warren (for hare coursing).[33]

Something of the settings of two of Henry's other palaces has been revealed through excavation. At Nonsuch (Surrey), large-scale excavation in the summers of 1959 and 1960 extended to embrace several important garden features,[34] while the gardens of Whitehall were partially excavated in the 1930s in advance of government office building.[35]

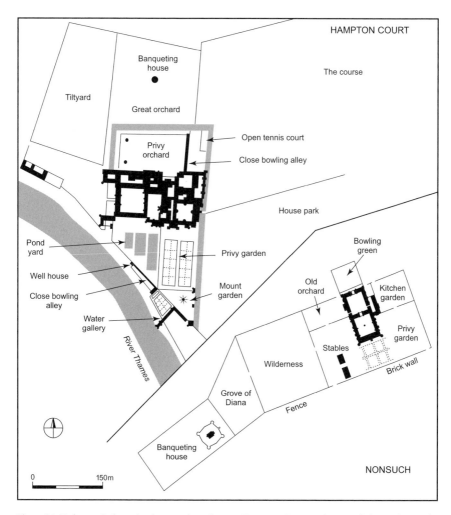

Figure 34. Tudor-period royal palaces and gardens at Hampton Court and Nonsuch (Surrey). Based on Biddle 1999, Biddle 2005 and Thurley 1993, with additions.

Relatively little is known of Wolsey's gardens at York Place (the ecclesiastical palace that pre-dated its rebuilding under Henry VIII as Whitehall), although a freestanding pavilion or banqueting house, known archaeologically from its massive arched foundations of brick, probably stood centrally within these, overlooking the river.[36] Henry VIII's Privy Garden at Whitehall has been characterised as a Renaissance reworking of a traditional model of *hortus conclusus*-type garden design.[37] Among the more important additions to the complex was a gallery between the Great Garden and Privy Gardens, which were decorated, like Hampton Court, with heraldic beasts on posts and rails.[38] In a wider context, Henry's palace was secluded through a series of land purchases that created a royal green belt of parkland, emphasising its isolation from the machinery of government in Westminster; royal rights to these areas were confirmed in an Act of Parliament of 1536 at the same time as the Liberty of the Tower was reconfirmed, showing intense interest in the exclusivity of palaces.[39]

Built from 1538 as a bizarre mishmash of medieval anachronism and Renaissance planning, Nonsuch 'Palace' (actually a 'privy palace' or hunting lodge) was the innermost of an intricately nested series of designed spaces comprising a suite of walled gardens and pleasure grounds entirely enveloped within the Little Park (272 hectares) and a larger Great Park (405 hectares).[40] The earlier manorial site and church of Cuddington were removed without trace, although ancient trees were retained, perhaps giving the parkland the appearance of being older than it really was.[41] While the residence itself was never completed the park was stocked with deer in November 1538, when paling was established, presumably to stop deer entering the site during construction. Two walled enclosures formed the heart of this designed landscape: one, around the palace buildings, was compartmentalised into a privy garden, kitchen garden and orchard; the other, adjoining to the west and of similar size, contained a 'wilderness' (*Figure 34*: bottom). Occupying a formerly sloping site levelled at great cost and effort, the construction of the terrace for the privy garden entailing the removal of some 24,000 cubic yards of spoil.[42] Detached to the west was a banqueting house, raised upon a revetted mound whose bastioned plan directly emulated the innovative Henrician artillery forts of the period.[43] A Parliamentary Survey of 1650 records that the central multi-storey timber-framed building was provided with large windows and surmounted with a lantern, while every corner of the site was provided with a 'balcone ... placed for prospect',[44] which, along with the pavilion's elevated position, confirm its function as a stage for observing activities in the surrounding park. Despite this relatively full understanding of the palace's setting, virtually nothing is known about the detail of the actual garden arrangements in Henry VIII's reign, such as the range of species grown, although more information is available following the sale of the grounds by the Crown in 1556.[45]

Opportunities for viewing these designed settings were often provided by galleries. Built in the first couple of years of the sixteenth century and depicted in detail on Wyngaerde's view of the site, those at Richmond Palace were particularly early, providing views both inwards onto the privy gardens and outwards over the Thames.[46] At The More, Rickmansworth (Hertfordshire), Wolsey is also known to have built a timber gallery 253 feet long which crossed the moat and terminated with two turrets in the garden, while Bridewell Palace in the City of London provides another early example.[47] Early Tudor palaces also incorporated the full panoply of sporting and recreational facilities, which were integrated into their gardens and pleasure grounds. The major sites featured their own tiltyards, complete with galleries and sometimes ostentatious towered pavilions (as at Greenwich and Hampton Court), as well as tennis courts, bowling alleys, cockpits, hawks' mews and archery butts.[48] Henry VIII's additions to the gardens at Greenwich included a water maze and tiltyard, while the park was stocked for a short time with peacocks.[49] While the sport of bowling is known from the thirteenth century, few if any formal bowling pavilions can be dated before *c*.1500, and the earliest examples are from royal contexts.[50] Besides the king's palaces, sporting facilities of this nature are found only in the residences of the most important magnates and favoured courtiers: the bishop of Winchester's palace at Southwark, for example, possessed a bowling alley with gallery and a tennis court by *c*.1550,[51] while Charles Brandon, the great favourite of Henry VIII, had a tiltyard built at Tattershall (Lincolnshire), showcasing his proximity to the king through the display of a discernibly royal activity.[52] Another good example is the *c*.100-metre-square brick-walled tiltyard enclosure laid out adjacent to Bradgate House (Leicestershire) for the first earl of Dorset *c*.1500.[53] Alongside these relatively well-studied examples, extensive expenditure on royal privy gardens is detailed across the full range of royal houses in the first half of the sixteenth century, including castles (Baynard's castle, London), manor houses (Chelsea, Middlesex) and palaces both newly built (Bridewell, London) and those adapted from existing properties (Eltham, Kent, West Horsley, Surrey, and Woking, Surrey).[54] Religious houses converted into royal residences, as, for example, Dartford (Kent), had their own pleasure grounds and it was not unknown for monastic gardens to be stripped and reused: the gardeners at Oatlands (Surrey) found use for six loads of fruit trees pillaged from Chertsey Abbey in 1538.[55]

Gentry landscapes

In non-royal contexts, polite landscapes of the sixteenth century are found at newly established power centres as well as old seats of medieval lordship recast as gentry houses, at places such as Basing House (Hampshire) and St Donat's (Glamorgan).[56] That so many residences of the period remained in the 'single pile' mould (that is, one room in width) ensured that domestic complexes arranged around courtyards remained common. Characteristic of the period was a tendency for the regularity of building plans to be extended to their surroundings in the form of compartmentalised gardens. This was not unprecedented in the medieval period, of course: walled court gardens at Apethorpe Hall (Northamptonshire), dating to the second half of the fifteenth century, were laid out in a compartmentalised, semi-geometric fashion that mirrored the layout of residential ranges.[57]

Also fundamental here is the transition after *c*.1500 from the 'inward-looking' to the 'outward-looking' house.[58] Growing rejection of the template of medieval hierarchical house design that gave an external impression of the building's internal planning saw the adoption of architectural forms that ensured emphasis on display to the outside world for aesthetic reasons.[59] The design of gardens and pleasure grounds was bound up with this process, as the formality of the gentry house's setting complemented the order of its architecture; and, conversely, buildings were designed with domestic facilities, such as state rooms with elaborate bay windows, that overlooked designed spaces.

The physical character of confiscated monastic properties presented new architectural opportunities for those reshaping these buildings as grand secular residences, many of which constituted the family's first major country seat.[60] Crucially, the experimentation and novelty embodied in the redesign of former monastic complexes such as Lacock (Wiltshire) and Titchfield (Hampshire) extended to treatment of their settings, while the Reformation lent many of these landscapes a new iconographic dimension. The sites of abbeys, priories and other monastic properties confiscated in the Dissolution have particular potential for the preservation of earthwork remains of sixteenth-century gardens associated with mansion houses. At Haughmond Abbey (Shropshire) for instance, the 'little cloister' adjacent to the abbot's lodging was converted into a small formal garden.[61] That many of the gentry houses carved out of monastic ruins were relatively short-lived features of the landscape, leaving no above-ground traces, can be a major barrier to the correct identification of associated garden arrangements, which can appear to lack context. Detailed field survey can also show that earthworks previously interpreted as monastic in origin relate to post-Dissolution garden layouts. This is the case at Byland Abbey (Yorkshire, North Riding), where a large pond on the edge of the precinct thought to relate to the monastic layout was part of the setting of a (lost) sixteenth-century gentry house.[62] At Lewes Priory (East Sussex), an enormous mount in the north-east corner of the precinct, some 50 metres in circumference around the base and *c*.14 metres high, had been frequently interpreted as a motte; it is now known to be part of a post-Dissolution garden layout associated with the (again lost) mansion 'Lords Place', which was built out of the monastic fabric.[63]

The laying out of formal gardens in settings with still-standing monastic fabric presented a contrast between new forms of design and archaic medieval imagery. Such referencing of the medieval past within early-sixteenth-century gardens represents a counterpoint to the 'museum gardens' displaying classical antiquities in the Elizabethan and Jacobean periods.[64] In addition, we should not underestimate the symbolic value of the monastic vestiges that were deliberately incorporated into these settings. At the Lincolnshire sites of Barlings and Kirkstead, for example, compartments containing 'ruin gardens' at residences reshaped by Charles Brandon were retained to showcase the suppression of the old religious order.[65] Many of the families indulging in the sixteenth-century boom in formal garden design did so not simply at one favoured gentry house, but across networks of properties. The grammar of formal garden design certainly put limits on what could be achieved, but we should not overlook the potential individuality of designs, nor variations in layout that relate to different properties maintained for different reasons, achieving different effects for different audiences. Also characteristic of the period was the more explicit design of routes of approach to display contrived sequences of symbols and images, the most obvious manifestation of which was a renewed interest in gatehouses.

Emphasis was placed on the provision of opportunities for the observation of these designed spaces from elevated positions, whether these were provided by raised or terraced walkways and prospect mounds or architectural spaces within residences and garden buildings. The long galleries and loggias commonly found in and around sixteenth-century buildings are important here: as well as forming corridors between the more private and public areas of houses and providing neutral venues for receptions and conversation, they were also intended to facilitate the appreciation of designed settings, sometimes quite explicitly.[66] For example, the six-bay loggia at Horton Court (Gloucestershire) dates to the 1520s and looked out on to a series of terraces and remodelled medieval fishponds.[67] Hallmarks of the newly built houses of courtiers, galleries were also inserted in ingenious ways into reused monastic buildings, as at Lacock (Wiltshire) and Neath (Glamorgan), where they overlooked formal gardens.

This obsession with elevated views is reflected in a slightly different way at sites such as Broughton castle (Oxfordshire), which was remodelled in the middle of the sixteenth century by Richard Fiennes to include a rooftop banqueting house that overlooked the garden, moat and surrounding parkland.[68] Viewing mounds sometimes highlighted a juxtaposition of the ordered garden environs and the more 'natural' surroundings of the landscape beyond. The sixteenth-century prospect mound at Burton Hall (Lincolnshire) commanded contrasting views over formal gardens and a designed wilderness, for example.[69] Rabbit warrens built close to gentry houses, sometimes with pillow mounds placed on crests or in other prominent locations, were also sometimes intended to be viewed from houses, at least in midland England.[70] An important site is Lyveden (Northamptonshire), where a sixteenth-century banqueting house or lodge (the 'New Bield') formed a point of interface between a garden landscape of formality attached to the gentry house (the 'Old Bield') and the more natural scenery of a hunting park and Rockingham Forest beyond.[71] Particularly ambitious is the arrangement at Sheriff Hutton castle (Yorkshire, North Riding), where two canals, each over 10 metres wide and running for over 200 metres, flank an earthen walkway that provided contrasting views over parkland to the south and the residential range and its formal gardens to the north. They seem likely to have been built for Henry Fitzroy, earl of Richmond and bastard son of Henry VIII, in the 1520s or 30s, although they form part of a multiphase designed landscape.[72]

Raglan (Monmouthshire) provides one of the most striking examples of an old seat of lordship whose setting was upgraded according to sixteenth-century tastes (*Black and White Plate 32*). Today, the site is by some measure the most perfectly preserved designed landscape of the period in Wales because of its post-Civil War abandonment.[73] Powis castle (Montgomeryshire) provides the comparison: a seat of lordship where occupation has been continuous, famous for its seventeenth-century gardens.[74] The most tangible physical remains of the spectacular new setting created for the third and fourth earls of Worcester at Raglan in the period 1549–1628 are a series of massive earthwork terraces cut

Plate 32. Aerial view of Raglan castle (Monmouthshire), showing ornamental garden features around the site including viewing terraces and the site of a mere. (© Crown copyright: Royal Commission on the Ancient and Historical Monuments of Wales)

into the slopes on the north-west side of the site. While now bare earthwork features, these were linked and accessed via steps, probably surmounted with balustrades, and ornamented with knots and summerhouses.[75] In the valley between castle and park, which the terraces overlooked, a large artificial mere contained a series of ornamental triangular and diamond-shaped islands. Similarly large-scale remodelling of castle grounds in the period are known at Kenilworth (Warwickshire), where a suite of parterre-type gardens was created on the north side of the curtain wall, forming part of a theatrical design rich in iconography constructed in anticipation of Elizabeth I's nineteen-day visit in 1575.[76] Kenilworth's redesigned setting, which included chases, parks, woods and ponds as well as the gardens themselves, was again clearly intended to accentuate contrasts in landscape texture, providing a variety of experiences to those moving through it and observing it from a multiplicity of intended viewpoints that included a bridge and arbours as well as the castle itself.[77]

Contemporary practical literature on estate management, such as the early-seventeenth-century texts *The English Husbandman* and *A New Orchard and Garden*, remind us that men and women of the middling sort also created gardens that enabled social class and identity to be negotiated in new ways.[78] Ordered but not strictly symmetrical arrangements of orchards and mounts on a modest scale were common, showing symbolic and aesthetic considerations to be inseparable from the practicalities of estate management; for the 'parish elite' of Tudor England and Wales there was clearly no rigid boundary between the landscape of production and the landscape of leisure. The full package of Tudor garden features was certainly not adopted wholesale in every case. In Wales most sixteenth-century gardens comprised enclosures within the vicinity of the gentry house, but with no axial relationship with the residence or formal relationship with each other.[79] The Vale of Clwyd is particularly rich in examples,[80] while another significant group of surviving early formal garden layouts can be found on Anglesey.[81] Key examples of sophisticated sixteenth-century designs attached to castles include Carew (Pembrokeshire), Cardiff (Glamorgan) and Laugharne (Carmarthenshire); new gentry houses with formal gardens of the period include Plas Machen (Monmouthshire) and Llantrithyd Place (Glamorgan), which displays walled terraces, a rectilinear arrangement of fishponds and an elaborate raised walkway linked to an elevated gazebo.[82] In Scotland, gardens of the period are more usually located in fortified enclosures attached to tower-houses.[83] Craigmillar castle, located on the crest of a ridge just south of Edinburgh, preserves the remains of a particularly fine late medieval noble landscape, with a tower-house set within later courts and accompanied by walled gardens, a separate terraced garden and a huge ornamental fishpond.[84] Other sixteenth-century gardens existed at Balgonie (Fife); Balvaird castle (Perthshire), Carberry Tower (Midlothian), Neidpath castle (Peeblesshire) and Seton palace (East Lothian), many incorporating terraces, which are a hallmark of Scottish designs of the period.[85] A slightly later arrangement is preserved at Edzell (Angus) (*Black and White Plate 33*), where the enclosed garden was complete by 1604; nearby there was a much earlier seat of lordship whose motte is intervisible with the site and may have been incorporated into the tower-top views as an antique point of reference.[86]

Finally, many larger sixteenth-century town houses possessed small formal gardens, some of which are shown in stylised form on John Speed's maps of the early seventeenth century. The City of London witnessed a flourishing of gardening as monastic sites bought up by civil servants and courtiers were converted into mansion houses complete with gardens that reused these properties in intriguing ways: examples include the Augustinian Friary in Broad Street, where a depiction of *c.*1559 shows an elaborate garden with a central fountain.[87] Similar arrangements are not unknown in Wales, and a geometric arrangement of gardens, including knot-like features, is depicted in Conwy between the mansion of Plas Mawr, constructed 1576–80, and the Edwardian town wall.[88] The fashion for garden galleries also extended to urban properties:

Plate 33. Edzell (Angus), showing the early Renaissance garden within a courtyard attached to the tower-house. (Photograph: Oliver Creighton)

in 1530 one surrounding a garden space was built at the Marquis of Exeter's London house by the Master Carpenter James Nedeham.[89] Set into the upper parts of buildings, usually at the rear, such constructions comprised one- or sometimes two-storey structures that flanked gardens, with glazed windows carefully positioned in relation to the view below.[90] The aping of royal garden features encompassed summerhouses as well; these became fashionable in the suburbs of London at the same time, a good example being the two octagonal brick-built structures constructed for Prior Bolton of St Bartholomew, Smithfield, at the priory estate (now Canonbury House, Islington) in the first quarter of the sixteenth century.[91]

The legacies of medieval designed landscapes

Many of the medieval designed landscapes discussed in the preceding chapters have been obliterated, or their appearance has been altered radically, by subsequent phases of landscaping and emparkment. Tangible features of the medieval past were, however, also physically reused in later designed landscapes in often quite deliberate ways. The images of medieval buildings were transformed in a very different way by painters in the eighteenth and nineteenth centuries who saw castles and their landscapes, in particular, as a source of fascination and depicted them in new ways as the Picturesque gave way to the Romantic style.[92]

Many medieval mottes have been remodelled in elaborate ways as features within post-medieval parks and gardens, one of the clearest cases being Marlborough (Wiltshire), where, perhaps as early as the sixteenth century, an elaborate spiral path cut into the mound made four circuits before ascending to a belvedere.[93] The great motte at Warwick was reused as the centrepiece of a walled garden of the seventeenth century.[94] At Antrim 'Castle' (Co. Antrim), a grand seventeenth-century house (now demolished), the relict earthwork of an Anglo-Norman motte in the demesne was incorporated into a set of formal gardens as a magnificent viewing mound complete with corkscrew path. Quite exceptionally, the gardens were not later swept aside by later parkland designed in the naturalistic style and survive substantially intact, complete with elaborate ornamental water features, as some of the very earliest extant formal gardens in the British Isles.[95] The motte at Topcliffe (Yorkshire, North Riding), known as 'Maiden Bower', was similarly landscaped with a spiral path, here to provide access to what was in effect an observation tower overlooking an elaborate series of late medieval water-based gardens.[96] The artificial mount known as Tout Hill in the precinct of Peterborough Abbey lay on the edge of a medieval garden, although the serpentine path cut into it seems to have been a post-medieval development.[97] At Dunham Massey (Cheshire) the motte is cut into by a series of tiers rather than a continuous pathway, while other variations include bowling greens constructed on flattened motte summits (Leicester castle and West Dean, Wiltshire) and ice houses inserted into the flanks of former castle mounds (Scraptoft, Leicestershire and Holdgate, Shropshire). What is intriguing, of course, is whether such reuse is in effect incidental, with the designers of formal gardens making utility out of large earthworks that would have been expensive to remove, or whether it represents a deliberate referencing of recognised power symbols of the past. Other relict medieval features were also reused: at Papworth St Agnes (Cambridgeshire), for instance, a moated manor site was converted into a formal enclosed garden through the insertion of prospect mounds in the angles of the moat and the addition of canal-like water features.[98] The reuse of medieval parish churches within post-medieval landscapes is a topic in its own right; examples include Mannington (Norfolk), where an eleventh-century church was incorporated into an ornamental woodland created by Horatio Walpole in the nineteenth century.[99]

The phrase 'Gothic Revival' is, of course, associated with the period following Horace Walpole's transformation of Strawberry Hill in the middle of the eighteenth century.[100] But this is not to say that a taste for the medieval past had been completely out of fashion in landscape design beforehand, and arguably many elite landscapes before *c.*1500 incorporated archaic medieval imagery (see p. 218). A remarkably early example of a pseudo-medieval garden was the 'fine garden' laid out on the site of the southern court of Dartington Hall (Devon) some time prior to 1682; the garden included a set of ruined arches designed to evoke an antique medieval atmosphere.[101] On a much larger scale, but also experimental, was the incorporation of the ruins of Fountains Abbey (Yorkshire, West Riding) into the designed landscape at Studley Royal. The parkland and water garden created by John Aislabie from 1717 to 1718 used the ruins as the visual climax of a tour of the estate, although they lay beyond its boundaries and were not included until later in the century, when his son partly 'restored' the medieval fabric for aesthetic effect.[102] At Sandbeck Park (Yorkshire, West Riding), vestiges of the former Cistercian house of Roche were altered by covering its exposed foundations to create a grassy surface from which the ruinous walls rose.[103] Perched on top of a sandstone crag rising above the Shropshire plains, the remains of Red Castle present a particularly clear example of a medieval ruin manipulated as a focus of interest within a later designed landscape. As part of the landscaping of the area around Hawkstone Hall in the final decades of the eighteenth century, the remains were not simply cleaned up but actively modified and augmented to create a visually appealing silhouette.[104] In the fashion for ruins from the middle of the eighteenth century a spectrum of possibilities existed between structures that were entirely fake and former medieval buildings that were left untouched. Completely fictitious and newly built were the 'castle ruin' of Hagley Hall (Worcestershire) and the gothic tower at Wimpole (Cambridgeshire); the castle-like structure of Alfred's Hall (in Cirencester Park, Gloucestershire) is something of a halfway house, in that it incorporates reused medieval windows in an otherwise fanciful creation.[105]

English landscape gardeners of the eighteenth century, such as Lancelot 'Capability' Brown and his successors, based many of their commissions on the sites of medieval deer parks, not infrequently retaining and actively incorporating the remnants of medieval buildings. The ruinous fabric of monasteries and castles formed picturesque points of interest in the settings of many country houses.[106] Scotney castle, on the High Weald of Kent, provides an excellent example. When a new house of the Hussey family, designed by Anthony Salvin, was built on the slopes above the castle in the 1830s, the derelict late-fourteenth-century building was partially dismantled to emphasise its medieval origins, forming a focal point within the carefully composed picturesque scene as viewed from the terrace of the family seat.[107] The changing relationship between the 'old' and 'new' castles at Sherborne (Dorset) in the late medieval and early post-medieval periods is another illustrative case in point. The 'new' castle originated as a medieval hunting lodge set within a deer park visible across the ornamental lake from the bishop's palace, to be transformed from the late sixteenth century into a grand country house. Following the disuse and, eventually, the partial demolition of the 'old' castle in the 1640s, the medieval ruins were carefully maintained and, in places 'enhanced' as features to enliven the setting of the Digby family's country seat.[108] In places, a fake curtain wall, complete with deliberately antiqued crenellations, was built on the lip of the old castle ditch in order to frame the idealised image of the medieval ruins. Other landscape parks of the early modern era featured pseudo-medieval grottoes and 'Gothick' cottages that were newly built to lend a contrived flavour of antiquity, while 'model villages' on their fringes were sometimes designed in a fake medieval style. While most of these reused medieval symbols were distinctively rural, it was not unknown for features from urban environments to find new homes in landscape parks. One of the clearest examples is the transportation in 1765 of the fifteenth-century cross that once stood at medieval Bristol's cross-roads to Stourhead (Wiltshire), where it completed a distinctively English scene.[109] In this particular context Alfred's Tower, a feature on one of the walks from Stourhead, is a reminder of the particular Englishness of this neo-medievalism – a heroic figure forever bound up with the birth of the English nation. The mid-eighteenth-century Temple of Liberty (or Gothic Temple) at Stowe (Buckinghamshire) can be viewed in a similar light. What is important here is that treatment of the past was never neutral. Whether real or fake, in all these cases elements of the 'medieval' landscape provided touchstones to a version of the past that was romanticised and idealised according to the tastes of the time.

The eighteenth century also saw many such polite landscapes and their grounds opened up to the paying public.[110] Beside famous examples such as Castle Howard, Chatsworth, Stowe and Stourhead, a place such as Sawley Park, created in the first half of the nineteenth century in the vicinity of Sawley Abbey (Lancashire), is a lesser-known example of a pseudo-medieval landscape explicitly intended for those willing to pay.[111] Medieval revivalism was present in twentieth-century gardens,[112] and heritage agencies continue to manipulate and refashion these landscapes in new ways. Romanticisation of the 'medieval' landscape is not dead: at Wigmore (Herefordshire), for example, a conservation plan implemented by English Heritage in the 1990s saw the reintroduction of ivy and other vegetation onto the castle remains in order to preserve a ruin shrouded by trees and foliage.

Chapter Seven Notes

[1] Hunt and Willis 1988.

[2] Whittle 1992, 13.

[3] For synthesis see Henderson 2005; for summary see Jennings 2005.

[4] RCHME Northamptonshire 1981, 103–9; Partida 2007, 50.

[5] Everson 1989b, 118.

[6] Woodfield 1991.

[7] See Bettey 1993, 45; Jennings 2005, 3, 25.

[8] See Everson and Williamson 1998, 147–50.

[9] Aston and Bettey 1998, 117–23.

[10] Mileson 2005, 23–4.

[11] See, for instance, Strong 1979.

[12] Strong 1999, 3.

[13] Taylor 1998b, 44; Everson 1991, 6.

[14] RCHME 1968–72; RCHME Northamptonshire 1975–84; Everson and Williamson 1998, 146.

[15] Brown and Taylor 1993, 108.

[16] Brown and Taylor 1993; RCHME Northamptonshire 1975, 6–8.

[17] Dix 1991.

[18] Hynd and Ewart 1983.

[19] Hawkyard 1977.

[20] Coope 1986, 46; Bond and Iles 1991, 39.

[21] Harding and Lambert 1994, 5.

[22] Coope 1986, 45–6; Guy 2006, 216–20.

[23] English Heritage Register of Parks and Gardens, No. GD1557.

[24] Chandler 1993, 186; see also Franklin 1989 on the earlier parks at Thornbury.

[25] Thurley 1997.

[26] Jennings 2005.

[27] Thurley 2003, 89.

[28] Colvin 1982, 26, 139.

[29] See Jennings 2005, 28–31.

[30] Thurley 2003, 89–99.

[31] Colvin 1982, 132, 138–9; Thurley 1995.

[32] Colvin 1982, 138.

[33] Thurley 2003, 97.

[34] Biddle 1961; 2005.

[35] Thurley 1999.

[36] Thurley 1999, 25–7.

[37] Thurley 1999, 62.

[38] Colvin 1982, 314–17; Thurley 1999, 59–62.

[39] See Thurley 1997.

[40] Biddle 1999, 145; see also Steane 1999, 91–3; Pattison 1998b, 40–2.

[41] Rackham 2001, 159.

[42] Colvin 1982, 190.

[43] Biddle 1961; Steane 1999, 119–20.

[44] Colvin 1982, 202.

[45] Biddle 1999.

[46] Colvin 1982, 17, 224, 228.

[47] Colvin 1982, 18, 166–8; Coope 1986, 46.

[48] Colvin 1982, 16; Thurley 1993, 179–93.

[49] Colvin 1982, 99; James 1990, 158.

[50] Woodfield 1991, 130–1.

[51] Phillpotts 2003, 301.

[52] Everson and Stocker 2003, 149.

[53] English Heritage Register of Parks and Gardens, No. GD1956.

[54] Colvin 1982; Thurley 1993.

[55] Colvin 1982, 207.

[56] Batey 1987; Whittle 1999.

[56] Smith *et al.* 2006; McOmish 2007, 27.

[58] See Cooper 1997.

[59] Cooper 1999, 93.

[60] Howard 2003.

[61] Taylor 1998b, 26; another illustrative example of a precinct transformed into compartmentalised formal garden associated with a post-Dissolution gentry house is Egglestone Abbey (Co. Durham): Dunn and Lax 2001.

[62] Pearson *et al.* 2004, 6–7, 10–11.

[63] Everson 2005, 21–2.

[64] Hepple 2001.

[65] Everson and Stocker 2003.

[66] Coope 1986, 59.

[67] Bond and Iles 1991, 39.

[68] English Heritage Register of Parks and Gardens, No. GD2090.

[69] Everson *et al.* 1991, 82; a similar effect might also be achieved through elevated garden buildings: see Everson and Stocker 2003, 155–6.

[70] Williamson 2007, 164–70.

[71] Brown and Taylor 1973, 160.

[72] Dennison and Richardson 2007–8b, 184–5.

[73] Kenyon 2003.

[74] Whittle 1992, 22–3.

[75] Whittle 1989, 88; MOLAS 2005.

[76] Johnson 2002, 155–8; Brown 2005b, 1.

[77] Woodhouse 1999.

[78] Munroe 2006; Roberts 1999, 89.

[79] Whittle 1992, 14.

[80] Briggs 1991.

[81] RCAHMW 1937, cliv.

[82] Whittle 1992, 14–20.

[83] Cruft 1991, 175.

[84] Douglas Simpson 1954, 9–11.

[85] Hynd 1984, 281.

[86] Cruft 1991, 176.

[87] Schofield 1999, 75–7.

[88] Whittle 1992, 21.

[89] Colvin 1975, 30.

[90] Schofield 1999, 81; Quiney 2003, 237.

[91] Schofield 1994, 90.

[92] Howard 1991.

[93] Field et al. 2001, 197–202.

[94] Jacques 2001, 51.

[95] Conway and Reeves-Smyth 1999, 156–7.

[96] Moorhouse 2003a, 200–1.

[97] English Heritage Register of Parks and Gardens, No. GD2824.

[98] Taylor 1974, 145–6.

[99] English Heritage Register of Parks and Gardens, No. GD2010.

[100] Batey 1991.

[101] Currie 2003a, 59.

[102] Coffin 1994, 30–2.

[103] Coffin 1994, 54–5.

[104] Duckers and Duckers 2006, 131–5.

[105] Gerrard 2003, 15–20.

[106] Batey 1994.

[107] Bisgrove 1990, 202–3.

[108] Davison 2001, 12–13, 22–4; Waymark 2001.

[109] Woodbridge 1982, 25, 45.

[110] Bettey 1993, 141–2.

[111] Hunt *et al.* 2005, 46–7.

[112] Elliot 2000.

Conclusions

The central tenet of this study has been that medieval elite landscapes were moulded not only according to the lifestyles of the members of society whose residences they surrounded, but also in a style that embodied an aristocratic world view within which the concepts of hierarchy, order and human control over nature were deeply ingrained. The structure of this book has been thematic, looking for evidence of landscape design using case studies of different dates from various parts of the British Isles. The first part of this conclusion takes a rather different approach, identifying some broad trends in the development of elite landscapes through time. How did the practice of elite landscape design change between the eleventh and sixteenth centuries and how does this relate to wider changes in the structure and outlook of medieval high society? The chapter concludes with a critique of the very notion of medieval 'designed landscapes', not in order to undercut or devalue in any way the arguments that have already been put forward in this volume, but to encourage future work on the subject that is critically aware. Accordingly, the final section attempts to identify some more specific future directions for research in the area.

Summary: evolution and tradition

What this study makes very clear is that there was no idealised 'template' of medieval elite landscape design; nor did the practice evolve in a simple linear sequence. Rather, an intricate pattern of regional differences can be observed, as the policies of landlords fitted in with, rather than cut against, the grain of landscape character. It is for these reasons that East Anglia, for example, was characterised by physically prominent lordship sites, settlement planning on common edges, and emparkment often involving the moulding of shallow river valleys.[1] The south-west peninsula saw borough, park and lordly residence often planned as discrete units that reflected the predominantly dispersed settlement pattern of Devon and Cornwall, while the medieval designed landscapes of that region usually lacked large-scale water features.[2] Designed landscapes were certainly not limited to lowland England, however, and were also present in borderland districts. In the case of the Anglo-Welsh Marches, for example, an upsurge of activity late in the thirteenth century and early in the fourteenth was characterised by the remodelling of established sites of lordship that were 'demilitarised' with garden earthworks and pleasure grounds.[3] There is a marked bias in the distribution of medieval gardens and designed landscapes in Wales towards the south-west and Pembrokeshire in particular, where something of a regional trend towards the manipulation of the surrounds of elite buildings perhaps existed.[4] But we should be careful not to see the familiar 'package' of elite features as the only means by which lords expressed their power and influence. In thirteenth- and fourteenth-century Ireland, for example, Anglo-Norman and Gaelic lords found quite different ways to express their influence physically. It is quite clear that, in organising their estates and residences, Gaelic lords put far less emphasis on the creation of permanent lordship sites for reasons of display, status and symbolism.[5] This provides a point of contrast not only with the situation in much of the rest of the British Isles, but also with medieval European elite society more generally,[6] and the circumstances that gave rise to the distinctive expression of Gaelic lordly power await serious and detailed study. While other variations in this kaleidoscopic pattern doubtless await identification, there is sufficient evidence to prove that, throughout the period, any underlying vocabulary of elite landscape design was clearly mediated by local and regional circumstances.

Despite the clear individuality and even idiosyncrasy of designs that reflected the personal circumstances of aristocratic lords, some broad trends can nonetheless be identified in the changing ways that designed landscapes were realised. One of the most striking observations on the upsurge in evidence for 'design' in the medieval landscape is that the practice was certainly not absent in the eleventh and twelfth centuries. The caricatured image of Norman castles as 'bare bastions of survival'[7] with no accompanying gardens or pleasure grounds is certainly no longer tenable. Elevated mottes and donjons of the period could be designed to impress adjacent communities and to be intervisible with large tracts of countryside. Being country houses as well as fortresses, Norman *capita* were sometimes positioned with an eye for dramatic effect, as exemplified by Castle Acre (Norfolk). At Montacute (Somerset), landscape reorganisation to create an elite setting around a Norman castle was in full flow by the close of the eleventh century, as the estate was forfeited soon after. Here, the Counts of Mortain had established a castle, borough and monastery, and provided their residence with vineyards, orchards and access to a park, while a rabbit warren occupied the earthworks of an Iron Age hillfort.[8]

The examples of Stow (Lincolnshire) and Manorbier (Pembrokeshire), meanwhile, show us that landscape design was a fact of life for a privileged minority by the end of the twelfth century, although the insight that Gerald of Wales affords us into how these settings were valued by contemporaries is exceptional. For this early period in general we have remarkably little direct evidence for how the aristocracy perceived their elite landscapes, although toponyms in aristocratic titles and place-names chosen for newly established estate centres again remind us that aesthetic observation of the countryside was not absent. In a wider geographical context, there were certainly commonalities in the practice of medieval gardening across north-west Europe, with an essentially similar range of plants in use, while the wider links of the Norman kings and aristocracy encouraged the diffusion of ideas. In an English context it is in the early Plantagenet period that more explicit evidence for interest in palace gardens emerges; at the residences of Arundel (West Sussex), and Marlborough (Wiltshire), for instance, landscaping included the laying of turf, and it is not out of the question that the favourable climate of the period may have been another factor behind the flourishing of gardening.[9]

From one point of view the increasing sophistication of noble gardens through the medieval period, in particular after *c*.1250, is part and parcel of the increasing importance of domestic and residential requirements within castle planning – symbols of a more secure and settled lifestyle. From another, however, it tells us about an increasingly aloof aristocracy that was progressively increasing the social distance between the household and the world beyond the walls. Particularly notable from the thirteenth century onwards is a trend towards the progressive physical withdrawal of the aristocracy. This is part of a pan-European phenomenon evident at key lordship sites in France, Germany and Scandinavia[10] and, in turn, part and parcel of a broader phenomenon of the increased privatisation of space, as manifested particularly clearly in the changing function of the hall and modes of domestic planning that enabled individuals to spend more time in individual rooms.[11] In Britain, one of the most striking trends in the chronology of medieval landscape design is the increasing desire of the social elite to isolate their residences and thereby segregate their households from the wider world. For example, while in the eleventh and twelfth centuries the topographies of planned villages integrated sites of lordship within their plan forms, later medieval examples show a distancing of lordship sites, if not their total removal and isolation.

In some cases water and moats were used to different extents within the social elite to isolate residences, while in other cases residences were physically removed from settlements. An exemplar is Goltho (Lincolnshire), where several centuries of uninterrupted lordly presence in an estate centre next to the parish church at the heart of a little clayland community were bought to an end early in the thirteenth century by the construction of a new moated manorial site 1 kilometre to the south on a new, uncluttered, site lying in splendid isolation within a newly created deer park.[12] Another factor that certainly led to the abandonment or relocation of some manorial sites from the middle of the fourteenth century was the growing trend towards the leasing of the demesnes with which they were directly associated.[13] There has been a tendency to explain the relocation of lordship sites solely in pragmatic terms, for instance on the grounds of defensive advantage or conditions of drainage, when aesthetic considerations might be equally if not more important. This period also saw more minor aristocrats engaged in the creation of pleasure grounds, as witnessed by the numerous surviving earthworks of 'moated sites' (lightly defended lordly residences surrounded by water-filled moats) adjoined by gardens, many of them dating to the thirteenth and fourteenth centuries.

It has been shown that links among the European nobility are important in explaining the changing character of parks and landscape design. It is well known that a pan-European horticultural exchange network was in operation for much of the period in question, with areas such as Burgundy and Islamic Spain playing particularly prominent roles at different times.[14] Direct evidence for the exchange of ideas about landscape design is harder to find, but anecdotal information might hold great importance: Edward II visited the magnificent but secluded Burgundian parkscape of Hesdin, for instance.[15]

The decline in direct demesne farming from the fourteenth century had particularly important effects on elite landscapes. Across Britain, the socio-economic circumstances of the post-Black Death period certainly signalled a watershed in park history, but this did not result in the outright 'decline' of these landscapes, as is sometimes proposed.[16] Falling seigneurial incomes meant that fewer parks were created than before and that once exclusively elite spaces were opened up to grazing and sometimes settlement. Yet new 'amenity' parks created after 1400 were some of the largest of all.[17] Furthermore, the increased leasing of demesnes, combined with higher wages and standards of living for the lower classes, ensured that increasingly luxurious foodstuffs became available to the lower classes. Lords keen to distance themselves socially from wealthy townspeople and yeoman farmers responded by exploiting resources beyond the reach of all but those in the highest echelons of medieval society, in particular 'exotic' wild birds. It is also from the end of the fourteenth century that many of our clearest examples of landscape design date, when several newly licensed castles were set in spectacular watery surrounds, many but not all of them built for the *nouveaux riche* and veterans of the French wars. The late fourteenth century was also characterised by royal park extensions as areas under Forest Law became increasingly threatened. A general increase in scale, sophistication and grandeur is apparent, especially at royal residences such at Windsor castle, for example, where Edward III invested heavily in the expansion of the Great Park and the construction of associated manor houses and lodges.

We might wonder whether the 'public face of lordship' expressed by impressive buildings and their contrived settings sometimes masked aristocratic families under pressure.[18] How often did seigneurial showmanship expressed through landscape reorganisation disguise financial difficulties or represent the pretensions of more minor families than these schemes of reorganisations outwardly proclaimed? This might be particularly relevant in the context of the post-1300 'crisis of feudalism',[19] when the inherent inability of lords to arrest economic downturn did not stop them creating ponds and parks and finding new ways of expressing the trappings of lordship on an escalating scale. A danger also exists of accepting too readily that physical changes to the landscape result from lordly planning and reorganisation. Peasants might be active agents in the planning of villages,[20] and might even found churches.[21] The limited access of peasant populations to parks may be taken as evidence of lordly control over everyday life, but, on the other hand, it reminds us that the seigneurial sphere was not hermetically sealed. Likewise, the location of parish churches within manorial *curiae* was a form of social control but is also another reason why high-status sites were far from totally socially exclusive spaces. Members of the lower classes entered the zone of lordship to worship as well as to carry out routine tasks such as the payment of rents and attendance at the manorial court. The successes of lords in some spheres should also not deflect our attention from the fact that the medieval landscape had its fair share of seigneurial enterprises that failed or never got off the ground, including partly completed building projects and the foundation of 'new' towns doomed to failure.

Emparkment strategies in the late fourteenth and fifteenth centuries often meant the total seclusion of country residences within great tracts of parkland.[22] Park boundaries may have become less permeable and there was also something of a tendency for the landscapes within to become progressively more open, with clearer lines of sight between residences and their surroundings, in contrast to earlier, more densely wooded, models, at least in southern Britain.[23] For this period, associations between licences to crenellate and permission to empark are often clear, as exemplified by the activities of William, Lord Hastings, in Leicestershire, where in 1474 he received permission to fortify three houses alongside the right to create massive accompanying parks at Ashby-de-la-Zouch (3,000 acres, 1,214 hectares), Bagworth (2,000 acres, 809 hectares) and Kirby Muxloe (2,000 acres, 809 hectares).[24] In other cases, emparkment coincided with major schemes of refurbishment at long-established seats of lordship. Park could come to house and house to park as lordship sites were removed and relocated.[25] At places like Berry Pomeroy (Devon) and Guildford (Surrey), secluded park lodges were transformed into more permanent residences. Through the transferral of lordship sites or the forced depopulation of their surrounds we see the heightening mystique of an increasingly reclusive elite.

Meanwhile, texts on the practice of hunting – the art of venery – show that hunting was becoming increasingly formalised through the fourteenth century and beyond, as a distinctive etiquette evolved with its own language and practices. This change was exemplified by texts such as the late-fourteenth-century French source *Livre de Chasse*, on which the early-fifteenth-century English text *The Master of the Game* was based.[26] In the fifteenth century the growing popularity of deer coursing within private parks may further reflect the developing formalisation of hunting, which was increasingly a spectator sport for a restricted elite.[27] The new structuring of outdoor activities mirrored the growing formality of life indoors and resulted in more sophisticated ways of sub-dividing parkland. It was this period that saw large gardens increasingly sub-divided not only into separate compartments but also into spheres of greater and lesser privacy, while elaborate water gardens were also found in association with later medieval bishops' palaces, in particular.[28]

Yet in trying to trace how elite landscapes evolved, it is also instructive to remember that these settings sometimes looked backwards to the past, often quite deliberately. Indeed, reference to and reuse of the past is a consistent theme in many of the landscapes explored in this book. The histories of landscapes and indeed the memories of communities could be manipulated through deliberately anachronistic references in the architecture and design of elite residences, giving the impression that buildings were older than they were. So much literature on castles, in particular, has concerned sites at the 'sharp end' of contemporary design and sophistication that we underestimate the extent to which medieval builders had a strong sense of the past, whether this was expressed in a new building or even by 'dressing up' a structure with earthworks to falsify a sense of antiquity. Notable are those mottes in England built after the twelfth century in a manner than can only have been deliberately old-fashioned: Skenfrith (Monmouthshire), Lydford (Devon) and Marshwood (Dorset) are good examples.[29] Long-term continuity in the occupation of lordship sites can also show how successive elites sought to connect with the past, emphasising not only the power but also the permanence of lordship. The clearest evidence comes from excavated Anglo-Norman castles that overlay earlier lordship sites. Links with symbols of the Roman imperial past could be expressed in the architecture of lordship sites and their settings, with the material culture of *Romanitas* presented as heritage.[30] In other cases Norman parish churches found new roles in late medieval designed settings, being used to reference the past in designed landscapes around sites such as Stokesay (Shropshire) and Whorlton (Yorkshire, North Riding). The phenomenon extends beyond the Middle Ages: at Ballylough (Co. Antrim) an early medieval crannog, Anglo-Norman motte, fifteenth-century tower-house and seventeenth-century estate house of the Plantation period are all closely juxtaposed.[31] Also relevant here is the arrogation of sites with glamorous and mythical medieval pasts, as exemplified by Tintagel (Cornwall) in the thirteenth century. Arthurian myth and the 'literary landscape' of romances are crucial to understanding the settings of sites such as Dunstanburgh (Northumberland) and perhaps Windsor (Berkshire) in the fourteenth century. Finally, we might well underestimate how antique earthworks of earlier 'abandoned' sites were integrated into and referenced within medieval elite landscapes. This phenomenon might extend beyond former medieval seats of lordship that were incorporated into the designed settings of later medieval castles (for example, William's Hill, near Middleham, Yorkshire, North Riding), to include relict earthworks such as siege castles (as at Corfe, Dorset), which would have been visible from residences.

'Designed' medieval landscapes?

It is only now that we are beginning to realise how widespread elite medieval landscapes were and appreciate the variety of different scales at which they operated. Nonetheless, despite the weight of evidence amassed here, an acceptance that the ensembles of elite features described in this study equate to medieval 'designed landscapes' still requires a considerable conceptual leap. It requires not only that we confront some deeply ingrained images of the parks and gardens of the period but also that we challenge 'dearly held notions of Renaissance innovation in this field'.[32] It requires us to revisit definitions of

medieval gardens and to consider the impact on the senses of magnificent residential buildings. It also requires us to look at outwardly 'functional' features
of the medieval landscape afresh and to think about how they and the animals, plants and trees within them were perceived by contemporaries other
than the estate officials who have left us documents concerned principally
with financial affairs. There is symmetry here: just as garden historians have
tended to overlook the importance of hunting to the design of eighteenth-
and nineteenth-century landscape parks, so too have medievalists underestimated the aesthetic and figurative dimension to features of the landscape
associated with the 'exploitation' of bird and animal 'resources'.

Yet characterisation of the elite buildings and spaces explored in this book as
'designed landscapes' will doubtless remain problematic to some for a number of
reasons. First, and most fundamental of all, the medieval elite had very different
belief systems and outlooks to their post-medieval equivalents and, from an art-
historical view, had quite different 'ways of seeing'. From this point of view, it is
hard to reconcile the actuality of medieval landscape 'design' with the sixteenth-
century origins of the word itself.[33] 'Design' as such was not an authentically
medieval concept. We must be always be careful not to confuse what may superficially appear to be evidence of landscapes composed partly for effect with the
organisation of the apparatus of estate management for reasons of ordered effi-
ciency, in the sorts of ways described in manuals available from the seventeenth
century onwards. It would also be erroneous to think that equivalents of the celebrated landscape gardeners of the eighteenth century were operating in the
medieval period. Financial accounts relating to major building operations provide insight into the activities of master masons and their networks of contacts,
and we are learning more about the individuals behind the practise of medieval
town planning.[34] But while it might seem paradoxical to conceptualise designed
landscapes without designers, the identities of the people who visualised and
created the landscapes around elite medieval buildings remain obscure.

If the concept of 'design' has its challenges, then so too does the word
'ornamental', which has also been applied to the types of landscape covered
in this book.[35] With the implication of arrangements of features intended for
show and decoration – somehow inanimate, without utility – it is also misleading. Crucially, we should avoid mono-functional interpretations of compositions of landscape features whose meanings were far more complex and cannot always be easily characterised. That functional and symbolic interpretations need not be mutually exclusive is exemplified by the case of the
medieval garden – or rather gardens – whose meanings could be contradic-
tory and, indeed, 'contested'.[36] Gardens meant different things to different
people, depending on their age, status, gender and viewpoint (see p. 45–6).

Of absolutely critical significance here is that the observation that the settings of medieval elite buildings had 'designed' qualities does not deny the
fact that these landscapes could serve utilitarian functions as well. An illuminating parallel is found in the landscape parks of the eighteenth and nine-

teenth centuries, many of which featured provision for hunting. Some of the most characteristic features of Brownian landscape parks reflect provision for animals and birds: thin perimeter belts of woodland provided cover for pheasants, while serpentine lakes were stocked with fish.[37] Utility and beauty were not necessarily in opposition: the functionality of these landscapes was, in effect, part of their symbolic value; the 'taskscapes' associated with them (whereby the lower classes worked in and around and interacted with the elite sphere) were part of the same. It might be tempting to argue that the balance between utility and aesthetics shifted towards the latter from the medieval to the post-medieval period, but this would be to present a false dichotomy. Sophisticated studies of landscapes should recognise that utilitarian and symbolic perspectives are not mutually exclusive but can co-exist, and that the two do not sit at opposite ends of a spectrum of land use.

The issue of scale is also important here. Designed landscapes of any date are embedded within their own wider settings, prompting us to question what the limits of these areas were. The designation of 'designed landscapes' as assets worthy of preservation and conservation in the modern world means that they must be identified as discrete zones, delimited by clear boundaries.[38] To think of any simple binary division between 'designed' and 'non-designed' areas of the landscape in the medieval past is nonsensical, however. Rather, the distinction is a fuzzy one. Parkscapes could contract as well as expand, while the visual linkages between elite zones and their wider environs are important, both in terms of the view from the workaday world inwards towards the perceived elite sphere, as well as the aristocratic view outwards from the estate centre. Decisions about which lines of sight were available, about which features could and could not be glimpsed from within and without, were integral to the practice of elite landscape design. Most anthropogenically altered landscapes of the medieval period were of course 'designed' in some sense, for instance in the form of planned field systems or regulated urban or rural settlements. Another consideration is therefore the level of complexity at which a tract of landscape can be characterised as 'designed', and whether this changed through time. When does an ensemble of essentially functional features associated with the apparatus of medieval estate management take on aesthetic characteristics and/or symbolic significance? It is suggested here that a rigid distinction is, again, unhelpful. Estate centres of different status existed on the same continuum of elite activity. From the majestic emparked surroundings of Windsor to the more modest show of status inherent in the decision to enclose a manor house and its gardens within a moat, we are looking at the same vocabulary of aristocratic landscape design. In addition there is not one scale of designed landscape but several, nested one within another: buildings were designed spaces in their own right, embedded within their own immediate settings, which were themselves suspended within wider territories and interlinked, often visually, with the settlements, scenery and the taskscapes of the working world. These considerations aside, the number of designed landscapes that existed can only be guessed at, but a figure of more than 1,000 has been suggested for England alone.[39]

We should also not necessarily think of medieval 'designed' landscapes as tracts of territory that were manipulated according to some preconceived and idealised blueprint, nor as necessarily resulting from a single phase of development or grand scheme. While Bodiam castle (Sussex) is by some measure the most widely quoted example of a medieval designed landscape, it should not be regarded as an idealised model applicable to other contexts. While it might be tempting to think of a 'template' of garden and landscape design 'exported' from England to other parts of the British Isles, parts of northern and western Britain that retained elements of Gaelic culture clearly drew on other influences, where lordship was expressed in fundamentally different ways. Dating landscape design is also intensely problematical. There is no escaping the fact that our evidence for when most of the elite landscapes covered in this study were created or modified is overwhelmingly circumstantial. Many examples are loosely dated at best, their potential points of origin in some cases spanning centuries.

But the fact that we might not be able to convincingly link the origins of particular elite settings with closely dateable phases of ownership history should not deny their medieval authenticity. The most scientific archaeological excavation and dating techniques would struggle to date some of the transient and ephemeral features with which the book has been concerned – garden beds, fishponds and swanneries, for example. There are a finite number of earthwork forms in the history of gardens and designed landscapes, and typological dating can be hazardous, leading us to question, for example, how many supposed sixteenth- and seventeenth-century designed landscapes could be earlier. For instance, prior to systematic archaeological study the well-preserved and supposedly well-known garden earthworks within Castle Garth, Cawood (Yorkshire, West Riding) were interpreted as seventeenth century in date. Yet analytical earthwork survey combined with documentary evidence showing the bishop's palace to have declined sharply after *c*.1530 demonstrates that they are medieval (see p. 62). In the absence of such evidence the symmetry and formality of the arrangement suggests a much later date.[40] Reconstruction of access routes from bare earthwork plans can also be hazardous. At Hopton (Shropshire), it is not clear whether a rectilinear walkway around a series of ornamental ponds served as a private recreational area or a designed formal route of approach, for example (see p. 115).[41] Even at Bodiam (East Sussex), the postulated single circuitous 'main approach' designed to show off the castle's watery setting cannot be accepted with absolute certainty.[42] Could it have been that the site had two routes of approach: a grand 'ornamental' one from the north that skirted a string of fishponds flanked by walkways; and another, more utilitarian in character, from the south towards the mill and postern gate, through the low end of the village?[43]

Caution is also needed because of the inherent temptation to assume that medieval designed landscapes resulted from one-phase projects brought to fruition. At sites such as Castle Bolton (Yorkshire, North Riding) (see p. 147), which was accompanied by successive parkland landscapes,[44] all the skills of landscape archaeology must be used to untangle complicated multi-layered landscapes, and the challenge is greater still when these relate to multi-phase buildings. Nor should we necessarily assume that elite landscapes were realised as intended. The medieval landscape had its share of partly completed, misguided and abandoned schemes. Many settings for elite buildings were also palimpsests, amalgamating features old as well as new, highlighting some and erasing others in a manner that reminds us that medieval treatment of the fabric of the past was never neutral or entirely pragmatic. This last point is important: while in some senses this book has traced the growing scale and sophistication of medieval designed landscapes, we should remember that these settings frequently looked backwards in time rather than 'anticipating' future developments in the manner of one of the great clichés of architectural and garden history. Medieval fascination with the past meant that monuments such as chapels and city gates could celebrate historical events, while the writings of men such as Henry of Huntingdon and William Worcester remind us of the existence of an embryonic medieval tourist industry focused on antiquities and ruins.[45] Neo-medievalism was particularly active in the designed landscapes of the fourteenth and fifteenth centuries, where a fascination with medieval heritage was displayed through anachronistic architecture and social ritual at places such as Dunstanburgh (Northumberland) and Windsor (Berkshire).

The relationships between 'real' medieval landscapes and those 'imagined' through literary and poetic sources are particularly intriguing and worthy of future detailed study. It is quite clear that a two-way process was at work: elite landscapes could be moulded with literary models in mind, as the examples of Tintagel and Woodstock show (see pp. 33 and 142), while conversely, idealised landscapes portrayed in romances and poetry sometimes made quite explicit references to real-life places. Equally, however, it is important not to try and read too much into the physical evidence available in the landscape, and link uncritically elements that can be observed within it to allegorical and idealised literary sources.

Phenomenologically inspired studies of prehistoric 'ritual' landscapes have been criticised for rhetorical arguments based on the supposed 'visibility' of monuments unsupported by rigorous field examination.[46] Studies of medieval landscapes must be careful not to fall into the same trap – for instance, attributing some great significance to the supposed 'visibility' of a certain type of landscape feature in one context but explaining away or ignoring its lack of visibility in another. The use of viewsheds of medieval sites generated through Geographical Information Systems (GIS) is a promising avenue for research and may ensure that future studies into the experiential dimension of medieval landscapes have some sort of empirical basis. This methodology can identify tracts of territory intervisible with buildings, although the technique is not without its theoretical as well as methodological problems.[47] It is inescapable, however, that archaeologists and historians perceive and interpret the landscape within the context of prevailing scholarship; archaeologists see what they want to see. Ideas change, but that is not all – sites and monuments transform too as they are rethought and fashions come and go: in the context of this field of study yesterday's moat is today's ornamental lake; siege-works of the past are viewing platforms of the present, and so on. At Ludgershall (Wiltshire), the outermost rampart of a ringwork castle has been reinterpreted as a garden walkway (see p. 136). At Nunney (Somerset) a bailey enclosure is now a series of ornamental earthworks (p. 82), as is also the case at Hopton (see p. 182). At Whittington (Shropshire) a motte is now a viewing platform (p. 68). A mere at Framlingham (Suffolk), once interpreted as a defensive feature, is now deemed primarily ornamental (see p. 191).

This survey of elite landscapes has endeavoured to take many of these various considerations on board. It has attempted to acknowledge the variety of scales at which designed landscapes were composed and experienced as well as the fact that their functional and symbolic meanings were intricately entwined. But the archaeological study of parks and gardens is still a relatively new field of study, and there is still more emphasis on the location, identification, cataloguing and recording of examples than on exploring their meanings. Many more examples of designed medieval landscapes undoubtedly remain to be identified and this book will hopefully inspire future work. We should remember, however, that designed landscapes of all periods seamlessly integrated residences and their immediate settings with their wider landscapes. To divide buildings from their physical contexts is artificial. A challenge for the future, therefore, is to build bridges between studies of landscapes and studies of buildings and accept that all provide windows into the medieval mindset. But realising this ideal will involve a rejection of the compartmentalisation of scholarship that has hindered our study of these aspects of the past. Categories of settlement and material culture have been studied separately: for example, castles, manor houses, moated sites and palaces have attracted their own literature, but commonalities are too often overlooked. Perhaps most important of all, the study of designed aspects of medieval landscape has great potential to open up lines of study relevant to British and European archaeology as a whole. This study has benefited from drawing on comparative evidence from continental Europe as well as western parts of the British Isles, but our understanding will also only advance if future studies examine medieval landscape design within this wider pan-European context. Comparative studies of different countries or regions represent one way forward,[48] but genuine Europe-wide syntheses are lacking.[49]

Did the landscapes with which this book has been concerned have aesthetic value to medieval contemporaries? While this precise term 'aesthetic' is a post-medieval innovation, the concept of perceiving beauty (as well as symbolism) within the landscape was not, and the answer must, emphatically, be 'yes'. There is clear evidence that the visual experience of many of the elite settings described here was carefully managed, both from the point of view of outsiders looking inwards towards buildings and their immediate settings and in the sense of buildings themselves providing contrived views. The important point here, however, is that these landscapes were valued for reasons far more complex than their prettiness. Overall, there is no escaping the fact that the notion of a pre-Renaissance culture of aesthetic landscape design is contentious. And while it is clear that the characterisation of landscape 'design' in the medieval period has value, the phrase should not be used loosely or imprecisely. Ultimately, however, there is a form of medieval ancestry to the quintessential parkland landscapes of the post-medieval period, not simply in the sense of continuous high-status occupation on the same sites, but in the very concept of manipulating vegetation, animals, water and earth to stamp design upon the land.

Chapter Eight Notes

[1] Liddiard 2005b, 51; Williamson 2006a, 127–31.

[2] Creighton and Freeman 2006, 117–19; Higham 2006, 90–1, 97–103.

[3] Whitehead 1995; Stamper 1996.

[4] Cadw 1994; 1995; 1998; 1999; 2000; 2002.

[5] O'Conor 2004, 251.

[6] Mallory and McNeill 1991, 306.

[7] McLean 1981, 91.

[8] Dunning 1974, 210; Fretwell 1988.

[9] James 1990, 50.

[10] Hansson 2006, 105–28.

[11] See Grenville 1997, 114–20.

[12] See Creighton 2005b, 21–7; the phenomenon is paralleled locally at places such as Lea: see Everson *et al.* 1991, 117–19.

[13] Gardiner 2007, 179–80.

[14] Hobhouse 1992, 70–95.

[15] Richardson 2007, 47.

[16] Rackham 2001, 158.

[17] Cantor and Hatherly 1979, 79; Platt 1988, 47.

[18] Dyer 2007, 73.

[19] Hilton 1990.

[20] Dyer 1985.

[21] Gardiner 2007, 172–3.

[22] Way 1997, 47; Mileson 2005, 23–4.

[23] Williamson 2007, 156.

[24] Peers 1986, 5.

[25] Rackham 1986, 129.

[26] Orme 1992, 137–40; Roberts 1997.

[27] Taylor 2004b, 52.

[28] Webb 2007, 192.

[29] Creighton 2005b, 66–7; Bowden 2005, 3.

[30] Wheatley 2004, 112–45.

[31] Mallory and McNeill 1991, 309–10.

[32] Cherry 2007, 413.

[33] Liddiard 2007a, 213.

[34] Lilley 2002; 2004.

[35] Taylor 2000.

[36] Gilchrist 1999.

[37] Williamson 1995, 130–40; 1997, 107, 113.

[38] Anthony 1996; the principal national records in the UK comprise English Heritage's *Register of Parks and Gardens of Special Historic Interest in England*, Historic Scotland's *Inventory of Gardens and Designed Landscapes*; and Cadw's *Register of Landscapes, Parks and Gardens of Special Historic Interest in Wales*.

[39] Liddiard 2007a, 206.

[40] Oswald 2005, 2.

[41] Bowden 2005, 8–10.

[42] See Taylor *et al.* 1990.

[43] See McNeill 2006, 127.

[44] Moorhouse 2003b, 329.

[45] Orme 2008b.

[46] See Fleming 2005.

[47] For a rare example, see Lowerre 2006 on GIS analysis of castle siting in the south-eastern midlands; see also Giles 2007, 108–10.

[48] Altenberg 2003; Hansson 2006.

[49] But see Chapelot and Fossier 1985 on the medieval rural landscape of Europe.

—— *Bibliography* ——

Aalen, F.H.A. 2006: *The North East*. London: English Heritage/Collins.

Aberg, A. (ed.) 1978: *Medieval Moated Sites*. London: Council for British Archaeology.

Ackerman, J.S. 1990: *The Villa: form and ideology of country houses*. London: Thames and Hudson.

Ainsworth, P. 2000: A passion for townscape: depictions of the city in a Burgundian manuscript of Froissart's *Chroniques*. In Ainsworth, P. and Scott, T. (eds), *Regions and Landscapes: reality and imagination in late medieval and early modern Europe*. Oxford: Peter Land, 69–111.

Albarella, U. and Thomas, R. 2002: They dined on crane: bird consumption, wild fowling and status in medieval England. *Acta Zoologia Cracoviensia* 45, 23–38.

Albers, L.H. 1991: The perception of gardening as art. *Garden History* 19.2, 163–74.

Alexander, C. 2002: The garden as occasional domestic space. *Signs* 27.3, 857–71.

Alexander, J. 1990: Labeur and paresse: ideological representations of medieval peasant labor. *The Art Bulletin* 72.3, 436–52.

Allcroft, E.A. 1908: *Earthwork of England*. London: MacMillan.

Allen, T. and Hiller, J. 2002: *The Excavation of a Medieval Manor House of the Bishops of Winchester at Mount House, Witney, Oxfordshire*. Oxford: Oxford Archaeology.

Almond, R. 1993: Medieval hunting: ruling classes and commonality. *Medieval History* 3, 147–55.

Altenberg, K. 2003: *Experiencing Landscapes: a study of space and identity in three marginal areas of medieval Britain and Scandinavia*. Stockholm: Almqvist & Wiksell International.

Andrews, M. 1999: *Landscape and Western Art*. Oxford: Oxford University Press.

Anthony, J. 1996: Protection for historic parks and gardens. *Garden History* 24.1, 3–7.

Appleton, J. 1975: *The Experience of Landscape*. London: Wiley.

Appleton, J. 1990: *The Symbolism of Habitat: an interpretation of landscape in the arts*. Seattle: University of Washington Press.

Armitage, P. and West, B. 1985: Faunal evidence from a late medieval garden well of the Greyfriars, London. *Transactions of the London and Middlesex Archaeological Society* 36, 107–36.

Ashbee, J.A. 2004a: The royal apartments in the inner ward at Conwy Castle', *Archaeologia Cambrensis* 153, 51–72.

Ashbee, J.A. 2004b: The chamber called gloriette' living at leisure in thirteenth-and fourteenth-century castles', *Journal of the British Archaeological Association* 157, 17–40.

Ashbee, J.A. 2006: Cloisters in English palaces in the twelfth and thirteenth centuries. *Journal of the British Archaeological Association* 59, 71–90.

Aspinall, A. and Pocock, J.A. 1995: Geophysical prospecting in garden archaeology: an appraisal and critique based on case studies. *Archaeological Prospecting* 2, 61–84.

Astill, G. 2002: Windsor in the context of medieval Berkshire. In Keen, L. and Scarff, E. (eds), *Windsor: Medieval archaeology, art and architecture of the Thames valley, British Archaeological Association Conference Transactions 25*. Leeds: Maney, 1–14.

Astill, G. and Grant, A. 1988: *The Countryside of Medieval England*. London: Blackwell.

Aston, M.A. 1970–72: Earthworks at the Bishop's Palace, Alvechurch, Worcestershire. *Transactions of the Worcestershire Archaeological Society* (third series) 3, 55–9.

Aston, M.A. (ed.) 1988: *Medieval Fish, Fisheries and Fishponds*, 2 vols. Oxford: BAR.

Aston, M.A. and Bettey, J. 1998: The post-medieval rural landscape c.1540–1700: the drive for profit and the desire for status. In Everson, P. and Williamson, T. (eds), *The Archaeology of Landscape*. Manchester: Manchester University Press, 117–38.

Austin, D. 1978: Excavations in Okehampton deerpark 1976–1978. *Proceedings of the Devonshire Archaeological Society* 36, 191–240.

Austin, D. 1988: Excavations and survey at Bryn Cysegrfan, Llanfair Clydogau, Dyfed, 1979. *Medieval Archaeology* 32, 130–65.

Austin, D. 2007: *Acts of Perception: a study of Barnard Castle in Teesdale*, 2 vols. Durham: Architectural and Archaeological Society of Durham and Northumberland.

Austin, D., Daggett, R.H. and Walker, M.J.C. 1980: Farms and fields in Okehampton park, Devon: the problems of studying medieval landscape. *Landscape History* 2, 39–57.

Bailey, M. 1988: The rabbit and the medieval East Anglian economy. *Agricultural History Review* 36.1, 1–20.

Barber, R. 2007: Why did Edward III hold the Round Table? The chivalric background. In Munby, J., Barber, R. and Brown, R. (eds), *Edward III's Round Table at Windsor: The house of the round table and the Windsor festival of 1344*. Woodbridge: Boydell, 84–99.

Barker, J.R.V. 1986: *The Tournament in England 1100–1400*. Woodbridge: Boydell.

Barker, L. 2004: *Orford Castle, Orford, Suffolk*. English Heritage Survey Report.

Barker, P.A. and Higham, R.A. 1982: *Hen Domen Montgomery: a timber castle on the Welsh border*. London: Royal Archaeological Institute.

Barnwell, P.S. 2007: The power of Peak Castle: cultural contexts and changing perceptions. *Journal of the British Archaeological Association* 160, 20–38.

Barnwell, P.S. and Everson, P. 2004: Landscapes of lordship and pleasure: the castle and its landscape setting. In Clarke, J., *Helmsley Castle*. London: English Heritage, 24–5.

Barron, W.R.J. (ed.) 1974: *Sir Gawain and the Green Knight*. Manchester: Manchester University Press.

Barry, T.B. 1977: *Medieval Moated Sites of S.E. Ireland*. Oxford: BAR.

Barry, T.B. 1987: *The Archaeology of Medieval Ireland*. London: Methuen.

Batey, M. 1987: Basing House Tudor garden. *Garden History* 15.2, 94–109.

Batey, M. 1991: Horace Walpole as modern garden historian: the President's lecture on the occasion of the Society's 25th anniversary AGM held at Strawberry Hill, Twickenham, 19 July 1990. *Garden History* 19.1, 1–11.

Batey, M. 1994: The Picturesque: an overview. *Garden History* 22.2, 121–32.

Beacham, M.J.A. 1990: Dovecotes in England: an introduction and gazetteer. *Transactions of the Ancient Monuments Society* 34, 85–131.

Beaumont, H.M. 1996: Tracing the evolution of an estate township: Barden in Upper Wharfedale. *The Local Historian* 26.2, 66–79.

Beck, C. and Casset, M. 2004: Résidences et environnement: les parcs en France du nord (XIIIe–XVe siècles). In Cocula, A. and Combet, M. (eds), *Château et Nature: actes du colloque d'Histoire et d'Archéologie de Périgueux*. Bordeaux: Ausonius Publications, 117–33.

Beck, C., Beck, P. and Duceppe-Lamarre, F. 2001: Les parcs et jardins des ducs de Bourgogne au XIVe siècle. In Renoux, A. (ed.), '*Aux Marches du Palais': actes du VIIe colloque international d'Archéologie Médiévale 1999*. Université du Maine: Publications du LHAM, 97–112.

Bell, C. 1994: New College Mound, Oxford. An archaeological investigation. *Garden History* 22.1, 115–19.

Bellamy, J. 1973: *Crime and Public Order in England in the Later Middle Ages*. London: Routledge and Kegan Paul.

Benton, J.R. 1992: The *Medieval Menagerie: animals in the art of the Middle Ages*. London: Abbeville Press.

Beresford, M. 1954: *The Lost Villages of England*. London: Lutterworth.

Beresford, M. 1967: *New Towns of the Middle Ages: Town Plantation in England, Wales and Gascony*. London: Lutterworth.

Beresford, M. 1971: *History on the Ground: six studies in maps and landscapes*. London: Methuen.

Beresford, M. and St Joseph, J.K.S. 1979: *Medieval England: an aerial survey*. Cambridge: Cambridge University Press.

Berners, J.B. (trans.) 1901–03: *The Chronicle of Froissart*. London: D. Nutt.

Bettey, J.H. 1993: *Estates and the English Countryside*. London: Batsford.

Bevan, B. 1994: Remote sensing of gardens and fields. In Miller, N.F. and Gleason, K.L. (eds), *The Archaeology of Garden and Field*. Philadelphia: University of Pennsylvania Press, 70–90.

Biddle, M. 1961: Nonsuch Palace 1959–60. *Surrey Archaeological Collections* 58, 1–20.

Biddle, M. 1969: Wolvesey: the *domus quasi palatium* of Henry de Blois in Winchester. *Chateau Gaillard* 3, 28–36.

Biddle, M. 1986: *Wolvesey: the old bishop's palace, Winchester*. London: HMSO.

Biddle, M. 1999: The gardens of Nonsuch: sources and dating. *Garden History* 27.1, 145–83.

Biddle, M. 2005: *Nonsuch Palace: the material culture of a noble restoration household*. Oxford: Oxbow.

Birrell, J. 1982: Who poached the king's deer? A study in thirteenth-century crime. *Midland History* 7, 9–25.

Birrell, J. 1992: Deer and deer farming in medieval England. *Agricultural History Review* 40.2, 112–26.

Bisgrove, R. 1990: *The National Trust Book of the English Garden*. London: Viking.

Blair, J. 2005: *The Church in Anglo-Saxon Society*. Oxford: Oxford University Press.

Bloch, M. 1967: The advent and triumph of the watermill. In Bloch, M. (ed.), *Land and Work in Mediaeval Europe*. London: Routledge, 136–68.

Blood, N.E. and Taylor, C.C. 1992: Cawood: an archiepiscopal landscape. *Yorkshire Archaeological Journal* 64, 83–102.

Bond, J. 1988a: Monastic fisheries. In M. Aston (ed.), *Medieval Fish, Fisheries and Fishponds*, 2 vols. Oxford: BAR, 69–112.

Bond, J. 1988b: Rabbits: the case for their medieval introduction into Britain. *Local Historian* 18.2, 53–7.

Bond, J. 1989: Water management in the rural monastery. In Gilchrist, R. and Mytum, H. (eds), *The Archaeology of Rural Monasteries*. Oxford: BAR, 83–112.

Bond, J. 1994: Forests, chases, warrens and parks in medieval Wessex. In Aston, M.A. and Lewis, C. (eds), *The Medieval Landscape of Wessex*. Oxford: Oxbow, 115–58.

Bond, J. 1998: *Somerset Parks and Gardens: a landscape history*. Tiverton: Somerset Books.

Bond, J. 2001: Production and consumption of food and drink in the medieval monastery. In Aston, M.A., Keevill, G. and Hall, T. (eds), *Monastic Archaeology: papers on the study of medieval monasteries*. Oxford: Oxbow, 54–87.

Bond, J. 2003: Somerset parks and gardens, 1500–1830: some addenda. In Wilson-North, R. (ed.), *The Lie of the Land: aspects of the archaeology and history of the designed landscape in the South West of England*. Exeter: Mint Press, 83–99.

Bond, J. 2004: *Monastic Landscapes*. Stroud: Tempus.

Bond, J. and Iles, R. 1991: Early gardens in Avon and Somerset. In Brown, A.E. (ed.), *Garden Archaeology*. London: Council for British Archaeology, 36–52.

Bond, J. and Tiller, K. 1997: *Blenheim: landscape for a palace*. Stroud: Sutton.

Booth, D. 2005: Garden history and archaeology in East Anglia. *Proceedings of the Cambridge Antiquarian Society* 94, 241–4.

Bowden, M. 1998: The conspicuous conversion of earlier earthworks in the design of parks and gardens. In Pattison, P. (ed.), *There by Design: field archaeology in parks and gardens*. Oxford: BAR, 23–6.

Bowden, M. 2005: *Hopton Castle, Shropshire: a survey of the earthworks*. English Heritage Survey Report.

Bradley, R. 1998: *The Significance of Monuments: on the shaping of human experience in Neolithic Britain and Europe*. London: Routledge.

Brann, M. 2004: *Excavations at Caerlaverock Old Castle 1998–9*. Dumfries: Dumfriesshire and Galloway Natural History and Antiquarian Society.

Breeze, A. 1997: *Medieval Welsh Literature*. Dublin: Four Courts Press.

Briggs, C.S. 1991: Garden archaeology in Wales. In Brown, A.E. (ed.), *Garden Archaeology*. London: Council for British Archaeology, 128–59.

Briggs, C.S. 1998: A new field of Welsh cultural heritage: inference and evidence in gardens and landscapes since *c*1450. In Pattison, P. (ed.), *There by Design: field archaeology in parks and gardens*. Oxford: BAR, 65–74.

Brighton, T. 1995: Chatsworth's sixteenth-century parks and gardens. *Garden History* 23.1, 29–55.

Brown, A.E. 1974: Higham Ferrers Castle – or otherwise. *Northamptonshire Past and Present* 5, 79–84.

Brown, A.E. (ed.) 1991: *Garden Archaeology*. London: Council for British Archaeology.

Brown, A.E. and Taylor, C.C. 1991: A relict garden at Linton, Cambridgeshire. *Proceedings of the Cambridge Antiquarian Society* 80, 62–7.

Brown, A.E. and Taylor, C.C. 1993: Cambridgeshire Earthwork Surveys VI. *Proceedings of the Cambridge Antiquarian Society* 82, 101–11.

Brown, G. 1998: Parklands as guardians of early landscapes: Highclere Castle, Hampshire. In Pattison, P. (ed.), *There by Design: field archaeology in parks and gardens*. Oxford: BAR, 7–12.

Brown, G. 2004: *Odiham Castle, Hampshire*. Swindon: English Heritage Investigation Report Series.

Brown, G. 2005a: *Halesowen Abbey and its Environs*. English Heritage Survey Report.

Brown, G. 2005b: *The Elizabethan Garden at Kenilworth Castle*. English Heritage Survey Report.

Brown, M. 2002: *Framlingham Castle, Framlingham, Suffolk*. English Heritage Survey Report.

Brown, M. and Pattison, P. 1997: *Framlingham Mere, Suffolk*. RCHME Survey Report.

Brown, P., King, P. and Remfry, P. 2004: Whittington Castle: the marcher fortress of the Fitz Warin family. *Transactions of the Shropshire Archaeological and Historical Society* 79, 106–27.

Brown, R.A. 1976: *English Castles*. London: Batsford.

Brown, R.A. 1984: Castle gates and garden gates. *Architectural History* 27, 443–5.

Brown, R.A. 1989: *Castles from the Air*. Cambridge: Cambridge University Press.

Butler, H.E. (trans.) 1949: *The Chronicle of Jocelin of Brakelond Concerning the Acts of Samson Abbot of the Monastery of St Edmund*. London: Thomas Nelson and Sons.

Cable, J. (ed.) 1971: *The Death of King Arthur*. London: Penguin.

Cadw 1994: *Gwent. Register of Landscapes, Parks and Gardens of Special Historic Interest in Wales*. Cardiff: Cadw.

Cadw 1995:*Clwyd. Register of Landscapes, Parks and Gardens of Special Historic Interest in Wales*. Cardiff: Cadw.

Cadw 1998: *Conwy, Gwynedd and the Isle of Anglesey. Register of Landscapes, Parks and Gardens of Special Historic Interest in Wales*. Cardiff: Cadw.

Cadw 1999: *Powys. Register of Landscapes, Parks and Gardens of Special Historic Interest in Wales*. Cardiff: Cadw.

Cadw 2000: *Glamorgan. Register of Landscapes, Parks and Gardens of Special Historic Interest in Wales*. Cardiff: Cadw.

Cadw 2002: *Carmarthenshire, Ceredigion and Pembrokeshire. Register of Landscapes, Parks and Gardens of Special Historic Interest in Wales*. Cardiff: Cadw.

Cahn, W. 1991: Medieval landscape and the encyclopedic tradition. *Yale French Studies* 80, 11–24.

Calkins, R.G. 1986: Piero de'Crescenzi and the medieval garden. In MacDougall, E.B. (ed.), *Medieval Gardens*. Washington: Dumbarton Oaks Research Library and Collection, 157–69.

Callou, C. 2003: *De la Garenne au Clapier: étude archéozoologique du lapin en Europe occidentale*. Paris: Publications Scientifiques du Muséum.

Cameron, K. 1961: *English Place-Names*. London: Batsford.

Campbell, B.M.S. 2000: *English Seigniorial Agriculture, 1250–1450*. Cambridge: Cambridge University Press.

Cantor, L.M. 1970–71: The medieval parks of Leicestershire. *Transactions of the Leicestershire Archaeological and Historical Society* 46, 9–24.

Cantor, L.M. 1982: *The English Medieval Landscape*. London: Croom Helm.

Cantor, L.M. 1983: *The Medieval Parks of England: a geography*. Loughborough: Loughborough University of Technology.

Cantor, L.M. and Hatherly, J. 1979: The medieval parks of England. *Geography* 64, 71–85.

Carter, H. 1969: Caernarvon. In Lobel, M.D. (ed.), *Historic Towns: Maps and Plans of Towns and Cities in the British Isles, with Historical Commentaries, from Earliest Times to 1800, Volume I*. London: Lovell Johns-Cook, Hammond and Kell Organization, 1–8.

Carus Wilson, E.M. 1947: The effects of the acquisition and of the loss of Gascony on the English wine trade. *Historical Research* 21 (63), 145–54.

Casset, M. 2003: Un mode de gestion de l'espace: les parcs à gibier en Normandie au Moyen Âge. *Annales de Normandie* 8, 153–70.

Casson, L.F. (ed.) 1949: *The Romance of Sir Degrevant*. Oxford: Oxford University Press.

Cazelles, R. and Rathofer, J. 1988: *Illuminations of Heaven and Earth: the glories of the Très Riches Heures du Duc de Berry*. New York: Harry N Abrams.

CBA 1997: Ornamental water garden found at Cheshire castle. *British Archaeology* 24.

Chandler, J. 1993: *John Chandler's Itinerary: Travels in Tudor England*. Stroud: Sutton.

Chapelot, J. 1998: *Le Château de Vincennes: une résidence royale au moyen age*. Paris: CNRS Editions.

Chapelot, J. and Fossier, R. 1985: *The Village and House in the Middle Ages*. Berkeley: University of California Press.

Charageat, M. 1951: Le Parc d'Hesdin, création monumentale du XIIIe siècle. *Bulletin de la Société de l'histoire de l'art Français (1950)*, Paris, 1951, 94–102.

Cherry, M. 2007: review article: *Greater Houses of England 1300–1500. Vol III: Southern England*. By Anthony Emery. *Antiquaries Journal* 87, 411–15.

Cherryson, A.K. 2002: The identification of archaeological evidence for hawking in medieval England. *Acta Zoologica Cracoviensia* 45, 307–14.

Christie, P.M. and Coad, J.G. 1980: Excavations at Denny Abbey. *Archaeological Journal* 137, 138–279.

Ciarallo, A. 2001: *Gardens of Pompeii*. Los Angeles: J. Paul Getty Museum.

Clark, K. 1949: *Landscape into Art*. London: John Murray.

Clark, W.B. 1992: *The Medieval Book of Birds: Hugh of Fouilloy's aviarum*. Binghamton: Center for Medieval and Early Renaissance Studies.

Clarke, C.A.M. 2006: *Literary Landscapes and the Idea of England, 700–1400*. Cambridge: Brewer.

Clay, R.M. 1914: *The Hermits and Anchorites of England*. London: Methuen.

Cobb, J.R. 1880: Old Hall, Monkton, Pembroke. *Archaeologia Cambrensis* 11, 248–52.

Coffin, D.R. 1994: *The English Garden: meditation and memorial*. Princeton: Princeton University Press.

Cohen, E. 1994: Animals in medieval perceptions: the image of the ubiquitous other. In Manning, A. and Serpell, J. (eds), *Animals and Human Society: changing perspectives*. London: Routledge, 59–80.

Cole, M.A., David, A.U.E., Linford, N.T., Linford, P.K. and Payne, A.W. 1997: Non-destructive techniques in English gardens: geophysical prospecting. In Jacques, D. (ed.), The techniques and uses of garden archaeology. *Journal of Garden History* 17.1, 26–39.

Colvin, H.M. (ed.) 1963: *The History of the King's Works, Volumes I and II, the Middle Ages*. London: HMSO.

Colvin, H.M. (ed.) 1975: *The History of the King's Works, Volume III, 1484–1660 (Part I)*. London: HMSO.

Colvin, H.M. (ed.) 1982: *The History of the King's Works, Volume IV, 1484–1660 (Part II)*. London: HMSO.

Colvin, H.M. 1986: Royal gardens in medieval England. In MacDougall, E.B. (ed.), *Medieval Gardens*. Washington: Dumbarton Oaks Research Library and Collection, 7–22.

Comito, T. 1971: Renaissance gardens and the discovery of paradise. *Journal of the History of Ideas* 32.4, 483–506.

Conway, M.G. and Reeves-Smyth, T. 1999: Excavations at Antrim Castle gardens, 1991 and 1994 – addendum. *Ulster Journal of Archaeology* 58, 159–76.

Cook, H. and Williamson, T. (eds) 1999: *Water Management in the English Landscape*. Edinburgh: Edinburgh University Press.

Coope, R. 1986: The 'long gallery': its origins, development, use and decoration. *Architectural History* 29, 43–72.

Cooper, N. 1997: The gentry house in the age of transition. In Gaimster, D. and Stamper, P. (eds), *The Age of Transition: the archaeology of English culture 1400–1600*. Oxford: Oxbow, 115–26.

Cooper, N. 1999: *Houses of the Gentry 1480–1680*. New Haven: Yale University Press.

Cooper, N. and Fletcher, M. 1995: *Godolphin and its Gardens*. London: RCHME.

Cooper, S. 1999: Ornamental structures in the medieval gardens of Scotland. *Proceedings of the Society of Antiquaries of Scotland* 129, 817–39.

Coppack, G. 1990: *Abbeys and Priories*. London: English Heritage/Batsford.

Coppack, G. 2006: *Abbeys and Priories*. Stroud: Tempus.

Coppack, G. and Aston, M.A. 2002: *Christ's Poor Men: the Carthusians in England*. Stroud: Tempus.

Cosgrove, D. 1984: *Social Formation and Symbolic Landscape*. London: Croom Helm.

Cosgrove, D. 1993: *The Palladian Landscape: geographical change and its cultural representations in sixteenth-century Venice*. University Park, Pennsylvania: Penn State University Press.

Cosgrove, D. and Daniels, S. (eds) 1988: *The Iconography of Landscape*. Cambridge: Cambridge University Press.

Coulson, C. 1990: Bodiam castle: truth and tradition. *Fortress* 10, 3–15.

Coulson, C. 2003: *Castles in Medieval Society: fortresses in England, France and Ireland in the central Middle Ages*. Oxford: Oxford University Press.

Crackles, F.E. 1986: Medieval gardens in Hull. *Garden History* 14.1, 1–5.

Crandell, G. 1993: *Nature Pictorialized*. Baltimore: John Hopkins University Press.

Crawford, O.G.S. 1953: *Archaeology in the Field*. London: Dent.

Creighton, O.H. 1998: *Castles and Landscapes: an archaeological survey of Yorkshire and the East Midlands*. University of Leicester: Unpublished PhD Thesis.

Creighton, O.H. 1999: Early castles in the medieval landscape of Rutland. *Transactions of the Leicestershire Archaeological and Historical Society* 73, 19–33.

Creighton, O.H. 2005a: Castles and castle-building in town and country. In Dyer, C. and Giles, K. (eds), *Medieval Town and Country 1100–1500*. Oxford: Society for Medieval Archaeology Monograph, 275–92.

Creighton, O.H. 2005b: *Castles and Landscapes: power, community and fortification in medieval England*. London: Equinox.

Creighton, O.H. and Freeman, J.P. 2006: Putting fortification in its place: castles and the medieval landscape of the south-west. In Turner, S. (ed.), *Medieval Devon and Cornwall: shaping an ancient countryside*. Bollington: Windgather, 104–22.

Creighton, O.H. and Higham, R.A. 2004: Castle studies and the 'landscape' agenda. *Landscape History* 26, 5–18.

Creighton, O.H. and Higham, R.A. 2005: *Medieval Town Walls: an archaeology and social history of urban defence*. Stroud: Tempus.

Crocker, A. 2005: Disparking the royal park at Guildford. *Surrey Archaeological Collections* 92, 187–215.

Crouch, D. 1992: *The Image of Aristocracy in Britain, 1000–1300*. London: Routledge.

Crouch, D. 2005: *Tournament*. London: Hambledon.

Cruft, C.H. 1991: The state of garden archaeology in Scotland. In Brown, A.E. (ed.), *Garden Archaeology*. London: Council for British Archaeology, 175–89.

Cummins, J. 2002: *Veneurs s'en vont en Paradis*: medieval hunting and the 'natural' landscape. In Howe, J. and Wolfe, M. (eds), *Inventing Medieval Landscapes: senses of place in western Europe*. Gainesville: University Press of Florida, 33–56.

Cunliffe, B. 1971: *Excavations at Fishbourne 1961–1969*, 2 vols. Leeds: Maney/Society of Antiquaries.

Cunliffe, B. 1998: *Fishbourne Roman Palace*. Stroud: Tempus.

Cunliffe, B. and Munby, J. 1985: *Excavations at Portchester Castle, Volume IV: Medieval, the inner bailey*. London: Society of Antiquaries.

Currie, C.K. 1989: The role of fishponds in the monastic economy. In Gilchrist, R. and Mytum, H. (eds), *The Archaeology of Rural Monasteries*. Oxford: BAR, 142–72.

Currie, C.K. 1990: Fishponds as garden features, c.1550–1750. *Garden History* 18.1, 22–46.

Currie, C.K. 1991: The early history of the carp and its economic significance in England. *Agricultural History Review* 39, 97–107.

Currie, C.K. 1993: The archaeology of the flowerpot in England and Wales, circa 1650–1950. *Garden History* 21.2, 227–46.

Currie, C.K. 1994: Earthworks at Compton Bassett, with a note on Wiltshire fishponds. *Wiltshire Archaeological and Natural History Magazine* 87, 96–101.

Currie, C.K. 2003a: Dartington Hall and Shilston Barton: archaeological excavation at two Devon gardens, 1991–2000. In Wilson-North, R. (ed.), *The Lie of the Land: aspects of the archaeology and history of the designed landscape in the South West of England*. Exeter: Mint Press, 51–65.

Currie, C.K. 2003b: Historic fishpond sites at Puttenham, with a provisional discussion of Surrey fishponds. *Surrey Archaeological Collections* 90, 273–94.

Currie, C.K. 2005: *Garden Archaeology*. York: Council for British Archaeology.

Currie, C.K. and Locock, M. 1991: An evaluation of archaeological techniques used at Castle Bromwich Hall, 1989–90. *Garden History* 19.1, 77–99.

Dallas, C. and Sherlock, D. 2002: *Baconsthorpe Castle, Excavations and Finds, 1951–1972*. Norwich: Norfolk Museums and Archaeology Service.

Daniels, S. 1988: The political iconography of woodland in late Georgian England. In Cosgrove, D. and Daniels, S. (eds), *The Iconography of Landscape*. Cambridge: Cambridge University Press, 43–82.

Darby, H.C. 1977: *Domesday England*. Cambridge: Cambridge University Press.

Darby, H.C. and Terrett, I.B. (eds) 1957: *The Domesday Geography of Eastern England*. London: Cambridge University Press.

Darlington, J. (ed.) 2001: *Stafford Castle: survey, excavation and research 1978–1998, Volume I – The Surveys*. Stafford: Stafford Borough Council.

Davies, D. 1988: The evocative symbolism of trees. In Cosgrove, D. and Daniels, S. (eds), *The Iconography of Landscape*. Cambridge: Cambridge University Press, 32–42.

Davison, B.K. 2001: *Sherborne Old Castle, Dorset*. London: English Heritage.

Dawson, G.J. 1976: *The Black Prince's Palace at Kennington, Surrey*. Oxford: BAR.

Deam, L. 2000: Landscape into history: the miniatures of the *Fleures des Histoires* (Brussels, B.R. ms. 9231–9232). In Ainsworth, P. and Scott, T. (eds), *Regions and Landscapes: reality and imagination in late medieval and early modern Europe*. Oxford: Peter Land, 113–37.

Dennison, E. (ed.) 2005: *Within the Pale: the story of Sheriff Hutton Park*. York: William Sessions.

Dennison, E. and Richardson, S. 2007–8a: Harewood castle survey. *Castle Studies Group Journal* 21, 167–71.

Dennison, E. and Richardson, S. 2007–8b: Sheriff Hutton – survey, recording and analysis. *Castle Studies Group Journal* 21, 172–88.

Dennison, E., Holloway, M. and Richardson, S. 2006: *Ravensworth Castle, Ravensworth, Yorkshire, North Riding: Management Plan*. Beverley: unpublished EDAS Ltd Archive Report.

Dennison, E., Richardson, S. and Matthews, E. 2007–8: Recent work on Yorkshire castles. *Castle Studies Group Journal* 21, 157–66.

Detsicas, A.P. 1972: Excavations at Eccles, 10th interim report. *Archaeologia Cantiana* 87, 101–10.

Dix, B. 1991: Towards the restoration of a period garden. In Brown, A.E. (ed.), *Garden Archaeology*. London: Council for British Archaeology, 60–72.

Dix, B. 2003: 'Come my spade': archaeology in historic gardens. In Wilson-North, R. (ed.), *The Lie of the Land: aspects of the archaeology and history of the designed landscape in the South West of England*. Exeter: Mint Press, 21–3.

Dix, B., Soden, I. and Hylton, T. 1995: Kirby Hall and its gardens: excavations in 1987–1994. *Archaeological Journal* 152, 291–380.

Dixon, P. 2002: The myth of the keep. In Meirion-Jones, G., Impey, E. and Jones, M. (eds), *The Seigneurial Residence in Western Europe AD c800–1600*. Oxford: BAR, 9–13.

Dixon, P. and Marshall, P. 2003: The great tower at Hedingham Castle: a reassessment. In Liddiard, R. (ed.), *Anglo-Norman Castles*. Woodbridge: Boydell, 297–306.

Dixon, P.J. 1997: Settlement in the hunting forests of southern Scotland in the medieval and later periods. In De Boe, G. and Verhaeghe, F. (eds), *Rural Settlements in Medieval Europe: papers of the Medieval Europe Brugge 1997 Conference*. Zellik: IAP Rapporten, 345–54.

Donald Hughes, J. 2003: Europe as consumer of exotic biodiversity: Greek and Roman times. *Landscape Research* 28.1, 21–31.

Doob, P. 1990: *The Idea of the Labyrinth from Classical Antiquity through the Middle Ages*. Ithaca: Cornell University Press.

Douglas Simpson, W. 1954: *Craigmillar Castle*. Edinburgh: HMSO.

Drew, J.H. 1963: Notes on the water system at Kenilworth Castle. *Transactions of the Birmingham and Warwickshire Archaeological Society* 81, 74–7.

Drury, J.L. 1976: Early settlement in Stanhope Park, Weardale. *Archaeologia Aeliana* (fifth series) 4, 139–49.

Duckers, P. and Duckers, A. 2006: *Castles of Shropshire*. Stroud: Tempus.

Dunn, C. and Lax, A. 2001: *The medieval and later landscape at Egglestone Abbey, Teesdale, County Durham*. English Heritage Survey Report.

Dunning, R.W. (ed.) 1974: *The Victoria History of the County of Somerset, Vol. III*. London: Oxford University Press.

Dyer, C. 1985: Power and conflict in the medieval village. In Hooke, D. (ed.), *Medieval Villages: a review of current work*. Oxford: Oxford University Committee for Archaeology Monograph No. 5, 27–32.

Dyer, C. 1997: Peasants and farmers: rural settlements and landscapes in an age of transition. In Gaimster, D. and Stamper, P. (eds), *The Age of Transition: the archaeology of English culture 1400–1600*. Oxford: Oxbow, 61–76.

Dyer, C. 2000a: Gardens and orchards in medieval England. In Dyer, C. (ed.), *Everyday Life in Medieval England*. London: Hambledon, 113–32.

Dyer, C. 2000b: The consumption of freshwater fish in medieval England. In Dyer, C. (ed.), *Everyday Life in Medieval England*. London: Hambledon, 101–11.

Dyer, C. 2006a: Gardens and garden produce in the later Middle Ages. In Woolgar, C.M., Serjeantson, D. and Waldron (eds), *Food in Medieval England: diet and nutrition*. Oxford: Oxford University Press, 27–40.

Dyer, C. 2006b: Seasonal patterns in food consumption in the later Middle Ages. In. Woolgar, C.M., Serjeantson, D. and Waldron, T. (eds), *Food in Medieval England: Diet and Nutrition*. Oxford: Oxford University Press, 201–14.

Dyer, C. 2007: The ineffectiveness of lordship in England, 1200–1400. *Past and Present* 195 (Supplement 2), 69–86.

Eade, J.C. (ed.) 1987: *Projecting the Landscape*. Canberra: Australian National University Humanities Centre Monograph.

Eco, U. 1986: *Art and Beauty in the Middle Ages*. New Haven: Yale University Press.

Elliot, B. 2000: Historical revivalism in the twentieth century: a brief introduction. *Garden History* 28.1, 17–31.

Elliott, R. 1997: Landscape and geography. In Brewer, D. and Gibson, J. (eds), *A Companion to the Gawain-Poet*. Cambridge: D.S. Brewer, 105–17.

Elliott-Binns, L.E. 1955: *Medieval Cornwall*. London: Methuen.

Ellis, P. 2000: *Ludgershall Castle, Wiltshire: a report on the excavations by Peter Addyman, 1964–1972*. Devizes: Wiltshire Archaeological and Natural History Society.

Elrington, C.R. (ed.) 1990: *The Victoria History of the County of Oxfordshire, Vol. XII*. Oxford: Oxford University Press for the University of London Institute for Historical Research.

Emery, A. 1970: *Dartington Hall*. Oxford: Clarendon Press.

Emery, A. 1996: *Greater Medieval Houses of England and Wales. Volume I: Northern England*. Cambridge: Cambridge University Press.

Emery, A. 2000: *Greater Medieval Houses of England and Wales. Volume II: East Anglia, Central England and Wales*. Cambridge: Cambridge University Press.

Emery, A. 2005: Late-medieval houses as an expression of social status. *Historical Research* 78.200, 140–61.

Emery, A. 2006: *Greater Medieval Houses of England and Wales. Volume III: Southern England*. Cambridge: Cambridge University Press.

Emery, A. forthcoming: Dartington Hall: a mirror of the nobility in late medieval Devon. *Archaeological Journal*.

English Heritage nd., *Register of Parks and Gardens of Special Historic Interest in England*. Swindon: English Heritage.

Esmonde Cleary, A.S. 1998: Roman Britain in 1997: England. *Britannia* 29, 381–432.

Everson, P. 1989a: Rural monasteries within the secular landscape. In Gilchrist, R. and Mytum, H. (eds), *The Archaeology of Rural Monasteries*. Oxford: BAR, 141–5.

Everson, P. 1989b: The gardens of Campden House, Chipping Campden, Gloucestershire. *Garden History* 17.2, 109–21.

Everson, P. 1991: Field survey and garden earthworks. In Brown, A.E. (ed.), *Garden Archaeology*. London: Council for British Archaeology, 6–19.

Everson, P. 1996a: Bodiam Castle, East Sussex: a fourteenth-century designed landscape. In Morgan Evans, D., Salway, P. and Thackray, D. (eds), *'The Remains of Distant Times', Archaeology and the National Trust*. London: Occasional Papers of the Society of Antiquaries of London, 66–72.

Everson, P. 1996b: Bodiam Castle, East Sussex: castle and designed landscape. *Château Gaillard* 16, 70–84.

Everson, P. 1996c: The after-life of monastic houses: the earthwork evidence. In. Sturman, C. (ed.), *Lincolnshire People and Places: essays in memory of Terence R. Leach, 1937–1994*. Lincoln: Society for Lincolnshire History and Archaeology, 13–17.

Everson, P. 1998: 'Delightfully surrounded with woods and ponds': field evidence for medieval gardens in England. In Pattison, P. (ed.), *There by Design: field archaeology in parks and gardens*. Oxford: BAR, 32–8.

Everson, P. 2003: Medieval gardens and designed landscapes. In Wilson-North, R. (ed.), *The Lie of the Land: aspects of the archaeology and history of the designed landscape in the South West of England*. Exeter: Mint Press, 24–33.

Everson, P. 2005: *Lewes Priory, Sussex: the post-Dissolution mansion and gardens of Lords Place*. English Heritage Survey Report.

Everson, P. and Stocker, D. 2003: The archaeology of vice-regality: Charles Brandon's brief rule in Lincolnshire. In Gaimster, D. and Gilchrist, R. (eds), *The Archaeology of Reformation, 1480–1580*. Leeds: Maney, 145–58.

Everson, P. and Stocker, D. 2007: St Leonard's at Kirkstead, Lincolnshire: the landscape of the Cistercian monastic precinct. In Gardiner, M. and Rippon, S. (eds), *Medieval Landscapes: landscape history after Hoskins, Volume 2*. Bollington: Windgather, 215–30.

Everson, P. and Williamson, T. 1998: Gardens and designed landscapes. In Everson, P. and Williamson, T. (eds), *The Archaeology of Landscape*. Manchester: Manchester University Press, 139–65.

Everson, P., Taylor, C.C. and Dunn, C.J. 1991: *Change and Continuity: rural settlement in north-west Lincolnshire*. London: HMSO.

Everson, P., Brown, G. and Stocker, D. 2000: The castle earthworks and landscape context. In Ellis, P. (ed.), *Ludgershall Castle, Wiltshire: a Report on the Excavations by Peter Addyman, 1964–1972*. Devizes: Wiltshire Archaeological and Natural History Society Monograph No. 2, 97–119.

Fairclough, G. 1992: Meaningful constructions – spatial and functional analysis of medieval buildings. *Antiquity* 66, 348–66.

Fairweather, J. (trans.) 2005: *Liber Eliensis: a history of the Isle of Ely from the seventh century to the twelfth*. Woodbridge: Boydell.

Farrar, L. 1998: *Ancient Roman Gardens*. Stroud: Sutton.

Faulkner, P. 1970: Some medieval archiepiscopal palaces. *Archaeological Journal* 127, 130–46.

Faulkner, P.A. 1963: Castle planning in the fourteenth century. *Archaeological Journal* 120, 215–35.

Field, D., Brown, G. and Crockett, A. 2001: The Marlborough Mount revisited. *Wiltshire Archaeological and Natural History Magazine* 94, 195–204.

Fish, S.K. 1994: Archaeological palynology of gardens and fields. In Miller, N.F. and Gleason, K.L. (eds), *The Archaeology of Garden and Field*. Philadelphia: University of Pennsylvania Press, 44–69.

Fisher, A. 2004: *Mazes and Labyrinths*. Princes Risborough: Shire.

Fisher, I. 2005: The heirs of Somerled. In Oram, R. and Stell, G. (eds), *Lordship and Architecture in Medieval and Renaissance Scotland*. Edinburgh: John Donald, 85–95.

Fleming, A. 2005: Megaliths and post-modernism: the case of Wales. *Antiquity* 79, 921–32.

Fleming, J.V. 1986: The garden of the Roman de la Rose: vision of landscape or landscape of vision? In MacDougall, E.B. (ed.), *Medieval Gardens*. Washington: Dumbarton Oaks Research Library and Collection, 201–34.

Fletcher, A.J. (ed.) 2002: *The Victoria History of the County of Northampton, Vol. V*. London: Victoria County History.

Foreman, B. and Dennison, E. 2005: *Within the Pale: the story of Sheriff Hutton Park*. York: William Sessions.

Foulds, T. 1997: 'A Garden called Paradise': variant street names and the changing townscape in later medieval Nottingham. *Transactions of the Thoroton Society* 101, 99–108.

Franklin, P. 1989: Thornbury woodlands and deer parks, part 1: earl of Gloucester's deer parks. *Transactions of the Bristol and Gloucestershire Archaeological Society* 107, 149–69.

Fredengren, C. 2002: *Crannogs*. Bray: Wordwell.

Frere, S.S. and St Joseph, J.K.S. 1983: *Roman Britain from the Air*. Cambridge: Cambridge University Press.

Fretwell, K. 1988: *Montacute Park and Garden Survey*. Taunton: National Trust.

Fretwell, K. 1995: Lodge Park, Gloucestershire: a rare surviving deer course and Bridgeman layout. *Garden History* 23.2, 133–44.

Fryde, E.B. 1996: *Peasants and Landlords in Later Medieval England, c.1380–c.1525*. Stroud: Alan Sutton.

Gandy, M. 2006: Editorial: water and landscape. *Landscape Research* 31.2, 117–19.

Gardiner, M. 2007: The origins and persistence of manor houses in England. In Gardiner, M. and Rippon, S. (eds), *Medieval Landscapes: landscape history after Hoskins, Volume 2*. Bollington: Windgather, 170–82.

Gautier, A. 2006: Game parks in Sussex and the Godwinesons. *Anglo-Norman Studies* 29, 51–64.

Gaydon, A.T. (ed.) 1968: *The Victoria History of the County of Shropshire, Vol. VIII*. London: Oxford University Press.

Gem, R. 1997: *English Heritage Book of St Augustine's Abbey, Canterbury*. London: English Heritage/Batsford.

Gerrard, C. 2003: *Medieval Archaeology: understanding traditions and contemporary approaches*. London: Routledge.

Gerrard, C. and Aston, M.A. 2007: *The Shapwick Project, Somerset: a rural landsape explored*. Leeds: Society for Medieval Archaeology.

Gilbert, J.M. 1979: *Hunting and Hunting Reserves in Medieval Scotland*. Edinburgh: John Donald.

Gilchrist, R. 1995: *Contemplation and Action: the other monasticism*. London: Leicester University Press.

Gilchrist, R. 1999: The contested garden: gender, space and metaphor in the English castle garden. In Gilchrist, R. (ed.), *Gender and Archaeology: contesting the past*. London: Routledge, 109–45.

Gilchrist, R. 2005: *Norwich Cathedral Close: The evolution of the English Cathedral landscape*. Woodbridge: Boydell.

Giles, K. 2007: Seeing and believing: visuality and space in pre-modern England. *World Archaeology* 39.1, 105–21.

Giorgi, J. 1997: Diet in late medieval and early modern London: the archaeobotanical evidence. In Gaimster, D. and Stamper, P. (eds), *The Age of Transition: the archaeology of English culture 1400–1600*. Oxford: Oxbow, 197–213.

Girouard, M. 1978: *Life in the English Country House*. New Haven: Yale University Press.

Goodall, J. 2006: *Warkworth Castle and Hermitage*. London: English Heritage.

Goodman, A.W. (ed.) 1927: *Chartulary of Winchester Cathedral*. Winchester: Warren.

Gracie, H.G. and Price, E.G. 1979: Frocester Court villa: second report. *Transactions of the Gloucestershire and Bristol Archaeological Society* 97, 9–64.

Grainge, W. 1871: *History and Topography of Harrogate and the Forest of Knaresborough*. London: John Russell Smith.

Gransden, A. 1972: Realistic observation in twelfth-century England. *Speculum* 47.1, 29–51.

Grant, A. 1988: Animal resources. In Astill, G. and Grant, A. (eds), *The Countryside of Medieval England*. Oxford: Blackwell, 149–87.

Graves, C.P. 2007: Sensing and believing: exploring worlds of difference in pre-modern England: a contribution to the debate opened by Kate Giles. *World Archaeology* 39.4, 515–31.

Green, J.A. 1997: *The Aristocracy of Norman England*. Cambridge: Cambridge University Press.

Green, J.R. 1892–4: Short History of the English People, 4 vols. London: MacMillan.

Greene, J.P. 1992: *Medieval Monasteries*. London: Leicester University Press.

Greig, J.R.A. 1986: The archaeobotany of the Cowick medieval moat, and some thoughts on moat studies. *Circaea* 4.2, 43–50.

Grenville, J. 1997: *Medieval Housing*. London: Leicester University Press.

Grönwoldt, R. 1977: Two tapestries of the Commander of the Teutonic Order, Hugo von Hohenlandenberg. *The Connoisseur* 196, 182–9.

Guy, N. 2005: The 18th Annual Conference held at Mullaghmore, Co. Sligo. *Castle Studies Group Bulletin* 18, 4–54.

Guy, N. 2006: Thornbury Castle. *Castle Studies Group Journal* 19, 205–34.

Hadfield, M. 1985: *A History of British Gardening*. London: Harmondsworth.

Hagopian van Buren, A. 1986: Reality and literary romance in the park of Hesdin. In MacDougall, E.B. (ed.), *Medieval Gardens*. Washington: Dumbarton Oaks Research Library and Collection, 117–34.

Halliday, F.E. (ed.) 1969: *Richard Carew of Anthony: the survey of Cornwall*. New York: Augustus M Kelley.

Hanawalt, B.A. 1988: Men's games, king's deer: poaching in medieval England. *Journal of Medieval and Renaissance Studies* 18.2, 175–93.

Hansell, P. and Hansell, J. 1988: *Doves and Dovecotes*. Bath: Millstream Press.

Hansson, M. 2006: *Aristocratic Landscape: the spatial ideology of the medieval aristocracy*. Stockholm: Almqvist and Wiksell International.

Harding, S. and Lambert, D. (eds) 1994: *Parks and Gardens of Avon*. Bristol: Avon Gardens Trust.

Hare, J.N. 1988: Bishop's Waltham Palace, Hampshire: William of Wykeham, Henry Beaufort and the transformation of a medieval episcopal palace. *Archaeological Journal* 145, 222–54.

Hare, J.N. 1990: *Bishop's Waltham Palace, Hampshire*. London: English Heritage.

Harley, J.B. 1988: Maps, knowledge and power. In Cosgrove, D. and Daniels, S. (eds), *The Iconography of Landscape*. Cambridge: Cambridge University Press, 277–312.

Harley, J.B. 1992: Deconstructing the map. In Barnes, T. and Duncan, J. (eds), *Writing Worlds: discourse, text and metaphor in the representation of landscape*. London: Routledge, 231–47.

Harris, E., Harris, J. and James, N.D.G. 2003: *Oak: a British history*. Bollington: Windgather.

Hartgroves, S. and Walker, R. 1988: Excavations in the Lower Ward, Tintagel Castle, 1986. *Cornish Studies* 16 (first series), 9–30.

Hartley, R.F. 1983: *Medieval Earthworks of Rutland*. Leicester: Leicestershire Museums Publications.

Harvey, J. 1981: *Medieval Gardens*. London: Batsford.

Harvey, J.H. 1984: Vegetables in the Middle Ages. *Garden History* 12.2, 89–99.

Harvey, J.H. 1985: The first English garden book: Mayster Jon Gardener's treatise and its background. *Garden History* 13.2, 83–101.

Harvey, J.H. 1989: Garden plants of around 1525: the Fromond list. *Garden History* 17.2, 122–34.

Harvey, J.H. 1992: Westminster Abbey: the Infirmarer's Garden. *Garden History* 20.2, 97–115.

Harvey, P.D.A. 1985: Mapping the village: the historical evidence. In Hooke, D. (ed.), *Medieval Villages: a review of current work*. Oxford: Oxford University Committee for Archaeology, 33–45.

Harvey, P.D.A. 1989: Initiative and authority in settlement change. In Aston, M.A. and Dyer, C. (eds), *The Rural Settlements of Medieval England*. Oxford: Blackwell, 31–43.

Harwood, R. 1985: *Chrétien de Troyes: Perceval or the Story of the Grail*. Athens: University of Georgia Press.

Hatcher, J. 1970: *Rural Economy and Society in the Duchy of Cornwall 1300–1500*. London: Cambridge University Press.

Hawkes, J. 1991: Poundisford Park, Pitminster. *Proceedings of the Somerset Archaeological and Natural History Society* 135, 158.

Hawkyard, A.D.K. 1977: Thornbury castle. *Transactions of the Bristol and Gloucestershire Archaeological Society* 95, 51–8.

Henderson, C. 1935: *Essays in Cornish History*. Oxford: Clarendon.

Henderson, P. 1999: The architecture of the Tudor garden. *Garden History* 27.1, 54–72.

Henderson, P. 2005: *The Tudor House and Garden: architecture and landscape in the sixteenth and early seventeenth centuries*. New Have: Yale University Press.

Henisch, B.A. 2002: Private pleasures: painted gardens on the manuscript page. In Howe, J. and Wolfe, M. (eds), *Inventing Medieval Landscapes: senses of place in western Europe*. Gainesville: University Press of Florida, 150–70.

Hepple, L.W. 2001: 'The museum in the garden': displaying classical antiquities in Elizabethan and Jacobean England. *Garden History* 29.2, 109–20.

Herring, P. 1997: *Godolphin Breage: an archaeological and historical survey*. Truro: Cornwall County Council.

Herring, P. 2003: Cornish medieval deer parks. In Wilson-North, R. (ed.), *The Lie of the Land: aspects of the archaeology and history of the designed landscape in the South West of England*. Exeter: Mint Press, 34–50.

Hewlett, G.P. and Hassell, J. 1971: Bishop's Waltham Dikes. *Proceedings of the Hampshire Field Club and Archaeological Society* 28, 29–40.

Hicks, C. 1993: *Animals in Early Medieval Art*. Edinburgh: Edinburgh University Press.

Higham, R.A. 2006: Landscapes of defence, security and status. In Kain, R.J.P. (ed.), *The South West*. London: English Heritage, 89–108.

Higham, R.A. and Barker, P. 2000: *Hen Domen, Montgomery: a timber castle on the English–Welsh border*. Exeter: Exeter University Press.

Higham, R.A., Allan, J.P. and Blaylock, S.R. 1982: Excavations at Okehampton castle, Devon, part two – the bailey. *Proceedings of the Devon Archaeological Society* 40, 19–151.

Hillier, W. and Hanson, J. 1984: *The Social Logic of Space*. Cambridge: Cambridge University Press.

Hilton, R. 2003: *Bond Men Made Free: medieval peasant movements and the English rising of 1381*. London: Routledge.

Hilton, R.H. 1990: Was there a general crisis of feudalism? In Hilton, R.H. (ed.), *Class Conflict and the Crisis of Feudalism: essays in medieval social history*. London: Verso, 166–72.

Hobhouse, P. 1992: *Plants in Garden History*. London: Pavilion.

Hoffman, R.C. 1993: The protohistory of pike in western culture. In Salisbury, J.E. (ed.), *The Medieval World of Nature: a book of essays*. London: Garland, 61–76.

Hoffman, R.C. 1996: Economic development and aquatic ecosystems in medieval Europe. *American Historical Review* 101.3, 631–69.

Holt, R. 1988: *The Mills of Medieval England*. Oxford: Blackwell.

Homes, C.H.I. 1973: Herefordshire vineyards. *Transactions of the Woolhope Naturalists' Field Club* 41, 9–13.

Hoogvliet, M. 2000: *Mappae Mundi* and the medieval hermeneutics of cartographical space. In Ainsworth, P. and Scott, T. (eds), *Regions and Landscapes: reality and imagination in late medieval and early modern Europe*. Oxford: Peter Land, 25–46.

Hooke, D. 1989: Pre-Conquest woodland: its distribution and usage. *Agricultural History Review* 37, 113–29.

Hooke, D. (ed.) 2000: *Landscape, the Richest Historical Record*. Birmingham: Society for Landscape Studies.

Hoppitt, R. 2007: Hunting Suffolk's parks: towards a reliable chronology of emparkment. In Liddiard, R. (ed.), *The Medieval Park: new perspectives*. Bollington: Windgather, 146–64.

Hoskins, W.G. 1955: *The Making of the English Landscape*. London: Hodder and Stoughton.

Howard, M. 2003: Recycling the monastic fabric: beyond the Act of Dissolution. In Gaimster, D. and Gilchrist, R. (eds), *The Archaeology of Reformation, 1480–1580*. Leeds: Maney, 221–34.

Howard, P. 1991: *Landscapes: the artists' vision*. London: Routledge.

Howe, J. and Wolfe, M. (eds) 2002: *Inventing Medieval Landscapes: senses of place in western Europe*. Gainesville: University Press of Florida.

Howes, L.L. 1997: *Chaucer's Gardens and the Language of Convention*. Gainesville: University Press of Florida.

Howes, L.L. 2002: Narrative time and literary landscapes in Middle English poetry. In Howe, J. and Wolfe, M. (eds), *Inventing Medieval Landscapes: senses of place in western Europe*. Gainesville: University Press of Florida, 192–207.

Hudson, H. and Neale, F. 1983: The Panborough charter, AD 956. *Proceedings of the Somerset Archaeological and Natural History Society* 127, 55–69.

Hull, P.L. (ed.) 1971: *The Caption of Seisin of the Duchy of Cornwall*. Exeter: Devon and Cornwall Record Society.

Hunt, A. and Brown, M. 2005: *Catley Priory, Lincolnshire: a Gilbertine House in the Witham Valley*. English Heritage Survey Report.

Hunt, A., Pollington, M., Dunn, C. and Pearson, T. 2005: *Sawley Abbey, Sawley, Lancashire: a Cistercian monastic precinct and post-medieval landscape*. English Heritage Survey Report.

Hunt, J.D. and Willis, P. 1988: *The Genius of the Place*. Cambridge: Massachusetts Institute of Technology.

Hunt, T.J. 1959–60: A thirteenth century garden at Rimpton. *Proceedings of the Somerset Archaeological and Natural History Society* 104, 91–5.

Hynd, N.R. 1984: Towards a study of gardening in Scotland from the 16th to the 18th centuries. In Breeze, D.J. (ed.), *Studies in Scottish Antiquity Presented to Stewart Cruden*. Edinburgh: John Donald, 269–84.

Hynd, N.R. and Ewart, G. 1983: Aberdour Castle gardens. *Garden History* 11.2, 93–111.

Ingold, T. 1993: The temporality of landscape. *World Archaeology* 25.2, 152–74.

Jacques, D. (ed.) 1997: The techniques and uses of garden archaeology. *Journal of Garden History* 17.1 (special issue).

Jacques, D. 2001: Warwick Castle grounds and park, 1743–60. *Garden History* 29.1, 48–63.

James, T.B. 1990: *The Palaces of Medieval England c.1050–1550: royalty, nobility, the episcopate and their residences from Edward the Confessor to Henry VIII*. London: Seaby.

James, T.B. (ed.) 2004: Medieval Britain and Ireland in 2003. *Medieval Archaeology* 48, 229–350.

James, T.B. and Gerrard, C. 2007: *Clarendon: landscape of kings*. Bollington: Windgather.

James, T.B. and Robinson, A.M. 1988: *Clarendon Palace: the history and archaeology of a medieval hunting palace and hunting lodge near Salisbury*. London: Society of Antiquaries.

Jamieson, E. and Jones, B.V. 2004: *Court House, East Quantoxhead, Somerset: a Jacobean manor house and its surrounding landscape*. English Heritage Survey Report.

Jamieson, F. 1994: The royal gardens of the palace of Holyroodhouse, 1500–1603. *Garden History* 22.1, 18–36.

Jamison, E. 1938: The Sicilian Norman kingdom in the mind of Anglo-Norman contemporaries. *Proceedings of the British Academy* 24, 237–85.

Jennings, A. 2004: *Medieval Gardens*. Swindon: English Heritage.

Jennings, A. 2005: *Tudor and Stuart Gardens*. London: English Heritage.

Jennings, A. 2006: *Roman Gardens*. London: English Heritage.

Johnson, M. 1996: *An Archaeology of Capitalism*. Oxford: Blackwell.

Johnson, M. 2002: *Behind the Castle Gate: from medieval to Renaissance*. London: Routledge.

Johnson, M. 2007: *Ideas of Landscape*. London: Blackwell.

Jope, E.M. 1951: Scottish influences in the North of Ireland: castles with Scottish features, 1580–1640. *Ulster Journal of Archaeology* 14, 31–47.

Kain, R.J.P. and Baigent, E. 1992: *The Cadastral Map in the Service of the State: a history of property mapping*. Chicago: University of Chicago Press.

Keevil, G.D. 2000: *Medieval Palaces: an archaeology*. Stroud: Tempus.

Keevill, G.D. and Linford, N. 1998: Landscape with gardens: aerial, topographical and geophysical survey at Hamstead Marshall, Berkshire. In Pattison, P. (ed.), *There by Design: field archaeology in parks and gardens*. Oxford: BAR, 13–22.

Keil, I. 1959–60: The garden at Glastonbury Abbey: 1333–4. *Proceedings of the Somerset Archaeological and Natural History Society* 104, 96–101.

Kelly, F. 1997: *Early Irish Farming*. Dublin: Dublin Institute for Advanced Studies.

Kenyon, J. 2003: *Raglan Castle*. Cardiff: Cadw.

King, A. 2001: Lordship, castles and locality: Thomas of Lancaster, Dunstanburgh Castle and the Lancastrian affinity in Northumberland, 1296–1322. *Archaeologia Aeliana* 29, 223–34.

King, C. 2003: The organization of social space in late medieval manor houses. *Archaeological Journal* 160, 104–24.

Kisling, V. 2001: *Zoo and Aquarium History: ancient animal collections to zoological gardens*. Boca Raton: CRC Press.

Landsberg, S. 1987: The re-creation of a medieval and a sixteenth-century garden in Hampshire. In Hedley, G. and Rance, A. (eds), *Pleasure Grounds: the gardens and landscapes of Hampshire*. Southampton: Milestone, 27–31.

Landsberg, S. 1996: *The Medieval Garden*. London: British Museum Press.

Langdon, J. 1994: Lordship and peasant consumerism in the milling of early fourteenth-century England. *Past and Present* 154, 3–46.

Langdon, J. 2004: *Mills in the Medieval Economy: England, 1300–1540*. Oxford: Oxford University Press.

Leach, P. 1977: Excavations at North Petherton, Somerset 1975. *Proceedings of the Somerset Archaeological and Natural History Society* 121, 9–39.

Leach, P.E. and Bevan, L. 1998: *Great Witcombe Roman Villa, Gloucestershire: a report on excavations by Ernest Greenfield, 1960–1973*. Oxford: Archaeopress.

Le Patourel, H.E.J. 1973: *The Moated Sites of Yorkshire*. London: Society for Medieval Archaeology.

Le Patourel, H.E.J. 1978a: Documentary evidence. In Aberg, A. (ed.), *Medieval Moated Sites*. London: Council for British Archaeology, 21–8.

Le Patourel, H.E.J. 1978b: The excavation of moated sites. In Aberg, A. (ed.), *Medieval Moated Sites*. London: Council for British Archaeology, 36–45.

Le Patourel, H.E.J. 1981: Moated sites in their European context. In Aberg, A. and Brown, A.E. (eds), *Medieval Moated Sites in North-West Europe*. Oxford: BAR, 1–18.

Le Patourel, H.E.J. 1991: Rural building in England and Wales. In Miller, E. (ed.), *The Agrarian History of England and Wales, III: 1348–1500*. Cambridge: Cambridge University Press, 820–919.

Leslie, M. 1993: An English landscape garden before 'the English landscape garden'? *Journal of Garden History* 13, 3–15.

Lewis, E. 1985: Excavations in Bishop's Waltham, 1967–78. *Proceedings of the Hampshire Field Club and Archaeological Society* 41, 81–126.

Lewis, J. 2000: *The Medieval Earthworks of the Hundred of West Derby: tenurial evidence and physical structure*. Oxford: BAR.

Liddiard, R. 2000a: Castle Rising, Norfolk: a 'landscape of lordship'. *Anglo-Norman Studies* 22, 169–86.

Liddiard, R. 2000b: *'Landscapes of Lordship': Norman castles and the countryside in medieval Norfolk, 1066–1200*. Oxford: BAR.

Liddiard, R. 2003: The deer parks of Domesday Book. *Landscapes* 4.1, 4–23.

Liddiard, R. 2005a: *Castles in Context: power, symbolism and landscape, 1066 to 1500*. Bollington: Windgather.

Liddiard, R. 2005b: The castle landscapes of Anglo-Norman East Anglia: a regional perspective. In Harper-Bill, C. (ed.), *Medieval East Anglia*. Woodbridge: Boydell, 33–51.

Liddiard, R. 2007a: Medieval designed landscapes: problems and possibilities. In Gardiner, M. and Rippon, S. (eds), *Medieval Landscapes: landscape history after Hoskins, Volume 2*. Bollington: Windgather, 201–14.

Liddiard, R. (ed.) 2007b: *The Medieval Park: new perspectives*. Bollington: Windgather.

Lilley, K.D. 2002: *Urban Life in the Middle Ages, 1000–1450*. London: Palgrave.

Lilley, K.D. 2004: Cities of God? Medieval urban forms and their Christian symbolism. *Transactions of the Institute of British Geographers* 29.3, 296–313.

Lobel, M.D. (ed.) 1957: *The Victoria History of the County of Oxford, Vol. IV*. London: Oxford University Press.

Longnon, J. and Cazelles, R. 1969: *Les Très Riches Heures du Duc de Berry, Musée Condé, Chantilly*. London: Thames and Hudson.

Loughlin, N. and Miller, K. 1979: *A Survey of Archaeological Sites in Humberside*. Hull: Humberside Libraries and Amenities for Humberside Joint Archaeological Committee.

Lowerre, A.G. 2006: Why here and not there? The location of early Norman castles in the south-eastern midlands. *Anglo-Norman Studies* 29, 121–44.

Luttrell, C. 1974: *The Creation of the First Arthurian Romance: a quest*. London: Edward Arnold.

McCann, J. 2000: Dovecotes and pigeons in English law. *Transactions of the Ancient Monuments Society* 44, 25–50.

McCarthy, M.R., Summerson, H.R.T. and Annis, R.G. 1990: *Carlisle Castle: a survey and documentary history*. London: HMSO.

McDiarmid, M.P. (ed.) 1973: *The Kingis Quair of James Stewart*. London: Heinemann.

McDonagh, B. 2007: 'Powerhouses' of the wolds landscape: manor houses and churches in late medieval and early modern England. In Gardiner, M. and Rippon, S. (eds), *Medieval Landscapes: landscape history after Hoskins, Volume 2*. Bollington: Windgather, 185–200.

MacDougall, E.B. 1986a: Introduction. In MacDougall, E.B. (ed.), *Medieval Gardens*. Washington: Dumbarton Oaks Research Library and Collection, 3–5.

MacDougall, E.B. (ed.) 1986b: *Medieval Gardens*. Washington: Dumbarton Oaks Research Library and Collection.

MacDougall, E.B. 1987: *Ancient Roman Villa Gardens*. Washington: Dumbarton Oaks Research Library and Collection.

MacGregor, A. 1996: Swan rolls and beak markings: husbandary, exploitation and regulation of *Cygnus olor* in England c.1100–1900. *Anthropozoologica* 22, 39–68.

MacGregor, P. 1983: *Odiham Castle 1200–1500, Castle and Community*. Gloucester: Alan Sutton.

MacIvor, I. and Gallagher, D. 1999: Excavations at Caerlaverock Castle, 1955–66. *Archaeological Journal* 156, 143–245.

McKean, C. 2001: *The Scottish Chateau: the country house of Renaissance Scotland*. Stroud: Sutton.

McLean, T.M. 1981: *Medieval English Gardens*. London: Collins.

McNeill, T. 1997: *Castles in Ireland: feudal power in a Gaelic world*. London: Routledge.

McNeill, T. 2002: Dunineny castle and the Gaelic view of castle building. *Chateau Gaillard* 20, 153–61.

McNeill, T. 2006: The view from the top. *Les Cahiers de l'Urbanisme*. Liege: Mardaga, 122–7.

McOmish, D. 2007: Landscape analysis around Apethorpe Hall. *Research News: Newsletter of the English Heritage Research Department* 5, 26–9.

Mallory, J.P. and McNeill, T.E. 1991: *The Archaeology of Ulster: from colonization to plantation*. Belfast: Institute of Irish Studies.

Maltby, M. 1982: Animal and bird bones. In Higham, R.A., Allan, J.P. and Blaylock, S.R., Excavations at Okehampton castle, Devon, part two – the bailey. *Proceedings of the Devon Archaeological Society* 40, 114–35.

Manley, J. and Rudkin, D. 2003: *Facing the palace: excavations in front of the Roman palace at Fishbourne (Sussex, UK), 1995–99*. Lewes: Sussex Archaeological Society.

Manning, R.B. 1993: *Hunters and Poachers: a cultural and social history of unlawful hunting in England, 1485–1640*. Oxford: Clarendon.

Markham, G. 1616: Maison Rustique *or Countrey Farme*. London.

Marshall, P. 2002a: The ceremonial function of the donjon in the twelfth century. *Chateau Gaillard* 20, 141–51.

Marshall, P. 2002b: The great tower as residence. In Meirion-Jones, G., Impey, E. and Jones, M. (eds), *The Seigneurial Residence in Western Europe AD c800–1600*. Oxford: BAR, 27–44.

Martin, G.H. 1995: *Knighton's Chronicle, 1337–1396*. Oxford: Clarendon Press.

Marvin, W.P. 1999: Slaughter and romance: hunting reserves in late medieval England. In Hanawalt, B.A. and Wallace, D. (eds), *Medieval Crime and Social Control*. Minneapolis: University of Minnesota Press, 224–52.

Meadows, I. 1996: Wollaston: the Nene valley, a British Moselle? *Current Archaeology* 150, 212–15.

Meek, M. 1984: *Tully Castle, County Fermanagh*. Belfast: Department of the Environment for Northern Ireland.

Mew, K. 2000: The dynamics of lordship and landscape as revealed in a Domesday study of the Nova Foresta. *Anglo-Norman Studies* 23, 155–66.

Miles, D., Palmer, S., Lock, G., Gosden, C. and Cromarty, A. 2003: *Uffington White Horse and its Landscape: investigations at White Horse Hill, Uffington, 1989–95, and Tower Hill, Ashbury, 1993–4*. Oxford: Oxford Archaeology.

Mileson, S. 2005: The importance of parks in fifteenth-century society. In Clark, L. (ed.) *Of Mice and Men: image, belief and regulation in late medieval England*. Woodbridge: Boydell, 19–38.

Mileson, S.A. 2007: The sociology of park creation in medieval England. In Liddiard, R. (ed.), *The Medieval Park: new perspectives*. Bollington: Windgather, 11–26.

Miller, N.F. and Gleason, K.L. (eds) 1994: *The Archaeology of Garden and Field*. Philadelphia: University of Pennsylvania Press.

Milln, J. 1993: Deer courses in medieval parks. *Past Times: Newsletter of the Stafford and Mid-Staffordshire Archaeological Society* 25, 2–4.

Mitchell, W.J.T. 1994: *Landscape and Power*. Chicago: University of Chicago Press.

Moffat, J.B., Thomson, B.S. and Fulton, J. 1989: *Sharp Practice 3: the third report on researches into the medieval hospital at Soutra, Lothian/Borders Region, Scotland*. Edinburgh: Soutra Hospital Archaeoethnopharmacological Research Project.

MOLAS (Museum of London Archaeology Service) 2005: *Raglan Castle, Monmouthshire, Wales, NP15, County of Monmouthshire: a landscape survey*. London: MOLAS unpublished report.

Mooney, L.R. and Arn, M.J. (eds) 2005: *James I of Scotland's The Kingis Quair and Other Prison Poems*. Kalamazoo: University of Michigan Press.

Moorhouse, S. 1984: Late medieval pottery plant-holders from eastern Yorkshire. *Medieval Archaeology* 28, 194–201.

Moorhouse, S. 1986: The Harewood landscape project. *Council for British Archaeology Forum* (1985), 10–15.

Moorhouse, S. 1989: Monastic estates: their composition and development. In Gilchrist, R. and Mytum, H. (eds), *The Archaeology of Rural Monasteries*. Oxford: BAR, 29–81.

Moorhouse, S. 1991: Ceramics in the medieval garden. In Brown, A.E. (ed.), *Garden Archaeology*. London: Council for British Archaeology, 100–17.

Moorhouse, S. 2003a: Anatomy of the Yorkshire Dales: decoding the medieval landscape. In Ottaway, P., Manby, T. and Moorhouse, S. (eds), *The Archaeology of Yorkshire: an assessment at the beginning of the 21st century; papers arising out of the Yorkshire Archaeological Resource Framework Forum Conference at Ripon, September, 1998*. Leeds: Yorkshire Archaeological Society, 293–362.

Moorhouse, S. 2003b: Medieval Yorkshire: a rural landscape for the future. In Ottaway, P., Manby, T. and Moorhouse, S. (eds), *The Archaeology of Yorkshire: an assessment at the beginning of the 21st century; papers arising out of the Yorkshire Archaeological Resource Framework Forum Conference at Ripon, September, 1998.* Leeds: Yorkshire Archaeological Society, 181–214.

Moorhouse, S. 2007: The medieval parks of Yorkshire: functions, contents and chronology. In Liddiard, R. (ed.), *The Medieval Park: new perspectives*. Bollington: Windgather, 99–127.

Morley, B. and Speak, S. 2002: Excavation and survey at Hylton Castle, Sunderland. *Archaeological Journal* 159, 258–65.

Morris, J.T. 2005: Red deer's role in social expression on the isles of Scotland. In Pluskowski, A. (ed.), *Just Skin and Bones? New perspectives on human–animal relations in the historical past*. Oxford: BAR, 9–18.

Morris, R.K. 1989: *Churches in the Landscape*. London: Dent.

Mosser, M. and Teyssot, G. (eds) 1991: *The History of Garden Design: the western tradition from the Renaissance to the present*. London: Thames and Hudson.

Mowl, T. 2004: *Gentlemen and Players: gardeners of the English landscape*. Stroud: Sutton.

MSRG 1995: Fieldwork and excavation 1995. *Medieval Settlement Research Group Report* 10, 25–46.

Muir, R. 2001: *Landscape Detective: discovering a countryside*. Bollington: Windgather.

Munby, L.M. 1977: *The Hertfordshire Landscape*. London: Hodder and Stoughton.

Munroe, J. 2006: Gender, class, and the art of gardening: gardening manuals in early modern England. *Prose Studies* 28.2, 197–210.

Murphy, P. and Scaife, R.G. 1991: The environmental archaeology of gardens. In Brown, A.E. (ed.), *Garden Archaeology*. London: Council for British Archaeology, 83–99.

Musty, J. 1886: Deer coursing at Clarendon Palace and Hampton Court. *Antiquaries Journal* 66.1, 131–2.

Nash, G. and Redwood, B. (eds) 2006: *Looking Beyond the Castle Walls: the Weobley Castle project*. Oxford: BAR.

Neal, D.S. 1971: Excavation at the palace and priory of King's Langley. *Hertfordshire Archaeology* 3, 31–73.

Neave, D.R.J. and Turnbull, D.K.M. 1992: *Landscaped Parks and Gardens of East Yorkshire 1700–1830*. Kingston-upon Hull: Georgian Society for East Yorkshire.

Neave, S. 1991: *Medieval Parks of East Yorkshire*. Beverley: Hutton Press.

Nenk, B.S., Margeson, S. and Hurley, M. 1995: Medieval Britain and Ireland in 1994. *Medieval Archaeology* 39, 180–293.

Nevanlinna, S. and Taavitsainen, I. (eds) 1993: *St Katherine of Alexandria: the late Middle English prose legend in Southwell Minster MS 7*. Cambridge: Brewer.

Nichols, S.G., Kablitz, A. and Calhoun, A. (eds) 2008: *Rethinking the Medieval Senses: heritage/fascinations/frames*. Baltimore: The John Hopkins University Press.

Noble, C. 1997: Norwich Cathedral Priory Gardeners' Accounts, 1329–1530. *Norfolk Record Society* 41, 1–94.

O'Conor, K.D. 1998: *The Archaeology of Medieval Rural Settlement in Ireland*. Dublin: Discovery Programme Monograph No. 3.

O'Conor, K.D. 2004: Medieval rural settlement in Munster. In Ludlow, J. and Jameson, N. (eds), *Medieval Ireland: the Barryscourt Lectures I–X*. Kinsale: Gandon Editions, 227–56.

O'Conor, K.D. and Murphy, M. 2006: Deerparks in medieval Ireland. *Eolas: The Journal of the American Society of Irish Medieval Studies* 1, 53–70.

O'Keeffe, T. 2000a: Ballyloughan, Ballymoon and Clonmore: three castles of c.1300 in County Carlow. *Anglo-Norman Studies* 23, 167–97.

O'Keeffe, T. 2000b: *Medieval Ireland: an introduction*. Stroud: Tempus.

O'Keeffe, T. 2004: Were there designed landscapes in medieval Ireland? *Landscapes* 5.2, 52–68.

O'Regan, H., Turner, A. and Sabin, R. 2005: Medieval big cat remains from the Royal menagerie at the Tower of London. *International Journal of Osteoarchaeology* 16.5, 385–94.

Oggins, R.S. 1993: Falconry and medieval views of nature. In Salisbury, J.E. (ed.), *The Medieval World of Nature: a book of essays*. London: Garland, 47–60.

Oosthuizen, S.M. and Taylor, C.C. 2000: Rediscovery of a vanished garden in Bassingbourn, Cambridgeshire, and the impact of the Lynne family on the medieval landscape. *Proceedings of the Cambridge Antiquarian Society* 89, 59–67.

Orme, N. 1992: Medieval Hunting: fact and fancy. In Hanawalt, B. (ed.), *Chaucer's England: literature in historical context*. Minneapolis: University of Minnesota Press, 133–53.

Orme, N. 2008a: Place and past in medieval England. *History Today* 58.7, 24–30.

Orme, N. 2008b: *Victoria County History of Cornwall, Vol II: religious history to 1559*. London: Victoria County History.

Orme, N. and Webster, M. 1995: *The English Hospital 1070–1570*. New Haven: Yale University Press.

Oschinsky, D. (ed.) 1971: *Walter of Henley, and other Treatises on Estate Management and Accounting*. Oxford: Clarendon.

Oswald, A. 2005: *Archaeological Investigation and Analytical Field Survey on Cawood Castle Garth, Cawood, Yorkshire, North Riding*. English Heritage Survey Report.

Oswald, A. and Ashbee, J. 2006: Dunstanburgh Castle – Northumberland's own Camelot? *Research News: Newsletter of the English Heritage Research Department* 4, 34–7.

Oswald, A., Ashbee, J., Porteous, K. and Huntley, J. 2006: *Dunstanburgh Castle, Northumberland: archaeological, architectural and historical investigations*. York: English Heritage Research Department Report.

Padel, O.J. 1981: The Cornish background of the Tristan stories. *Cambridge Medieval Studies* 1, 53–81.

Padel, O.J. 1988: Tintagel in the twelfth and thirteenth centuries. *Cornish Studies* 16, 61–6.

Page, W. (ed.) 1906: *The Victoria History of the County of Northampton, Vol. II*. London: Archibald Constable.

Page, W. (ed.) 1908a: *The Victoria History of the County of Rutland, Vol. I*. London: Archibald Constable.

Page, W. (ed.) 1908b: *The Victoria History of the County of Warwickshire, Vol. II*. London: Archibald Constable.

Page, W. (ed.) 1923: *The Victoria History of the County of Yorkshire, North Riding, Vol. II*. London: Archibald Constable.

Papworth, M. 2003: Archaeological recording on historic gardens by the National Trust. In Wilson-North, R. (ed.), *The Lie of the Land: aspects of the archaeology and history of the designed landscape in the South West of England*. Exeter: Mint Press, 12–20.

Parker, G. 1981–82: The medieval hermitage of Grafton Regis. *Northamptonshire Past and Present* 6, 247–52.

Parker, J.H. 1851–59: *Some Account of Domestic Architecture in England*, 3 vols. Oxford: James Parker.

Parsons, J.C. 1995: *Eleanor of Castile: queen and society in thirteenth-century England*. New York: St Martin's Press.

Partida, T. 2007: The early hunting landscapes of Northamptonshire. *Northamptonshire Past and Present* 60, 44–60.

Pattison, P. (ed.) 1998a: *There by Design: field archaeology in parks and gardens*. Oxford: BAR.

Pattison, P. 1998b: Giant steps: fieldwork in London's royal parks. In Pattison, P. (ed.), *There by Design: field archaeology in parks and gardens*. Oxford: BAR, 39–46.

Payne, A. 1990: *Medieval Beasts*. London: British Library.

Payne, N. 2003: *The Medieval Residences of the Bishops of Bath and Wells, and Salisbury*. University of Bristol unpublished PhD thesis.

Pearsall, D. 1977: Hunting scenes in medieval illuminated manuscripts. *The Connoisseur* 196, 170–82.

Pearsall, D. and Salter, E. 1973: *Landscapes and Seasons of the Medieval World*. London: Elek.

Pearse, R. 1963: *The Ports and Harbours of Cornwall*. St Austell: H.E. Warne.

Pearson, T., Ainsworth, S. and Oswald, A. 2004: *An Archaeological Assessment of Earthworks at Byland Abbey, Yorkshire, North Riding*. English Heritage Survey Report.

Peers, C. 1986: *Kirby Muxloe Castle*. London: English Heritage.

Peers, C.R. 1921–22: Harlech Castle. *Transactions of the Honourable Society of Cymmrodorion*, 63–82.

Pestell, T. 2004: *Landscapes of Monastic Foundation: the establishment of religious houses in East Anglia c.650–1200*. Woodbridge: Boydell.

Pevsner, N. and Williamson, E. 1984: *The Buildings of England: Leicestershire and Rutland*. Harmondsworth: Penguin.

Phillpotts, C. 2003: The houses of Henry VIII's courtiers in London. In Gaimster, D. and Gilchrist, R. (eds), *The Archaeology of Reformation, 1480–1580*. Leeds: Maney, 299–309.

Platt, C. 1982: *The Castle in Medieval England and Wales*. London: Secker and Warburg.

Platt, C. 1988: *Medieval England: a social history and archaeology from the conquest to 1600AD*. London: Routledge.

Pluskowski, A. 2002: Predators in robes: materialising and mystifying hunting, predation and seclusion in the northern European medieval landscape. In Helmig, G., Scholkmann, B. and Untermann, M. (eds), *Centre, Region, Periphery: Proceedings of the International Conference of Medieval and Later Archaeology, Basel, Switzerland*, vol. 2. Basel: Archäologische Bodenforschung Basel-Stadt, 243–7.

Pluskowski, A. 2007: The social construction of medieval park ecosystems: an interdisciplinary perspective. In Liddiard, R. (ed.), *The Medieval Park: new perspectives*. Bollington: Windgather, 63–78.

Pollock, D. 2004: The bawn exposed: recent excavations at Barryscourt. In Ludlow, J. and Jameson, N. (eds), *Medieval Ireland: the Barryscourt Lectures I–X*. Kinsale: Gandon Editions, 149–75.

Poore, D. and Wilkinson, D. 2001: *Beaumont Palace and the White Friars: excavations at the Sackler Library, Beaumont Street, Oxford*. Oxford: Oxford Archaeology.

Port, G. 1987: *Rochester Castle*. London: English Heritage.

Poulton, R. 2005: *A Medieval Royal Complex at Guildford: Excavations at the castle and palace*. Guildford: Surrey Archaeological Society.

Pounds, N.J.G. 1982–84: *The Parliamentary Survey of the Duchy of Cornwall*, 2 vols. Exeter: Devon and Cornwall Record Society.

Powell, W.R. (ed.) 1966: *The Victoria History of the County of Essex, Vol. V*. London: Oxford University Press for the Institute of Historical Research.

Power, E. (trans.) 1928: *The Goodman of Paris: a moral and domestic economy*. London: Routledge.

Prendegast, E.D.V. 1984: The history of the Abbotsbury duck decoy. *Proceedings of the Dorset Natural History and Archaeological Society* 106, 51–62.

Prestwich, M. 1980: *The Three Edwards: war and state in England 1272–1377*. London: Methuen.

Priestley, S.G. and Turner, R.C. 2003: Three castles of the Clare family in Monmouthshire during the thirteenth and fourteenth centuries. *Archaeologia Cambrensis* 152, 9–52.

Probert, S. 2004: *Okehampton Castle and Park*. English Heritage Survey Report.

Prummel, W. 1997: Evidence of hawking (falconry) from bird and mammal bones. *International Journal of Osteoarchaeology* 7.4, 333–8.

Querrien, A. 2003: Pêche et consommation du poisson en Berry au Moyen Âge. *Bibliothèque de l'École des Chartes* 161: 409–35.

Quest-Ritson, C. 2001: *The English Garden: a social history*. London: Penguin.

Quiney, A. 2003: *Town Houses of Medieval Britain*. New Haven: Yale University Press.

Rackham, O. 1976: *Trees and Woodland in the British Landscape*. London: Dent.

Rackham, O. 1986: *The History of the Countryside*. London: Dent.

Rackham, O. 2001: *Trees and Woodland in the British Landscape: the complete history of Britain's trees, woods and hedgerows*. London: Pheonix Press.

Rackham, O. 2004: Pre-existing trees and woods in country-house parks. *Landscapes* 5.2, 1–15.

Radford, C.A.R. 1935: Tintagel: the castle and Celtic monastery, interim report. *Antiquaries Journal* 40.4, 401–19.

Rahtz, P.A. 1969: Excavations at King John's Hunting Lodge, Writtle, Essex, 1955–1957. London: Society for Medieval Archaeology.

RCAHMW 1937: *An Inventory of Ancient Historical Monuments in Anglesey*. London: HMSO.

RCAHMW 1982: *An Inventory of the Ancient Monuments in Glamorgan. Volume III: Medieval Secular Monuments. Part II: Non-Defensive*. Cardiff: HMSO.

RCAHMW 2000: *An Inventory of the Ancient Monuments in Glamorgan. Volume III – Part 1b: Medieval Secular Monuments. The Later Castles: from 1217 to the present*. Cardiff: HMSO.

RCHAMS 1963: *Stirlingshire: an inventory of the ancient monuments*, 2 vols. Edinburgh: HMSO.

RCHME 1916–23: *An Inventory of the Historical Monuments in Essex*, 4 vols. London: HMSO.

RCHME 1926: *An Inventory of the Historical Monuments in Huntingdonshire*. London: HMSO.

RCHME 1931–34: *An Inventory of the Historical Monuments in Herefordshire*, 3 vols. London: HMSO.

RCHME 1952–75: *An Inventory of the Historical Monuments in the County of Dorset*, 5 vols. London: HMSO.

RCHME 1968–72: *An Inventory of the Historical Monuments in the County of Cambridge*, 2 vols. London: HMSO.

RCHME 1975–84: *An Inventory of the Historical Monuments in the County of Northampton*, 6 vols. London: HMSO.

RCHME 1990: *Whorlton Castle, Holy Cross Church, Whorlton Village and Environs, Hambleton District, North Yorkshire*. Unpublished report, National Monuments Record Centre, Swindon.

Reaney, P.H. 1960: *The Origins of English Place-Names*. London: Routledge.

Rees, S.E. 1996: The secret garden. *Heritage in Wales* 6, 11–13.

Rees, S.E. 1999a: *Haverfordwest Priory*. Cardiff: Cadw.

Rees, S.E. 1999b: The Augustinian Priory. In Miles, D. (ed.), *A History of the town and county of Haverfordwest*. Gomer: Llandysul, 68–71.

Reeve, M.M. and Thurlby, M. 2005: King John's Gloriette at Corfe Castle. *Journal of the Society of Architectural Historians* 64.2, 168–85.

Reeves, C. 1995: *Pleasures and Pastimes in Medieval England*. Stroud: Alan Sutton.

Reeves-Smyth, T. 2004: Irish gardens and gardening before Cromwell. In Ludlow, J. and Jameson, N. (eds), *Medieval Ireland: the Barryscourt Lectures I–X*. Kinsale: Gandon Editions, 97–143.

Renn, D. 1969: *Three Shell Keeps: Launceston, Restormel, Totnes*. London: HMSO.

Rhys, E. (ed.) 1908: *The Itinerary through Wales by Giraldus Cambrensis*. London: Dent.

Richardson, A. 2003a: Corridors of power: a case study in access analysis from medieval England. *Antiquity* 77.296, 373–84.

Richardson, A. 2003b: Gender and space in medieval palaces c.1160–1547: a study in access analysis and imagery. *Medieval Archaeology* 47, 131–65.

Richardson, A. 2005: *The Forest, Park and Palace of Clarendon, c.1200–c.1650: reconstructing an actual, conceptual and documented Wiltshire landscape*. Oxford: BAR.

Richardson, A. 2007: 'The king's chief delights': a landscape approach to the royal parks of post-conquest England. In Liddiard, R. (ed.), *The Medieval Park: new perspectives*. Bollington: Windgather, 27–48.

Rieser, M. 1946: The language of shapes and sizes in architecture or on morphic semantics. *The Philosophical Review* 55.2, 152–73.

Rigold, S.E. 1957: *Nunney Castle, Somerset*. London: HMSO.

Riley, H. 2006: *The Historic Landscape of the Quantock Hills*. Swindon: English Heritage.

Riley, H. and Wilson-North, R. 2003: From pillow mounds to parterres: a revelation at Cerne Abbas. In Wilson-North, R. (ed.), *The Lie of the Land: aspects of the archaeology and history of the designed landscape in the South West of England*. Exeter: Mint Press, 100–6.

Roberts, E. 1985: Alresford Pond, a medieval canal reservoir: a tradition asserted. *Proceedings of the Hampshire Field Club and Archaeological Society* 41, 127–38.

Roberts, E. 1986: The Bishop of Winchester's fishponds in Hampshire, 1150–1400: their development, function and management. *Proceedings of the Hampshire Field Club and Archaeological Society* 42, 125–38.

Roberts, E. 1988: The Bishop of Winchester's deer parks in Hampshire 1200–1400. *Proceedings of the Hampshire Field Club and Archaeological Society* 44, 67–86.

Roberts, E. 1993: The Bishop of Winchester's fishponds and deer parks. *Proceedings of the Hampshire Field Club and Archaeological Society* 49, 229–31.

Roberts, E. 1995: Edward III's lodge at Odiham, Hampshire. *Medieval Archaeology* 39, 91–106.

Roberts, I. 2002: *Pontefract Castle: archaeological excavations 1982–86*. Morley: West Yorkshire Archaeological Service.

Roberts, J. 1997: *Royal Landscape: the gardens and parks of Windsor*. London: Yale University Press.

Roberts, J. 1999: The gardens of the gentry in the late Tudor period. *Garden History* 27.2, 89–108.

Roberts, J. 2001: 'Well Temper'd Clay': constructing water features in the landscape park. *Garden History* 29.1, 12–28.

Robinson, M. and Wilson, B. 1987: Survey of environmental archaeology in the south midlands. In Keeley, H.C.M. (ed.), *Environmental Archaeology: a regional review*, vol. 2. London: English Heritage Occasional Paper 1, 16–100.

Rodwell, K. and Bell, R. 2005: *Acton Court: the evolution of an early Tudor courtier's house*. London: English Heritage

Rodwell, W. 2005: 'Begun while the Black Death raged…' The Vicars' Close at Wells. In Domino, C. (ed.), *Vicars Choral at English Cathedrals: history, architecture and archaeology*. Oxford: Oxbow, 112–37.

Rooney, A. 1997: The hunts in Sir Gawain and the Green Knight. In Brewer, D. and Gibson, J. (eds), *A Companion to the Gawain-Poet*. Cambridge: D.S. Brewer, 157–63

Rose, P. 1994: The medieval garden at Tintagel Castle. *Cornish Archaeology* 33, 170–82.

Rowe, A. 2007: The distribution of parks in Hertfordshire: landscape, lordship and woodland. In Liddiard, R. (ed.), *The Medieval Park: new perspectives*. Bollington: Windgather, 128–45.

Rowley, T. 1999: *The Normans*. Stroud: Tempus.

Ruggles, D.F. 1999: *Gardens, Landscape and Vision in the Palaces of Islamic Spain*. University Park, Pennsylvania: Penn State University Press.

Russell, W.M.S. and Russell, C. 1991: English turf mazes, Troy and the labyrinth. *Folklore* 102.1, 77–88.

Ryder, P. 1979: Ravensworth Castle, North Yorkshire. *Yorkshire Archaeological Journal* 51, 81–100.

Rynne, C. 2004: Technological change in Anglo-Norman Munster. In Ludlow, J. and Jameson, N. (eds), *Medieval Ireland: the Barryscourt Lectures I–X*. Kinsale: Gandon Editions, 33–63.

Sales, J. 1995: Garden restoration past and present. *Garden History* 23.1, 1–9.

Salisbury, J.E. (ed.) 1993: *The Medieval World of Nature: a book of essays*. London: Garland.

Salisbury, J.E. 1994: *The Beast Within: animals in the Middle Ages*. London: Routledge.

Salzman, L.F. 1937: *The Victoria History of the County of Sussex*, *Vol. IX*. London: Oxford University Press for the Institute of Historical Research.

Saunders, A. 1980: Lydford Castle, Devon. *Medieval Archaeology* 24, 123–86.

Saunders, A. 2006: *Excavations at Launceston Castle, Cornwall*. Leeds: Society for Medieval Archaeology.

Saunders, C.J. 1993: *The Forest of Medieval Romance: Avernus, Broceliande, Arden*. Cambridge: Brewer.

Saunders, T. 1990: The feudal construction of space: power and domination in the nucleated village. In Samson, R. (ed.), *The Social Archaeology of Houses*. Edinburgh: Edinburgh University Press, 181–96.

Scheibe, R. 1997: The major professional skills of the dove in the Buke of the Howlat. In Houwen, L.A.J.R. (ed.), *Animals and the Symbolic in Medieval Art and Literature*. Gronigen: Egbert Forsten, 107–37.

Schofield, J. 1984: *The Building of London: from the conquest to the great fire*. London: British Museum.

Schofield, J. 1994: *Medieval London Houses*. New Haven: Yale University Press.

Schofield, J. 1999: City of London gardens, 1500–c.1620. *Garden History* 27.1, 73–88.

Seeley, D. and Phillpotts, C. 2006: *Winchester Palace: excavations at the Southwark residence of the Bishops of Winchester*. London: Museum of London Archaeology Service.

Serjeantson, D. 2006: Birds: food and a mark of status. In Woolgar, C.M., Serjeantson, D. and Waldron, T. (eds), *Food in Medieval England: diet and nutrition*. Oxford: Oxford University Press, 131–47.

Serjeantson, D. and Woolgar, C.M. 2006: Fish consumption in medieval England. In Woolgar, C.M., Serjeantson, D. and Waldron (eds), *Food in Medieval England: diet and nutrition*. Oxford: Oxford University Press, 102–30.

Serpell, J. and Paul, E. 1994: Pets and the development of positive attitudes to animals. In Manning, A. and Serpell, J. (eds), *Animals and Human Society: changing perspectives*. London: Routledge, 127–44.

Ševčenko, N.P. 2002: Wild animals in the Byzantine park. In Littlewood, A., Maguire, H. and Wolschke-Bulmahn, J. (eds), *Byzantine Garden Culture*. Washington: Dumbarton Oaks, 69–86.

Shanks, M. 1992: *Experiencing the Past*. London: Routledge.

Sheail, J. 1971: *Rabbits and their History*. Newton Abbot: David and Charles.

Shortt, H.S. 1965: *Old Sarum*. London: HMSO.

Silvester, R.J., Courtney, P. and Rees, S.E. 2004: Castell Blaenllynfi, Brecknock: a Marcher castle and its landscape. *Archaeologia Cambrensis* 153, 75–103.

Smith, N. 2000: *Bronsil Castle, Eastnor, Herefordshire: a survey of the remains of a 15th-century mansion, its surrounding moat, and ponds*. English Heritage Survey Report.

Smith, N. 2002: *Dyrham Park, South Gloucestershire: an archaeological earthwork survey*. English Heritage Survey Report.

Smith, P., Morrison, K., Hill, N., McOmish, D., Cattell, J., Cole, E. and Edgar, J. 2006: *Apethorpe Hall, Apethorpe, Northamptonshire: Survey, Research and Analysis*, 2 vols. English Heritage Research Department Report.

Smyser, H.M. 1956: The domestic background to Troiluis and Criseyde. *Speculum* 31.2, 297–315.

Soderberg, J. 2004: Wild cattle: red deer in the religious texts, iconography, and archaeology of early medieval Ireland. *International Journal of Historical Archaeology* 8.3, 167–83.

Spandl, K. 1998: Exploring the round houses of doves. *British Archaeology* 35.

Stalley, R. 1987: *The Cistercian Monasteries of Ireland*. New Haven: Yale University Press.

Stamper, P. 1988: Woods and parks. In Astill, G. and Grant, A. (eds), *The Countryside of Medieval England*. Oxford: Blackwell, 128–48.

Stamper, P. 1996: *Historic Parks & Gardens of Shropshire*. Shrewsbury: Shropshire Books.

Steane, J. 1974: *The Northamptonshire Landscape*. London: Hodder and Stoughton.

Steane, J. 1975: The medieval parks of Northamptonshire. *Northamptonshire Past and Present* 5, 211–33.

Steane, J. 1988: The royal fishponds of medieval England. In M. Aston (ed.), *Medieval Fish, Fisheries and Fishponds*, 2 vols. Oxford: BAR, 39–68.

Steane, J. 1995: Stonor – a lost park and garden found. *Oxoniensia* 59, 449–70.

Steane, J. 1999: *The Archaeology of the Medieval English Monarchy*. London: Routledge.

Steane, J. 2001: *The Archaeology of Power*. Stroud: Tempus.

Steane, J.M. and Bryant, G.F. 1975: Excavations at the deserted medieval settlement at Lyveden. *Journal of the Northampton Museum and Art Gallery* 12, 3–160.

Stewart-Brown, R. 1912: The royal manor and park of Shotwick. *Transactions of the Historic Society of Lancashire and Cheshire* 64, 82–142.

Stocker, D. 2006: *The West*. London: English Heritage/Collins.

Stocker, D. and Everson, P. 2003: The straight and the narrow way: fenland causeways and the conversion of the landscape in the Witham Valley. In Carver, M. (ed.), *The Cross Goes North: processes of conversion in northern Europe, AD300–1300*. Woodbridge: York Medieval Press, 271–88.

Stocker, D. and Stocker, M. 1996: Sacred profanity: the theology of rabbit breeding and the symbolic landscape of the warren. *World Archaeology* 28.2, 265–72.

Stone, D.J. 2006: The consumption and supply of birds in late medieval England. In. Woolgar, C.M., Serjeantson, D. and Waldron, T. (eds), *Food in Medieval England: diet and nutrition*. Oxford: Oxford University Press, 148–61.

Strong, R. 1979: *The Renaissance Garden in England*. London: Thames and Hudson.

Strong, R. 1999: Foreword: the Renaissance garden in England reconsidered. *Garden History* 27.1, 2–9.

Sweetman, D. 1999: *The Medieval Castles of Ireland*. Woodbridge: Boydell.

Sykes, N. 2004a: The dynamics of status symbols: wildfowl exploitation in England AD 410–1550. *Archaeological Journal* 161, 82–105.

Sykes, N. 2004b: Zooarchaeology and the Norman Conquest. *Anglo-Norman Studies* 27, 185–97.

Sykes, N. 2005: Hunting for the Anglo-Normans: zooarchaeological evidence for medieval identity. In Pluskowski, A. (ed.), *Just Skin and Bones? New perspectives on human–animal relations in the historical past*. Oxford: BAR, 73–80.

Sykes, N. 2007: Animal bones and animal parks. In Liddiard, R. (ed.), *The Medieval Park: new perspectives*. Bollington: Windgather, 49–62.

Taylor, A.J. 1950: *Raglan Castle*. London: HMSO.

Taylor, A.J. 2003: *Conwy Castle and Town Walls*. Cardiff: Cadw.

Taylor, C.C. 1972: Medieval moats in Cambridgeshire. In Fowler, P.J. (ed.), *Archaeology and the Landscape: essays for L.V. Grinsell*. London: John Baker, 237–48.

Taylor, C.C. 1974: *Fieldwork in Medieval Archaeology*. London: Batsford.

Taylor, C.C. 1983a: *The Archaeology of Gardens*. Aylesbury: Shire.

Taylor, C.C. 1983b: *Village and Farmstead: a history of rural settlement in England*. London: George Philip.

Taylor, C.C. 1989a: Somersham Palace, Cambridgeshire, a medieval landscape for pleasure? In Bowden, M., Mackay, D. and Topping, P. (eds), *From Cornwall to Caithness: some aspects of British field archaeology, papers presented to Norman V. Quinnell*. Oxford: BAR, 211–24.

Taylor, C.C. 1989b: Spaldwick, Cambridgeshire. *Proceedings of the Cambridge Antiquarian Society* 78, 71–5.

Taylor, C.C. 1991: Garden archaeology: an introduction. In Brown, A.E. (ed.), *Garden Archaeology*. London: Council for British Archaeology, 1–5.

Taylor, C.C. 1996: The archaeology of gardens and designed landscapes. In Morgan Evans, D., Salway, P. and Thackray, D. (eds), *'The Remains of Distant Times', Archaeology and the National Trust*. London: Occasional Papers of the Society of Antiquaries of London, 59–65.

Taylor, C.C. 1998a: From recording to recognition. In Pattison, P. (ed.), *There by Design: field archaeology in parks and gardens*. Oxford: BAR, 1–6.

Taylor, C.C. 1998b: *Parks and Gardens of Britain: a landscape history from the air*. Edinburgh: Edinburgh University Press.

Taylor, C.C. 2000: Medieval ornamental landscapes. *Landscapes* 1.1, 38–55.

Taylor, C.C. 2004a: A late seventeenth-century garden at Babraham, Cambridgeshire. *Proceedings of the Cambridge Antiquarian Society* 93, 143–50.

Taylor, C.C. 2004b: Ravensdale Park, Derbyshire, and medieval deer coursing. *Landscape History* 26, 37–57.

Taylor, C.C. 2006: Landscape history, observation and explanation: the missing houses in Cambridgeshire villages. *Proceedings of the Cambridge Antiquarian Society* 95, 121–32.

Taylor, C.C., Everson, P. and Wilson-North, R. 1990: Bodiam Castle, Sussex. *Medieval Archaeology* 34, 155–7.

Tebbutt, C.F. 1974: King's Standing, Ashdown Forest. *Sussex Archaeological Collections* 112, 30–3.

Terra Nova 2002: *A Geoarchaeological study of Whittington Castle, Shropshire*. Unpublished report.

Thacker, C. 1979: *The History of Gardens*. London: Croom Helm.

Theis, J. 2001: The 'ill kill'd' deer: poaching and social order in *The Merry Wives of Windsor*. *Texas Studies in Literature and Language* 43.1, 46–73.

Thiébaux, M. 1974: *The Stag of Love: the chase in medieval literature*. Ithaca: Cornell University Press.

Thomas, K. 1983: *Man and the Natural World: changing attitudes in England 1500–1800*. London: Allen Lane.

Thomas, N. 2000: *Restormel Castle, a Re-appraisal*. Draft report, Cornwall Historic Environment Service.

Thomas, P.D. 1996: The Tower of London's royal menagerie. *History Today* 46.8, 29–35.

Thomas, R. 2005: *Animals, Economy and Status: integrating zooarchaeological and historical data in the study of Dudley Castle, West Midlands (c.1100–1750)*. Oxford: Archaeopress.

Thompson, H.V. 1994: The rabbit in Britain. In Thompson, H.V. and King, C.M. (eds), *The European Rabbit: the history and biology of a successful colonizer*. Oxford: Oxford University Press, 64–107.

Thompson, M.W. 1964: Reclamation of waste ground for the Pleasance at Kenilworth Castle. *Medieval Archaeology* 8, 222–3.

Thompson, M.W. 1965: Two levels of the Mere at Kenilworth Castle. *Medieval Archaeology* 9, 156–61.

Thompson, M.W. 1989: The green knight's castle. In Harper-Bill, C., Holdsworth, C. and Nelson, J.L. (eds), *Studies in Medieval History Presented to R. Allen Brown*. Woodbridge: Boydell, 317–26.

Thompson, M.W. 1997: Castles. In Brewer, D. and Gibson, J. (eds), *A Companion to the Gawain-Poet*. Cambridge: D.S. Brewer, 119–30.

Thompson, M.W. 1998: *Medieval Bishops' Houses in England and Wales*. London: Ashgate.

Thorpe, L. (trans) 1978: *Gerald of Wales: the journey through Wales and the description of Wales*. London: Penguin.

Thurley, S. 1993: *The Royal Palaces of Tudor England: architecture and court life, 1460–1547*. New Haven: Yale University Press.

Thurley, S. (ed.) 1995: *The King's Privy Garden at Hampton Court, 1689–1995*. London: Apollo.

Thurley, S. 1997: Whitehall Palace and Westminster 1400–1600: a royal seat in transition. In Gaimster, D. and Stamper, P. (eds), *The Age of Transition: the archaeology of English culture 1400–1600*. Oxford: Oxbow, 93–104.

Thurley, S. 1999: *Whitehall Palace: an architectural history of the royal apartments, 1240–1698*. New Haven: Yale University Press.

Thurley, S. 2003: *Hampton Court: a social and architectural history*. New Haven: Yale University Press.

Ticehurst, N.F. 1957: *The Mute Swan in England*. London: Cleaver-Hume.

Tilley, C. 1994. *A Phenomenology of Landscape: places, paths and monuments*. Oxford: Berg.

Tolley, T. 1991: Eleanor of Castile and the 'Spanish' style in England. In Ormrod, W.M. (ed.), *England in the Thirteenth Century: proceedings of the 1989 Harlaxton Symposium*. Stamford: Paul Watkins, 167–92.

Toulmin Smith, L. (ed.) 1906–10: *The Itinerary of John Leland in or about the years 1535–1543*. London: George Bell and Sons.

Treen, C. and Atkin, M. 2005: *Wharram: a study of settlement on the Yorkshire Wolds. Water Resources and their Management*. York: York University Archaeological Publications.

Trollope, E. 1858: Notices on ancient and medieval labyrinths. *Archaeological Journal* 15, 216–35.

Turner, R.C. 1991: *Lamphey Bishop's Palace. Llawhaden Castle*. Cardiff: Cadw.

Turner, R.C. 2004: The great tower, Chepstow Castle, Wales. *Antiquaries Journal* 84, 223–317.

Turner, R.C. 2006a: *Chepstow Castle*. Cardiff: Cadw.

Turner, R.C. 2006b: The upper bailey. In Turner, R.C. and Priestley, S. 2006: The hunting preserves. In Turner, R.C. and Johnson, A. (eds), *Chepstow Castle: its history and buildings*. Woonton: Logaston Press, 71–80.

Turner, R.C. and Priestley, S. 2006: The hunting preserves. In Turner, R.C. and Johnson, A. (eds), *Chepstow Castle: its history and buildings*. Woonton: Logaston Press, 185–98.

Turner, R.C., Sale, C.B. and Axworthy Rutter, J.A. 1988: A medieval garden at the Belgrave Moat, Cheshire. *Journal of the Chester Archaeological Society* 69, 59–77.

Van Dam, J.E.M. 2001: Status loss due to ecological success. Landscape change and the spread of the rabbit. *Innovation – The European Journal of Social Science Research* 4.2, 157–70.

Van Dam, J.E.M. 2002: New habitats for the rabbit in Northern Europe, 1300–1600. In Howe, J. and Wolfe, M. (eds), *Inventing Medieval Landscapes: senses of place in western Europe*. Gainesville: University Press of Florida, 57–69.

Van Damme, D. and Ervynck, A. 1988: Medieval ferrets and rabbits in the castle of Laarne (East Flanders, Belgium): a contribution to the history of a predator and its prey. *Helinium* 208, 278–84.

Van de Noort, R. and O'Sullivan, A. 2006: *Rethinking Wetland Archaeology*. London: Duckworth.

Van de Noort, R. and O'Sullivan, A. 2007: Places, perceptions, boundaries and tasks: rethinking landscapes in wetland archaeology. In Barber, J. *et al.* (eds), *Archaeology from the Wetlands: recent perspectives*. Edinburgh: Society of Antiquaries of Scotland, 79–89.

Van Laun, M. 1981: A medieval vineyard in Herefordshire? *Transactions of the Woolhope Naturalists' Field Club* 43, 355–6.

Varley, W.J. 1973: Giant's Hill, Swine: the excavations of 1960–1. *Yorkshire Archaeological Journal* 45, 142–8.

Veale, E.M. 1957: The rabbit in England. *Agricultural History Review* 5, 85–90.

Wacher, J. 1974: *The Towns of Roman Britain*. London: Batsford.

Wainwright, A. forthcoming: *Invented History: revision and fabrication in the historic landscapes of eighteenth-century parks in south-west England*.

Warner, G. 1912: *Queen Mary's Psalter: Miniatures and Drawings by an English Artist of the 14th Century, Reproduced from Royal MS 2 B VII in the British Museum*. London: Longmans.

Warry, J. 1988: The ancient history of rabbits. *Local Historian* 18.1, 5–15.

Waterhouse, R. 2003: Garden archaeology in south Devon. In Wilson-North, R. (ed.), *The Lie of the Land: aspects of the archaeology and history of the designed landscape in the South West of England*. Exeter: Mint Press, 66–82.

Waterman, D.M. 1959: Tully Castle. *Ulster Journal of Archaeology* 22, 123–7.

Watts, K. 1998: Some Wiltshire deer parks. *Wiltshire Archaeological and Natural History Magazine* 91, 90–102.

Watts, M. 2002: *The Archaeology of Mills and Milling*. Stroud: Tempus.

Way, T. 1997: *A Study of the Impact of Imparkment on the Social Landscape of Cambridgeshire from c1080 to 1760*. Oxford: BAR.

Waymark, J. 2001: Sherborne, Dorset. *Garden History* 29.1, 64–81.

Webb, D. 2007: *Privacy and Solitude in the Middle Ages*. London: Hambledon Continuum.

Wheatley, A. 2004: *The Idea of the Castle in Medieval England*. York: York Medieval Press.

White, T.H. 1954: *The Book of Beasts*. London: Jonathan Cape.

Whitehead, D. 1995: Some connected thoughts on the parks and gardens of Herefordshire before the age of landscape gardening. *Transactions of the Woolhope Naturalists' Field Club, Herefordshire* 48, 193–223.

Whitehead, D. and Patton, J. (eds) 2001: *A Survey of Historic Parks and Gardens in Herefordshire*. Herefordshire Gardens Trust.

Whitely, M. 1999: Relationship between garden, park and princely residence in medieval France. In Guillaume, J. (ed.), *Architecture, Jardin, Paysage*. Paris: Picard, 91–102.

Whitmore, M. and Robertson, D. 2002: Excavations at Swannington Hall, 2002. *Norfolk Archaeology* 45, 97–104.

Whittle, E.H. 1988: *The Creation of a Historic Garden at Tretower Court*. Unpublished Cadw report.

Whittle, E.H. 1989: The Renaissance gardens of Raglan Castle. *Garden History* 17.1, 83–94.

Whittle, E.H. 1991: *Tretower Court, Sir Richard Vaughan's garden*. Cardiff: Cadw.

Whittle, E.H. 1992: *The Historic Gardens of Wales*. London: HMSO.

Whittle, E.H. 1999: The Tudor gardens at St Donat's Castle, Glamorgan, South Wales. *Garden History* 27.1, 109–26.

Whittle, E.H. and Robinson, D.M. 1991: *Tretower Court: Sir Roger Vaughan's Garden*. Cardiff: Cadw.

Whitworth, A. 1993: Yorkshire dovecotes and pigeon lofts: a preliminary survey. *Yorkshire Archaeological Journal* 65, 75–89.

Williams, R.J. and Zeepvat, R.J. 1994: *Bancroft*. Aylesbury: Buckinghamshire Archaeological Society.

Williamson, T. 1995: *Polite Landscapes: gardens and society in eighteenth-century England*. Stroud: Alan Sutton.

Williamson, T. 1997: Fish, fur and feather: man and nature in the post-medieval landscape. In Barker, K. and Darvill, T. (eds), *Making English Landscapes: Papers presented to Christopher Taylor at a symposium held at Bournemouth University on 25th March 1995*. Oxford: Oxbow, 92–117.

Williamson, T. 1998: *The Archaeology of the Landscape Park: garden design in Norfolk, England, c.1680–1840*. Oxford: Archaeopress.

Williamson, T. 1999: Gardens, legitimation, and resistance. *International Journal of Historical Archaeology* 3.1, 37–52.

Williamson, T. 2001: Chatsworth, Derbyshire. *Garden History* 29.1, 82–90.

Williamson, T. 2006a: *East Anglia*. London: English Heritage/Collins.

Williamson, T. 2006b: *The Archaeology of Rabbit Warrens*. Princes Risborough: Shire.

Williamson, T. 2007: *Rabbits, Warrens and Archaeology*. Stroud: Tempus.

Williamson, T. and Bellamy, L. 1987: *Property and Landscape: a social history of land ownership and the English countryside*. London: George Philip.

Williamson, T. and Loveday, R. 1988: Rabbits or ritual? Artificial warrens and the Neolithic long mound tradition. *Archaeological Journal* 145, 290–313.

Willis-Bund, J.W. (ed.) 1902: *The Black Book of St David's*. London: Cymmrodorion Record Series.

Wilson, C. 2002: The royal lodgings of Edward III at Windsor Castle: form, function, representation. In Keen, L. and Scarff, E. (eds), *Windsor: medieval archaeology, art and architecture of the Thames valley*, British Archaeological Association Conference Transactions 25. Leeds: Maney, 15–94.

Wilson, D.R. 1991: Old gardens from the air. In Brown, A.E. (ed.), *Garden Archaeology*. London: Council for British Archaeology, 20–35.

Wilson-North, R. (ed.) 2003: *The Lie of the Land: aspects of the archaeology and history of the designed landscape in the South West of England*. Exeter: Mint Press.

Wiltshire Archaeological and Natural History Society 1998: Excavation and fieldwork in Wiltshire, 1996. *Wiltshire Archaeological and Natural History Magazine* 91, 152–66.

Winchester, A.J.L. 2007: Baronial and manorial parks in medieval Cumbria. In Liddiard, R. (ed.), *The Medieval Park: new perspectives*. Bollington: Windgather, 165–84.

de Winter, P. 1983: Castles and town residences of Philip the Bold, Duke of Burgundy (1364–1404). *Artibus et Historiae* 4.8, 95–118.

Wood, M. 1965: *The English Mediaeval House*. London: Dent.

Woodbridge, K. 1982: *The Stourhead Landscape: Wiltshire*. Stourhead: National Trust.

Woodfield, C. and Woodfield, P. 1988: *Lyddington Bede House*. London: English Heritage.

Woodfield, P. 1991: Early buildings in gardens in England. In Brown, A.E. (ed.), *Garden Archaeology*. London: Council for British Archaeology, 123–37.

Woodhouse, E. 1999: Kenilworth, the Earl of Leicester's pleasure grounds following Robert Laneham's letter. *Garden History* 27.1, 127–44.

Woolgar, C.M. 1999: *The Great Household in Late Medieval England*. New Haven: Yale University Press.

Woolgar, C.M. 2001: Fast and feast: conspicuous consumption and the diet of the nobility in the fifteenth century. In Hicks, M. (ed.), *Revolution and Consumption in Late Medieval England*. Woodbridge: Boydell and Brewer, 7–25.

Woolgar, C.M. 2006: *The Senses in Medieval England*. New Haven: Yale University Press.

Wrathmell, S. 1989: *Wharram: a study of settlement on the Yorkshire Wolds. Medieval Peasant Farmsteads*. York: York University Archaeological Publications.

Wright, J. 2008: *Castles of Nottinghamshire*. Nottingham: Nottinghamshire County Council.

Yapp, B. 1981: *Birds in Medieval Manuscripts*. London: British Library.

Yarrow, A. 2003: *Corfe Castle*. Warrington: The National Trust.

Young, C.R. 1974: The Forest Eyre in England during the thirteenth century. *American Journal of Legal History* 18.4, 321–31.

Zeepvat, R.J. 1988: Fishponds in Roman Britain. In Aston, M.A. (ed.), *Medieval Fish, Fisheries and Fishponds*, 2 Vols. Oxford: BAR, 17–26.

Zink, M. 2008: The place of the senses. In Nichols, S.G., Kablitz, A. and Calhoun, A. (eds), *Rethinking the Medieval Senses: heritage/fascinations/frames*. Baltimore: The John Hopkins University Press, 93–101.

— *Index* —